DISCARDED

The Phonology of
Pennsylvania German English
as Evidence of
Language Maintenance and Shift

The Phonology of Pennsylvania German English as Evidence of Language Maintenance and Shift

Achim Kopp

SUP

Selinsgrove: Susquehanna University Press
London: Associated University Presses

© 1999 by Associated University Presses, Inc.

All rights reserved. Authorization to photocopy items for internal or personal use, or the internal or personal use of specific clients, is granted by the copyright owner, provided that a base fee of $10.00, plus eight cents per page per copy is paid directly to the Copyright Clearance Center, 222 Rosewood Drive, Danvers, Massachusetts 01923. [1–57591–006–3/99 $10.00 + 8¢ pp, pc.]

Associated University Presses
440 Forsgate Drive
Cranbury, NJ 08512

Associated University Presses
16 Barter Street
London, WC1A 2AH, England

Associated University Presses
P.O. Box 338, Port Credit
Mississauga, Ontario
Canada L5G 4L8

The paper used in this publication meets the requirements
of the American National Standard for Permanence of Paper
for Printed Library Materials Z39.48–1984.

Library of Congress Cataloging-in-Publication Data

Kopp, Achim, 1961–
    The phonology of Pennsylvania German English as evidence of language maintenance and shift / Achim Kopp.
        p.   cm.
    Includes bibliographical references (p.) and index.
    ISBN 1-57591-006-3 (alk. paper)
    1. Pennsylvania Dutch—Languages. 2. English language—Pennsylvania—German elements. 3. English language—Pennsylvania—Phonology. 4. English language—Dialects—Pennsylvania. 5. German Americans—Pennsylvania—Language. 6. Pennsylvania German dialect—Influence. 7. German language—Influence on English. 8. Languages in contact—Pennsylvania. 9. Code switching (Linguistics). 10. Bilingualism—Pennsylvania. I. Title.
PE3102.P45K66 1999
427'.9748—dc21   98-30641
                                                                                                     CIP

PRINTED IN THE UNITED STATES OF AMERICA

Meinen Eltern und Geschwistern in Liebe und Dankbarkeit

To Kristen and Fabian, with love

Contents

Acknowledgments	9
1. Introduction	13
2. The Influence of Pennsylvania German on the Phonology of English	63
3. The Effects of Language Competence, Acquisition, and Use on Maintenance and Shift	134
4. Language Attitudes: A Matched-Guise Test	210
5. Synthesis and Conclusion	276
Appendix: Questionnaire	290
Notes	310
Bibliography	325
Index	334

Acknowledgments

This volume is a revised version of a dissertation accepted by the *Neuphilologische Fakultät* of Ruprecht-Karls-Universität, Heidelberg, Germany, in partial fulfillment of the requirements for the degree of *Dr. phil.* in 1994. The two readers were Prof. Dr. Beat Glauser (*Anglistisches Seminar*) and Prof. Dr. Klaus J. Mattheier (*Germanistisches Seminar*).

In the entire course of the production of this study I received invaluable support from numerous individuals and agencies. I wish to thank Prof. M. Lois Huffines, who during a one-year stay at Bucknell University, Lewisburg, Pennsylvania, in 1985–86 introduced me to the Pennsylvania German culture and first brought me to the homes of local Amish, Mennonite, and nonsectarian Pennsylvania German families. I would like to express my sincere appreciation to Prof. Dr. Hans Käsmann (Universität Heidelberg), who guided me in the production of my *Staatsexamen* thesis, a research report on the literature until 1988, the groundwork for the present study. I am grateful to Prof. Dr. Klaus J. Mattheier for his invaluable advice during the setup of the questionnaire and for many other helpful suggestions and initiatives during and after the completion of the dissertation. The greatest thanks I owe to Prof. Dr. Beat Glauser, who, as my thesis adviser, has given me unyielding support and encouragement over many years. Through his critical and insightful comments he taught me to examine the data from more than just one perspective.

Thanks also to my Heidelberg friends and colleagues Dr. Walter Sauer and Volker Mohr for their most helpful suggestions. In addition, I am indebted to Dr. Thomas J. Badey and my brother Bernd for their technical assistance. A special note of gratitude is reserved for Prof. Joseph C. Salmons (University of Wisconsin–Madison), who provided me with numerous insightful comments, invaluable suggestions, and bibliographical references for the final revision of this volume.

Acknowledgments

My dissertation was financially supported by a two-year scholarship from Heidelberg University in accordance with the Baden-Württemberg *Landesgraduiertenförderungsgesetz*. The fieldwork in Pennsylvania between October 1989 and May 1990 was made possible through a grant from the *Deutscher Akademischer Austauschdienst (DAAD)*. My sincere thanks go to Prof. Hans Feldmann and Susquehanna University Press for accepting the manuscript for publication. I would also like to thank Dean Douglas W. Steeples of the College of Liberal Arts of Mercer University for a research and development grant which I received during the final production stage of this book.

I wish to express my special and warmest thanks to all my informants in central Pennsylvania. Without their cooperation and patience this study would not have been possible. I will never forget their kindness and hospitality, which made fieldwork truly rewarding and pleasurable.

Finally, I would like to thank my wife, Kristen B. Peterec, not only for her great patience and invaluable comments during proofreading, but also for her moral support and wonderful friendship throughout the production of this volume.

The Phonology of Pennsylvania German English as Evidence of Language Maintenance and Shift

1
Introduction

Chapter 1 is divided into three major parts. A general outline of the goals and the core argument of the text will be followed by a description of the historical development of the Pennsylvania German area and the informants' present-day lifestyle. In the final section, the fieldwork methods will be presented together with a detailed description of all fifty informants.

OUTLINE

The goal of this study is to describe the linguistic behavior of six multigeneration families living at the northern edge of the Pennsylvania German area in Pennsylvania. Three main cultural groups will be focused on: nonsectarian Pennsylvania Germans, sectarian Pennsylvania Germans, and non-Pennsylvania Germans. Generally speaking, in the nonsectarian group only the oldest generation is bilingual (Pennsylvania German and English), while younger members are nonfluent in Pennsylvania German or have no competence in this language at all. By contrast, all the members of the sectarian group are bilingual, as they learn Pennsylvania German natively and English in their early school years at the latest. Non-Pennsylvania Germans are monolingual speakers of English.

Although the sectarian Pennsylvania Germans' lifestyle may be fascinating, they are of relatively lesser interest in sociolinguistic terms. Their stable diglossia prevents extraordinary linguistic changes. By contrast, the nonsectarian group is currently undergoing dramatic change, which will eventually culminate in language death, and is at the center of this investigation. The non-Pennsylvania German informants, who are entirely monolingual, represent the oldestablished non-German element in the region. Monolingual speakers of English whose families recently moved into the area from other parts of the United States will not be considered.

Most of the older publications on the languages of the Pennsylvania Germans focused on only one of the two main varieties.[1] The first Pennsylvania German-to-English dictionaries and word lists appeared as early as the last quarter of the nineteenth century (Horne 1875, Rauch 1879, Lins 1887). The largest ones still in print are Lambert 1924 (reprinted 1977) and Stine 1990. The latter has an English-to-Pennsylvania German counterpart compiled by Beam (1985).

Pennsylvania German grammars were published by Frey (1942) and by Buffington and Barba (1965). The latter has become accepted as a guideline for Pennsylvania German orthography, which, nevertheless, has remained unstandardized to the present day. In 1954 Reed and Seifert published their *Linguistic atlas of Pennsylvania German*. Authors dealing with all aspects of Pennsylvania German include Buffington (1937) and Springer (1943). Reed investigated its phonology (1947) and morphology (1948). The influence of English on the Pennsylvania German lexicon was described by Schach (1951).

Pennsylvania German English has attracted linguists' attention as well. Early publications are Tucker (1934), Struble (1935), and Page (1937). In addition, general works on American English, such as those by Mencken (first edition: 1919) and Kurath (1949), contain examples of Pennsylvania German English.

More recent studies tend to follow Frey (1945), who, when examining the linguistic situation of the Amish, turned his attention to sociolinguistic issues. In Germany the Essen Delaware Project Team under the directorship of Enninger brought out numerous publications in the 1980s describing an Old Order Amish community in Delaware. Among them were Enninger 1984 and 1985a, Enninger and Wandt 1982, and Raith 1982, to mention only four. By contrast, Seel's book (1988) on the Pennsylvania German lexicon is again a purely linguistic study. Van Ness (1990) describes a variety of Pennsylvania German spoken in West Virginia, and Meister Ferré (1994) that of a group of Old Order Amish from Lancaster County, Pennsylvania.

In the United States, Huffines has been one of the most prominent figures in Pennsylvania German research over the last decade. After starting out with studies on Pennsylvania German English (1980a, 1984a–d, 1986a and b), she has recently turned her attention toward Pennsylvania German (1989, 1990a, 1991, 1992), always with the view on the larger sociolinguistic context. Finally, Louden's dissertation (1988) also goes beyond a purely linguistic description, giving insight into the sociolinguistic context of sectarian communities, although ultimately pursuing an argument about syntactic change. Important recent articles on the English varieties spoken in German-American communities include Wilson 1980 (Texas German English) and Shields 1985 and

1987 (lexical aspects in Pennsylvania German English). An excellent overview and comparison of data from several German-speaking areas can be found in Howell 1993.

Like some of its more recent forerunners, the present study is sociolinguistic; it differs from them in that it juxtaposes up to four generations of six families living in the same area, thus extending an apparent-time approach over different cultural subgroups. Differences between the generations reflect patterns of linguistic change. The continuous tension between maintenance and shift influences the people's rules of language use, their language attitudes, and, ultimately, their language behavior. In fact, all three factors are interdependent and greatly influence each other.

This basic assumption is reflected in the structure of the study. Chapter 1 gives a short overview of the historical, cultural, and linguistic developments of the Pennsylvania German area as well as an introduction to the six informant families.

In chapter 2 the phonology of Pennsylvania German English is described on the basis of a word list elicited with the help of picture cards. The older generations of the nonsectarians display the most contact phenomena whereas the English of the younger nonsectarians, all the sectarians, and all the non-Pennsylvania Germans is considerably less marked. The fact that the English variety of the sectarians, who live in relative isolation from the mainstream society,[2] approaches the regional standard more closely than that spoken by the older nonsectarians forms part of the "Pennsylvania German paradox."

These linguistic findings will be accounted for with the aid of sociolinguistic instruments, specifically a language use analysis and an attitude test. Chapter 3 deals with language competence, acquisition, and use and shows how the various subgroups differ in their patterns. This analysis makes use of such different models as Fishman (1964, 1965, 1972; domains), Gal (1978a, 1978b, 1979; interlocutors), and, to a certain extent, Milroy (first edition: 1980, second edition: 1987; network). A qualitative evaluation shows that the sectarians' language use is strictly governed by domains, which results in relatively stable (diglossic) bilingualism. By contrast, the nonsectarian group, because of its changing acquisition patterns, is presently undergoing a rapid language shift from Pennsylvania German to English, resulting in the eventual death of the minority language.

In chapter 4 the results of a *matched-guise test* are presented. This technique, which was first developed by Lambert (Lambert et al. 1960, Lambert 1967), represents a fine instrument to measure language attitudes. The data reveal a generally more positive attitude toward Pennsylvania German and ethnically marked English on the solidarity dimension than on the status dimension. The stereotype of the "dumb Dutchman" is more widespread in the oldest nonsectarian generation than among the sectarians and the younger nonsectarians. The latter even have a positive attitude toward their dying culture, which may result in a certain degree of ethnic marking.

Chapter 5 attempts a synthesis between the linguistic and the sociolinguistic results. The phonological differences found in the informants' varieties of English are reflected in the differences they show in the areas of language use and language attitude. At the end of the study an attempt is made to integrate the phonological findings into a larger theory of language change in a contact situation and to make predictions about possible future linguistic developments within the groups studied in this survey.

The present study makes use of both quantitative and qualitative methods of fieldwork. While the questionnaire was designed to make concrete data counts possible, Dorian's (1981) qualitative approach of ethnomethodology was used as a subsidiary method in the form of several occasions of participant observation.

The underlying theme is languages in contact, more specifically a majority language (English) in contact with a minority language (Pennsylvania German). The most visible results of this contact situation are imposition and convergence on a linguistic level, and shift, with its ultimate stage, language death (cf. Dorian 1981), on a sociolinguistic level.

A number of concepts play only a marginal role. The area in which Pennsylvania German is spoken could be said to form a *speech island* (following the term *Sprachinsel* used in German linguistics) within the English-speaking surroundings. A speech island could be tentatively defined as "a communicative unit smaller than the surrounding society in which the process of linguistic assimilation is decelerated."

However, it depends on the definition of the term *speech community*[3] whether one would consider the area in which the informants live as one speech island or as several separate ones. Following Kloss (1977), the major criterion for a speech community is the existence of a common language. In this case, Pennsylvania German would form a single speech island. According to Gumperz (1968), additional factors such as social contacts and a common identity are important. In this sense, the present examination deals with at least two separate Pennsylvania German speech islands, namely the nonsectarian and the sectarian ones. Although the concepts of speech island, speech community, and social network will not be at the center of the present investigation (as the focus is on small, well-structured sections of the community, that is, six families), Gumperz's definition appears to be more suitable. It also includes those (younger) nonsectarian informants who have no active competence in Pennsylvania German but are still part of the community's social network.

The region in question was settled by speakers of two main languages: German and English. The various German dialects underwent a process of linguistic leveling and developed into Pennsylvania German, which until a few decades ago was the dominant language of the speakers of German origin. The beginning shift to English is marked by a phase of bilingualism. Today, however, this bilingualism is more and more being lost, especially in the nonsectarian group. The shift is occurring not only on account of increasing numbers of monolingual English speakers coming to live in the area, but also because a large subgroup of the Pennsylvania Germans have stopped raising their children in German-speaking environments.

All the informants speak English; those who know Pennsylvania German are bilingual. Since Ferguson (1959), the concept of bilingualism has been distinguished from that of diglossia.[4] Bilingualism is said to exist when a speaker or a group of speakers uses two separate languages. In a diglossic society the two languages are used in clearly defined domains or roles. It will be seen that diglossia and bilingualism exist in only two of the informant families (the sectarians), while three were found to be partly bilingual (the nonsectarians), and one fully monolingual (the non-Pennsylvania Germans).

The overwhelming direction of language shift is from Pennsylvania German to English. Especially for past generations of the nonsectarian group, a good knowledge of Pennsylvania German generally meant poor competence in English. Today, the more closely speakers approach the regional standard of English, the less Pennsylvania German they tend to know. *Regional standard* in this study refers to northern Midland usage, the variety of American English spoken in central Pennsylvania (cf. Kurath 1949, 31).

Linguistically, this study focuses on phonology rather than morphology, syntax, and lexicon, and within phonology on English rather than on Pennsylvania German. Wherever Pennsylvania German forms are cited, the orthographical system suggested by Buffington and Barba (1965) is used.

The ultimate goal is to show how the different social patterns of the three subgroups correlate with linguistic differences. It will be attempted to lay out the strategies applied by the two major groups of Pennsylvania Germans in dealing with their cultural and linguistic heritage, that is, language maintenance and shift.[5] Most importantly, this study will go beyond a mere description of linguistic facts. With the help of a sociolinguistic approach, it will try to facilitate a deeper understanding of the processes of change.

HISTORICAL AND SOCIOCULTURAL BACKGROUND

GERMAN IMMIGRATION TO PENNSYLVANIA

On 4 March 1681 King Charles II of England signed the Charter of Pennsylvania, in which he granted to William Penn all the land between Lord Baltimore's province of Maryland and the duke of York's province of New York. The king owed William Penn's father, Admiral Sir William Penn, sixteen thousand pounds. In compensation, William Penn accepted a new colony, named in honor of his father, as a haven in the New World for his persecuted fellow believers, the members of the Society of Friends or, as they were commonly known, the Quakers. The new colony included the land between the thirty-ninth and forty-second degrees of north latitude, and from the Delaware River westward for five degrees of longitude (Stevens 1976, 8; figure 1.1). To find settlers for his new land, Penn not only campaigned in England, but also in Holland and in the Lower Rhine region, using pamphlets in which he promised religious tolerance, economic freedom, and political independence. In 1671–72, and again in 1677, Penn himself traveled to Germany, looking for supporters of the Friends' beliefs. In 1678 a group of Mennonites—who after a long period of persecution had made their homes in Krefeld, a German town well-known for its religious tolerance—came into contact with the English Quaker Stephen Crisp. Subsequently, a small congregation of Quakers, some of them former Mennonites, regularly met to worship in Krefeld.

In 1682 and 1683 six members of this circle bought land from William Penn. In 1683 they sailed to Pennsylvania aboard the *Concord*, together with thirteen other families from Krefeld. On 6 October 1683 they reached Philadelphia and, under the leadership of the Frankfurt pietist Franz Daniel Pastorius, founded nearby Germantown, the first German-speaking settlement in North America.

In the following years hundreds of Mennonite, Amish, and Pietist families followed from Germany. By 1790 three thousand Germans lived in Germantown. In all, almost one hundred thousand Germans came to the British colonies in North America during the colonial period, the majority to Pennsylvania. The major reason for this exodus was

Introduction 19

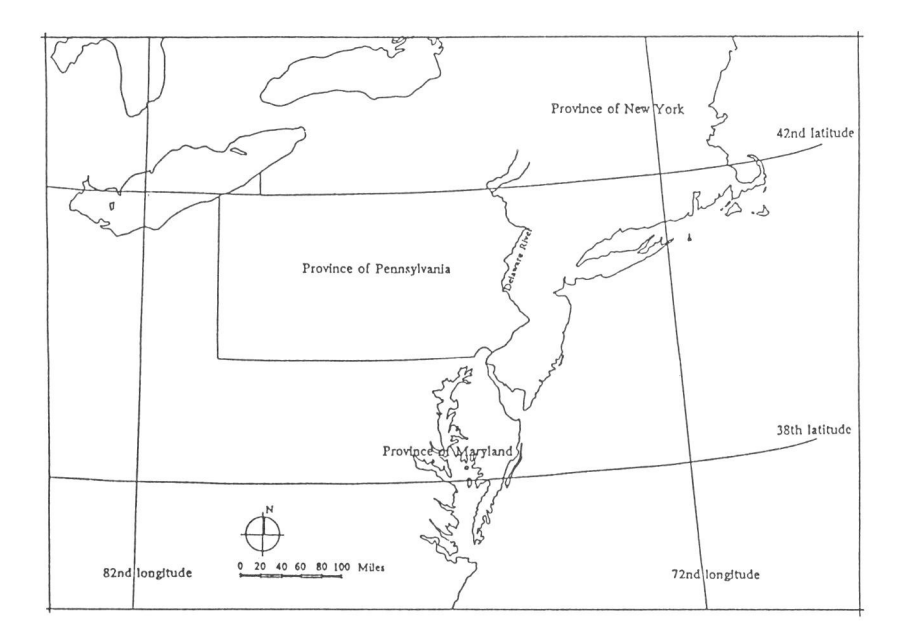

Figure 1.1: The province of Pennsylvania

the unstable socioeconomic situation in Germany after the Thirty Years' War (1618–48).

In Germany, certain territories were more tolerant than others toward different religious beliefs, thus attracting large numbers of members of religious minority groups. One of those states was the Palatinate under Elector Karl-Ludwig, who ruled from 1650 to 1680. During his reign, Swiss and Alsatian Anabaptists as well as Moravian Hutterites, among others, came to live in the Palatinate alongside the members of the large official confessions, the Lutherans, the Reformed, and the Catholics. Karl-Ludwig made the religious minorities pay for his tolerance in the form of a tax.

However, under his successor, who was Catholic, religious tolerance ceased. This and the cold winter of 1708–09 led to the beginning of the largest emigration wave from the Palatinate to Pennsylvania. Between 1717 and 1732 an estimated three thousand Mennonites left the Palatinate (Hostetler 1993, 52). It was not only Mennonites who emigrated, but also Lutherans, Reformed, Amish, Schwenkfelders, and even Catholics. Besides the Palatinate they came from the Lower Rhine, Alsace, Baden, Hesse, and Switzerland.

The classic emigration route led down the Rhine to Holland, and from there to England, where the emigrants often had to wait for months until their journey across the Atlantic Ocean began. To the present day, this route down the Rhine valley is marked by Palatinate speech islands in the form of a number of towns around Krefeld (Raith 1982, 11).

The majority of the emigrants had to earn their crossing as so-called *redemptioners*. American landowners paid for the journey of the emigrants, who, in return, promised to work for a certain number of years without pay (indentured servitude). In those days the Dutch and English authorities called any German emigrant coming down the Rhine a *Paalzer* 'Palatine' (cf. Standard German *Pfälzer*). As the emigrants were mostly poor, the term soon acquired a derogatory meaning (*see* Yoder 1980).

Independently from both the group emigration and the redemptioner system, another group of Germans came to America toward the end of the colonial time. They were German soldiers who fought on both sides in the Revolutionary War. Many of them, like Friedrich Wilhelm von Steuben, the drillmaster of Washington's army, remained in the New World, while those who returned triggered new waves of emigrations through their favorable reports.

The negative experiences of the "1709 Palatines" with the British authorities led the vast majority of German emigrants to avoid New York and the New England states until the nineteenth century. During the whole of the eighteenth century, emigrants from the Palatinate preferred Pennsylvania as their new home. Many of those families who did try to settle in the Hudson Valley eventually came to Pennsylvania in secondary migrations. By the time of the American Revolution, the Germans formed one-third of the population of Pennsylvania.

The *Pennsylvania Germans*, as they came to be known, settled heavily in the interior counties of Northampton, Berks, Lancaster, Lehigh, and neighboring areas (figure 1.2). Their skill and industry transformed the region into a rich farming country, contributing greatly to the expanding prosperity of the province.

The dominant group among their neighbors were the English Quakers, who settled predominantly in the southeastern counties, with Philadelphia as the center of intellectual and commercial life. The Scotch-Irish,[6] whose tide of immigration was strong between 1728 and the American Revolution, were the third important ethnic group. They pushed first into central and western Pennsylvania. Together with their fellow Scots from Scotland they numbered about seventy thousand at the end of the colonial era (approximately one-fourth of the population). Finally, the Welsh, French Huguenots, and Irish, together with the Dutch

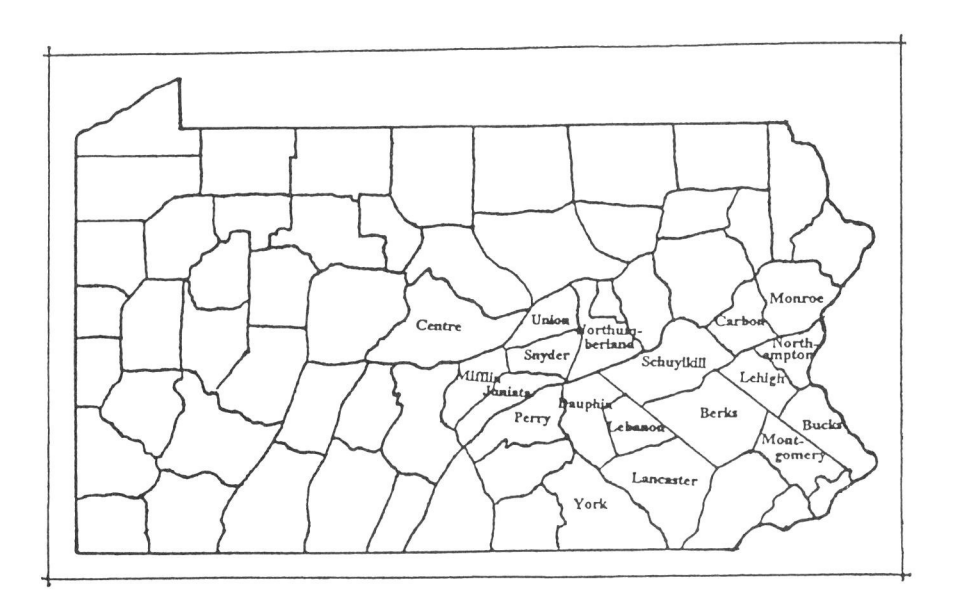

Figure 1.2: Distinctively Pennsylvania German counties in Pennsylvania

and Swedes, contributed in smaller numbers to the development of colonial Pennsylvania (Stevens 1976, 10).

DEFINING THE PENNSYLVANIA GERMANS

Attempting to answer the question of who the Pennsylvania Germans are, Gilbert (1962, 13) quotes a definition by a Lehigh County judge:

> A Pennsylvania German is the descendant of German immigrants, who migrated to America from the Rhenish Palatinate or from Switzerland...before the Revolutionary War and who has retained the characteristics—in language, accent, character and customs, or any of them—of his German ancestors.

This definition stresses three aspects of the question, which will be looked at in some detail.

First, as far as the historical aspect is concerned, the Revolutionary War constitutes an important borderline. Together with the later Napoleonic Wars in Europe, it checked the coming of Germans to America for more than thirty years. Also, the Napoleonic Wars mark the first modern expression of a German national concept.

In the colonial period[7] whole groups of immigrants arrived, often tied together by their religious beliefs and/or extreme economic hardship in their former homeland. They settled in rural areas and maintained their group structure in the New World, a fact essential for the maintenance of their native language. Apart from the relatively early Pennsylvania German speech island, the German language survived in Texas and in parts of the Midwest and the Great Plains, again because of group rather than individual immigration.

During the mass emigrations of the nineteenth and twentieth centuries, when 5.5 and 1.5 million Germans, respectively, emigrated to the United States, the relatively loose structure of the communities and the emigrants' fast assimilation in the large cities (e.g., New York, Philadelphia, and Chicago) prevented a prolonged maintenance of their native German language. Even the existence of so-called *Little Germanies*, sections with a high proportion of German immigrants in the large cities and also in smaller ones, such as Milwaukee, Cincinnati, and St. Louis, did not prevent the loss of the German language.

The second important aspect is space. The lack of an exact delimitation in the definition makes it clear that the geographic distribution of the Pennsylvania Germans in the New World has to be defined in rather broad terms. Numerous groups of Pennsylvania Germans have, to the present day, moved on from the original southeastern Pennsylvania counties, usually in search of new farmland.

Not only did they settle in other parts of Pennsylvania, such as the central Pennsylvania counties Union, Northumberland, and Schuylkill (the homes of the families under investigation), but also in other states, such as Virginia, Delaware, Maryland, Iowa, Ohio, North Carolina, Kentucky, Indiana, Michigan, Wisconsin, Kansas, Oklahoma, North Dakota, and Illinois. Today, groups of Pennsylvania Germans, whose ancestors left the Conestoga Valley near Lancaster in 1793, are even found in Waterloo and Perth Counties, Ontario, Canada.

In view of the problems concerning a definition of the term *Pennsylvania German*, it is obvious that the question of numbers is extremely difficult to answer. According to Gilbert (1962, 14), the descendants of the approximately one hundred thousand prerevolutionary German and Swiss settlers numbered between eight and ten million in the early

1960s. Taking geographic origin together with language as a criterion for group membership, Gilbert counted approximately three hundred thousand Pennsylvania Germans with active and an additional four hundred thousand with passive competence in Pennsylvania German in the 1960s.

As the terms *active* and *passive language competence* are extremely arbitrary, an estimation of the present number of Pennsylvania Germans will not be attempted here. It will be seen, however, that the number of nonsectarian Pennsylvania Germans with either active or passive competence in Pennsylvania German is decreasing dramatically. Native speakers of Pennsylvania German in this group will die out within the next couple of decades. However, this does not mean that there will be no more native speakers of Pennsylvania German in the future. The sectarian group continues using Pennsylvania German as their native language, and, owing to a large increase in population, not only secures the survival of this variety, but also its spread and an overall increase of the number of its users.

The third aspect of Gilbert's definition to deserve special attention is that language seems to play an important role. The genesis of Pennsylvania German has long been an object of dispute among researchers. Most scholars agree that the early southern German and Swiss settlers brought their local dialects to the New World and often had very little knowledge of Standard German. Toward the end of the eighteenth century, when immigration stopped for a few decades, the southern German dialects spoken in Pennsylvania underwent a process of leveling. Uncommon features found in only one or few dialects generally disappeared.

This development resulted in a dialect that could be easily used and understood by all speakers and came to be known as *Pennsylfaanisch Deitsch* 'Pennsylvania German' (cf. Standard German *Pennsylvaniadeutsch*). In popular language use and also in older academic publications this variety has been termed *Pennsylvania Dutch*. However, the term *Dutch*, which has been a source of confusion to the present day, has nothing to do with the Dutch language, but is merely an adaptation of the dialect word *Deitsch* 'German' (cf. Standard German *deutsch*).

The basis of Pennsylvania German is the West Middle German (specifically Rhine Frankish) dialect of *Pfälzisch*,[8] mixed with some Alemannic influences. The question of dominance of a certain variety of *Pfälzisch* and, more generally, the principle behind the genesis of Pennsylvania German, has long been disputed. Based on a number of comparative studies of phonology and lexicon (e.g., Veith 1968), many researchers have come to the conclusion that indeed one local variety of *Pfälzisch* played a dominant role in the rise of Pennsylvania German,

24   Introduction

namely, the dialect spoken in the eastern Palatinate, more specifically around the city of Mannheim (figure 1.3). However, the underlying process was not adaptation to the variety spoken by the majority of speakers. Instead, the Mannheim area dialect seems to have had the largest amount of compromise forms (*Ausgleichsformen*) and the highest prestige[9] among the German-speaking settlers in colonial Pennsylvania.

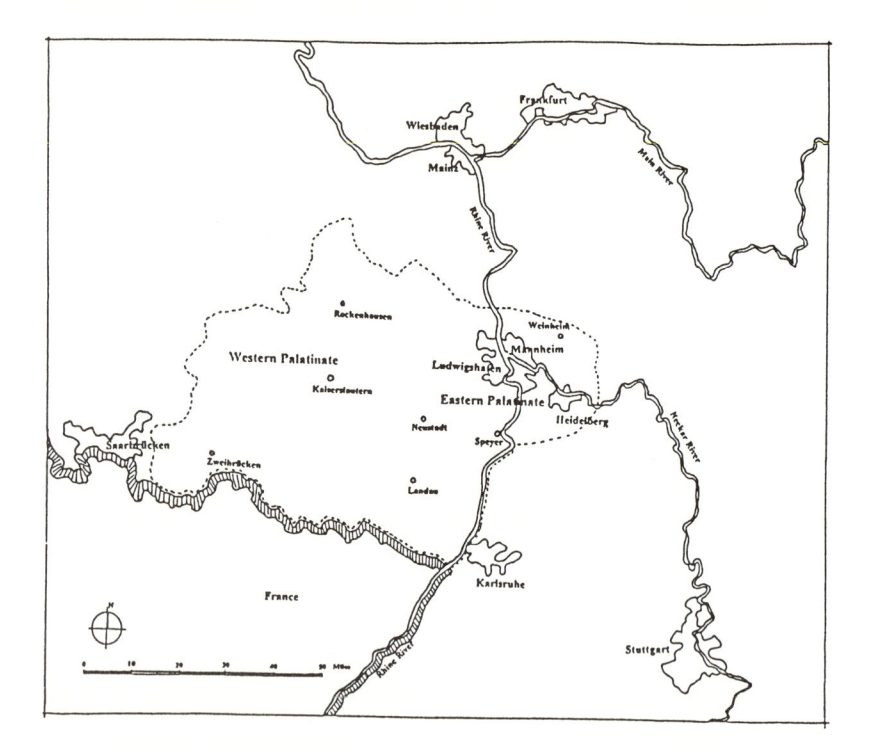

Figure 1.3: The Palatinate

All the other German dialects brought to Pennsylvania were leveled generally in the direction of the Mannheim variety. Leveling was most complete in Lancaster County, where linguistically distant groups, such as Mennonites from the Palatinate and Amish from Switzerland, lived side by side. In those areas where the original varieties were more similar, the need for leveling was smaller. In part, this explains geographic variation within Pennsylvania German.[10]

THE NONSECTARIANS

The term *nonsectarian Pennsylvania Germans* refers to groups of speakers whose ancestors were members of the established Protestant churches in Germany, mainly the Lutheran and Reformed Churches. The first Lutheran and Reformed German settlers came to Pennsylvania after 1750. Their churches, which were centrally organized, had both the right to ordain ministers and the control over confirmation and excommunication.

Unlike the sectarians, members of the Lutheran and Reformed Churches practice child baptism. The common language furthered tendencies toward the unification of the Lutherans and the Reformed, who were closely related theologically, and hindered efforts to bring about a union between the Lutherans and the Church of England. The Reformed Church, which was influenced by Zwingli and Calvin, was more militantly Protestant, emphasizing its differences to the Catholic Church more strongly than the Lutheran Church did. The Reformed settled predominantly in Montgomery County, the Lutherans mainly in Lehigh and Northampton Counties (Raith 1982, 12).

Today, however, members of the two denominations are found all over the Pennsylvania German area. From the very beginning, many church buildings were used jointly by Lutheran and Reformed congregations until in 1968 the Union Church was dissolved. The Reformed Church has been renamed *United Church of Christ*.

THE SECTARIANS

The one group most outsiders associate with the Pennsylvania Germans are the sectarians. They call themselves *Plain People* in allusion to their plain way of living within the framework of their Christian belief. There are many different groups living in the Pennsylvania German area, differing among each other both in their degrees of progressiveness and in their origin.

Some of the smaller sectarian denominations include the Church of the Brethren, whose members are also called *Dunker* 'Dunkards' (cf. Standard German *tunken* 'dip') because of the total immersion in a river at their baptism. Another small group were the Seventh Day Baptists, founded by Konrad Beissel from Eberbach, who, between 1728 and 1733, built Ephrata Cloister in Lancaster County, where the group flourished until 1814. In 1734 the Schwenkfelders, who were persecuted in Silesia and Saxony, settled in Montgomery County. The Moravian

Brethren, or Herrnhuters, who began immigrating to Pennsylvania in 1735, did not come as persecuted dissidents, but predominantly as missionaries. The origins of this group date back to the Czech prereformer Johannes Hus (1369–1415). Their main settlement in Pennsylvania was Bethlehem. The Rappists, who in 1805 founded Harmony, Pennsylvania, and in 1825 the nearby town of Economy, arrived in the nineteenth century. The Zoarists, Amanites, and Hutterites predominantly settled outside Pennsylvania.

None of these sects became as important for the linguistic and cultural development of Pennsylvania as did the Mennonites and the Amish. They have always attracted people's interest because of their traditional lifestyle, which sets them apart from their fellow Americans. Recent major publications include Hostetler (1993) and Kraybill (1989) on the Amish and Redekop (1989) on the Mennonites.

Both sects derive from the European Anabaptists, who, as forerunners of the free-church movement, were heavily persecuted. The Anabaptist contemporaries of Martin Luther did not recognize the state church as their model, but the early Christian communities. Common characteristics of both Amish and Mennonites, showing their shared Anabaptist roots, are adult baptism, tight organization, plain and simple lifestyle, strong religious beliefs, renunciation of the world, resistance against oaths, and pacifism. The latter two attitudes were the source of numerous conflicts between the Anabaptist groups and the ruling powers not only in Europe, but also on American soil, especially in times of war.

The founder of the Mennonites was the Frisian Menno Simons (1492–1559), who resigned from Roman Catholic priesthood in 1536 and became an important Anabaptist leader. Prior to their unification in the sixteenth century, two groups of Anabaptists were found in Europe, one in Switzerland (Swiss Brethren) and one in the Netherlands. In 1525 both groups had broken independently with Zwingli's Reformed Church because of the Anabaptists' refusal to baptize their children. Each believer, they held, should voluntarily and consciously join the church as an adult. Their goal was the separation of state and church in order to avoid any threat to the freedom of conscience.

Anabaptism spread particularly among simple peasants. The tremendous losses during the Peasant Wars (1524–25), in which southern and central German peasants unsuccessfully attempted to break the power of the ruling classes, strengthened rather than weakened the Anabaptists. When Martin Luther, who rejected the peasants' interpretation of the New Testament as a justification of their actions, joined the rulers, the peasants opposed him. The subsequent persecutions were one reason for the originally militant Anabaptists to become pacifists. The 1527 Schleitheim Confession, the movement's religious manifesto, reflects the change from an established to a free church. In its fourth article a long paragraph is found concerning the separation of the plain congregation from the rest of society in all areas of life, in worship, at meetings, in wine taverns, and in financial commitments (Enninger 1985b, 142).

The history of the Anabaptists' persecutions through Luther's and Zwingli's followers is recorded in Thieleman Jens van Braght's *The Bloody Theatre; or, Martyrs Mirror of the Defenseless Christians*. Originally published in Dutch in 1660, it was translated and printed in German in Ephrata Cloister in 1748 under the title *Märtyrerspiegel der Tauffs Gesinnten*. To the present day this book is found in numerous Mennonite households.

Between 1650 and 1671 as well as between 1709 and 1711 a large number of Mennonites emigrated from the Swiss cantons Zurich and Bern to the Palatinate. As religious tolerance was limited even in this relatively liberal state, between three and five thousand of them moved on to the New World between 1707 and 1756. They formed the second large wave of Mennonite immigrants after the group from the Lower Rhine, who had founded and built Germantown between 1683 and 1705. For all of these and other Mennonite immigrants from Holland, Germany, Alsace, and Switzerland, Lancaster County, Pennsylvania, became a new home.

From there their descendants migrated to the western states during the eighteenth and nineteenth centuries. After 1793 and especially in 1806–7, a number of Mennonite families emigrated from Pennsylvania to Waterloo County, Ontario, Canada, where they were offered cheap land and exemption from military service. After the Napoleonic Wars the flow of Mennonite immigration bypassed Pennsylvania and moved into other American states. The history of Mennonite migrations not only includes the streams mentioned above, but also migrations to Prussia, Russia, and from there to North and South America.[11]

After numerous splits caused by disagreements over questions of faith and opening to the world, the Mennonites who live in the United States today consist of a large number of small subgroups. Among other things, they differ in language use. The three largest Mennonite groups in North America today are the (Old) Mennonite Church, the General Conference Mennonite Church, and the Mennonite Brethren Church (Redekop 1989, 39ff.).

While the latter was formed by immigrants from Russia, the ancestors of the first two groups came from Switzerland and the Palatinate. Single subgroups are usually united in so-called *conferences*, such as the

Lancaster Conference in Lancaster County, Pennsylvania. Numerous schisms within the local conferences have brought about more or less conservative lines, such as the Reformed or New Mennonites and the Old Order Mennonites. The former originated in Strasburg, Pennsylvania, in 1812. The latter line consists of numerous subgroups, some of which have as few as two hundred members.[12]

The two main branches of the Old Order Mennonites are the Wisler Mennonites (since 1872) and the Pike or Stauffer Mennonites (since 1845). The Wisler Mennonites consist of the Groffdale Conference Mennonites (also called *Wenger Mennonites* or *Wengerites*), the Weaverland Conference (also called *Horning Mennonites*), and several smaller groups such as the Reidenbach Mennonites. The relatively progressive Weaverland Conference allows its members to own cars, which, however, can have neither chrome parts nor colorful bodies, thus giving rise to the name *Black Bumper Mennonites*. The Groffdale Conference insists on horse-and-buggy transportation; as a result, the members of this group are also called *Team Mennonites* or, in Pennsylvania German, *Fuhreleit* 'coachpeople' (cf. Standard German *Fuhrleute*).

The various degrees of progressiveness are reflected by various degrees of preservation of the German dialect. While the fairly progressive Horning Mennonites have long since switched to English in their worship service and often have only passive competence in Pennsylvania German, the Wenger Mennonites continue to use Bible High German[13] and Pennsylvania German in church and Pennsylvania German among themselves in everyday life.

Some conservative groups use the horse and buggy for transportation, but tractors for working the fields. The latter, however, have steel wheels to prevent their use on macadam roads. These groups use cars only if driven by an outsider. They reject Sunday school and worldly clothing, and the women wear bonnets. They have been supporting missionary work since 1912. Their worship services, in which the old Anabaptist ritual of foot washing is still practiced, are held in churches. Married men, unmarried men, married women, and unmarried women all use different entrances to reach the separated sections of seating in church. Ministers, bishops, and deacons are chosen by lot from among the members of the community. The language of the service is Pennsylvania German, with readings from the Luther Bible and High German hymns, which are sung a cappella. The conservative Mennonites reject formal education beyond eighth grade. Their school language is English.

Unlike the conservative groups, less traditional Mennonites, often members of the (Old) Mennonite Church, have long operated Sunday schools and supported missionary work. Although they are generally in favor of conscientious objection, some members fought in World War II.

Higher education is common; the group even established twelve colleges in the United States and Canada, such as Bethel College in North Newton, Kansas, and Goshen College in Elkhart, Indiana (Redekop 1989, 178ff.). The women wear head coverings only in the church service. During the hymns, an organ is used, and services are conducted exclusively in English.

The Amish split from the Mennonites before their emigration from Europe. The division began when the Swiss religious refugee Jacob Ammann came to Alsace and complained about a lack of discipline in faith. Between 1693 and 1697 a dispute arose between Ammann and the Mennonite leader Hans Reist over the issue of *Meidung* 'shunning, ban' (cf. Standard German *meiden* 'avoid').

Among the Mennonites a member could be banned from communion only for offenses against the Bible or group conventions. Jacob Ammann extended the ban to both the social and the domestic domains. Whoever was banned could neither speak nor do business with their fellow group members. Within the family, banned persons had to eat at a separate table and sleep in a separate room until they had repented their sins and were fully reaccepted by the community. Other innovations of Ammann's include the introduction of foot washing, communion twice a year instead of once, simpler attire, unity of dress, the prohibition of men to cut their beards, and the excommunication of members who attended services of the state churches.

Thus, some of the Alsatian congregations split from the Swiss and southern German ones and, with reference to their leader's name, adopted the name *Amische*. While the schism was soon overcome in Europe, it still survives among the descendants of the emigrants to North America.

Today's Amish derive primarily from two peak immigration periods, one in the eighteenth (1727–70) and the other in the nineteenth century (1815–60; Hostetler 1993, 50). Like the Mennonites, the Amish in present-day Pennsylvania lead their lives separate from the world.[14]

To illustrate some characteristics of their lifestyle, the Old Order Amish will be described here. Between 1862 and 1878 they split from the rest of their group as a conservative branch. To the present day they use horse-and-buggy transportation. Their buggies differ in form and style from those of other plain groups, and among each other from state to state. Like conservative Mennonites, Old Order Amish use cars only as passengers on long-distance rides, for example, to visit out-of-state relatives, a pattern of behavior springing from the desire for separation from the outside world.

The Old Order Amish differ in hairstyle and dress from other plain groups, for instance, the Mennonites. The women, who in public always keep their hair tied together in a knot, wear plain black, blue, or brown dresses and big matching bonnets according to the community's dress code. They do not wear jewelry. Amish people cut their hair themselves. Unlike the Mennonites, whose male adults usually have clean-shaven faces, the married Old Order Amish men do not shave except for the moustache, which was seen as a characteristic of a soldier. For the same reason, Old Order Amish do not have buttons on their clothes, but prefer to use hooks and eyes. Instead of a belt, the men wear suspenders. In the summer they wear a straw hat, in the winter a black felt hat.

Similar to the women's dresses, plain colors are found on the fences, the buggies, and inside the house, where wallpaper, curtains, and pictures are not allowed on the walls. The beds are covered with colorful quilts artistically sewn together from small pieces of cloth. Old Order Amish do not allow their baptized members to go to the movies, use bicycles or musical instruments, or have a radio, television, or telephone in the house. Because they hold that the only purpose of the radio is to catch the weather forecast—which is very important for a farmer—a radio set is allowed in the barn. A number of communities share so-called *phone shanties* with telephones for commercial and emergency use.

Many Old Order Amish refuse to be photographed or taped. Although in some areas tobacco is one of their main crops, Amish people themselves do not smoke. The Old Order Amish use horses to till their fields. They reject formal education beyond eighth grade. Their families often have close to ten children, of whom the youngest son inherits the farm. The older sons acquire their own land with the help of their father. The Old Order Amish abstain from forming farm cooperatives with their worldly neighbors and avoid having electrical wires and telephone lines coming into their homes just as they refuse to take out life insurance or to put lightning rods on their roofs. The reasons for this are their fear of the "unequal yoke," that is, the fear to be improperly connected with outsiders, and their absolute trust in God's justice.

Old Order Amish homes are lit by gas lights, which, together with the gas canister, are often installed on casters and can easily be moved to wherever light is needed in the house. As the bedrooms and often the livingroom remain unheated in the winter, the large kitchen forms the center of the house. Like the Mennonites, the Amish are famous for neighborly help in times of need. One obvious example for this group solidarity is the barn raising, in which all the members of a community build a barn or house in one day for one of their families.

Every two weeks the Old Order Amish conduct their worship services[15] on the farm of a member of their district, a district consisting of about thirty-five families. The host family thoroughly cleans their house before the service, sometimes removing partitions between rooms. The service, which is followed by a meal for the whole community, takes place on Sunday morning from eight to twelve. Only the closest relatives stay during the afternoon and for Sunday night dinner.

During the service, men and women sit separated on backless benches arranged in rows in the kitchen, the livingroom, and the parents' bedroom. The minister often stands on the threshold between the two largest rooms. The service begins with the unison, a cappella singing of a number of hymns from the *Ausbund*, which originally was the hymnbook of both the Mennonites and the Amish, but is now exclusively used by the latter. It was first printed in 1564. An enlarged edition was published in Schaffhausen, Switzerland, in 1583. The *Ausbund* only contains the words of the hymns; the respective tunes have been handed down orally from generation to generation, which has caused some slight deviations between different Amish communities. Similar to the *Martyrs Mirror* mentioned earlier, a great number of the 140 hymns from the *Ausbund* recall the persecutions of the early Anabaptists.

The service continues with a short sermon, silent prayer, and the deacon reading the Scripture. Hymns and Bible passages are in High German (rendered with a Pennsylvania German pronunciation), but the leaders' elaborations and admonishments are in Pennsylvania German. The one-hour main sermon, called *es schwere Deel* 'the hard part' (cf. Standard German *der schwere Teil*), is at the center of the service. It is followed by comments from other leaders, a lengthy prayer, the blessing, and the announcement of the place of the next service. The youngest members leave the service first, the oldest last, the men before the women.

Only few Amish groups celebrate their worship services in churches. They are called *Church Amish* as opposed to the *House Amish*, described above. They split off as a more progressive line in 1927. Subgroups of the Church Amish are the *Beachy Amish*, the *Amish Mennonites*, and the *Weavertown*. These groups allow their members to have electricity and telephones in the house, a tractor, and even cars. Their dress, however, is traditional. A few smaller groups, generally referred to as *New Amish*, represent various departures from the Old Order Amish. Like the Church Amish, they prefer a more modern lifestyle than the House Amish.

INFORMANT FAMILIES

The three nonsectarian Pennsylvania German families interviewed live in the Mahantango Valley, a fertile area of rolling hills covering about 145 square miles situated in southern central Pennsylvania, forty miles north of the state capital, Harrisburg (figure 1.4).
Politically, this area belongs to southern Northumberland County, northern Dauphin County, and western Schuylkill County. These three counties were created in 1772, 1785, and 1811, respectively, from parts of the earlier Lancaster and Berks Counties, situated in the south of the Mahantango Valley and incorporating the fertile Great Valley.

The Mahantango Valley is confined by a fifteen-mile stretch of the Susquehanna River in the west, Line Mountain in the north, and Mahantango Mountain in the southeast. From a bird's-eye view, the confining lines have the shape of a horseshoe. In the wider part, starting from the river and stretching fifteen miles to the east, the Hooflander Mountain and Fisher Ridge divide the valley into two parts, namely the Schwaben Creek Valley in the north and the Mahantango Valley in the south. Both valleys are named after creeks that flow through them from east to west.

On the entire riverside of the valley, there is no bridge linking the east bank of the Susquehanna with the west bank. The nearest bridges are twenty miles north in Sunbury, where the north and the west branches of the Susquehanna River unite, and twenty-five miles south toward Harrisburg. The biggest roads in the valley are Route 147 along the Susquehanna River, leading from Sunbury to Harrisburg, Route 225 in the northwestern part, and Route 125 in the extreme eastern part, all running from north to south. The roads running from west to east toward the tip of the horseshoe are all small country roads.

The ridges of Line Mountain and Mahantango Mountain are broken by only a small number of gaps (e.g., Line Mountain near Dornsife and Mahantango Mountain near Pillow and Klingerstown). These mountain gaps used to be Indian trails crossing the valley, such as the Tulpehocken Path, which led over fifty miles from Womelsdorf in Berks County to the old Indian town of Shamokin, the present-day Sunbury, in Northumberland County. The Indian agent Conrad Weiser, who had his home in Womelsdorf, and Shikallamy, chief of the Iroquois, are among the first recorded travelers of the Tulpehocken Path, which was first mentioned as early as 1728. The name *Mahantango* is derived from *Mohantango*, which in the language of the Delaware Indians (Lenni Lenape) means "where we ate plentiful meat" (Heckewelder 1833).

Unlike in the so-called *coal region* beyond Line Mountain a few miles northeast, no coal has been found in the Mahantango Valley. The

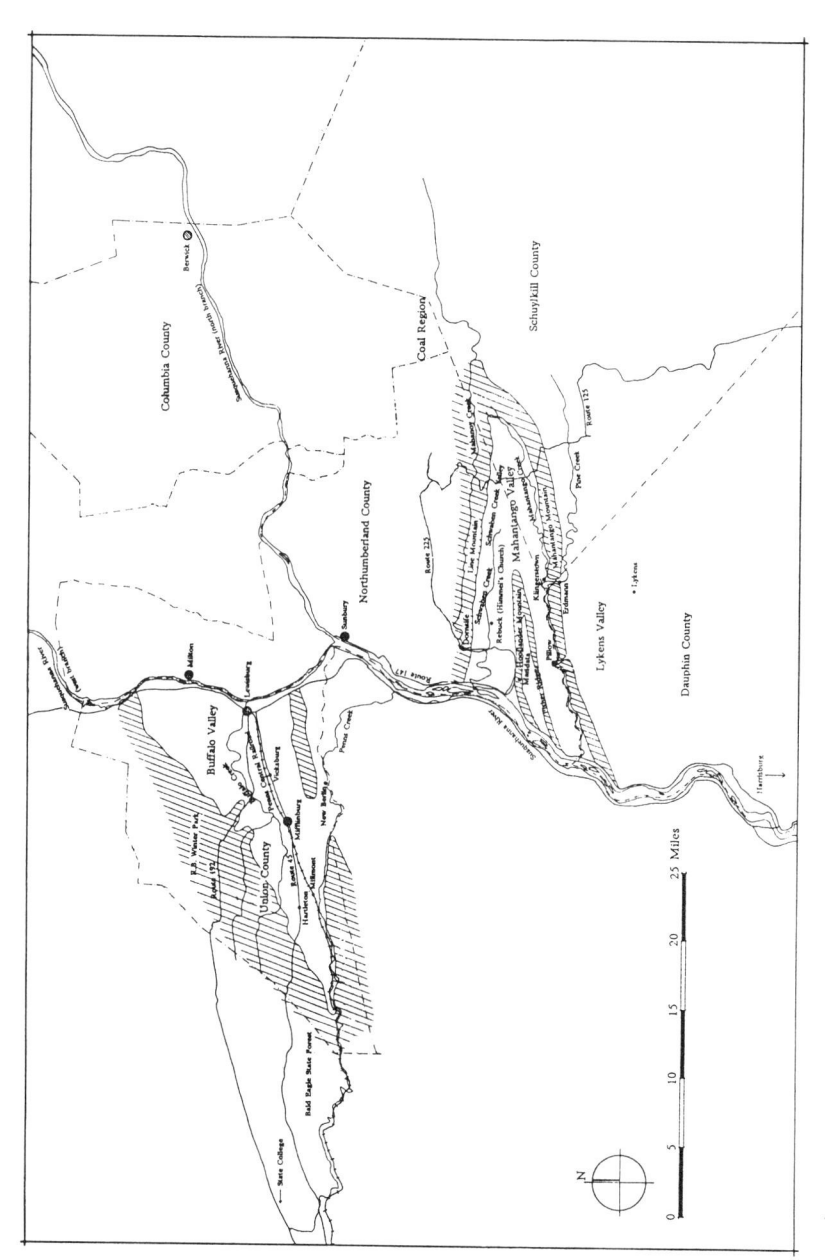

Figure 1.4: Areas of fieldwork in central Pennsylvania

area has thus been spared many of the influences of industrialization, urbanization, and the tourist industry. Unlike in Lykens Valley, the valley south of Mahantango Mountain, no sectarian Pennsylvania Germans have ever settled in the Mahantango. The land is still owned largely by the descendants of the Lutheran and Reformed settlers who came during the eighteenth century.

To illustrate the historical development of the Mahantango Valley, two major landmarks built and frequented for centuries by the ancestors of the nonsectarian Pennsylvania German families interviewed for the present study will be described in more detail: Himmel's Church and Klingerstown.

Himmel's Church[16] is situated near Rebuck in the Schwaben Creek Valley. It was the first church and school north of Blue Mountain. Begun in 1776, the Himmel's Church protocol is the oldest church record in existence in Pennsylvania outside Philadelphia.

William Penn's legal claim to all the land that is now Pennsylvania may have been valid in England; it was not, however, in any sense binding on the Native Americans who had lived there for many centuries. Maybe it was his sense of justice and his religious principles that led Penn to buy the land step by step from the Indians. In 1736, after several treaties moving the frontier in a northwesterly direction, Blue Mountain north of Harrisburg formed the northern border. In 1749 the chiefs of the Iroquois, Delaware, and Shawnee Indians granted a deed, which extended the frontier to the first mountain north of the mouth of Mahanoy Creek. Thus, Line Mountain became the northern boundary of Pennsylvania and remained so until 1768.

The majority of the first German pioneers to settle south of Line Mountain represented two groups of people: those who immigrated to America between 1749 and 1768, and those whose ancestors had first settled at the Schoharie River in New York and from there had migrated to the Tulpehocken region south of Blue Mountain in 1723.

In 1774 the people living on the Schwaben Creek erected a log church and a log schoolhouse. The first schoolteacher was Carl Heinrich Kaufmann, who in all probability had arrived in Philadelphia from Rotterdam in 1754 aboard the *Brothers*, and whose eighth-generation descendant, informant 13, is presently a schoolteacher in the Mahantango Valley. The original school building was used as a school until 1870, when the public school system was adopted. Nineteen members of the Himmel's Church congregation served on the side of the Americans in the Revolutionary War.

The first pastor, the Reverend John Michael Enterlein, who was educated at the University of Leipzig, served as the Lutheran pastor from 1773 to 1787. It was he who began the protocol. From the beginning, during almost the whole time of its existence, a Lutheran and a Reformed minister served at Himmel's Church simultaneously. Although the United States started coining silver dollars in 1794 and copper cents in 1793, all the Himmel's Church financial records before 1813 are still in pounds, shillings, and pence.

In 1818 the log church was replaced by a large stone church, which was one of few churches in the area to have a pipe organ. This instrument was also used in the new frame church erected on the same site in 1904. In January 1959, however, a fire destroyed both the instrument and the church. Since 1960, a new brick building has been the home of the present Lutheran and United Church of Christ congregations.

Klingerstown,[17] or *Klingerschtedtel* (cf. Standard German *Städtchen* 'little town'), as it is called in Pennsylvania German, is situated on the southern side of the Mahantango Valley, close to a narrow gap through Mahantango Mountain. The Tulpehocken Path used to lead through this natural gap. Today, the road connecting the Mahantango Valley with Lykens Valley still follows Pine Creek, which flows northward toward its junction with Mahantango Creek. The area became known as *Spread Eagle*, possibly because the configuration formed by the stream junction resembled a large bird.

In 1749 the Penn family purchased the area from the Iroquois Indians. The Penns reserved a tract of 1,200 acres for their own use, which they called *Spread Eagle Manor*. In 1750 the proprietary survey of Spread Eagle Manor was completed, and the land surrounding the manor was thrown open for purchase by land-seeking immigrants. With the end of the French and Indian War (1754–63), the stage was set for the Klingers to enter the scene.

Klingerstown is named after Alexander Klinger, who, along with his brother Johannes Philipp, arrived in Philadelphia aboard the *Albany* in September 1749. The brothers immigrated from Pfaffen-Beerfurth, a town in the Odenwald in southern Germany. In 1780, after a number of years spent in Reading, Pennsylvania, Alexander Klinger purchased land in Upper Mahantango Township, in what was then Berks County and became Schuylkill County in 1811. This purchase included the land where the village of Klingerstown is now located.

In 1807 one of Alexander Klinger's sons laid out a town and began to sell lots. The new town in the wilderness was originally called *Waynetown*, then *Elizabethtown*, and finally *Klingerstown*. The local Lutheran and Reformed congregations were organized as early as 1787 and met in the home of Johannes Philipp Klinger. In 1801 the congregation built the first Union Church building on land donated by Johannes Philipp Klinger. It was situated south of the gap through Mahantango Mountain, near the present village of Erdman, and served as the church building of both Klingerstown and Erdman. In the cemetery beside the church, a continuous line of the male descendants of Johannes Philipp Klinger are buried. In 1895 a new building replaced the original church; it continued to be used by the Lutheran and Reformed congregations in common worship services.

In 1968 the Union Church was dissolved and a new Lutheran congregation organized and chartered. Although the actual name of the church is *Zion Lutheran Church*, most locals to the present day refer to it as *Klinger's Church*.

Even though the Pennsylvania Germans living in the present-day Mahantango Valley are deeply rooted in the frontier tradition described above, there is nothing in their outer appearance to distinguish them from non-German rural inhabitants of the United States. Unlike the sectarian Pennsylvania Germans, they do not wear plain clothes, nor do they reject modern technology. Nevertheless, the descendants of the German immigrants are characterized by a certain cultural loyalty and various degrees of language competence.

As a rule, the generation of today's grandparents is the last to speak Pennsylvania German natively. Their children were the first to learn English as their native language, but on the whole they still have a good active and passive command of Pennsylvania German. The next generation only heard Pennsylvania German from their grandparents, which was usually not enough to enable them to pass any Pennsylvania German on to their own children. As a result, there is a rapid decline not only in native speakers, but also in semispeakers, which, among the group of the nonsectarian Pennsylvania Germans, will ultimately lead to language loss, that is, the death of Pennsylvania German. Various degrees of competence in Pennsylvania German lead to different degrees of interference with English.

There are a number of historical reasons for the demise of Pennsylvania German, two of which should be mentioned here. In the 1830s English-language preaching and public schools began to replace the original German worship services and church schools. Approximately a century later the widespread anti-German attitude in the United States in connection with World Wars I and II made a great number of families raise their children in English rather than Pennsylvania German. During World War I, German was forbidden in schools, churches, over the telephone, and in semipublic places (Rippley 1976, 187). Intimidations of cititens of German descent were the order of the day, particularly in the Midwest and the Great Plains, where many of the newer German-speaking immigrants lived. After World War II Americans of German descent again found it a handicap to admit to German background, although not on account of the same open hostility. Rather, ethnic pride in being German was gone (Rippley 1976, 214).[18]

While the outlay of old pioneer homesteads, which were originally built in stone rather than wood, would indicate whether the owner had immigrated from Germany or Britain,[19] the present-day houses of the nonsectarian Pennsylvania Germans do not differ from those of other Americans. Like most modern American farms, the appearance of the Pennsylvania German ones in the Mahantango Valley is dominated by high silos. Nevertheless, the original Pennsylvania German bank barn and the numerous smaller buildings such as smoke houses and outhouses are still found on almost every farm. Unlike the barns used by the sectarians, many nonsectarian barns are decorated with so-called *barn-signs* or *hex-signs* (*hex* 'witch', cf. Standard German *Hexe*), which are supposed to keep away evil spirits and date back to preemigration times in Europe.

In the winter a few families still have home butcherings, in which typical Pennsylvania German foods such as *Summerwascht* 'bologna' (cf. Standard German *Sommerwurst* 'summer sausage') and *Pannhaas* 'scrapple' (cf. Standard German *Panhas*) are prepared. Only in some of the more traditional households does the menu still include German dishes such as *Schnitz and Gnepp* 'sliced and dried apples and dumplings' (cf. Standard German *Schnitz* 'slice', *Knopf* 'dumpling') and *Schnitzboi* 'snitz pie'.

Only some forms of the old Pennsylvania German folk art survive. While some women still quilt, the art of cabinetmaking, once flourishing in the Mahantango Valley (*see* Weiser and Sullivan 1980), and the artistic drawing of *Daafschei* 'baptismal certificates' (cf. Standard German *Taufscheine*) in so-called *Fraktur* 'Pennsylvania German calligraphy'[20] are skills of the past. There is a sizeable corpus of Pennsylvania German literature, both poetry and prose. During many family reunions and on other occasions short skits—rather crude little comedies depicting rural life—are put on stage. The Pennsylvania German Society (founded in 1891), the Pennsylvania German Folklore Society (founded in 1935), and other organizations try to preserve the cultural heritage.

Of the old German holidays only few are still celebrated. Apart from the Church holidays, the two occasions particularly observed were *Fasnacht* 'Shrove Tuesday' (cf. Standard German *Fastnacht*) and *Grundsaudag* 'Groundhog Day' (cf. Standard German *Grundsautag*). At *Fasnacht* the school children were allowed to lock out their teacher from the one-room schoolhouse. The last person in a family to get up that morning would be called *Fasnacht*. Today, however, *Fasnacht* is nothing more than the word for *doughnut*, and in some more traditional households doughnuts are prepared on Shrove Tuesday.

According to old folk beliefs, the *Grundsau* 'groundhog, woodchuck' comes out of its hole on Groundhog Day, 2 February, and acts as an indicator of when spring will begin. If it sees its shadow, it will continue its hibernation, thereby indicating that the beginning of springlike weather is still six weeks away.

The so-called *Versammling* 'assembly, meeting' (cf. Standard German *Versammlung*), the annual gathering of male speakers of Pennsylvania German for food and entertainment, has been another big occasion to the present day. In April 1990 the *Siwweunfatzichscht Yarlich Fersommling der Pennsylfawnish Deitsche–Unner Mahanoy un Nochberschaft* 'forty-seventh annual gathering of the Pennsylvania Germans–Lower Mahanoy and surrounding area' was held in Lykens, Pennsylvania. Among all the *Grundsau* and *Versammling* lodges, this is the one that includes the area of the Mahantango Valley. Although the old rule of speaking only Pennsylvania German at the *Versammlinge* is no longer strictly followed, these gatherings are still a popular facet in the attempts to preserve a dying language and culture.

In the middle of the twentieth century, the rural one- and two-room schoolhouses disappeared in the Mahantango Valley. Today, after elementary school, almost all the students attend the modern Line Mountain High School near Mandata in the western part of the valley. Here they come into contact with fellow students from outside the valley, that is, from the coal region beyond the mountains to the northeast. The cultural clash between the Protestant Pennsylvania Germans and the Catholic or Orthodox descendants of Croatians, Ukrainians, Slovaks, Italians, and other immigrants have led to a number of strong personal experiences of the younger informants, two of whom are now teachers at Line Mountain High School. While before World War II most people in the Mahantango Valley were farmers and did not go beyond eighth-grade education, the members of the present parent generation were the first to attend colleges and universities outside the valley. The number of marriages with outsiders has increased, and many people have left the valley.

Today the spectrum of professions in the Mahantango Valley equals that of any other rural area in the United States. However, to the present day, there are no big industries or fast-food restaurants in the valley. The villages and towns are admininstered by boards of supervisors. The main denominations are Lutheran and United Church of Christ. Regular church services are conducted in English, Pennsylvania German being used by only a few congregations approximately once a year for nostalgic reasons. A large number of German tombstones in the cemeteries give proof of the former dominance of German in the domain of the church. During a time of transition in the early nineteenth century, some tombstones were inscribed in both German and English. However, there are no stones inscribed in Pennsylvania German, which used to be a spoken language only.

The two sectarian families interviewed live in Buffalo Valley, an area sixty miles north of Harrisburg (see figure 1.4). In size it almost matches the Mahantango Valley, but lies on the western side of the Susquehanna River, approximately twenty miles upriver on the west branch. Buffalo Valley is a wide, relatively flat area stretching almost twenty miles from east to west. The natural boundaries are the west branch of the Susquehanna River in the east, and the hills and mountains of the Bald Eagle State Forest in the north, west, and south. Broad openings in the mountains are found in the north along the river toward Milton and in the south toward the town of New Berlin.

The largest town in the vicinity is Lewisburg, situated on the eastern edge of Buffalo Valley along the Susquehanna River. The major town inside the valley is Mifflinburg on Route 45, running from Lewisburg in the east to State College in the west. The Penns Central Railroad line runs in the same direction. The only other east-west connection through the valley is Route 192 from Lewisburg to R. B. Winter Park, leading through the mountains to State College. The biggest creeks are Buffalo Creek in the north and Penns Creek in the south, both running toward the Susquehanna River from west to east. A great number of covered bridges, which are typical of this part of Pennsylvania, can be found here. All of Buffalo Valley belongs to Union County, founded in 1813. Until 1855 the county seat was New Berlin and has been Lewisburg ever since.

The two informant families living in Buffalo Valley belong to the sectarian groups of the Mennonites and the Amish. The Mennonite family lives on two farms around Hartleton. They are Old Orders, more specifically members of the Groffdale Conference, that is, one of the most conservative Mennonite groups. The most prominent markers of their conservatism are horse-and-buggy transportation, plain dress, neither television nor radio in the houses, no curtains, eighth-grade education only, steel wheels on the tractors, use of Bible High German and Pennsylvania German in church, and Pennsylvania German as their native language.

On the other hand, the Mennonite informants do not completely reject modern technology and worldly lifestyle. Electricity from the public power supply, telephones in the houses, electric lights, freezers, electric knives, wallpaper, colorful pictures and calendars on the walls, and colorful toys for the children are just a few modern items they have accepted.

In 1968 the present grandparent generation moved to Buffalo Valley to buy cheap land. Before, members of the family had been living on farms near Leola, New Holland, and Ephrata, all in Lancaster County, Pennsylvania, for many generations. However, after several splits, their own land in Lancaster County had become too small to be divided any further, and new land was too expensive to buy.

The Amish family lives on two farms near Mifflinburg in the center of Buffalo Valley. The older generation and their unmarried children are New Order Amish, while the younger married couple interviewed has joined the Beachy Amish.

The New Order Amish informants use horse-and-buggy transportation, wear plain dress, have neither radio nor television in their homes, and conduct their worship services in German in the homes of their members. On the other hand, they have made a number of concessions to modernity. Public electricity, telephones in their houses, freezers, electric milking machines, Sunday school, and Bible classes distinguish them from more conservative Amish groups. Through their use of tractors with rubber tires and by allowing their members to fly in airplanes, they are more progressive than their Old Order Mennonite neighbors, described above.

The young couple that joined the Beachy Amish has opened its lifestyle even more to the world. Only the woman wears plain clothing with bonnet and dress, while the husband wears conventional blue jeans. They have neither radio nor television in their house, but own a car. Electricity, telephone, freezer, curtains, and pictures on the wall are taken for granted. The service they attend takes place in a church building and is entirely in English.

The present grandparent generation lived on farms near Leola in Lancaster County, Pennsylvania, until 1967 and near Honeybrook in Chester County, Pennsylvania, until 1976, before they bought new land and established a new farm in Buffalo Valley. As in the case of the Mennonite informants, the present parent generation moved out of their parents' farm after marriage, and built a new one in the vicinity.

In Buffalo Valley, like elsewhere in the Pennsylvania German area, the sectarian farms and shops are situated among the homes of the non-sectarians. Most Mennonites and Amish are farmers, but when new land became scarce, other farm-related trades and professions arose, such as carpenter or chicken catcher.[21] Today, a number of sectarian carpenters specialize in building gazebos. Other sectarian craftsmen meet the specific needs of their communities as buggy builders, hatmakers, bookbinders, or harness store owners. Bible bookstores are often run by farmers and their families.

All church offices are honorary and held along with the regular profession. No member of the sectarian families interviewed has an academic profession, as neither the Mennonite nor the Amish family belongs to a community allowing its members to go beyond eighth-grade education. The schoolteachers are usually young women around the age of nineteen, who teach in one-room schoolhouses until they get married and have children. One of the Mennonite informants was the schoolteacher in her community from 1979 to 1982.

There are several one-room schoolhouses in Buffalo Valley. Each school has approximately twenty-five students. The children of the Mennonite family attend Sunny Side Mennonite School in Millmont, which lies just across the road for some of them. The Amish children interviewed presently attend the Mennonite school in Hartleton.

The language used in these schools is English. Many children, unless they have older brothers and sisters, learn English at school. Pennsylvania German is only used on the playground and on the way to and from school. Subjects taught are reading, writing, arithmetic, and Bible studies. The children of all eight grades are together in one room and instructed by the teacher in small groups, while the other grades do quiet work.

On Saturday afternoon the Mennonite community offers a special reading course of the German Bible and hymn book especially for younger people who have some deficiencies in reading and pronouncing Bible High German. The Mennonite community has modern churches near Hartleton and Vicksburg.

Pennsylvania German is the native language of all the members of the sectarian families interviewed. It is used in the domains of family and worship service, and in almost all in-group interaction. English, on the other hand, is the variety used in dealing with outsiders as well as in school. Through the strict use of the varieties in certain domains, the survival of Pennsylvania German is secured for years to come. However, there are first indications of changes; the use of English in the church service of the Beachy Amish is a case in point.

Most members of the non-Pennsylvania German family live in Lewisburg, Pennsylvania, on the west branch of the Susquehanna River (see figure 1.4). One branch of the family originates from Berwick, a slightly larger industrial town thirty miles east on the north branch in Columbia County. Three informants belonging to the grandparent generation still live in a rural area outside Berwick.

While Berwick is an industrial town with a large power station and railroad industry, Lewisburg today is a wealthy residential town of approximately fifteen thousand inhabitants. Since 1855 it has been the county seat of Union County. Named after its founder Ludwig (Lewis) Derr, Lewisburg was laid out in 1785 and incorporated as a borough in 1822. Its main street, Market Street, forms part of an important east-west highway crossing the Susquehanna River at Lewisburg.

Today the town is known as the site of a Federal Penitentiary and for Bucknell University, which was established as the University of Lewisburg in 1846 by Pennsylvania Baptists. In 1886 it was renamed *Bucknell University* in honor of William Bucknell, a major benefactor.

Lewisburg is situated too far on the edge of the Pennsylvania German heartland to have a German character. The influx and influence of English-speaking inhabitants was so strong that the town was English-speaking from its very beginning, while the German language was thriving in the more isolated and rural Mahantango Valley, situated only thirty miles south. Attracting English speakers from all parts of the United States and overseas, the university may also have contributed to this development. Today Bucknell has 3,500 students and 250 faculty members and is considered one of the nation's more competitive undergraduate institutions.

Even though student life takes place primarily on Bucknell's 330-acre campus, the linguistic situation of the town of Lewisburg is completely different from that of the other informant families. Pennsylvania German is practically nonexistent, and the regional standard of English is far more prevalent than an English variety influenced by Pennsylvania German. The only place to hear this variety in town is the Farmers' Market, which takes place every Wednesday and is frequented, among others, by sectarian and nonsectarian farmers and salespeople from the surrounding areas. Members of nonsectarian family 3 have a regular butcher stall at the Lewisburg Farmers' Market.

The ancestors of the non-Pennsylvania German family came from England, Ireland, Wales, and the Palatinate. Owing to the large number of Pennsylvania Germans in the counties south of Union County, most local families can claim at least some German ancestry. However, in the case of this particular family, intermarriage with members of non-German groups was strong, and Pennsylvania German has not been the native language for many generations. None of the present family members understands as much as a single word of Pennsylvania German. All the informants are Protestants, one branch of the family belonging to the Pentecostal, the other to the United Methodist denominations.

As compared to the nonsectarian and particularly the sectarian groups, the non-Pennsylvania Germans are characterized by higher individual mobility. Many of them have lived or been stationed in other parts of the country. None of the members of this group are farmers. Their professions range from welder and mechanic to nurse, computer specialist, and accountant. All the informants attend or have attended public consolidated schools. The children go to the elementary school in Lewisburg. All the informants are monolingual speakers of English.

Fieldwork

All data were collected between October 1989 and May 1990. The winter months were chosen to enable the predominantly rural informants to have time for the interviews. In spite of some overlaps, the basic order was nonsectarian Pennsylvania Germans first, then the non-Pennsylvania Germans, and finally the sectarians.

Before the actual interviews, three pilot interviews were conducted to test the questionnaire and to record voices for the matched-guise test. The contacts were established with the help of Professor M. Lois Huffines from Bucknell University. All the informants in the pilot interviews, three nonsectarians and a Mennonite, were members of a Pennsylvania German discussion group meeting once every month at Susquehanna University in Selinsgrove, Pennsylvania, about fifteen miles south of Lewisburg.

Contacts with nonsectarian family 2 had existed since 1986. However, with the help of Professor Huffines, the first meeting in October 1989 was arranged with the young couple from family 3, who run the butcher stand at the Lewisburg Farmers' Market. After this first contact to the informants was established, it proved easy to approach other family members. Without exception, all groups were extremely keen on talking to a German, and, at least in the case of the Pennsylvania German informants, talking to someone who came from the country of their forefathers. Soon after the interviews with family 3 had begun, the contacts with the "old" friends in family 2 were reestablished. From here, it was easy to find access to family 1, which is distantly related to family 2.

A comparable non-Pennsylvania German family was difficult to find as it had to be local, without strong German ancestry, and of a socioeconomic background similar to the Pennsylvania German families. It took until March 1990 before a suitable family was contacted with the help of a local friend.

At about the same time, contacts with the sectarian families were established. The first contact with the Mennonites was made at a farm sale through the agency of the local veterinarian. The Amish family were old friends from the fieldworker's first stay four years earlier.

QUESTIONNAIRE

The questionnaire consisted of three major parts: (1) language, (2) language use and network, (3) language attitude.

The language part was itself subdivided into three sections. Section 1.1 contained a large number of questions to elicit discourse on topics such as language, childhood, school, spare time/traveling, work, and old traditions. While each interview started out in English, the last two topics could be dealt with in English or Pennsylvania German[22] according to the informants' language competence. Section 1.2 consisted of a list of phonologically relevant English words to be elicited with the help of flashcards. In section 1.3 the sectarian informants were invited to read a brief passage from the German Bible and a hymn from the *Ausbund* to test their competence in Bible High German.

The part on use and network opened with personal data (2.1) and questions about the structure of the informant's family (2.2), which were followed by a large integrated section on social network and language use (2.3).

The first section of part 3 consisted of direct questions concerning the informants' attitudes toward the Pennsylvania German language and culture (3.1). Section 3.2 was a matched-guise test of language attitudes.

Three large sections of the questionnaire correspond with the three central chapters of the present study, namely the word list of section 1.2 (chapter 2), the questions on network and language use of section 2.3 (chapter 3), and the matched-guise test of section 3.2 (chapter 4). The fourth part to be thoroughly evaluated consists of sections 2.1 and 2.2, which refer to the informants' personal data and identify their position in the family structure. These results will be presented in the section below, on informants.

Those sections of the questionnaire that are relevant for the present study are reprinted in the appendix.

In retrospect, it is clear that, like in most empirical examinations, the questionnaire contains some deficiencies. The obsolescence of the questionnaire is the fieldworkers' eternal and inevitable dilemma.[23] At the same time, through this phenomenon they have the comforting certainty that in the course of their fieldwork they have learned something new about their informants.

Gathering as complete data as possible turned out to be one of the most difficult problems. Completeness of the information is particularly essential for the method of implicational scaling used in chapters 2 and 3. A high degree of empty cells makes reliable interpretation difficult.

When the questionnaire was set up, it was decided that the language use questions should strictly ask about the facts. Thus, two typical questions were "Do you speak Pennsylvania German to your grandfather?" and "Do you speak Pennsylvania German to your grandson?" If the informant did not have a grandfather or a grandson, the respective question was treated as inapplicable. One could argue that the empty cells produced through this method could have been avoided by rephrasing the questions as "Did you speak Pennsylvania German to your grandfather when he was still alive?" and "How would you speak to your grandson if you had one?" However, it was decided that such hypothetical questions would have resulted in highly unreliable data that could not have been verified. Empty cells appeared to be the lesser of the two evils, particularly since the fieldworker has the chance to interpret them according to the knowledge he has of a given informant's language behavior.

INFORMANTS

Of the fifty informants interviewed, the twenty-eight nonsectarians (informants 1–28) are members of three separate families. Family 1 comprises twelve informants, family 2 nine, and family 3 seven. The twelve sectarians (informants 29–40) belong to two families, one being Mennonite, the other Amish. Finally, ten informants (informants 41–50) are members of a single non-Pennsylvania German family.

The nonsectarian Pennsylvania German informants are numbered according to generation (a through d) rather than family as the various generations differ in their patterns of language acquisition, thus forming clusters in many tables and scales. By contrast, the various generations of the sectarian and the non-Pennsylvania German families differ neither in acquisition patterns nor in language competence; they were therefore ordered according to family. If the generation is given nevertheless, this is meant to help the reader to locate the individual informant within the family tree.

All in all, there are seven groups of informants:

(1) Nonsectarian generation a:
Native speakers of Pennsylvania German, acquired English as their second language in early childhood. The group includes eight informants (1–8), two of them male and six female. They range in age from sixty to seventy-nine years. They were the first generation to raise their children

in English. Six of the informants speak predominantly Pennsylvania German today, two use more English.

(2) Nonsectarian generation b:
Members of the first generation to have English as their native language. Most of the eight informants (9–16) have near-native competence in Pennsylvania German, which they usually acquired through listening to their parents and older relatives. The four male and four female informants range in age from thirty-seven to eighty-three years. They use Pennsylvania German only with the older members of the community, but speak English with their age peers and younger people.

(3) Nonsectarian generation c:
Members of the second generation to have English as their native language. Most of the seven informants (17–23) have only rudimentary competence in Pennsylvania German, of which their grandparents were often the only source. They were usually addressed in English by all relatives and members of the community. The four male and three female informants range in age from twenty-three to fifty-four years. One informant (19) married into family 1 from a non-Pennsylvania German background. These informants can understand some Pennsylvania German, but never speak it.

(4) Nonsectarian generation d:
Members of the third generation to have English as their native language. Only two of the five informants (24–28) have rudimentary competence in Pennsylvania German, which, as in the case of some members of the c-generation, shows interference from a high school knowledge of Standard German. The three youngest informants are monolingual speakers of English. The one male and four female informants range in age from five to thirty-one years. They use English in all social situations.

(5) Sectarian family M:
Members of a Mennonite family with Pennsylvania German as their native language. English was acquired during the first year at school at the latest. The seven informants (29–35) belong to three generations, ranging in age from six to fifty-seven years; three are male, four female. They all belong to the Old Order Mennonite group (church service held in German). The usual group-internal variety is Pennsylvania German. English is used almost exclusively with outsiders and at school.

Introduction

(6) Sectarian family A:
Members of an Amish family with Pennsylvania German as their native language. English was acquired during the first year at school at the latest. Of the five informants (36–40), three are male and two female, ranging in age from seventeen to fifty-two years. They belong to two generations. While three informants are members of the New Order Amish group (worship service in German), two younger ones recently joined the more progressive Beachy Amish congregation (service in English). Within their own community, the informants normally use Pennsylvania German. Only the Beachy Amish couple raises their children in English.[24] With outsiders and at school, the language is always English.

(8) Non-Pennsylvania Germans:
Members of a local family without immediate Pennsylvania German ancestry. The ten informants (41–50) belong to four generations and range in age from five to eighty-one years. There are five male and five female informants, all of them monolingual speakers of English.

Short individual descriptions of all the informants will follow, concentrating on family, gender, age, and generation along with other social data. In addition, information about places of residence, education, profession, and relatives will be presented. At the end of each characterization, the informants' linguistic profiles will be given.

Informant 1:
Family 1, nonsectarian, male, 77, a-generation (married to informant 2), Lutheran;
has lived in the Mahantango Valley all his life;
eighth-grade education (public one-room school);
retired farmer;
ten brothers and sisters, seven children, twenty-four grandchildren, sixteen great-grandchildren;
native speaker of Pennsylvania German, heavily accented English.

Informant 2:
Family 1, nonsectarian, female, 77, a-generation (married to informant 1), Lutheran;
has lived in the Mahantango Valley all her life;
eighth-grade education (public one-room school);
farmer's wife;
nine brothers and sisters, youngest child in the family (born twenty-one years after her oldest brother), seven children, twenty-four grandchildren, sixteen great-grandchildren;
native speaker of Pennsylvania German, heavily accented English.

Informant 3:
Family 1, nonsectarian, female, 77, a-generation, widowed, United Church of Christ;
has lived in the Mahantango Valley all her life;
eighth-grade education (public one-room school);
farmer's wife;
seven brothers and sisters, two children, seven grandchildren, six great-grandchildren;
native speaker of Pennsylvania German, accented English.

Informant 4:
Family 2, nonsectarian, male, 71, a-generation (married to informant 5), Lutheran;
has lived in the Mahantango Valley almost all his life; served in Germany for two years in World War II;
eighth-grade education (public one-room school);
retired car mechanic and plumber;
five brothers and sisters, four children, two grandchildren;
native speaker of Pennsylvania German, heavily accented English.

Informant 5:
Family 2, nonsectarian, female, 68, a-generation (married to informant 4), Lutheran;
has lived in the Mahantango Valley all her life;
eighth-grade education (public one-room school);
retired factory and school cafeteria worker;
one brother, four children, two grandchildren;
native speaker of Pennsylvania German, heavily accented English.

Informant 6:
Family 2, nonsectarian, female, 74, a-generation, widowed, Lutheran;
has lived in the Mahantango Valley all her life;
eighth-grade education (public one-room school);
farmer's wife and retired factory worker;
five brothers and sisters, three children, seven grandchildren;
native speaker of Pennsylvania German, heavily accented English.

Informant 7:
Family 3, nonsectarian, female, 79, a-generation, widowed, Lutheran;
has lived in the Mahantango Valley all her life;
high school education;
housewife;
three brothers and sisters, four children, eleven grandchildren, eighteen great-grandchildren;
native speaker of Pennsylvania German, heavily accented English.

Introduction

Informant 8:
Family 3, nonsectarian, female, 60, a-generation (married to informant 15, a member of the b-generation), Lutheran;
has lived in the Mahantango Valley all her life;
high school education;
housewife, retired toy factory worker;
six brothers and sisters, three children, ten grandchildren;
native speaker of Pennsylvania German, heavily accented English.

Informant 9:
Family 1, nonsectarian, female, 57, b-generation, widowed, Lutheran;
has lived in the Mahantango Valley all her life;
eighth-grade education (mostly public one-room school);
housewife and part-time worker in the area;
six brothers and sisters, four children, four grandchildren;
native speaker of English, accented; very good command of Pennsylvania German.

Informant 10:
Family 1, nonsectarian, male, 54, b-generation (married to informant 11), Lutheran;
has lived in the Mahantango Valley almost all his life (apart from technical institute and military service);
two years at technical institute after high school;
car mechanic, owner of gas station and school bus business;
one brother, three children, three grandchildren;
native speaker of English, accented; very good command of Pennsylvania German; on the board of the *Yaahrlich Versammling*.

Informant 11:
Family 1, nonsectarian, female, 53, b-generation (married to informant 10), Lutheran;
has lived in the Mahantango Valley all her life;
high school education;
housewife and part-time secretary in family business;
six brothers and sisters, three children, three grandchildren;
native speaker of English, accented; fair command of Pennsylvania German.

Informant 12:
Family 2, nonsectarian, female, 83, b-generation, widowed, Lutheran;
has lived in the Mahantango Valley all her life;
eighth-grade education (public one-room school);
housewife;
five brothers and sisters, two children, eight grandchildren, five great-grandchildren;
native speaker of English, accented; had an English great-grandmother in whose house her father grew up; very good command of Pennsylvania German.

Informant 13:
Family 2, nonsectarian, male, 49, b-generation, single, Lutheran;
has lived in the Mahantango Valley all his life;
university education (M.A.);
high school teacher;
three brothers and sisters;
native speaker of English, slightly accented; good command of Pennsylvania German; very interested in Pennsylvania German culture and language.

Informant 14:
Family 2, nonsectarian, male, 54, b-generation (married to informant 22, a member of the c-generation), Lutheran;
has lived in the Mahantango Valley almost all his life (apart from military service and university);
university education (M.A.);
high school teacher;
two brothers and sisters, four children;
native speaker of English, slightly accented; very good command of Pennsylvania German; very interested in Pennsylvania German culture and language; tried to raise his youngest son in Pennsylvania German.

Informant 15:
Family 3, nonsectarian, male, 61, b-generation (married to informant 8, a member of the a-generation), Lutheran;
has lived in the Mahantango Valley all his life;
high school education;
construction equipment operator;
three brothers, three children, ten grandchildren;
native speaker of English, accented; very good command of Pennsylvania German; very interested in Pennsylvania German culture and language.

Informant 16:
Family 3, nonsectarian, female, 37, b-generation (married to informant 23, a member of the c-generation), United Church of Christ;
has lived in the Mahantango Valley almost all her life (apart from four years at college);
university education (B.A.);
housewife and sales assistant in family butcher shop;
three brothers and sisters, two children;
native speaker of English, slightly accented; slight command of Pennsylvania German.

Informant 17:
Family 1, nonsectarian, male, 35, c-generation, single, Lutheran;
has lived in the Mahantango Valley all his life;

high school education;
farmer, family butcher;
three brothers and sisters;
native speaker of English, accented; good command of Pennsylvania German.

Informant 18:
Family 1, nonsectarian, male, 30, c-generation (married to informant 19, a non-Pennsylvania German), Lutheran;
has lived in the Mahantango Valley all his life;
high school education;
car mechanic and school bus operator (family business);
two brothers and sisters, one child;
native speaker of English, hardly accented; very slight command of Pennsylvania German; some knowledge of Standard German through high school.

Informant 19:
Family 1, non-Pennsylvania German, female, 30, c-generation (married to informant 18), Greek Catholic;
grew up near Shamokin, Pennsylvania (coal region) in a family with a Slovak and Italian background, has lived in the Mahantango Valley since her marriage in 1980;
university education (M.A.);
school counselor;
two brothers and sisters, one child;
native speaker of English, unaccented; no command of Pennsylvania German at all.

Informant 20:
Family 1, nonsectarian, male, 26, c-generation (married to informant 21), Lutheran;
has lived in the Mahantango Valley all his life;
high school education;
car mechanic and school bus operator (family business);
two brothers and sisters;
native speaker of English, hardly accented; very slight command of Pennsylvania German; some knowledge of Standard German through high school.

Informant 21:
Family 1, nonsectarian, female, 23, c-generation (married to informant 20), Lutheran;
has lived in the Mahantango Valley all her life;
high school education;
secretary;
two brothers and sisters;
native speaker of English, hardly accented; no command of Pennsylvania German.

Informant 22:
Family 2, nonsectarian, female, 54, c-generation (married to informant 14, a member of the b-generation), Mormon (converted from Lutheran in 1983);
has lived in the Mahantango Valley almost all her life;
high school education;
housewife, voluntary work with handicapped children, former hairdresser;
one brother, four children;
native speaker of English, slightly accented; good command of Pennsylvania German; consciously used Pennsylvania German with her husband for some time after their marriage.

Informant 23:
Family 3, nonsectarian, male, 37, c-generation (married to informant 16, a member of the b-generation), United Church of Christ;
has lived in the Mahantango Valley almost all his life (apart from four years at college);
university education (B.A. in geology);
butcher (family business);
two brothers and sisters, two children;
native speaker of English, slightly accented; slight command of Pennsylvania German; some knowledge of Standard German through high school.

Informant 24:
Family 1, nonsectarian, female, 5, d-generation, Greek Catholic;
has lived in the Mahantango Valley all her life;
kindergarten;
native speaker of English, unaccented; has learned a few Pennsylvania German songs, numbers, and words from her grandparents and great-grandparents.

Informant 25:
Family 2, nonsectarian, female, 31, d-generation, single, Lutheran;
has lived in the Mahantango Valley all her life;
college education (B.A.);
poultry plant manager;
three brothers and sisters;
native speaker of English, hardly accented; slight command of Pennsylvania German; some knowledge of Standard German through high school.

Informant 26:
Family 2, nonsectarian, female, 27, d-generation, single, Lutheran;
has lived in the Mahantango Valley all her life;
community college education (Associate Degree);
clerk;
three brothers and sisters;

Introduction 53

native speaker of English, hardly accented; very slight command of Pennsylvania German; some knowledge of Standard German through high school.

Informant 27:
Family 3, nonsectarian, male, 11, d-generation, United Church of Christ;
has lived in the Mahantango Valley all his life;
sixth grade at junior high school;
one sister;
native speaker of English, unaccented; knows fewer Pennsylvania German expressions than his younger sister (informant 28).

Informant 28:
Family 3, nonsectarian, female, 9, d-generation, United Church of Christ;
has lived in the Mahantango Valley all her life;
third grade at elementary school;
one brother;
native speaker of English, unaccented; has learned a few Pennsylvania German expressions from her grandparents.

Informant 29:
Family M, sectarian, male, 57, a-generation (married to informant 30), Old Order Mennonite;
grew up in Lancaster County, established a farm in Buffalo Valley in 1968 at the age of thirty-six;
eighth-grade education (public one-room school);
farmer;
six brothers and sisters, fourteen children, twenty-seven grandchildren;
native speaker of Pennsylvania German; hardly accented English.

Informant 30:
Family M, sectarian, female, 55, a-generation (married to informant 29), Old Order Mennonite;
grew up in Lancaster County, moved to Buffalo Valley in 1968 at the age of thirty-four;
eighth-grade education (public one-room school);
farmer's wife;
twelve brothers and sisters, fourteen children, twenty-seven grandchildren;
native speaker of Pennsylvania German; hardly accented English; as the youngest child, she learned English from her brothers and sisters before she went to school.

Informant 31:
Family M, sectarian, male, 37, b-generation (married to informant 32), Old Order Mennonite;
grew up in Lancaster County, moved to Buffalo Valley in 1962 at the age of ten;

eighth-grade education (public one-room school);
farmer;
seven brothers and sisters, four children;
native speaker of Pennsylvania German; hardly accented English.

Informant 32:
Family M, sectarian, female, 27, b-generation (married to informant 31), Old Order Mennonite;
grew up in Lancaster County, moved to Buffalo Valley in 1968 at the age of six;
eighth-grade education (Mennonite and Amish two-room school);
farmer's wife, from 1979 to 1982 teacher at Mennonite one-room school;
thirteen brothers and sisters, four children;
native speaker of Pennsylvania German; hardly accented English.

Informant 33:
Family M, sectarian, male, 12, b-generation, Old Order Mennonite;
has lived in Buffalo Valley all his life;
seventh grade at Mennonite one-room school;
thirteen brothers and sisters;
native speaker of Pennsylvania German; hardly accented English.

Informant 34:
Family M, sectarian, female, 22, b-generation, married, Old Order Mennonite;
born in Lancaster County, moved to Buffalo Valley in 1967 at three months of age;
eighth-grade education (Mennonite one-room school);
housewife;
thirteen brothers and sisters, one child;
native speaker of Pennsylvania German; hardly accented English.

Informant 35:
Family M, sectarian, female, 6, c-generation, Old Order Mennonite;
has lived in Buffalo Valley all her life;
first grade at Mennonite one-room school;
three brothers and sisters;
native speaker of Pennsylvania German; currently learning English at school and through contact with older children and outsiders.

Informant 36:
Family A, sectarian, male, 52, a-generation (married to informant 37), New Order Amish;
grew up in Lancaster County, lived in Chester County from 1968 to 1976, established a farm in Buffalo Valley in 1976 at the age of thirty-nine;
eighth-grade education (public one-room school);

Introduction 55

farmer;
eleven brothers and sisters, nine children, ten grandchildren;
native speaker of Pennsylvania German; hardly accented English.

Informant 37:
Family A, sectarian, female, 51, a-generation (married to informant 36), New Order Amish;
grew up in Lancaster County, lived in Chester County from 1968 to 1976, moved to Buffalo Valley in 1976 at the age of thirty-eight;
eighth-grade education (public one-room school);
farmer's wife;
thirteen brothers and sisters, nine children, ten grandchildren;
native speaker of Pennsylvania German; hardly accented English.

Informant 38:
Family A, sectarian, male, 29, b-generation (married to informant 39), Beachy Amish (converted from New Order Amish after marriage in 1984);
born in Lancaster County in 1960, lived in Chester County from 1968 to 1976, has lived in Buffalo Valley since 1976, first on his father's farm, since 1984 on his own farm;
eighth-grade education (first two grades at Amish and Mennonite one-room school, then public school);
farmer;
eight brothers and sisters, two children;
native speaker of Pennsylvania German; hardly accented English.

Informant 39:
Family A, sectarian, female, 30, b-generation (married to informant 38), Beachy Amish (converted from New Order Mennonite after marriage in 1984; parents originally Amish, converted to New Order Mennonite when informant was three years old);
grew up in central Ohio, has lived in Buffalo Valley since 1984;
eighth-grade education (public schools);
farmer's wife;
eight brothers and sisters, two children;
native speaker of Pennsylvania German; unaccented English.

Informant 40:
Family A, sectarian, male, 17, b-generation, single, New Order Amish;
born in Chester County in 1972, has lived in Buffalo Valley since 1976;
eighth-grade education (Mennonite one-room school);
farmhand on his father's farm;
eight brothers and sisters;
native speaker of Pennsylvania German; hardly accented English.

Informant 41:
Family N, non-Pennsylvania German, female, 81, a-generation, widowed, Protestant;
has lived in Berwick all her life;
university education;
retired schoolteacher;
one brother and one sister, three children, six grandchildren, seven great-grandchildren;
monolingual English (regional standard); virtually no knowledge of Pennsylvania German although father had Pennsylvania German as his second language.

Informant 42:
Family N, non-Pennsylvania German, male, 63, b-generation, married (divorced from informant 44), Independent Bible Church (Protestant);
has lived in Berwick almost all his life (apart from two years of military service);
high school education;
retired development engineer;
two brothers and sisters, three children and two stepchildren, six grandchildren;
monolingual English (regional standard).

Informant 43:
Family N, non-Pennsylvania German, male, 50, b-generation (married to informant 44), Pentecostal Church (Protestant);
born and raised in Columbia County near Berwick, two years of military service, lived in Texas for ten years until the age of twenty-nine, has lived near Berwick ever since;
high school education;
retired equipment operator, mechanic, and construction worker;
five half-brothers and -sisters, one stepchild, two grandchildren;
monolingual English (regional standard); strong interest in Amish culture (distant German ancestors on his mother's side).

Informant 44:
Family N, non-Pennsylvania German, female, 52, b-generation (married to informant 43, divorced from informant 42), Pentecostal Church (Protestant);
has lived near Berwick all her life;
high school education with one year of college;
retired nurse;
two brothers and sisters, one child, two grandchildren;
monolingual English (regional standard); strong interest in Amish culture (distant German ancestors on her mother's side).

Informant 45:
Family N, non-Pennsylvania German, male, 54, b-generation (married to informant 46), United Methodist Protestant Church (converted from Reformed);

Introduction 57

born and raised in Columbia County near Berwick, four years of military service, spent another four years near Berwick until the age of twenty-eight, has lived in Lewisburg ever since;
university education (B.A.);
accountant;
ten brothers and sisters, one child, two grandchildren;
monolingual English (regional standard); distant German ancestors on his father's side, but no knowledge of German.

Informant 46:
Family N, non-Pennsylvania German, female, 52, b-generation (married to informant 45), United Methodist Protestant Church;
grew up in Berwick, spent four years in Washington, D.C., and another four years in Berwick, has lived in Lewisburg ever since;
high school education;
housewife;
one child, two grandchildren;
monolingual English (regional standard).

Informant 47:
Family N, non-Pennsylvania German, male, 31, c-generation (married to informant 48), Protestant;
born and raised in Berwick, lived in Pottstown, Pennsylvania, for three years, has lived in Lewisburg since the age of twenty-six;
six months of trade school after high school;
welder;
four half-brothers and -sisters, two children;
monolingual English (regional standard).

Informant 48:
Family N, non-Pennsylvania German, female, 30, c-generation (married to informant 47), Protestant;
born in Washington, D.C., lived in Berwick until the age of three, has lived in Lewisburg ever since with short interruptions (college);
university education (B.A.);
housewife, used to work with computers;
two children;
monolingual English (regional standard).

Informant 49:
Family N, non-Pennsylvania German, male, 8, d-generation, Protestant;
spent the first three years of his life in Berwick and Pottstown, Pennsylvania, has lived in Lewisburg ever since;

third grade at elementary school;
one sister;
monolingual English (regional standard).

Informant 50:
Family N, non-Pennsylvania German, female, 5, d-generation, Protestant;
spent the first three months of her life in Pottstown, Pennsylvania, has lived in Lewisburg ever since;
kindergarten;
one brother;
monolingual English (regional standard).

Figure 1.5 is a summary of the informants' main social data. From left to right, the six columns give the informants' identification number, family, generation, age, gender, and the variety they use predominantly during a normal workday.

In the column marking the family, the numbers "1," "2," and "3" represent the three nonsectarian Pennsylvania German families; the letters "M," "A," and "N" designate the Mennonite, the Amish, and the non-Pennsylvania German families, respectively.

In the column marking the generation, "a" indicates, in the case of the nonsectarian families, all the members of the generation having Pennsylvania German as their native language. The letter "b" designates those informants who belong to the first generation to have English as their native language. The letter "c" represents the second generation having English as their first language, and "d" the third. In the case of the Mennonite, Amish, and non-Pennsylvania German families, "a," "b," and "c" merely differentiate between the grandparents', parents' and children's generations and, therefore, appear in parentheses.

In the column marking the language variety, "PG" indicates that the informants report that they use more Pennsylvania German than English on a normal workday; "E" represents the predominant use of English.

Informant	Family	Generation	Age	Sex	Variety
1	1	a	77	m	PG
2	1	a	77	f	PG
3	1	a	77	f	E
4	2	a	71	m	PG
5	2	a	68	f	PG
6	2	a	74	f	PG
7	3	a	79	f	PG
8	3	a	60	f	E
9	1	b	57	f	PG/E
10	1	b	54	m	E
11	1	b	53	f	E
12	2	b	83	f	E
13	2	b	49	m	E
14	2	b	54	m	E
15	3	b	61	m	E
16	3	b	37	f	E
17	1	c	35	m	E
18	1	c	30	m	E
19	1/N	(c)	30	f	E
20	1	c	26	m	E
21	1	c	23	f	E
22	2	c	54	f	E
23	3	c	37	m	E
24	1	d	5	f	E
25	2	d	31	f	E
26	2	d	27	f	E
27	3	d	11	m	E
28	3	d	9	f	E
29	M	(a)	57	m	PG
30	M	(a)	55	f	PG
31	M	(b)	37	m	PG
32	M	(b)	27	f	PG
33	M	(b)	13	m	PG
34	M	(b)	22	f	PG
35	M	(c)	6	f	PG
36	A	(a)	52	m	PG
37	A	(a)	51	f	PG
38	A	(b)	29	m	PG
39	A	(b)	30	f	PG
40	A	(b)	17	m	PG
41	N	(a)	81	f	E
42	N	(b)	63	m	E
43	N	(b)	50	m	E
44	N	(b)	52	f	E
45	N	(b)	54	m	E
46	N	(b)	52	f	E
47	N	(c)	31	m	E
48	N	(c)	30	f	E
49	N	(d)	8	m	E
50	N	(d)	5	f	E

Figure 1.5: List of informants with social data

1 (nonsectarian family 1) = 12
2 (nonsectarian family 2) = 9
3 (nonsectarian family 3) = 7
A (Amish) = 5
M (Mennonite) = 7
N (non-Pennsylvania German) = 11

a = 13
b = 20
c = 10
d = 7

f (female) = 28
m (male) = 22

E (English) = 32
PG (Pennsylvania German) = 19

INTERVIEWS

The size of the questionnaire necessitated two interview sessions per informant. In most cases, they were held within a few days of each other.

At the first session, the fieldworker would introduce himself, sometimes by showing some pictures of his home area, to create a more relaxed atmosphere for the informants. Then, normally, sections 1.1, 1.2, 2.1, and 3.1 were dealt with for approximately two hours. These were the questionnaire parts that had to be tape-recorded.

During the second session, which also lasted about two hours, usually sections 2.2, 2.3, and 3.2 were completed; no tape recording was involved. While the fieldworker filled out part 2 on the spot according to the informants' answers, section 3.2 was completed by the informants themselves. This matched-guise test was especially popular and could easily be administered in groups. The language samples were played with a cassette player.

Very frequently, after the "official" parts of the interview, the informants asked the fieldworker to stay for lunch or dinner with the family. This offered an opportunity for extensive participant observation.

The various parts of the questionnaire, except for 3.2, were usually completed in one-to-one interviews, particularly the word list (1.2) and the attitude questions (3.1). With married couples, section 1.2 was sometimes recorded together, which led to a more natural conversation, the informants forgetting about the interview and at times talking to each other rather than only to the fieldworker.

These group interviews were one way to avoid what Labov calls the *observer's paradox*.[25] Another part of the strategy to create a relaxed atmosphere was to conduct the interviews in the informants' homes and to use a very small tape recorder, which was kept out of the informants' view as much as possible. The tape recorder was a Sony Walkman Professional WM-D3 with a small but extremely sensitive microphone, which could easily be left out of the interviewees' reach. The tapes were conventional audiotape cassettes, ninety minutes in length. They had to be turned over only once during the course of an average session. This way the informants were reminded of the interview situation as little as possible.

Participant observation showed that the informants used the same language during the interviews as in less formal situations. The fact that the interviewer spoke the Palatinate dialect of German natively created the situation of a conversation with a group member for most informants.

Housewives and retired informants were usually interviewed in the morning. Most interviews with the younger informants had to be conducted in the evening, as they had to go to work during the day. Without exception, the informants were cooperative and extremely friendly. Once the interviews had begun in a family, other family members became curious and did not mind being interviewed as well. On the whole, the interviews were easier with older people, as their experience of life provided a rich reservoir of topics and anecdotes.

PARTICIPANT OBSERVATION

The quantitative data are the most important instrument to account for the linguistic phenomena. Their greatest advantage is that these data are perfectly comparable for all the informants.

Nevertheless, qualitative methods were applied in two ways. Since Dorian's apprehensions against questionnaire self-reports[26] were taken very seriously, all questions (with the exception of those in the matched-guise test) were asked in an interview setting. Thus, it was possible to ask the informants for illustrations of, or reasons for, their answers when it was felt to be necessary.

Still, it seemed important to have a further instrument to judge the validity of the informants' self-reports. As the fieldworker was unable to live with his informants over a period of many years,[27] a large number of occasions of participant observation served as a control mechanism instead; the fieldworker took an active part in a number of group interactions such as church services, Sunday school, school lessons, Bible classes, birthday parties, Thanksgiving Day, family reunions, the *Versammling*, home butcherings, hunting camps, horse auctions, and farm sales.

Although no tape recordings or questionnaires were involved, these activities do give important evidence of the informants' actual language behavior. The results of the participant observations, which were noted down immediately after each activity, put the self-reports on language use and competence into perspective. They will be compared with the quantitative data in the respective chapters.

Further, the participant observations facilitated deeper insights into the cultural life of the various groups. The most important occasions of participant observation are given in chronological order in figure 1.6.

Month	Family	Activity
October	–	Annual Pennsylvania German church service at Richfield Methodist Church, Snyder County, Pennsylvania
November	3	Thanksgiving Day in the Mahantango Valley
December	2	Deer hunting in the Mahantango Valley; afterwards home butchering of deer meat
January	1	Home butchering (pork and beef) at grandparents' farm
February	M	Farm sale in Buffalo Valley
	M	Saturday afternoon lesson in Bible High German for adult Mennonites at Sunny Side School in Millmont
	M	Mennonite church service at Mountain View Church in Buffalo Valley
March	3	English church service and Sunday school at St. Michael's Lutheran Church, Klingerstown
	M	Driver for Old Order Mennonite to farm machinery sale in Lancaster County, Pennsylvania
April	M	Lessons at Sunny Side School (Mennonite one-room schoolhouse) in Millmont
	N	
	1,2,3	Family birthday party for one of the children
	M	Yarlich Fersommling at Lykens, Pennsylvania: Pennsylvania German songs, speeches, skits, and food (open to male speakers only)
May	N	Horse auction at Middleburg, Snyder County, Pennsylvania
	1	Family at son's first Little League Baseball game in Lewisburg
July	1,2	Weekend stay at family hunting camp in northern Pennsylvania
		Family reunion at Himmel's Church

Figure 1.6: Participant observation October 1989 through July 1990

2

The Influence of Pennsylvania German on the Phonology of English

In this chapter linguistic data will be presented that reflect some of the differences in speech found among the informants. The focus will be on the informants' English in general and on phonological features in particular. The extent to which these phonological differences can be attributed to the speakers' contact with Pennsylvania German will have to be decided from case to case.

Phonology was chosen because peculiarities in this area are striking to the listener, and phonological features can be gathered more easily and objectively than features from the other linguistic levels.[1]

After a brief description of how the data were collected, the phonetic inventories of both the informants' Pennsylvania German and English varieties will be drawn up. A general presentation of the data, including a discussion of the phonetic contexts, will be followed by some theoretical remarks on the nature of the marked features identified. The next two subchapters will give quantitative and qualitative analyses of the data. In the latter, implicational scaling will be used to show how the material structures both the informants and the phonological features. Chapter 2 will be rounded off by a comparison with previous studies and a synopsis.

METHODOLOGY: DATA COLLECTION

The goal in section 1.2 of the interview was twofold. On the one hand, a way had to be found to help the informants to speak in a style as close to casual speech[2] as possible. Therefore, the use of a reading text had to be ruled out. For the same reason, the informants could not simply be asked to read aloud words in a word list or even minimal pairs. On the other hand, it was imperative that highly comparable phonological data be collected. For this reason, the usual practice of examining free speech did not appear to be desirable. This method would not have consistently rendered the features in the same phonological contexts for all the informants. In the end, the best method appeared to be the use of flashcards. Section 1.2 was administered directly after the free interviews during the first session held with each informant.[3]

The informants were presented with fifty-five flashcards showing easily identifiable objects. Some of them belonged to a set of the sort typically used at elementary schools to teach students how to read, others were self-produced with the help of pictures taken from a children's dictionary. Flashcards that tended to elicit the wrong words in the pilot interviews were replaced.

There was still the problem that the informants would give the names of the objects in a careful style. Moreover, it would have been difficult to make plausible that the fieldworker wanted to hear English words; some informants might have suspected a hidden intelligence test.

The informants were therefore first asked for the Pennsylvania German word for each object. If they knew it, the English equivalent was asked for and given as a sort of afterthought, that is, in a casual way; after all, for the informant, the question had already been answered. If the informant did not know the Pennsylvania German word, it was all the more plausible to ask for the English version. Normally, in such situations, the informants gave it without being specifically asked.

This method even worked with the small group of monolingual Pennsylvania German informants and the non-Pennsylvania German ones, who tried to help the fieldworker with the German expressions as best they could. As a positive side effect of asking for the Pennsylvania German words first, the number of correct answers was a good indication of each informant's lexical competence in Pennsylvania German.

The objects on the flashcards were chosen in such a way as to elicit words with a relatively high potential for phonological interference from Pennsylvania German. From earlier conversations and interviews the fieldworker had a vague idea about which phonemes tended to be realized differently by speakers who were in contact with Pennsylvania German. Thus, the test could be aimed directly at specific features, which then did or did not prove to be relevant. The phonemes and their possible phonetic realizations, together with the fifty-five target words, all listed in questionnaire section 1.2 (see appendix), are summarized in figure 2.1.

The Influence of Pennsylvania German on English Phonology 65

Phoneme	Phonetic realization		Target words
	AmE	PGE	
/dʒ/	[dʒ]	[tʃ]	jug (word-initial)
			pigeon (word-internal)
			cabbage (word-final)
/b,d,g/ /_#	[b,d,g]	[b̥,d̥,g̊] or [p,t,k]	tub, bed, egg
/z/	[z]	[s]	zoo (word-initial)
			houses (word-internal)
			boys, girls, pigs (word-final)
/w/	[w]	[v]	well, wagon, wheel
/v/	[v]	[w]	vegetables, valentine
/θ/	[θ]	[s]	thistle (word-initial)
			author (word-internal)
			south (word-final)
/ð/	[ð]	[d]	that (word-initial)
			feather (word-internal)
			smooth (word-final)
/r/ /_#	[ɾ]	ø	car, bear
/_C			bird
/_s			stars
/ʒ/	[ʒ]	[ʃ]	measure, pleasure
/v/ /_#	[v]	[f]	glove, hive
/l/	[ɫ]	[l]	ladder (before vowel)
			milk (before consonant)
			hill (word-final)
/ou/	[ou]	[oᵘ] or [oː]	goat, soap
/eɪ/	[eɪ]	[eˑ] or [eː]	cake, gate
/ʌ/	[ʌ]	[ʌ]	cup, sun
/au/	[au]	[aᵘ], [aᵊ], or [aː]	mouse, crown
/aɪ/	[aɪ]	[aᵊ] or [aː]	mice, lion
/u/	[u]	[y] or [u]	book, wolf
unstressed /ɪ/ /_#	[ɪ]	[j], [ə], or [e]	family, baby
/Vː/ or /V+off-glide/	[Vː] or [V+off-glide]	[Vːə] or [V+off-glide+ə]	key (/iː/), saw (/ɑː/), shoe (/uː/), pie (/aɪ/), tray (/eɪ/), boy (/ɔɪ/), cow (/au/), crow (/ou/)

Figure 2.1: Phonemes, their realizations in the regional standard (AmE) and in Pennsylvania German English (PGE), and target words

Section 1.2 was conducted with forty-five of the fifty informants. For various reasons, five informants (27, 33, 34, 40, 41) chose not to take part in this section of the interview.

Phonetic Inventories

The whole conversation covering section 1.2 was tape-recorded. All the English and Pennsylvania German target words were transcribed in a narrow IPA transcription (cf. IPA 1957). Before the evaluation of the relevant interferences, the data collected from all the informants were used to establish the phonetic inventories of the two language varieties: English and Pennsylvania German. These two systems, which include all the sounds that occurred in the data, consist of monophthongs (figure 2.2), diphthongs (figure 2.3), and consonants (figure 2.4).

Neither of these phonetic inventories represents that of a single speaker. They are merely lists of sounds received from all the informants taken together. Particularly the inventories for English represent a broad variety of speakers on a continuum from the regional standard to heavily marked Pennsylvania German English.

In each depiction, the English inventory is given on the left-hand side, the Pennsylvania German one on the right. The question of whether the bilingual informants have internalized one phoneme system for both their varieties or have two overlapping systems (cf. Weinreich 1953, 8f.) is difficult to answer. The frequent occurrence of loan words further complicates this question. Moreover, the different varieties used by the various subgroups would require a differentiated, individual examination. Competence in Pennsylvania German and acquisition history appear to play an important role. For the purposes of this chapter, a common core of sounds has been established, marked in bold type in each of the three figures.

Figure 2.2 includes long, short, and unstressed monophthongs. In the lists of sample words these groups are depicted separately. Sometimes half-length (ˑ) occurs. A few sounds within each list deserve special mentioning.

The following vowels only occur in (Pennsylvania German) English: [ɜː] (g*ir*ls), [æ] (c*a*bbage), [ʌ] (c*u*p), and unstressed [ɪ] (famil*y*). Two others are present in Pennsylvania German only: [ɔ] (V*o*ggel 'bird') and [ɐ] (Fedd*er* 'feather'). In each case, these vowels occur in loan words from the other language only and have therefore not been included in the common core.

All in all, four centralized vowels occur in the informants' varieties of English, namely [ɜː] (g*ir*ls), [ə] (feath*er*), [ʌ] (c*u*p), and [ɪ] (for unstressed final [ɪ] as in famil*y*). Of these, only [ə] (Koppch*e* 'cup') is also present in Pennsylvania German, along with another centralized vowel, [ɐ] (Fedd*er* 'feather').

The Influence of Pennsylvania German on English Phonology 67

Pennsylvania German English

Pennsylvania German

Sample words:

		PGE	PG
Long:	[iː]	wh*ee*l	K*ie*h 'cows'
	[eː]	c*a*ke	L*ee*b 'lion'
	[ɑː]	st*a*rs	M*a*riye 'morning'
	[ɜː]	g*i*rls	–
	[ɔː]	b*oa*rd	R*aa*d 'wheel'
	[oː]	g*oa*t	R*o*t 'advice'
	[uː]	sh*oe*	Sch*uh* 'shoe'
	[u̟ː]	sh*oe*	Sch*uh* 'shoe'
Short:	[ɪ]	p*i*geon	D*i*schdel 'thistle'
	[ɛ]	w*e*ll	B*e*tt 'bed'
	[æ]	c*a*bbage	–
	[ɑ]	l*o*t	H*a*tz 'heart'
	[ʌ]	c*u*p	–
	[ʌ̟]	c*u*p	K*o*ppche 'cup'
	[ɔ]	–	V*o*ggel 'bird'
	[ʊ]	b*oo*k	B*u*ch 'book'
	[ʊ̝]	b*oo*k	B*u*ch 'book'
Unstressed:	[ɪ̈]	famil*y*	–
	[ə]	feath*er*	Koppch*e* 'cup'
	[ɐ]	–	Fedd*er* 'feather'

Figure 2.2: Monophthongs occurring in the informants' varieties of English and Pennsylvania German (common core in bold type)

In both varieties a considerable number of informants had an advanced /ʌ/, marked as [ʌ̟] (c*u*p; K*o*ppche 'cup'), which in its quality goes toward [ʊ], without being rounded. Thus, there is a continuum from [ʌ] via [ʌ̟] to [ʊ].

A raised variant of /ʊ/, marked as [ʊ̝] (b*oo*k; B*u*ch 'book'), and an advanced variant of /uː/, marked as [u̟ː] (sh*oe*; Sch*uh* 'shoe'), are fairly frequent. They also occur in Pennsylvania German English as well as Pennsylvania German, forming continua in both varieties. Which vowel

68   The Influence of Pennsylvania German on English Phonology

is used appears to depend, especially in English, on the degree of markedness and also on the target words. The continua are accounted for in the vowel charts by the fact that all the variants are given (e.g., [ʊ] and [ʊ̈]).

English and Pennsylvania German differ most in their diphthong inventories (figure 2.3). Because of the broad spectrum of English varieties found among the informants, no fewer than six closing diphthongs occur: [aɪ] (m*i*ce), [ɔɪ] (b*oy*), [oɪ] (b*oy*), [eɪ] (c*a*ke), [aʊ] (m*ou*se), and [oʊ] (cr*ow*). Of these, the latter three can also be realized with the second element as merely an off-glide ([eⁱ], [aᵘ], and [oᵘ]) or even as long monophthongs ([eː], [aː], and [oː]). As is generally true for American English, there are no centring diphthongs.

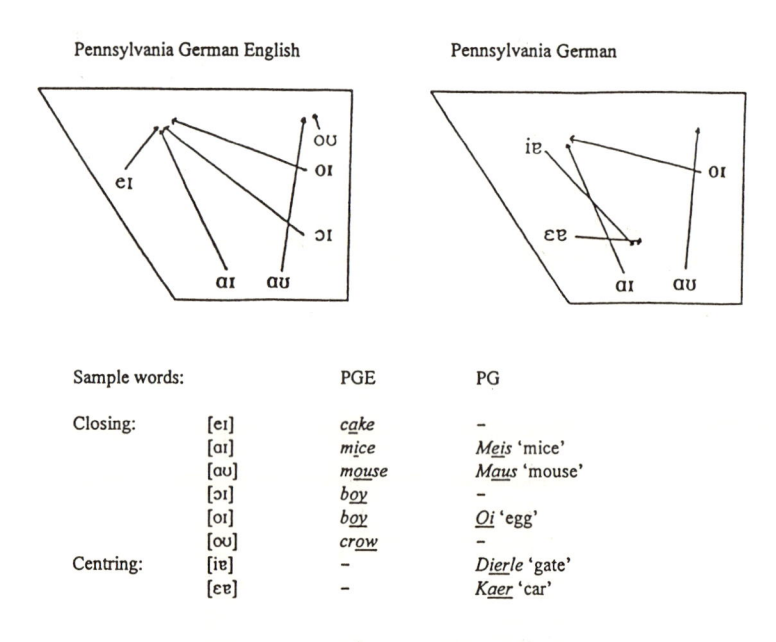

Sample words:		PGE	PG
Closing:	[eɪ]	c*a*ke	–
	[aɪ]	m*i*ce	M*ei*s 'mice'
	[aʊ]	m*ou*se	M*au*s 'mouse'
	[ɔɪ]	b*oy*	–
	[oɪ]	b*oy*	*Oi* 'egg'
	[oʊ]	cr*ow*	–
Centring:	[iɐ]	–	D*ie*rle 'gate'
	[ɛɐ]	–	K*ae*r 'car'

Figure 2.3: Diphthongs occurring in the informants' varieties of English and Pennsylvania German (common core in bold type)

In the Pennsylvania German varieties, the number of diphthongs is reduced to five: [aɪ] (M*ei*s 'mice'), [aʊ] (M*au*s 'mouse'), [ɔɪ] (*Oi* 'egg'), [iɐ] (D*ie*rle 'gate'), and [ɛɐ] (K*aer* 'car'). One reason for the lower number is that instead of [eɪ] and [oʊ], the long monophthongs [e:] and [o:] are always found. In the case of [aʊ], the monophthongal form ([ɔ:]) occurs only occasionally.[4] Two special diphthongs present in Pennsylvania German but not in English are the centring diphthongs [iɐ] and [ɛɐ].

Among the consonants (figure 2.4), the phones [x] (K*uch*e 'cake') and [ç] (Mill*ich* 'milk') and the bilabial sound [β] (Wa*gg*e 'wagon') are found only in Pennsylvania German. The phoneme /r/ is realized as a retroflex sound ([ɻ]) throughout the informants' varieties of English (c*r*own), whereas in Pennsylvania German the retroflex /r/ occurs beside the trilled version ([ʀ]; B*r*unne 'well'). Their distribution is as follows: All the sectarian informants and the younger nonsectarians have [ɻ]; only the older nonsectarians (particularly native speakers of Pennsylvania Germans and members of the b-generation) preserve the old trilled version. However, some of them have [ɻ], and even mixing of the two variants occurs with individual speakers.[5]

The following sounds occur in the informants' English only: [θ] (*th*istle), [ð] (fea*th*er), [z] (*z*oo), [ʒ] (plea*s*ure), [dʒ] (*j*ug), and [w] (*w*ell). Additionally, devoiced, unaspirated lenis consonants, usually in word-final position, occur in Pennsylvania German English only; they are marked as [b̥] (tu*b*), [d̥] (be*d*), [g̊] (e*gg*), [z̥] (girl*s*), [ʒ̊] (mea*s*ure), and [d̥ʒ̊] (cabba*ge*). Thus, there is a continuum from the unvoiced fortis consonants [p], [t], [k], [s], [ʃ], and [tʃ] via [b̥], [d̥], [g̊], [z̥], [ʒ̊], and [d̥ʒ̊] to the voiced lenis consonants [b], [d], [g], [z], [ʒ], and [dʒ].

While in the English varieties [p], [t], and [k] are unaspirated behind /s/ (*sp*ot, *st*ar, *sch*ool), the same is true for these sounds in Pennsylvania German behind /ʃ/ (Gsch*p*ass 'pleasure', Sch*t*aern 'star', Sch*kl*aaf 'slave'). In both varieties a glottal stop [ʔ] is present, usually in word-final position as a realization of /d/ or /t/ (be*d*; Be*tt* 'bed').

In the informants' varieties of English, the phoneme /l/ is realized as [l] (clear /l/) or [ɫ] (dark /l/) before a vowel (*l*adder). Word-finally (hi*ll*) and before a consonant (mi*l*k), [ɫ] is more frequent. In these positions, [l] is found mainly in the English of nonsectarian native speakers of Pennsylvania German. In Pennsylvania German [l] prevails (*L*eeder 'ladder', Wo*lf* 'wolf', Hiwwe*l* 'hill'), but [ɫ] also appears in all positions, particularly in the speech of sectarians and nonfluent nonsectarians.

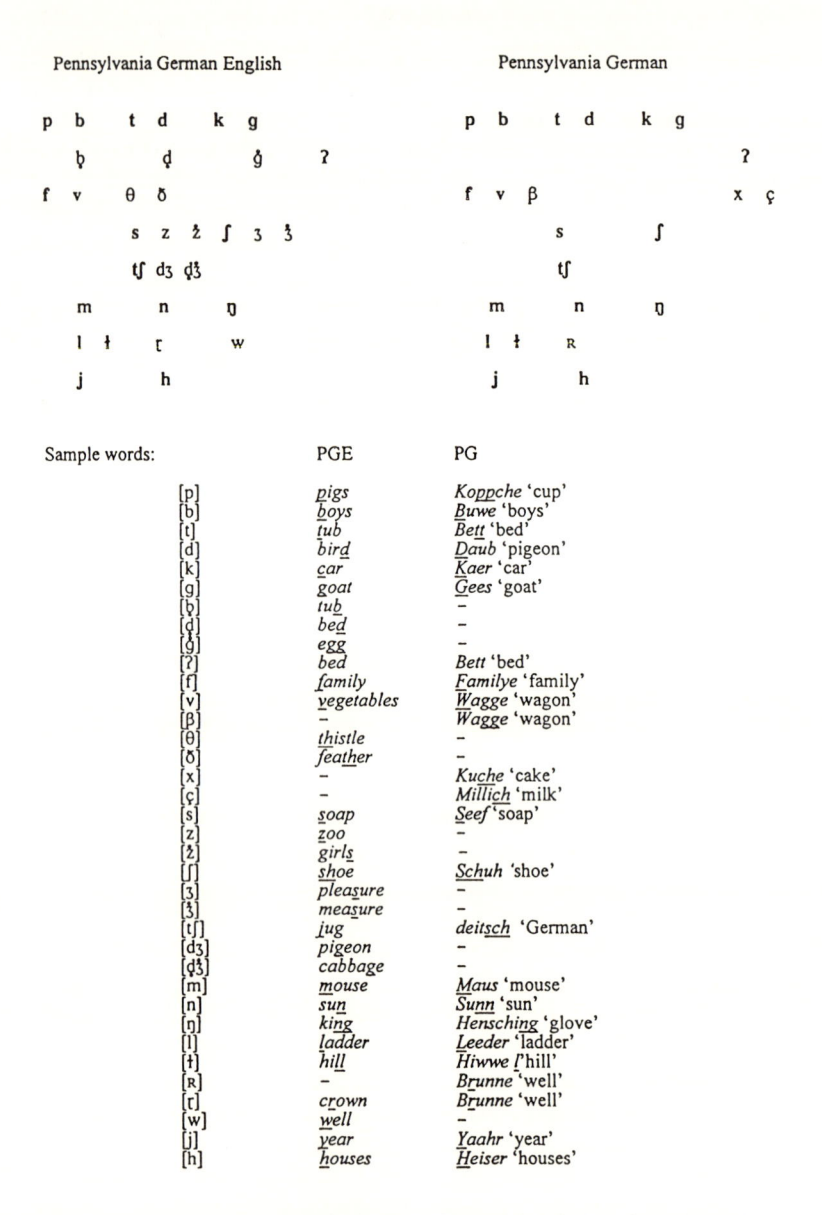

70 The Influence of Pennsylvania German on English Phonology

Pennsylvania German English							Pennsylvania German						
p	b	t	d	k	g		p	b	t	d	k	g	
	ɓ		ɗ		ɠ	ʔ							ʔ
f	v	θ	ð				f	v	β			x	ç
		s	z	ʐ	ʃ	ʒ	ʑ			s		ʃ	
		tʃ	dʒ	dʑ					tʃ				
m		n		ŋ			m		n		ŋ		
l	ɫ	ɾ		w			l	ɫ		R			
j		h					j		h				

Sample words: PGE   PG

[p]	pigs	Koppche 'cup'
[b]	boys	Buwe 'boys'
[t]	tub	Bett 'bed'
[d]	bird	Daub 'pigeon'
[k]	car	Kaer 'car'
[g]	goat	Gees 'goat'
[ɓ]	tub	–
[ɗ]	bed	–
[ɠ]	egg	–
[ʔ]	bed	Bett 'bed'
[f]	family	Familye 'family'
[v]	vegetables	Wagge 'wagon'
[β]	–	Wagge 'wagon'
[θ]	thistle	–
[ð]	feather	–
[x]	–	Kuche 'cake'
[ç]	–	Millich 'milk'
[s]	soap	Seef 'soap'
[z]	zoo	–
[ʐ]	girls	–
[ʃ]	shoe	Schuh 'shoe'
[ʒ]	pleasure	–
[ʑ]	measure	–
[tʃ]	jug	deitsch 'German'
[dʒ]	pigeon	–
[dʑ]	cabbage	–
[m]	mouse	Maus 'mouse'
[n]	sun	Sunn 'sun'
[ŋ]	king	Hensching 'glove'
[l]	ladder	Leeder 'ladder'
[ɫ]	hill	Hiwwe l'hill'
[R]	–	Brunne 'well'
[ɾ]	crown	Brunne 'well'
[w]	well	–
[j]	year	Yaahr 'year'
[h]	houses	Heiser 'houses'

Figure 2.4: Consonants occurring in the informants' varieties of English and Pennsylvania German (common core in bold type)

The Data

A close examination of the target words (figure 2.1) reveals that thirty-seven of them have the potential for phonological interference in features for which they were not originally collected. These thirty-seven words are given in figure 2.5 together with their respective categories.

Feature	Target word
[tʃ] for [dʒ]	*vegetables* (word-internal)
[p,t,k] for [b,d,g]	*bird, jug*
[s] for [z]	*houses, stars, vegetables* (word-final)
[v] for [w]	*wolf*
⌀ for [ɾ]	*author, feather, measure, pleasure, ladder* (word-final); *girls* (before consonant)
[l] for [ɫ]	*valentine, pleasure, glove, lion, family* (before vowel); *girls, vegetables, wolf* (before consonant); *well, wheel, thistle* (word-final)
[oː] for [oʊ]	*crow*
[eː] for [eɪ]	*tray, baby*
[ʌ] for [ʌ]	*jug, tub, glove*
[ɑː] for [aʊ]	*houses, south, cow*
[ɑː] for [aɪ]	*valentine, hive, pie*
[Vːə] for [Vː]	*zoo*

Figure 2.5: Target words with potential interferences in additional features

No additional words were present for the features [w] for [v], [s] for [θ], [d] for [ð], [ʃ] for [ʒ], [f] for [v], [ʊ̈] for [ʊ], and [ɹ] for [ɾ]. To ensure a full evaluation of the data, the above thirty-seven target words will be incorporated into the data overview.

Moreover, in the course of the interviews it became clear that the speech of a number of informants was marked by the feature [ṳː] for [uː], for which originally no target word was provided. However, the three words *zoo*, *smooth*, and *shoe*, which were all used to test other features, will be taken to provide the necessary data.

All in all, the following discussion will cover the data for twenty phonological categories tested with the help of ninety-five target words. They will be presented in the order given in figure 2.1.

72   The Influence of Pennsylvania German on English Phonology

The two lines on top of figures 2.6–21 give the informants' social groups along with their identification numbers. Underneath, the symbol "+" indicates that the marked form was present; "–" means that the regional-standard feature occurred. An empty cell indicates that the target word was not received. The symbol "°" marks all cases of devoiced lenis consonants. Qualitative differences in diphthongs were marked in the following way: "1" stands for [eːⁱ], [oːᵘ], or [ɑːᵘ]; "2" for [eⁱ], [oᵘ], or [ɑᵘ]; and "3" for [eⁱ], [oᵘ], or [ɑᵘ], respectively. Finally, "4" represents the diphthong [əʊ]. All percentages are based only on the forms received for the target words and have been rounded to whole numbers. The target words are ordered from top to bottom according to the degree of markedness.

The first phonological feature is [tʃ] for [dʒ] (figure 2.6). It was tested in word-initial (*jug*), word-internal (*pigeon, vegetables*)⁶ and word-final positions (*cabbage*).

Figure 2.6: [tʃ] for [dʒ] in *cabbage, vegetables, pigeon, jug*

The absence of the voiced affricate in the Pennsylvania German phoneme system and in the English variety of predominantly those nonsectarians who have native or near-native competence in Pennsylvania German is an indication of phonological interference. Altogether, 64 of 150 forms received (over 42%) are marked in that they feature [tʃ] or [d̥ʒ̊].

The unvoiced fortis consonant is present most often in *vegetables*, that is, word-internally (nineteen instances = 42%). In *pigeon*, [tʃ] is

The Influence of Pennsylvania German on English Phonology   73

found no more than seven times (29%), which, however, may be due to the fact that the target word was not received twenty-one times, *dove* or *bird* being given instead. Almost as often as in *vegetables*, namely sixteen times (41%), the marked variant is found in *cabbage*, that is, word-finally. In word-initial position (*jug*), [tʃ] is present twelve times (28%).

The devoiced lenis consonant ([d̥ʒ̊]) is found most often in word-final position (five times = 13%). Word-internally it occurs twice in *pigeon* (8%) and once in *vegetables*. In word-initial position it is found twice (5%). In all, the highest proportion of marked variants is found in word-final position (twenty-one instances = 54%), closely followed by the target word *vegetables*, representing word-internal position (twenty instances = 44%). Word-initially, marked variants are present fourteen times (33%). The word *pigeon* was received too infrequently to yield representative information (nine instances of marked variants = 37%).

The highest proportion of [tʃ] is found among the members of the nonsectarian a- and b-generations. The marked variant is never present in the speech of the non-Pennsylvania Germans. The full amount of marking is found for informants 3 and 5 (nonsectarian a-generation), informant 10 (nonsectarian b-generation), and informant 29 (Mennonite). Among the informants belonging to the younger nonsectarian generations and the sectarians, the devoiced lenis consonant appears with relatively greater frequency. Thus, the transition zone between marked and unmarked is established quantitatively as well as qualitatively.

The second feature is [p,t,k] for word-final [b,d,g] (figure 2.7).[7] These unvoiced final plosives are a general feature of German including Pennsylvania German (*Auslautverhärtung*). In some instances, devoiced lenis consonants ([b̥,d̥,g̊]) are found as an intermediate stage. Like the fortis consonants, they will be regarded as marked variants.

While in many nonstandard varieties of American English the glottal stop ([ʔ]) alternates with /t/, in the present set of data [ʔ] was received three times in the word *bed*, that is, as a variant of final /d/. Therefore, [ʔ] has to be regarded as a marked feature, most likely as a realization of an unvoiced [t], which itself is a marked variant of /d/. In all, 59 of 218 forms received (27%) show some degree of marking ([p,t,k], [b̥,d̥,g̊], or [ʔ]).

For final /g/ the fortis consonant [k] is found in the speech of thirteen informants (31%) and the devoiced lenis [g̊] in the speech of three (7%) in the target word *jug*. The results for *egg* are similar, namely nine instances of [k] (20%) and six of [g] (14%).

74   The Influence of Pennsylvania German on English Phonology

	Nonsectarian a	b	c	d	Sectarians	Non-Pennsylvania Germans
Informant	1 2 3 4 5 6 7 8	9 10 11 12 13 14 15 16	17 18 19 20 21 22 23	24 25 26 28	29 30 31 32 35 36 37 38 39	42 43 44 45 46 47 48 49 50
jug	* * * + * + + *	* * * + + + * *	- - - - - - -	- - - -	* * - * - - - - -	- - - - - - - - -
egg	* * * * * * + *	* * + + + + * *	- - - - - - -	- * + *	* * - - - - - - -	- - - - - - - - -
tub	* * * + * + + *	* + + * + + + *	- - - - - - -	- - * *	* - - - - - - - -	- - - - - - - - -
bed	? ? * + + * + -	* + - * + + + *	? - - - - - -	- * - *	* - - - - - - - -	- - - - - - - - -
bird	- - - - - - - -	- - - - - - - -	- - - - - - -	- - - -	- - - - - - - - -	- - - - - - - - -

	*	(?)	*	-	not received
jug	13 (31%)	0 (0%)	3 (7%)	26 (62%)	3
egg	9 (20%)	0 (0%)	6 (14%)	29 (66%)	1
tub	12 (27%)	0 (0%)	2 (4%)	31 (69%)	0
bed	7 (15%)	3 (7%)	4 (9%)	31 (69%)	0
bird	0 (0%)	0 (0%)	0 (0%)	42 (100%)	3

* * [p,t,k]
* - [b̥,d̥,g̊]
- * [b,d,g]

Figure 2.7: [p,t,k] for [b,d,g] in *jug, egg, tub, bed, bird*

Fourteen instances of marked variants are found for final /b/ (31%). Twelve informants have the fortis consonant [p] (27%), and two the devoiced lenis [b̥] (4%).

Final /d/ in *bed* is realized as a fortis consonant [t] by seven informants (15%), as a devoiced lenis [d̥] by four (9%), and as a glottal stop [ʔ] by three informants (7%). No informant had a marked variant in *bird*, which may be due to the different phonetic environment, /d/ being preceded by /r/.

All in all, the numbers of marked variants are distributed quite equally (between 31% and 38% if *bird* is neglected). There are fourteen instances for /b/ (*tub*) and /d/ (*bed*), and fifteen and sixteen for /g/ (*egg* and *jug*, respectively). Thus, as there are no salient differences in terms of marked realization between the three consonants /b,d,g/, it seems justified to group them together.

The consistency of the nonsectarian a-generation in the realization of final /b/ as [p] (*tub*) and /g/ as [k] (*jug*) is particularly remarkable (seven and six of eight informants, respectively). In the case of /d/ (*bed*), the nonsectarian b-generation seems to use the fortis consonant more consistently, while the a-generation sometimes has the devoiced lenis or the glottal stop. However, the pattern is not clear enough to make a differentiation between final /b/, /d/, and /g/ imperative.

Marked variants are found for all the members of the nonsectarian a-generation, six of the eight informants belonging to the nonsectarian b-

The Influence of Pennsylvania German on English Phonology 75

generation (informants 9–12, 14, 15), one member of the nonsectarian c-generation (informant 17), and three of the d-generation. The latter three are two sisters with rudimentary competence in Pennsylvania German (informants 25, 26) and a five-year-old monolingual girl (informant 24). In addition, two Mennonite informants (29, 31) show traces of marking.

In sum, unvoicing of final /b,d,g/ is found almost exclusively in the English of the nonsectarian informants, rarely with the sectarians, and never with the non-Pennsylvania Germans. The highest rates of marking are scored by the a- and b-generations. The members of the c- and d-generations, who typically have much lower indices of translation competence, have no more than one or two instances of marked variants.

The feature [s] for [z][8] also belongs with the group of unvoiced for voiced sounds. The share of marked forms ([s] or [ž]) is 99 of 271 words received (over 36%). The large number of empty spaces in figure 2.8 indicates that the target words were far from ideal. Six of them relied on plural forms to create the appropriate phonetic environments, and in many cases the informants hit the right words but gave them in the singular.

Intervocalically (*houses*), [s] appears thirteen times (50%) and [ž] once. The target word was not received nineteen times.

For word-final /z/ the distribution of variants is as follows. In *boys*, where the fricative follows a vowel, [s] is found thirteen times (39%) and [ž] three times (9%). The target word was not received twelve times. In *houses*, where final /s/ also follows a vowel, the marked forms are somewhat less frequent. Here, [s] occurs nine times (33%) and [ž] once, while the target word was not given eighteen times.

In *houses*, where the fricative occurs in both word-internal and word-final position, the distribution of the variants is usually uniform, that is, [haʊzɪz], [haʊsɪs] or [haʊžɪž]. However, while [haʊsɪz] occurs five times (informants 14, 19, 25, 28, 35), [haʊzɪs] is not found in the corpus.

In *pigs*, where /z/ follows a lenis consonant, the fortis appears eleven times (31%), the devoiced lenis three times (8%); the target word was not received nine times. Whenever /z/ is realized as [s], the preceding /g/ appears as [k]. Similarly, in those cases where /z/ is devoiced, it is preceded by devoiced [g̊]. In all other cases [gz] occurs.

In *girls*, where /z/ follows a lateral, [s] is present ten times (27%) and [ž] six times (16%); the target word was not given eight times. The scores of /z/ after [l] in *vegetables* are different with respect to the devoiced form; [s] occurs thirteen times (30%), [ž] once, and once the target word was not received.

76   The Influence of Pennsylvania German on English Phonology

	Nonsectarian a	b	c	d	Sectarians	Non-Pennsylvania Germans
Informant	1 2 3 4 5 6 7 8	9 10 11 12 13 14 15 16	17 18 19 20 21 22 23	24 25 26 28	29 30 31 32 35 36 37 38 39	42 43 44 45 46 47 48 49 50
houses	+ · + · · + · ·	+ · · · · · + + ·	+ · + · · · ·	+ ·	· - - - - - · ·	- - - - - - - - -
boys	+ · · + · · + + ·	+ - · - + + -	· + - - - - ·	· ·	- + - - - - -	- - - - - - - - -
houses	+ + · + · + +	+ · · · + +	+ · - - - ·	· ·	· - - - - -	- - - - - - - - -
pigs	+ · + + + ·	· + · + · + ·	+ · - - - ·	· ·	+ · · - - - ·	· - - - - - - - -
girls	+ · + + + + + ·	+ · · · · · · +	+ · - - - ·	· · · ·	+ · - - - · · ·	- - - - - - - - -
vegetables	+ · + + + · · +	+ + · · + · + · ·	+ · - - - - ·	· - -	+ · - - - - -	- - - - - - - - -
stars	+ · · + + + ·	+ · - - - ·	+ · - - - ·	· · ·	+ · - - - -	- - - - - - - - -
zoo	+ ·	- · + · - · - ·	+ · - - - ·	- - -	+ · - - - -	- - - - - - - - -

	+	*	-	not received
houses	13 (50%)	1 (4%)	12 (46%)	19
boys	13 (39%)	3 (9%)	17 (52%)	12
houses	9 (33%)	1 (4%)	17 (63%)	18
pigs	11 (31%)	3 (8%)	22 (61%)	9
girls	10 (27%)	6 (16%)	21 (57%)	8
vegetables	13 (30%)	1 (2%)	30 (68%)	1
stars	6 (19%)	2 (7%)	23 (74%)	14
zoo	7 (19%)	0 (0%)	30 (81%)	8

+ = [s]
* = [ž]
- = [z]

Figure 2.8: [s] for [z] in *houses, boys, pigs, girls, vegetables, stars, zoo*

Finally, the scores for /z/ after /r/ (*stars*) are [s] six times (19%), [ž] twice (7%); fourteen times the target word was not given.

Word-initially (*zoo*), the unvoiced variant is present in seven cases (19%); the devoiced lenis does not appear. In eight instances the target word was not received.

In sum, the marked variants appear considerably less often word-initially (seven times = 19%) than in word-internal (fourteen times = 54%) and in word-final positions (thirteen times = 37% on average). The six target words where the feature is word-final show less variation (*boys*: sixteen instances = 48%, *girls*: sixteen instances = 43%, *pigs*: fourteen instances = 39%, *houses*: ten instances = 37%, *vegetables*: fourteen instances = 32%, *stars*: eight instances = 26%). Thus, the quality of the sounds preceding the fricative does not seem to be as significant as its position.

Only a few linguistically rather conservative informants (2, 7, 10, 13, 15, 17, 29) have the unvoiced variant in word-initial position. Wherever [s] is present word-initially, it also appears in the other positions when all the target words were received. If informants with fewer

The Influence of Pennsylvania German on English Phonology   77

marked variants in their speech have isolated unvoiced or devoiced forms, they are found in word-internal and word-final position rather than word-initially.

The marked variant [s] is present most often in the speech of members of the nonsectarian a-generation, and, to a lesser extent, the b-generation. The share of the other groups of informants in [s] is negligible. The only exceptions are informant 17, a member of the nonsectarian c-generation, and informant 29, a Mennonite. The proportion of the variant [ž] is higher in the nonsectarian c- and d-generations. The use of the devoiced lenis consonant by the younger generations may be regarded as the qualitative reflection of the state of transition from marked to regional-standard variants.

Among the 175 forms received in the category [v][9] for [w] (figure 2.9), thirty-two (over 18%) are marked ([v]). The twelve informants who have [v] include all eight members of the nonsectarian a-generation as well as informants 12, 14, 15 (nonsectarian b-generation) and 17 (nonsectarian c-generation).

Figure 2.9: [v] for [w] in *wolf, wheel, well, wagon*

Five times the marked variant appears in all four target words (*well, wagon, wheel, wolf*), namely in the speech of informants 1–3, 7, and 12. Informants 6 and 15 both feature [v] three times, informant 5 has it twice, while informants 4, 8, 14, and 17 have only one instance each.

The reverse feature, [w] for [v], was also tested. The target word *vegetables* was received from all the informants, but was never pro-

78   The Influence of Pennsylvania German on English Phonology

nounced with a [w]. Although *valentine* was not given twenty times, where it was received the first consonant was invariably [v].

The features [s] for [θ] and [d] for [ð], which were both tested in word-initial, word-internal, and word-final positions, are not only phonetically related; they also show similar results. As the Pennsylvania German phoneme system includes neither /θ/ nor /ð/ (*see* figure 2.4), the linguistically most conservative informants substitute the articulatorily "easier" variants [s] and [d] for [θ] and [ð].

Figure 2.10 gives the distribution of the feature [d] for [ð]. Of the 129 words received, 33 (almost 26%) include a marked form ([d], [s], or [θ]).

	Nonsectarian a	b	c	d	Sectarians	Non-Pennsylvania Germans
Informant	1 2 3 4 5 6 7 8	9 10 11 12 13 14 15 16	17 18 19 20 21 22 23	24 25 26 28	29 30 31 32 35 36 37 38 39	42 43 44 45 46 47 48 49 50
that	+ + + - + - + -	+ + - - - - - -	- - - - - - -	- - - -	- + - - - - - - -	- - - - - - - - -
feather	+ - - + + + - -	- - - + + - - -	- - - - - - -	- - - -	- - - - - - - - -	- - - - - - - - -
smooth	s s s 0 s 0 -	0 - 0 0 0 s s -	0 - - 0 - 0 -	- - - -	0 - - - s - - -	- - - - - - - - -

	+	[s]	[θ]	-	not received
that	9 (21%)	0 (0%)	0 (0%)	33 (79%)	3
feather	7 (16%)	0 (0%)	0 (0%)	38 (84%)	0
smooth	0 (0%)	7 (17%)	10 (24%)	25 (59%)	3

+ = [d]
- = [ð]

Figure 2.10: [d] for [ð] in *that, feather, smooth*

The sound [d] is substituted for [ð] by twelve informants. Seven of them belong to the nonsectarian a-generation (informants 1–7), four are members of the b-generation (informants 9–11, 15), and one is Amish (informant 39). This substitution occurs nine times (21%) in word-initial position (*that*) and seven times (16%) word-internally (*feather*). In four cases (informants 1, 2, 5, 9), both words have [d].

The variant [d] in *feather* could quite naturally be seen as an interference phenomenon, the pronunciation being influenced by Pennsylvania German *Fedder* 'feather'. However, [d] for [ð] is a general feature of nonstandard American English, especially in unstressed syllables or in unstressed sentence position (Raith 1981, 39).

Thus, in the case of informant 39, who is a member of the b-generation of the Amish family and grew up in a Mennonite community

The Influence of Pennsylvania German on English Phonology   79

in Ohio, the variant [d] for [ð] in *that* should probably be regarded as a general feature of nonstandard American English rather than a marker of Pennsylvania German ethnicity; no other sectarian informant shows any trace of marked variants for /ð/ or /θ/.

By contrast, markedness in these two phonemes plays a large role in the case of the nonsectarian informants, specifically in the two older generations.

The realization of the phoneme /ð/ is split. In the target words *that* and *feather*, sixteen instances of [d] were counted. The word *smooth*, where the feature occurs in word-final position, turned out to be a special case. The marked variant is [s], not [d] (seven instances = 17%). Ten informants (24%) take an intermediate step, namely [θ] for [ð], that is, they substitute the unvoiced for the voiced sound.

Only two nonsectarian native speakers of Pennsylvania German (informants 4, 7) have [θ]; all the other occurrences of this sound are in the nonsectarian b-generation (informants 9, 11–13), the c-generation (informants 17, 20, 22), or the Mennonite b-generation (informant 29). The seven informants who realize unvoiced /θ/ as [s] belong to the a-generation (informants 1–3, 6), the b-generation (informants 14, 15), and the Amish family (informant 36).[10]

As *smooth* turned out to constitute a case of [s] for [ð] no fewer than seven times,[11] it will be included in the discussion of *thistle, author,* and *south* (figure 2.11). The share of marked forms ([s]; [θ] in *smooth*) is 29 of 159 forms (over 18%).

Figure 2.11: [s] for [θ] in *thistle, smooth, south, author*

80   The Influence of Pennsylvania German on English Phonology

In no case do all four words show the marked variant: [s] never occurs word-internally (*author*). In word-initial position (*thistle*), [s] is present seven times (21%), word-finally seven times in *smooth* (17%) and five times in *south* (12%). The fact that whenever [s] is found in *south*, it is also present in *smooth* indicates a high degree of consistency.

Among the informants with the highest rate of three marked target words, there are three members of the nonsectarian a-generation (informants 1, 3, 6) and one of the b-generation (informant 15). Apart from informant 36, a sectarian, only those belonging to the nonsectarian a- or b-generations have [s] for [θ].

No informant exhibited ∅ for [r], neither in word-final position (*car, bear, author, feather, measure, pleasure, ladder*), nor before /s/ (*stars*) or other consonants (*bird, girls*).

Among the seventy-six forms received in the category [ʃ] for [ʒ] (figure 2.12), there are twenty-eight marked forms (almost 37%). Thirteen informants have [ʃ] in both target words; only informant 4 has the devoiced lenis [ʒ̊] instead of the fully marked [ʃ] in *pleasure*.

Figure 2.12: [ʃ] for [ʒ] in *measure, pleasure*

Thus, the informants are clearly divided into two groups. Those who have the marked variant consist of all eight members of the nonsectarian a-generation, four members of the nonsectarian b-generation (informants 9, 12, 14, 15), and one of the c-generation (informant 17). Outside the nonsectarian group, the marked variant was also found in the speech of informant 31, who belongs to the Mennonite b-generation. All the other informants show the unmarked variant.

The Influence of Pennsylvania German on English Phonology   81

Word-final [f] for [v] was not present in the data, neither in *glove* nor in *hive*. *Glove* was not received nineteen times, as many informants gave the plural form where the fricative was no longer in word-final position.

The results of [l] for [ɫ] differ greatly depending on context (figure 2.13). The three positions tested are before a vowel (*ladder, valentine, pleasure, glove, lion, family*), before a consonant (*milk, girls, vegetables, wolf*), and word-finally (*hill, well, wheel, thistle*).

	Nonsectarian a	b	c	d	Sectarians	Non-Pennsylvania Germans
Informant	1 2 3 4 5 6 7 8	9 10 11 12 13 14 15 16	17 18 19 20 21 22 23	24 25 26 28	29 30 31 32 35 36 37 38 39	42 43 44 45 46 47 48 49 50
family						
lion						
valentine						
ladder						
thistle						
vegetables						
wolf						
well						
girls						
milk						
hill						
wheel						
pleasure						
glove						

	+	−	not received
family	42 (95%)	2 (5%)	1
lion	41 (93%)	3 (7%)	1
valentine	23 (92%)	2 (8%)	20
ladder	29 (66%)	15 (34%)	1
thistle	10 (27%)	27 (73%)	8
vegetables	5 (12%)	38 (88%)	2
wolf	2 (5%)	39 (95%)	4
well	2 (4%)	43 (96%)	0
girls	1 (3%)	36 (97%)	8
milk	1 (2%)	43 (98%)	1
hill	1 (2%)	42 (98%)	2
wheel	0 (0%)	45 (100%)	0
pleasure	0 (0%)	43 (100%)	2
glove	0 (0%)	44 (100%)	1

+ = [l]
− = [ɫ]

Figure 2.13: [l] for [ɫ] in *family, lion, valentine, ladder, thistle, vegetables, wolf, well, girls, milk, hill, wheel, pleasure, glove*

Prevocalically, /l/ shows an extremely diverse pattern of distribution. The three target words *family, lion,* and *valentine* score similar results. In this group [l] prevails, [ɫ] occurring only twice in *family* (5%), three times in *lion* (7%), and twice in *valentine* (8%). The latter target word, however, has a relatively high rate of twenty instances in which it was not received.

In *ladder* twenty-nine informants (66%) have [ɫ], fifteen [l]. However, the feature [l] for [ɫ] runs through all social groups without structuring the informants. Social parameters such as community, age, and gender do not seem to play a role for the distribution.

Pleasure and *glove* display exactly the opposite pattern. In both these words, [l] is not present at all, with only one and two instances in which the words were not received. The reason for this incongruity appears to be phonological; the /l/ in *family, lion, valentine,* and *ladder* is either word-initial or preceded by a vowel, in *family*, where both /fæmɪlɪ/ and /fæmlɪ/ occur, also by a nasal. In each of these words, /l/ is at the beginning of a syllable. By contrast, a plosive precedes in *pleasure* and *glove*, which may trigger the realization of /l/ as [ɫ].

To sum up, the realization of prevocalic /l/ appears to be governed by two major rules. If prevocalic /l/ is preceded by a plosive, the allophone [ɫ] is present. If, on the other hand, /l/ before a vowel marks the beginning of a syllable, it is realized as [l] in most cases. The exceptions seem to be idiosyncratic; their number can vary considerably from word to word. This may be taken as an indication that in a word like *ladder* [l] and [ɫ] are free variants not only within the speech community but also within the individual speakers.

By contrast, the feature [l] for [ɫ] is significant both before a consonant and word-finally. In these positions, Pennsylvania German has both [l] and [ɫ], while the regional standard of English only allows [ɫ].

In preconsonantal position, [l] for [ɫ] appears five times in *vegetables* (12%), twice in *wolf* (5%), once in *girls*, and once in *milk*. With one exception (informant 31, a Mennonite), all the informants showing this feature belong to the nonsectarian a-generation (informants 1–4, 6, 7). Only two informants (1, 4) have [l] in two of the four words.

Word-finally, [l] for [ɫ] is found ten times in *thistle* (27%), twice in *well* (4%), once in *hill*, and never in *wheel*. Once again, most of the nine informants exhibiting [l] are members of the nonsectarian a-generation (informants 1–7). The other two belong to the nonsectarian b-generation (informant 12) and the Amish family (informant 39). As before, only two informants (4, 5) have [l] in two target words. Therefore, both before a consonant and word-finally, [l] for [ɫ] has to be regarded as a very sporadic feature.

The large number of marked variants in *thistle* is conspicuous. In this word, a second marking was found. Eight informants realized the intermediate <t> (/θɪsdəl/) rather than /θɪsəl/). Among them, no fewer

The Influence of Pennsylvania German on English Phonology 83

than six (informants 1–4, 12, 39) also have [l]. At first sight, this realization could be merely regarded as a spelling pronunciation. However, except for informant 12, all the informants are native speakers of Pennsylvania German; the Pennsylvania German equivalent has /d/ or /t/, depending on syllabic break: *Dischdel* /dɪʃdəl/ 'thistle', *Dischdle* /dɪʃtlə/ 'thistles'.

Figure 2.14 shows the occurrence of [oː] for [oʊ]. The continuum ranging from the diphthong [oʊ] (regional standard; *see* Kurath and McDavid 1961, Maps 20f., and Kurath 1972, 62) to the most heavily marked monophthong [oː] includes three intermediate stages. All of them, [oᵘ], [oˑᵘ], and [oːᵘ], are regarded as marked forms. In addition, the diphthong [əʊ] is present in the speech of a number of sectarian and non-Pennsylvania German informants. Because of its centralized first component, this diphthong is counted as an unmarked variant.[12]

Figure 2.14: [oː] for [oʊ] in *crow, goat, soap*

With sixteen instances of [oː] (38%), *crow* shows the highest number of monophthongs. They are present in the speech of all eight members of the nonsectarian a-generation, informants 9–11, 14, 15 (b-generation), informant 17 (c-generation), and informants 29, 31 (Mennonites). Only one intermediate variant is found for *crow*, that is, [oːᵘ] for informant 30, a Mennonite woman. Thus, the overall score of marked forms is seventeen (40%). Five informants, namely 32, 35 (a young Mennonite woman and her six-year-old daughter), as well as 45, 47, 49 (all non-Pennsylvania Germans), have [əʊ] (12%).

In *goat*, thirteen informants have the monophthong (30%); this group includes all the members of the nonsectarian a-generation except informant 3. The monophthong is also found in the speech of informants 9, 12, 14, 15 (nonsectarian b-generation), 17 (c-generation), and 30 (sectarian). Informant 10, a member of the nonsectarian b-generation, is the only informant to have [oːᵘ]. [oᵓᵘ] is found in the speech of informants 29, 31, and 38, all of whom are sectarians (7%), while informants 3, 11, and 13 (nonsectarian a- and b-generations) have [oᵘ] (7%). All in all, twenty realizations of *goat* (46%) are marked. The diphthong [əʊ] is found four times (9%); it occurs in the speech of informants 32, 35, 37 (all sectarians), and 45 (non-Pennsylvania German).

In *soap*, the monophthong appears only eleven times (24%). Of the eight a-generation informants, six (1, 2, 4–7) have [oː]. The monophthong is also present in the speech of informants 12, 14, 15 (nonsectarian b-generation) and 30, 31 (sectarians). [oːᵘ] occurs three times (7%), namely in the speech of informants 8 (nonsectarian a-generation), 10 (b-generation), and 17 (c-generation). Informants 25 (nonsectarian d-generation) and 29 (Mennonite) have [oᵓᵘ] (4%). [oᵘ] is found for informants 3 (a-generation), 9, 11, 13 (all b-generation; 9%). Altogether, like in *goat*, twenty realizations are marked. Informants 32, 35, and 37, all of whom are sectarians, have [əʊ] (7%).

In sum, the share of marked variants ([oː], [oːᵘ], [oᵓᵘ], or [oᵘ]) is 57 of 131 forms (almost 44%). It is highest in the nonsectarian a-generation and declines rapidly in the other groups. Likewise, the a-generation shows the highest proportion of pure monophthongs, while intermediate variants are found in all the subgroups other than the non-Pennsylvania Germans. This allows us to establish the transition zone not only quantitatively, but also qualitatively. The older Mennonites show a tendency toward marked forms. [əʊ] is found most often in the speech of younger sectarians and in that of the non-Pennsylvania Germans.

The distribution of the variable [eː] for [eɪ] (figure 2.15) is similar to that of [oː] for [oʊ]. Again, a monophthong is found instead of a diphthong in marked speech. The variation ranges from the regional-standard diphthong [eɪ] via three sounds where the second component is merely an off-glide and which differ only in the length of the first element ([eᶦ], [eᵎ], and [eːᶦ]) to the monophthong [eː]. Of all these, the first is counted as the regional-standard form (*see* Kurath and McDavid 1961, Maps 18f., and Kurath 1972, 62); the others are regarded as marked variants. Quite generally, however, both [oː] for [oʊ] and [eː] for [eɪ] are fairly frequently found in (conservative) regional and social dialects of

The Influence of Pennsylvania German on English Phonology   85

Informant	Nonsectarian a 1 2 3 4 5 6 7 8	b 9 10 11 12 13 14 15 16	c 17 18 19 20 21 22 23	d 24 25 26 28	Sectarians 29 30 31 32 35 36 37 38 39	Non-Pennsylvania Germans 42 43 44 45 46 47 48 49 50
baby	+ + + + + + + +	+ + 1 + - - + 2 -	+ - - - - - -	- + - -	+ + 2 - - - - - -	- - - - - - - - -
gate	+ + + + + + + +	+ + 1 + - + - -	+ - - - - - -	- 2 1 -	+ 1 + - - - - - -	- - - - - - - - -
tray	+ + + + + + + +	+ + + 3 - - - + -	+ - - - - - -	- - - -	- + + + + 2 - 2	- - - - - - - 2 -
cake	+ + 3 + 3 + + +	3 + + 3 - - - + -	+ - - - - - -	- - - -	+ + + - - - - 2 -	- - - - - - - - -

	+	1	2	3	-	not received
baby	16 (40%)	1 (2%)	2 (5%)	0 (0%)	21 (53%)	5
gate	16 (38%)	3 (7%)	1 (2%)	0 (0%)	22 (53%)	3
tray	17 (38%)	0 (0%)	3 (7%)	1 (2%)	24 (53%)	0
cake	15 (33%)	0 (0%)	1 (2%)	4 (9%)	25 (56%)	0

+ = [eː]
1 = [eːⁱ]
2 = [eᵉ]
3 = [eⁱ]
- = [eɪ]

Figure 2.15: [eː] for [eɪ] in *baby, gate, tray, cake*

English across North America, and within the United States particularly in the upper Midwest.[13]

Baby shows sixteen instances of monophthongs (40%). They occur in the speech of all the members of the nonsectarian a-generation except for informant 8 (target word not received), of four members of the b-generation (informants 9, 10, 12, 14), one of the c-generation (informant 17), one of the d-generation (informant 25), and three Mennonites (informants 29, 30, 35). Informant 11 (nonsectarian b-generation) shows [eːⁱ]; informants 15 (b-generation) and 31 (Mennonite) have [eᵉ] (5%). In all, a marked form occurs nineteen times (47%).

In *gate* the monophthong is present sixteen times (38%), occurring in the speech of all eight members of the nonsectarian a-generation, four members of the b-generation (informants 9, 10, 12, 14, 15), one of the c-generation (informant 17), and two Mennonites (informants 29, 31). Informants 11 (nonsectarian b-generation), 26 (d-generation), and 30 (Mennonite) have [eːⁱ] (7%). Informant 25, the sister of informant 26, has [eᵉ]. Altogether, twenty realizations (47%) are marked.

Seventeen informants (38%) have the monophthong in *tray*. They are all the members of the nonsectarian a-generation, four of the b-generation (informants 9–11, 15), one of the c-generation (informant 17), and four Mennonites (informants 30–32, 35). In addition, three informants (37, 39, 49; = 7%) show the intermediate form [eᵉ]. While the appearance of informants 37 and 39, who are both Amish, in this list is

86   The Influence of Pennsylvania German on English Phonology

already remarkable, the fact that informant 49, a young non-Pennsylvania German, has a marked form, is highly unusual. Informant 12, a member of the nonsectarian b-generation, has [eⁱ]. Thus, a total of twenty-one realizations of *tray* (47%) are marked.

For *cake*, fifteen instances (33%) of monophthongs are found, namely for six members of the nonsectarian a-generation (informants 1, 2, 4, 6–8), four of the b-generation (informants 10, 11, 14, 15), one of the c-generation (informant 17), one of the d-generation (informant 25), and two Mennonites (informants 29, 30). One Amish informant (38) has [eⁱ]; four nonsectarians (informants 3 and 5, a-generation; informants 9 and 12, b-generation) have [eⁱ] (9%). Thus, a total of twenty forms (44%) are marked.

The word *vegetables* was not included in figure 2.15, as its regional-standard form does not contain /eɪ/. Nevertheless, informants 1 and 2 had [e] and [eː], respectively, instead of [ə] for <a>. Most probably the monophthongs constitute realizations of the diphthong /eɪ/. Those variants might be regarded as general features of nonstandard English. All the other informants had [ə].

In sum, all four target words score approximately the same amount of marked variants (between 44% and 47%). Phonetic environment does not seem to play a significant role. In most cases, the members of the nonsectarian a- and b-generations have the pure monophthong; with the exception of informants 13 and 16, all of them have some marked variant. The same is true for one informant (17) belonging to the nonsectarian c-generation and two informants (25 and 26, who are sisters) belonging to the d-generation. The tendency toward the monophthong is also found in the speech of several sectarian informants belonging to both the a- (informants 29, 30) and the b-generation (informants 31, 38).

The variant [ʌ̟] for [ʌ][14] found in marked speech (figure 2.16) constitutes an advanced /ʌ/ reaching toward [ʊ]. The overall share of [ʌ̟] is 94 of 220 forms received (almost 43%). Of the five target words, four (*cup, jug, tub, glove*) score similar results. The marked feature appears twenty-eight times in *cup* (62%), twenty-five times in *jug* (60%), twenty-one times in *tub* (47%), and nineteen times in *glove* (43%).

Sun shows a totally different result. Here, only informant 15 has [ʌ̟]. From the evidence of the other four target words, it appears quite safe to assume that in the word *sun* certain phonetic restrictions—possibly the following nasal—prevent the marked feature from appearing more frequently. However, the one case cited above shows that [ʌ̟] is not altogether impossible before /n/.

The Influence of Pennsylvania German on English Phonology 87

Figure 2.16: [ʌ] for [ʌ] in *cup, jug, tub, glove, sun*

The word *sun* appears in the synopses given by Kurath and McDavid (1961, 60–63) for speakers from four places situated in central Pennsylvania. In three cases the vowel is marked as [ʌ]; in no case is there an indication of [ʌ] in the regional standard of this area.

The sound [ʌ] is found in the speech of the majority of informants, namely thirty-two. Only informants 16 (nonsectarian b-generation), 21 (nonsectarian c-generation), 24, 26, 28 (nonsectarian d-generation), 39 (sectarian), 19, and 45–50 (non-Pennsylvania Germans) do not have the marked variant. One informant (15) has [ʌ] in all five target words; six informants (20, 22, 35, 38, 43, 44) have only one instance of the marked variant. From informant 1 through 15 (nonsectarian a- and b-generations), there is no case of fewer than three target words with [ʌ].

For two reasons, the feature [ɑː] for [ɑʊ] (figure 2.17) has to be clearly separated from [oː] for [oʊ] and [eː] for [eɪ]. Not only is it less prevalent in the present sample, but also quite generally so in the American English dialects. According to Kurath and McDavid (1961, Maps 28f.), there are no traces of [ɑː] for [ɑʊ] in the area under examination.

In the continuum of articulation from the standard realization [ɑʊ] to the most heavily marked [ɑː], three intermediate steps are found, namely [ɑᵘ], [ɑˑᵘ], and [ɑːᵘ]. Together with the final stage [ɑː], these variants are considered to be marked.

All in all, the five target words show quite similar results. With twenty instances of [ɑː] (46%), *south* has the highest proportion of

88   The Influence of Pennsylvania German on English Phonology

	Nonsectarian a	b	c	d	Sectarians	Non-Pennsylvania Germans
Informant	1 2 3 4 5 6 7 8	9 10 11 12 13 14 15 16	17 18 19 20 21 22 23	24 25 26 28	29 30 31 32 35 36 37 38 39	42 43 44 45 46 47 48 49 50
south	. . . . . 2 . .	. . . .	. . . .	. . 1	. . . . 1 .	. . . 1 2 . 2 . 2 2
crown	. . . .	. . . .	. . . .	. . . .	. . . .	. . . . 2 . .
cow	1	2 . . . 2 . 2 .	. . . .	. 2 . .	. 1 2	. 2 . . . .
houses	 3	. . . .	. 1	1 . . .	. . . 2	. . . .
mouse	. . . .	2 . . 3	. . . .	. . . 1	. . . .	. . . .

	.	1	2	3	-	not received
south	20 (46%)	3 (7%)	5 (12%)	0 (0%)	15 (35%)	2
crown	14 (31%)	0 (0%)	1 (2%)	0 (0%)	30 (67%)	0
cow	11 (25%)	2 (4%)	6 (13%)	0 (0%)	26 (58%)	0
houses	11 (25%)	2 (5%)	1 (2%)	1 (2%)	29 (66%)	1
mouse	11 (26%)	1 (2%)	1 (2%)	1 (2%)	29 (68%)	2

. = [ɑ]
1 = [ɑːᵘ]
2 = [ɑːᵒ]
3 = [ɑː]
- = [aʊ]

Figure 2.17: [ɑː] for [aʊ] in *south, crown, cow, houses, mouse*

monophthongs. They occur in the speech of all the members of the nonsectarian a-generation except for informant 6, all the members of the b-generation except for informants 15 and 16, as well as informants 17, 18, 23 (c-generation), 26 (d-generation), 30, 36 (sectarians), and 43 (non-Pennsylvania German). In addition, [ɑːᵘ] (7%) is found for informants 28 (nonsectarian d-generation), 38 (Amish), and 44 (non-Pennsylvania German). Informant 6 (nonsectarian a-generation) and informants 45, 47, 49, 50 (all non-Pennsylvania Germans) have [ɑːᵘ] (12%). In all, this adds up to twenty-eight cases (65%) of marked variants, by far the highest number among all five target words. The frequency of the marked variants in *south* among the non-Pennsylvania German informants is remarkable.

Crown shows fourteen instances (31%) of the monophthong. They are found with all the members of the nonsectarian a-generation, informants 9, 10, 12, 14 (b-generation), 17 (c-generation), and 29 (Mennonite). Moreover, informant 49, a young non-Pennsylvania German, has [ɑːᵘ]. All in all, these are fifteen instances (33%) of marked forms.

In *cow* the monophthong appears eleven times (25%), namely in the speech of all the members of the nonsectarian a-generation (except for informants 1 and 8), informants 10, 14 (b-generation), 17, 18 (c-generation), and 29 (Mennonite). In addition, two intermediate forms are present. Informants 1 (nonsectarian a-generation) and 30 (sectarian) have [ɑːᵘ] (4%); informants 9, 13, 15 (b-generation), 25 (d-generation), and 39 (Amish) display [ɑʳᵘ] (13%). Altogether, there are nineteen cases (42%) of marked variants.

Houses shows a similar distribution. Informants 1–6 (nonsectarian a-generation) have the monophthong, as well as informants 10, 14 (b-generation), 17 (c-generation), and 29, 30 (sectarians), bringing the percentage of [ɑː] to 25%. Four instances of intermediate forms are present. Informants 18 (c-generation) and 24 (d-generation) have [ɑːᵘ] (5%), informant 32 (Mennonite) has [ɑʳᵘ], and informant 8 (a-generation) has [ɑᵘ]. Altogether, fifteen marked variants (34%) are found.

In *mouse* the monophthong is present eleven times (26%); it occurs in the speech of all the members of the nonsectarian a-generation except for informant 8, of informants 10, 13 (b-generation) and 17, 18 (c-generation). In addition, informant 28 (d-generation) has [ɑːᵘ], informant 9 (b-generation) [ɑʳᵘ], and informant 12 (b-generation) [ɑᵘ]. In all, for *mouse*, fourteen of forty-three forms (32%) are marked. They all come from members of the nonsectarian group.

The overall share of marked forms is ninety-one forms (over 41%). No fewer than thirty-four informants vary in some way from the regional-standard form in at least one target word. The group comprises all the nonsectarian native speakers of Pennsylvania German, all the members of the nonsectarian b-generation except for informant 16, three of the c-generation (informants 17, 18, 23), all four members of the d-generation, all but three members of the sectarian group, and even six of the nine members of the non-Pennsylvania Germans.

Particularly the appearance of marked forms in the speech of informants 28, 43–45, 47, 49, and 50, who are all monolingual English speakers, the latter six even with no speakers of Pennsylvania German in their family and therefore minimal exposure to that language, shows that certain features typical of nonsectarian Pennsylvania German English enter the speech of other speakers living in the area.

At the same time, the pure monophthong is most widespread among the members of the nonsectarian a- and b-generations as well as informants 17 (c-generation) and 29, 30 (Mennonites). Most other informants have intermediate variants, usually in single target words. Thus, the quantitative decrease in marked forms is reflected by qualitative changes.

Huffines (1984b, 98) calls the prevalence of the marked monophthongal variant "a recent development."[15] This seems rather

90 The Influence of Pennsylvania German on English Phonology

doubtful for two reasons. First, the fact that the members of the a- and b-generations are clearly in the majority and that the monophthong only sporadically occurs in the younger generations rules out a recent development and a stable variable, independent of the factor age. Quite on the contrary, figure 2.17 indicates that the marked variant is dying out. There is no reason to assume that an innovation starts with the oldest, linguistically most conservative generations. Secondly, there is a simpler explanation for the presence of the monophthong in the speech of those nonsectarians who have good competence in Pennsylvania German. The realization of Standard German /aʊ/ in Pennsylvania German is split into the diphthong [aʊ] and the monophthong [ɔː]. The feature [ɑː] for [aʊ] can therefore be regarded as an interference or contact phenomenon.

Unlike the other sounds discussed, [ɑː] for [aɪ] is extant neither in the regional standard of the area nor in Pennsylvania German English. The monophthong was not found in any of the five target words (*mice, lion, valentine, hive, pie*). Of these, *valentine* has a high proportion of unreceived target words, namely twenty.

The feature [ʉ] for [ʊ] (figure 2.18) is far more frequent in *book* (ten instances = 23%) than in *wolf* (two instances = 5%).

Figure 2.18: [ʉ] for [ʊ] in *book, wolf*

In all, the marked variant [ʉ] is present in twelve of eighty-five forms received (over 14%). It is found in the speech of five of the eight members of the nonsectarian a-generation (informants 1, 2, 4, 6, 8), one member of the c-generation (informant 17), and four sectarian informants (29, 32, 35, 37). In two cases (informants 1, 4), both target words show the marked variant; in the other eight cases, [ʊ̝] is found in *book* only.

As could be seen in the monophthong charts of figure 2.2, the marked variants of short [ʊ] and long [uː], that is, [ʊ̝] and [u̟ː], are very similar qualitatively. [ʊ̝] is a raised variant of [ʊ], while [u̟ː] is an advanced variant of cardinal vowel number eight.

The variant [u̟ː] for [uː] (figure 2.19) occurs twenty-two times in *shoe* (49%), twelve times in *zoo* (32%), and ten times in *smooth* (24%). At first sight, the numerical discrepancy between *shoe* and *zoo*, with /uː/ in word-final position, is rather surprising. The high frequency of the marked variant in *shoe* may be accounted for by the fact that exactly the same pronunciation is used for the Pennsylvania German word *Schuh* 'shoe'. In all cases where informants pronounced English *shoe* with the marked variant, they also had [u̟ː] in Pennsylvania German *Schuh*, provided they knew the word. Both variants of /uː/, [uː] and [u̟ː], are present in Pennsylvania German (*see* figure 2.2).

	Nonsectarian a	b	c	d	Sectarians	Non-Pennsylvania Germans
Informant	1 2 3 4 5 6 7 8	9 10 11 12 13 14 15 16	17 18 19 20 21 22 23	24 25 26 28	29 30 31 32 35 36 37 38 39	42 43 44 45 46 47 48 49 50
shoe				∂∪ – – ∂∪		
zoo				∂∪ + ∂∪ ∂∪		
smooth						

	+	[∂ʊ]	–	not received
shoe	22 (49%)	2 (4%)	21 (47%)	0
zoo	12 (32%)	3 (8%)	22 (60%)	8
smooth	10 (24%)	0 (0%)	32 (76%)	3

+ = [u̟ː]
– = [uː]

Figure 2.19: [u̟ː] for [uː] in *shoe, zoo, smooth*

Three members of the nonsectarian d-generation (informants 24, 26, 28) have diphthongal [∂ʊ] in word-final position, a total of two instances in *shoe* (4%) and three in *zoo* (8%). This sound, which does not occur in Pennsylvania German, is not regarded as a marked variant.

Altogether, the share of the marked variant ([u̟ː]) is 44 of 124 (over 35%). Only two informants (2, 11) have the marked variant in all three words. The prevalence of members of the nonsectarian a-generation is not as strong as with other features. Rather, [u̟ː] is just as much a marker of the speech of the b-generation and, particularly, of the sectarian in-

92   The Influence of Pennsylvania German on English Phonology

formants. The younger nonsectarians have a lower proportion of the marked form. [u̞ː] is not extant in the speech of the non-Pennsylvania Germans.

The second-last feature to be discussed is [ɪ̞] for unstressed [ɪ], that is, lowering in word-final position (figure 2.20). A total of eighteen instances of [ɪ̞] are found in both *baby* (45%) and *family* (41%).

Informant	Nonsectarian a 1 2 3 4 5 6 7 8	b 9 10 11 12 13 14 15 16	c 17 18 19 20 21 22 23	d 24 25 26 28	Sectarians 29 30 31 32 35 36 37 38 39	Non-Pennsylvania Germans 42 43 44 45 46 47 48 49 50
baby	+ + + - + + +	- + + - - + -	+ - - - - - -	- + - -	- - ə + + + -	+ - - - - - -
family	+ + ə - - ə + ə	+ + + + + - + -	+ - - - - - + -	+ - -	- + - - - ə + + -	+ + - - - - - -

	+	[ə]	-	not received
baby	18 (45%)	1 (2%)	21 (53%)	5
family	18 (41%)	4 (9%)	22 (50%)	1

+ = [ɪ̞]
- = [ɪ]

Figure 2.20: [ɪ̞] for [ɪ] in *baby, family*

In five cases, the quality of the marked variant proved to be [ə] rather than [ɪ̞]. [ə] occurs once in *baby* (informant 35) and four times (9%) in *family* (informants 3, 6, 8, 36).

All in all, forty-one of the eighty-four forms received (almost 49%) are marked. Seventeen informants have such a variant in both target words. The twenty-four informants displaying at least one marked form include all eight members of the nonsectarian a-generation (apart from informant 4) as well as the b-generation (apart from informants 14, 16), two informants belonging to the nonsectarian c-generation (informants 17, 22), two belonging to the d-generation (informants 25, 28), five sectarians (informants 30, 35–38), and two non-Pennsylvania Germans (informants 42, 43).

Five informants (9, 13, 28, 30, 35) have a marked variant in one target word and the regional-standard variant in the other. Three of them (informants 28, nonsectarian d-generation; 30 and 35, sectarian) belong to groups which tend to be in the middle of the continuum between the members of the nonsectarian a-generation, whose English is heavily marked, and the non-Pennsylvania Germans, whose English pronunciation generally includes few nonstandard features.

The Influence of Pennsylvania German on English Phonology   93

The last phonological variant, epenthetic [ə] after long vowels and diphthongs in word-final position (figure 2.21), appears twice in *key* (5%) and twice in *shoe* (4%). In the other seven target words (*saw, zoo, pie, tray, boy, cow, crow*), [Vːə] never occurs. In all, the marked variant is found in 4 of 386 forms received (just over 1%). *Zoo* and *boy* have a relatively high rate of eight and seven unreceived target words, respectively.

	Nonsectarian a	b	c	d	Sectarians	Non-Pennsylvania Germans
Informant	1 2 3 4 5 6 7 8	9 10 11 12 13 14 15 16	17 18 19 20 21 22 23	24 25 26 28	29 30 31 32 35 36 37 38 39	42 43 44 45 46 47 48 49 50
key	- + + - - - - -	- - - - - - - -	- - - - - - -	- - - -	- - - - - - - - -	- - - - - - - - -
shoe	- + - - - - - -	- - - - - - - -	- - - - - - -	- + - -	- - - - - - - - -	- - - - - - - - -
saw	- - - - - - - -	- - - - - - - -	- - - - - - -	- - - -	- - - - - - - - -	- - - - - - - - -
zoo	- - - - - - - -	- - - - - - - -	- - - - - - -	- - - -	- - - - - - - - -	- - - - - - - - -
pie	- - - - - - - -	- - - - - - - -	- - - - - - -	- - - -	- - - - - - - - -	- - - - - - - - -
tray	- - - - - - - -	- - - - - - - -	- - - - - - -	- - - -	- - - - - - - - -	- - - - - - - - -
boy	- - - - - - - -	- - - - - - - -	- - - - - - -	- - - -	- - - - - - - - -	- - - - - - - - -
cow	- - - - - - - -	- - - - - - - -	- - - - - - -	- - - -	- - - - - - - - -	- - - - - - - - -
crow	- - - - - - - -	- - - - - - - -	- - - - - - -	- - - -	- - - - - - - - -	- - - - - - - - -

	+	-	not received
key	2 (5%)	42 (95%)	1
shoe	2 (4%)	43 (96%)	0
saw	0 (0%)	45 (100%)	0
zoo	0 (0%)	37 (100%)	8
pie	0 (0%)	45 (100%)	0
tray	0 (0%)	45 (100%)	0
boy	0 (0%)	38 (100%)	7
cow	0 (0%)	45 (100%)	0
crow	0 (0%)	42 (100%)	3

+ = [Vːə]
- = [Vː]

Figure 2.21: [Vːə] for [Vː] in *key, shoe, saw, zoo, pie, tray, boy, cow, crow*

Epenthetic [ə] is present in the speech of two members of the nonsectarian a-generation (informants 2, 3) and one member of the nonsectarian d-generation (informant 25). Informant 2 has the feature in two target words (*key* and *shoe*), informant 3 in one (*key*) and informant 25 also in one (*shoe*). Huffines's observations[16] are in line with the presence of epenthetic [ə] in the speech of informant 25.

ETHNICALLY MARKED FEATURES: INTERFERENCE VERSUS CONTACT PHENOMENA

Of the nineteen variables originally tested (*see* figure 2.1), fifteen proved to be present in the speech of the forty-five informants. In addition, the material shows that [u̜ː] for [uː] is a marked feature. Only the variables [w] for [v], ∅ for [r], [f] for [v], and [ɑː] for [ɑɪ] were not found.

Based on the general phonetic inventories established earlier, the following examination gives a concrete overview of which of the sixteen nonstandard variants found in the informants' varieties of English also appear in Pennsylvania German.

The sound [tʃ] is found in Pennsylvania German in both native words (*deitsch* [daɪtʃ] 'German') and in loan words from English (*tschaae* [tʃɑːə] 'chew'). It also represents [dʒ] in English loan words or names (*tschumbe* [tʃʊmbə] 'jump', *John* [tʃɑn]). Neither the voiced affricate [dʒ] nor its devoiced variant [d̥ʒ̊] are extant in unmarked Pennsylvania German.

In Pennsylvania German, there are no word-final lenis consonants ([b,d,g]). Following the German rule of unvoicing of word- and syllable-final plosives (*Auslautverhärtung*), only [p], [t], and [k] are present in final position (*Graab* [gʁɔːp] 'grave', *Raad* [ʁɔːt] 'wheel', *Schlaag* [ʃlɔːk] 'stroke'). Neither are devoiced lenis consonants ([b̥,d̥,g̊]) found. In positions other than word- or syllable-final, [b], [d], and [g] are, of course, present, for instance, *Bu* [bu̜ː] 'boy', *Dierle* [diʋlə] 'gate', *Gees* [geːs] 'goat'.

Like in most southern German dialects, [s] is present in Pennsylvania German (*Seef* [seːf] 'soap'), whereas [z] and [ž] do not occur.

Equally, [w] is not a phoneme of Pennsylvania German, unless in carefully pronounced borrowings; [v], however, is present in Pennsylvania German (*Wagge* [vɔβə] 'wagon').

The fricatives [θ] and [ð] are not regular phonemes of Pennsylvania German. They may only occur in markedly pronounced borrowings from English. Usually, however, [s] or [d] take their place, which, of course, are both phonemes of Pennsylvania German, as is shown by the minimal pair *Seel* [seːl] 'soul' vs. *Deel* [deːl] 'part'.

The English nonstandard variant [ʃ] (for [ʒ]) is present in Pennsylvania German (*Schul* [ʃu̜ːl] 'school'), whereas the standard variant [ʒ] is found only occasionally in English borrowings pronounced in a markedly English way. The devoiced variant [ʒ̊] is not a phoneme of Pennsylvania German.

Dark /l/ ([ɫ]) is found word-finally in the Pennsylvania German varieties even of the native speakers, both nonsectarians and sectarians (*Hiwwel* [hɪvəɫ] 'hill'). Only the general use of [l] before a vowel and before a consonant (*Leeder* [leːdɐ] 'ladder', *Wolf* [vɔlf] 'wolf') and by some very conservative speakers (e.g., informant 4) even in word-final position indicates that originally [l] was found in all positions.

In the cases of [oː] and [eː] (for [oʊ] and [eɪ]), the English nonstandard variants (the monophthongs) are present in Pennsylvania German, for example, in *Owed* [oːvət] 'evening' and *schee* [ʃeː] 'beautiful', while the English standard variants (the diphthongs) do not exist in Pennsylvania German.

The nonstandard variant [ʌ] (for [ʌ]) is found in Pennsylvania German words, such as *Koppche* [kʌpçə] 'cup' and *Kopp* [kʌp] 'head'.

Unlike [eɪ] and [oʊ], the diphthong [aʊ] is present in the Pennsylvania German sound system (*laut* [laʊt] 'loud'); the same is true for the English nonstandard variant, the monophthong [ɑː] (*Mariye* [mɑːʀjə] 'morning'). The distribution of Standard German /aʊ/ in Pennsylvania German follows the pattern of *Pfälzisch*: Middle High German /uː/ has become [aʊ] (*Maus* [maʊs] 'mouse'), while Middle High German /ou/ is represented by [ɔː] (*Fraa* [fʀɔː] 'woman'). In Pennsylvania German English, the potential for the monophthongal realization is expanded to all /aʊ/-sounds, regardless of their origin. It should be noted, however, that the monophthong is [ɑː] rather than [ɔː].

Both the standard and the nonstandard variants of the feature [u̞] for [ʊ]) are found in Pennsylvania German (*dumm* [dʊm], [du̞m] 'stupid'). The same is true for the long vowels ([u̞ː] for [uː]; *Schulmeeschder* [ʃuːɫmeːʃdɐ], [ʃu̞ːɫmeːʃdɐ] 'teacher').

The nonstandard variant [ɪ̞] for word-final unstressed [ɪ] is not present in Pennsylvania German, as opposed to the variant [ə], which was occasionally found as an alternative (*Familye* [fəmɪljə] 'family').

Finally, epenthetic [ə] after long vowels and diphthongs was not observed in the Pennsylvania German varieties spoken by the informants.

In sum, of the sixteen marked variants found in the informants' English, fourteen also occur in Pennsylvania German. Only lowering of word-final /ɪ/ ([ɪ̞] for [ɪ]) and epenthetic [ə] after long vowels ([Vːə] for [Vː]) have no equivalents. Because of the high proportion of correlations between Pennsylvania German English and Pennsylvania German, the German dialect can be assumed to play a certain role in the distribution of the marked variants among the informants. Therefore it seems to be justified to use the term *ethnically marked features*.

96   The Influence of Pennsylvania German on English Phonology

Even though two of the variants do not occur directly in Pennsylvania German, they can nevertheless be regarded as ethnically marked, as they occur in Pennsylvania German English but not in the regional standard. They can therefore serve as easily as group identifiers as the fourteen features mentioned above.

Figure 2.22 groups the sixteen ethnically marked features.

Pennsylvania German English and Pennsylvania German:	
Unvoiced consonants: Fricatives:	[s] for [z]
	[ʃ] for [ʒ]
Affricates:	[tʃ] for [dʒ]
Word-final plosives:	[p,t,k] for [b,d,g]
Monophthongs:	[oː] for [oʊ]
	[eː] for [eɪ]
	[ɑː] for [ɑʊ]
Other consonants:	[d] for [ð]
	[s] for [θ]
	[v] for [w]
	[l] for [ɫ]
Other vowels:	[ʌ] for [ʌ]
	[ʊ] for [u]
	[uː] for [uː]
Pennsylvania German English only:	
Word-final lowering:	[ɹ] for [ɪ]
Epenthetic [ə]:	[Vːə] for [Vː]

Figure 2.22: Groups of ethnically marked features

It is a truism that linguistic change can be internally and externally induced. Internally induced change is due to system-internal pressures, for instance, a tendency toward symmetry in a phoneme system. Externally induced change results from pressure from outside, for example, in a language contact situation.

Those fourteen ethnically marked variants that can be assumed to be supported by the use of the same forms in Pennsylvania German can be termed *interferences*.[17]

However, postulating an explicit causal relationship would appear to go too far. The interferences are not necessarily "caused" by a speaker's simultaneous competence in Pennsylvania German. There are at least two reasons for this view. First, some of the features appear in the English of non-Pennsylvania Germans with no active or passive competence in this language. Secondly, as was shown above, two other variables do not even have equivalents in Pennsylvania German.

It would therefore be more precise to use the somewhat broader expression *contact phenomena*[18] instead of the term *interferences*. The former may equally affect bilinguals, semispeakers, and monolinguals.

QUANTITATIVE ANALYSIS

In figures 2.23–28, the scores of phonetic markedness for selected subgroups will be presented. They will be based on the data presented earlier in this chapter.

In the calculations of the percentages, each fully marked variant (represented by "+" in figures 2.6–21) was counted as 1. All unmarked forms ("–"), including the diphthong [əʊ] ("4"), were counted as 0. The sounds [ʔ] in the category [p,t,k] for [b,d,g][19], [s] in [d] for [ð], and [ə] in [ɪ] for [ɪ] were treated like fully marked variants. Devoicing of lenis consonants (" ° ")[20] and [θ] in the feature [d] for [ð] were counted as 0.5. The intermediate variants between (marked) monophthongs and (unmarked) diphthongs were counted as 0.25 ("3"), 0.5 ("2"), and 0.75 ("1"). Target words that were not received remained unconsidered.

Most importantly, each figure gives the percentage of ethnically marked forms, illustrated in a graph. In addition, the rate of markedness, calculated according to the details given above, the number of target words that were received, the number of cells, that is, the total number of target words, and the number of informants are given for each subgroup.

Figure 2.23 compares the percentages of the twenty marked variants for the nonsectarian, sectarian, and non-Pennsylvania German informants.

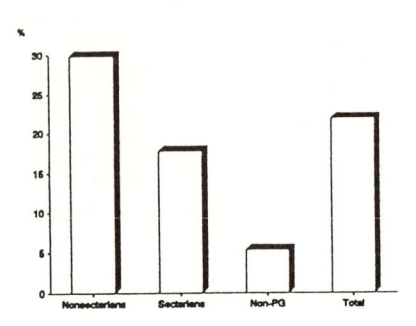

Group	Nonsectarians	Sectarians	Non-PG	Total
Percentage	29.9	17.8	5.3	22.0
Rate of markedness	669.50	136.75	46.50	852.75
Target words	2242	770	870	3882
Cells	2470	855	950	4275
Informants	26	9	10	45

Figure 2.23: Percentages of ethnically marked variants in the English of the nonsectarian, sectarian, non-Pennsylvania German informants, and all the informants together

The percentage of phonetic markedness is almost twice as high in the nonsectarian group (29.9%) as in the sectarian group (17.8%). Since the non-Pennsylvania German informants are all monolingual speakers of English, their score of 5.3% supports the view that the marked features can be regarded as contact phenomena. The percentage of marked variants for all the informants taken together is 22%.

Figures 2.24–26 examine the results of various generations of the nonsectarian, sectarian, and non-Pennsylvania German groups of informants. It becomes clear that generation membership is most significant for the score of phonetic markedness in the nonsectarian group.

Figure 2.24 shows that in the nonsectarian group the a-generation's score is by far the highest (51.6%); the b-generation still has almost one-third of all possible ethnically marked variants in its English variety

The Influence of Pennsylvania German on English Phonology 99

(30.6%). The c-generation scores almost exactly half the percentage of the b-generation, namely 14.5%. The d-generation's score (7.7%) is reduced by approximately another 50% as compared to its parent generation.

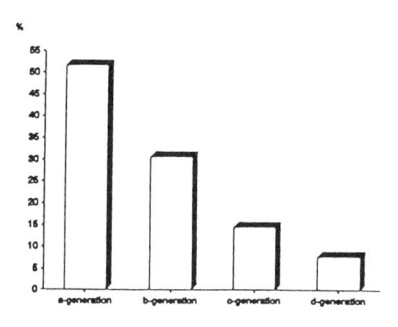

Generation	a	b	c	d
Percentage	51.6	30.6	14.5	7.7
Rate of markedness	351.25	216.25	77.00	25.00
Target words	681	707	530	324
Cells	760	760	570	380
Informants	8	8	6	4

Figure 2.24: Percentages of ethnically marked variants in the English of the four nonsectarian generations

Figure 2.25 gives the scores of the three generations of the sectarian families. Although there is a tendency of decline of phonological variants between the a- and the b-generation, it is much less striking than in the nonsectarian group. The sectarian a-generation scores 20.2% of ethnically marked variants, the b-generation 14.7%, and the c-generation 20.8%.[21]

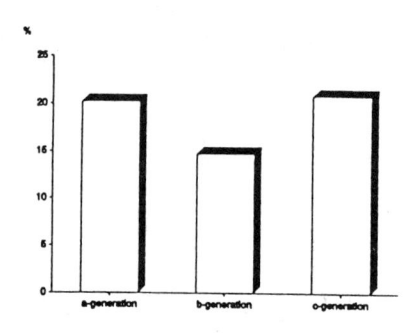

100   The Influence of Pennsylvania German on English Phonology

Generation	a	b	c
Percentage	20.2	14.7	20.8
Rate of markedness	70.25	51.50	15.00
Target words	348	350	72
Cells	380	380	95
Informants	4	4	1

Figure 2.25: Percentages of ethnically marked variants in the English of the three sectarian generations

To complete the picture, figure 2.26 shows the three generations of the non-Pennsylvania German group. No informant belonging to the a-generation took part in this section of the interview; the figure shows the results of the b-, c-, and d-generations only.

The phonological data of the non-Pennsylvania German informants correlate only partly with age. The b-generation has the highest percentage of ethnically marked variants (6.6%). The score of the d-generation (4.5%) is even slightly higher than that of the c-generation (3.9%).

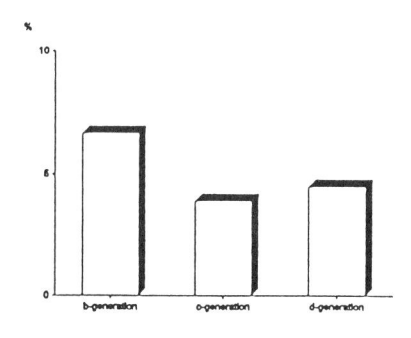

Generation	b	c	d
Percentage	6.6	3.9	4.5
Rate of markedness	28.00	10.50	8.00
Target words	422	270	178
Cells	475	285	190
Informants	5	3	2

Figure 2.26: Percentages of ethnically marked variants in the English of three non-Pennsylvania German generations

Figure 2.27 gives a breakdown of the scores of the sectarian group by the Mennonite and the Amish families.

The scores of 22.8% of ethnically marked variants for the Mennonites and 11.6% for the Amish differ more significantly than the great similarity of their lifestyles would suggest. Although the Mennonite family interviewed is Old Order and the Amish family belongs to the New Order branch, the actual difference in religious and social conservatism is minimal.

According to previous studies (e.g., Raith 1981), the more distant a sectarian group is from mainstream society, the less its English variety is characterized by ethnic marking. The present study shows that the same degree in conservatism does not automatically lead to the same degree of ethnic markedness. On the contrary, even though the couple representing the youngest generation of the Amish family has chosen to join the Beachy Amish group with its more modern lifestyle, the degree of ethnic markers in the Amish family is still lower than in the Mennonite family.[22]

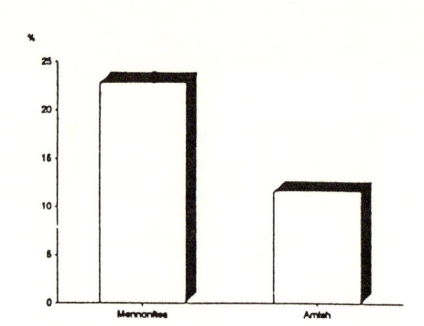

Family	Mennonites	Amish
Percentage	22.8	11.6
Rate of markedness	96.75	40.00
Target words	424	346
Cells	475	380
Informants	5	4

Figure 2.27: Percentages of ethnically marked variants in the English of the two sectarian families

Finally, a breakdown into the two genders is given in figure 2.28. As compared to all the juxtapositions of data for various social groups presented so far, the difference in markedness between the English of the male and the female informants is extremely small (1.8%). The slightly higher rate for the male informants is in line with previous studies,[23] which show that men generally use more nonstandard forms than women. All in all, however, gender is one of the less significant social factors for the distribution of ethnically marked features in the present examination.

The Influence of Pennsylvania German on English Phonology   103

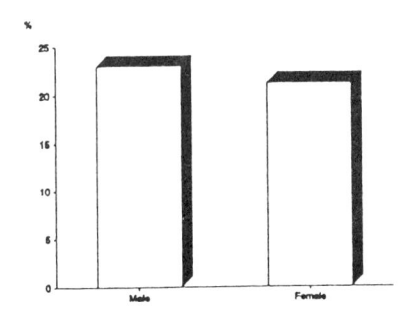

Gender	Male	Female
Percentage	23.0	21.2
Rate of markedness	375.75	477.00
Target words	1635	2247
Cells	1805	2470
Informants	19	26

Figure 2.28: Percentages of ethnically marked variants in the English of male and female informants

QUALITATIVE ANALYSIS

IMPLICATIONAL SCALING

With the help of frequency analysis it was possible to form group averages, which facilitated preliminary generalizations. In a second step, more precise insight will be gained through implicational scaling.[24]

In figure 2.29, the forty-five informants, together with their social data, are ordered horizontally. The symbols are the same as in figure 1.5. In addition, the line "PG words" indicates the number of target words the informants were able to give in Pennsylvania German, thus providing an index of their competence.

The seventy-six target words are arranged vertically. The words belonging to those features for which no ethnic variant was extant have been disregarded. The relevant feature in each word is marked by underlining and, if necessary, indicated with phonetic symbols. Pluses indicate that the ethnically marked feature is present; minuses stand for

104 The Influence of Pennsylvania German on English Phonology

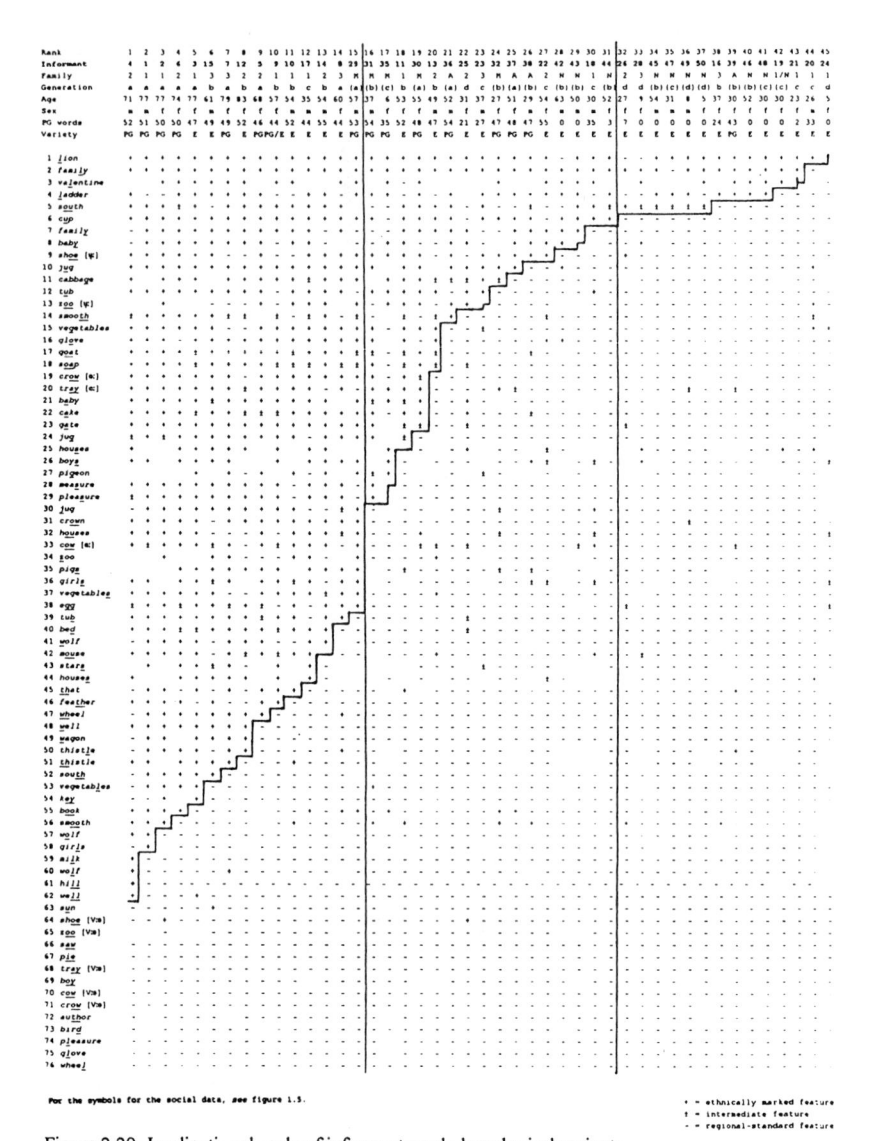

Figure 2.29: Implicational scale of informants and phonological variants

regional-standard variants. "±" means that an intermediate form (e.g., a devoiced plosive, a diphthong with an off-glide) occurred.

Figure 2.29 orders both informants and phonological data implicationally, that is, generally speaking, rows with greater numbers of pluses precede those with smaller numbers, and the same holds for the columns. This means that the pluses concentrate in the top left-hand corner, the minuses on the bottom right, separated by the gradation line. Minor changes in the order of rows and columns were made to ensure the optimal arrangement of the data.

In a perfect scale, the value "+" implies pluses in all the cells above and to the left. Conversely, the value "−" means that minuses also appear in all the cells below and to the right. Thus, for instance, the presence of the feature [ʌ] for [ʌ] in *jug* (rank 10) in the speech of informant 37 (rank 25) implies that the same informant is also likely to show all the ethnically marked features in words 1–9. Further, all the informants ordered to the left of informant 37 are expected to have [ʌ] for [ʌ] as well. Thus, the implicational scale shows how some features control others which are hierarchically subordinate.

In reality, few implicational arrangements scale perfectly. Figure 2.29 also contains error cells, for instance, pluses to the right of the gradation line and minuses to its left. Target words that were not received (empty cells) and some intermediate forms prevent a complete fit as well.

To find out whether figure 2.29 represents a valid and meaningful scalogram, its reproducibility, or scalability,[25] has been determined. All the pluses and plus-minuses to the right of the gradation line as well as all the minuses to its left are regarded as error cells. Likewise, all the unreceived forms are counted as such.

The resulting scalability of 0.86 may well be considered satisfactory, especially since the unreceived (and therefore undetermined) forms constitute a large portion of the error cells. As nonlinguistic, that is, the social, data have not been used to establish the informants' order in the scale, they can be used as an additional explanatory instrument without circularity of argument.

Those informants who show a large number of pluses (and are therefore located on the left) sound more "dutchified," that is, speak English with a stronger Pennsylvania German accent than informants who have more minuses. Similarly, the further to the bottom of the scale a feature is, the less frequently it occurs.

Despite the gradation line, the implicational scale represents a continuous spectrum of linguistic variety. This continuum will be structured and described with reference to both the phonological variants along the vertical and the informants along the horizontal.

106 The Influence of Pennsylvania German on English Phonology

ORDER OF PHONOLOGICAL FEATURES

In this chapter the order of the phonological features is established on the basis of the seventy-six target words. In some cases, the phonetic contexts are significant for the interaction of the features.

From top to bottom in figure 2.29, the marked variants are characterized by increasing instability. The features in rows 1–8 are even present in the English of monolingual informants. By contrast, all the marked variants in rows 64–76 do not occur even in the speech of the most "dutchified" sounding informants.

The feature [l] for [ɫ] is one of the most heterogeneous ones in the scale. In the four target words in rows 1–4 (*lion, family, valentine, ladder*), where /l/ appears before a vowel and is not preceded by a plosive, clear /l/ is present in the speech of almost all the informants. However, the considerable number of error cells, particularly in *ladder*, is likely to be an indication of free variation in this phonetic context.

The second group, situated in the center of the continuum, includes *thistle* (row 50), *vegetables* (row 53), and *girls, milk, wolf, hill, hell* (rows 58–62). In these words, /l/ occurs before a consonant or word-finally. Here, ethnically marked [l] is present only in the speech of the most "dutchified" informants, that is, members of the nonsectarian a-generation, sometimes of a single speaker.

Finally, the third group is found at the end of the continuum (rows 74–76). In the target words *pleasure, glove*, and *wheel*, /l/ is always realized as [ɫ]. In the former two words, the preceding plosive seems to be responsible, as /l/, although followed by a vowel, is still dark.

The target words testing the feature [ʌ̞] for [ʌ] are found in the top part of the continuum, specifically in rows 6 (*cup*), 10 (*jug*), 12 (*tub*), and 16 (*glove*). Only *sun* (row 63) does not follow this pattern.

The two target words for the feature word-final [ɪ̞] for [ɪ], *family* and *baby*, are located in rows 7 and 8. The marked forms reach as far as informants 42 and 43, those non-Pennsylvania German informants with the highest degree of ethnic marking.

Two of the three words testing the feature [ṳː] for [uː] are found in the upper part, namely *shoe* in row 9 and *zoo* in row 13. Only *smooth* (row 56), where the vowel is word-internal, does not fit well into the pattern of the scale. Although there are no fewer than ten occurrences of the ethnically marked form, their distribution does not reflect the social groups of informants.

The four words testing [tʃ] for [dʒ] are all found in the upper half of the scale. They form two groups, the first with *cabbage* in row 11 and *vegetables* in 15, and the second with *pigeon* in row 27 and *jug* in 30.

The close linguistic relationship of the next two features (monophthongs for diphthongs) is reflected by their position in the scale. The three target words for the feature [oː] for [oʊ] (*goat, soap, crow*) in rows 17–19 are directly followed by all four target words testing [eː] for [eɪ] (*tray, baby, cake, gate*) in rows 20–23.

The target words testing the feature [s] for [z] cluster in three groups in the center of the continuum. *Houses* (word-internal) and *boys* form the first group in rows 25 and 26. The large middle group consists of *zoo, pigs, girls,* and *vegetables* in rows 34–37. The third group is formed by *stars* and *houses* (word-final) in rows 43 and 44.

The two target words for the feature [ʃ] for [ʒ], *measure* and *pleasure*, are found next to each other in rows 28 and 29.

Three of the five target words for the feature [ɑː] for [aʊ] are located side by side in rows 31–33, namely *crown, houses,* and *cow*. *Mouse* is found just a little further down, in row 42. The only target word that does not follow the pattern is *south* in row 5, for which ethnically marked forms were found even in the speech of several non-Pennsylvania German informants.

The three cases representing the feature fortis for lenis consonant (word-final [p,t,k] for [b,d,g]) are located next to each other in rows 38–40, in the order *egg, tub, bed*. Between each of them there is a difference of one informant. The assumption that [k] for [g] is the most stable feature of the three is supported by the fact that *jug* is located further up in row 24. For *bird* (row 73), no occurrence of the ethnically marked form is found.

The target words containing the feature [d] for [ð] (*that, feather*) are located in rows 45 and 46. Word-initially the feature reaches just one informant further than word-internally. In *smooth*, where the feature is in word-final position, the marked forms turned out to be [s] or, intermediately, [θ]. Since this target word is located far higher (row 14), it seems safe to conclude that [s]/[θ] for word-final [ð] is more stable than [d] for initial or internal [ð].

Three of the four target words testing the feature [v] for [w] are found next to each other in rows 47–49, namely *wheel, well,* and *wagon*. In *wolf,* located in row 41, the feature appears to be slightly more stable.

Of the three words for the feature [s] for [θ], two (*thistle, south*) are located next to each other in rows 51 and 52. As was the case with [d] for [ð], the feature reaches one informant further in word-initial position. In the target word *author*, that is, word-internally, the feature is not extant (row 72). It is interesting to regard *smooth* in row 14 under the aspect of [s] for [θ]; moving this row between *thistle* and *south* would result in no more than three additional error cells.

The feature [ʊ̈] for [ʊ] (*book, wolf*) occupies rows 55 and 57. Although the words appear almost next to each other, there is a certain quantitative difference. *Book*, like *smooth* immediately below, is characterized by a large number of ethnically marked forms to the right of the gradation line.

Of the nine target words testing the feature [Vːə] for [Vː], seven can only be ordered arbitrarily, since no marked variants occur (rows 65–71: *zoo, saw, pie, tray, boy, cow, crow*). *Shoe* (row 64) has two sporadic occurrences of epenthetic [ə]. Only in *key*, located in row 54, the feature appears to be somewhat more stable.

The following four features, for which no marked forms were found, have been disregarded: [w] for [v] (*vegetables, valentine*); ɸ for [ɾ] (word-finally: *car, bear, author, feather, measure, pleasure, ladder*; before a consonant other than /s/: *bird, girls*; before /s/: *stars*); word-final [f] for [v] (*glove, hive*); and [ɑː] for [ɑɪ] (*mice, lion, valentine, hive, pie*).

The order of the features given in figure 2.30 is established in an attempt to group the relevant target words of the continuum.

The features at the beginning (1–3) and at the end (13–19) of figure 2.30 are hard to group. In the center, however, two distinct clusters can be identified. On ranks 4 and 5 two monophthongal articulations of diphthongs are located ([oː] for [oʊ] and [eː] for [eɪ]). A third one is found further down in the scale, on rank 10. Unlike /aʊ/, the diphthongs /oʊ/ and /eɪ/ are not part of the Pennsylvania German phoneme inventory. The center of the scale is dominated by the results of four unvoicing processes (6: [tʃ] for [dʒ]; 9: [ʃ] for [ʒ]; 11: [s] for [z]; 12: final [p,t,k] for [b,d,g]). Such qualitative groupings appear to be more significant than groupings according to phonetic environments, that is, word-initial, word-internal, and word-final position.

Especially in the middle and right-hand parts of figure 2.29, a number of intermediate variants are located along or close to the gradation line. Here, phonological features and informants form what could be called a qualitative transition zone.

The five phonological changes listed under (19) in figure 2.30 ([w] for [v], ɸ for [ɾ], [f] for [v] in word-final position, [l] for [ɫ] before a vowel if it is itself preceded by a plosive, and [ɑː] for [ɑɪ]) are not characteristic of the informants' English; particularly the latter two do not seem to be markers of Pennsylvania German English at all. By contrast, the former three changes have been claimed to be so elsewhere in the literature.[26]

The Influence of Pennsylvania German on English Phonology   109

Rank	Phonological feature		Target words
(1)	[l] for [ɫ]	before vowel if not itself preceded by a plosive	lion, family, valentine, ladder
(2)	[ɪ] for [i]	in word-final position	family, baby
(3)	[s]/[θ] for [ð]	in word-final position	smooth
(4)	[o:] for [oʊ]		goat, soap, crow
(5)	[e:] for [eɪ]		tray, baby, cake, gate
(6)	[tʃ] for [dʒ]		cabbage, vegetables, pigeon, jug
(7)	[ʌ] for [ʌ]		cup, jug, tub, glove, sun
(8)	[u:] for [u:]		shoe, zoo, smooth
(9)	[ʃ] for [ʒ]		measure, pleasure
(10)	[a:] for [aʊ]		south, crown, houses, cow, mouse
(11)	[s] for [z]		houses, boys, zoo, pigs, girls, vegetables, stars
(12)	[p,t,k] for [b,d,g]	in word-final position	jug, egg, tub, bed
(13)	[d] for [ð]	in word-initial and word-internal position	that, feather
(14)	[v] for [w]		wolf, wheel, well, wagon
(15)	[s] for [θ]	in word-initial and word-final position	thistle, south, smooth
(16)	[ʊ] for [ʊ]		book, wolf
(17)	[l] for [ɫ]	before consonant and in word-final position	thistle, vegetables, girls, milk, wolf, hill, well
(18)	[V:ə] for [V:]	only for /i:/ and /u:/	key, shoe
(19)	[w] for [v]		vegetables, valentine
	ø for [r]	before /s/ and other consonants, and in word-final position	car, bear, author, feather, measure, pleasure, ladder, bird, girls, stars
	[f] for [v]	in word-final position	glove, hive
	[l] for [ɫ]	before vowel if itself preceded by a plosive	pleasure, glove
	[a:] for [aɪ]		mice, lion, valentine, hive, pie

Figure 2.30: Order of phonological features

Based on the apparent-time[27] approach used in the present study (i.e., the examination of various generations), the order of the phonological features in figure 2.29 from top to bottom can be understood as an order in time. The variables that were not received and are located at the bottom (except for the last two) have practically died out already. The feature [V:ə] for [V:], for which the fewest marked forms were found, might be expected to be the next feature to disappear.

Accordingly, the feature [l] for [ɫ] before a vowel (if not preceded by a plosive) on the extreme left would be the last one to disappear during the process of change in the direction of the regional standard. The fact that this feature is found in the speech of the various generations of all the social groups represented in the present study, that is, nonsectarians, sectarians, and even non-Pennsylvania Germans, shows how firmly it is embedded in the speech of the area.

This argument, of course, presupposes two assumptions: first, that the phonological variables in figure 2.29 represent change in progress; and, second, that the scale indeed reflects passage of time. The structure of the informants according to social groups and age, as will be described in the following, supports the validity of these assumptions.

ORDER OF INFORMANTS

As is indicated by the two vertical lines in figure 2.29, the phonological data divide the informants into three large groups of roughly the same size. The first line, between informants 29 and 31, is determined by a sizeable difference in ethnically marked variants. Between these informants, the gradation line runs vertically along a string of nine pluses, the largest continuous stretch in the entire scale. The second line, between informants 44 and 26, is drawn immediately to the left of a group of six informants for whom the positive area ends with [ɑː] for [ɑʊ] in *south* on rank 5. Here the longest continuous horizontal stretch of the gradation line is found.

Roughly speaking, the first line separates the nonsectarian native speakers of Pennsylvania German from the sectarians, while the second line divides the sectarians from the non-Pennsylvania Germans. Those nonsectarians who were raised with English as their native language are scattered all over the three areas.

The first group, comprising the first fifteen ranks, includes all the members of the nonsectarian a-generation: those nonsectarians who had Pennsylvania German as their first language show the largest number of phonological interferences of Pennsylvania German in their English. Six of those speakers report that they predominantly use Pennsylvania German to the present day. The other two are a woman whose husband has died (informant 3) and a woman (informant 8) whose husband is not a native speaker of Pennsylvania German, so that on a normal workday today they both speak more English around the house than in the past. The eight members of the nonsectarian a-generation are between sixty and seventy-nine years old, and all show a high translation rate; of fifty-five English target words, they were able to translate between forty-six and fifty-two into Pennsylvania German.

Among the first fifteen informants there are also five members of the nonsectarian b-generation (informants 9, 10, 12, 14, 15), one member of the c-generation (informant 17), and even a Mennonite (informant 29). These informants share high translation rates (between forty-four and fifty-five words), but all of them (except for the Mennonite and informant 9) report that they speak more English than Pennsylvania German on average today.

Informant 9, a widow who lives together with her son (informant 17), reports that during a normal workday she uses Pennsylvania German as much as English. At home the languages are English and Pennsylvania German; with her parents, who live on a nearby farm, she speaks predominantly Pennsylvania German. The informant has a part-time job at the chicken house of one of her brothers, where a certain amount of the conversations with her fellow workers, many of whom are relatives, are also in Pennsylvania German.

Informant 10 also acquired Pennsylvania German in early childhood at home from his parents, who spoke Pennsylvania German to each other.

Even though informant 12 is the oldest informant in the sample (eighty-three years of age), she is a member of the nonsectarian b-generation because of her acquisition history. Nevertheless, her translation rate of fifty-two words is as high as the best of the a-generation. The number and quality of phonological variables in her English establish her in the center of the group of heavily marked speakers.

Informant 14, a high-school teacher who is very interested in the Pennsylvania German culture and language, is situated toward the end of this group. He used to address his youngest son only in Pennsylvania German. The son, who died in a car accident at the age of twenty-one, was free to answer in English and also spoke English with his mother and brothers and sisters. Although he must have been by far the youngest living Pennsylvania German to whom a parent consistently spoke in the German variety, his active competence in Pennsylvania German was far from native, as the fieldworker could ascertain during his first contacts with family 2 in 1986.

Informant 15 is the husband of Pennsylvania German native informant 8. He reports that he learned Pennsylvania German in his early school years from his age peers.

At first glance, the appearance of informant 17 (c-generation) in the group including his grandparents (informants 1 and 2), from whom he learned the German variety, is rather surprising. His position among the most conservative speakers becomes plausible if one keeps in mind that this thirty-five-year-old unmarried farmer is strongly rooted to the soil, still lives with his mother (informant 9), and only once in his life went on a longer journey, namely a high- school trip to Canada. As the family butcher in charge of all the home butcherings of family 1 during the months of December and January, he functions as a preserver of old traditions. Together with his elders, informant 17 is a good example of decreasing ethnic markedness over the generations. While informant 17 is located on rank 12, his mother (informant 9) is on rank 10 with two more features, and his maternal grandparents (informants 1 and 2) are located on ranks 2 and 3 with no fewer than fourteen and twelve additional features, respectively.

The only informant in the first group who does not belong to the nonsectarian Pennsylvania Germans is informant 29, an a-generation Mennonite, on rank 15. In comparison with the other sectarian informants, his speech is characterized by an unusual degree of ethnic markedness, making it more conservative.

The middle section, comprising sixteen informants, starts with informant 31, a Mennonite, on rank 16 and reaches down to informant 44, a non-Pennsylvania German, on rank 31. It includes all the sectarian informants except for informants 29 and 39. The latter, who is located in the lower zone, is the second-generation Amish woman who originally came from Ohio and used to be a New Order Mennonite before she married into the Amish family.

Among the sectarians, age or membership in a certain generation do not play the same role for the order of the informants. The couple representing the oldest Amish generation (informants 36 and 37) has fewer ethnically marked variants than three and four other sectarians, respectively, who are younger.

While gender is not a significant factor for the order of the sectarian informants either, the distinction between the Amish and the Mennonite families shows clearly. Apart from informant 36, all the Amish informants are located lower in the scale than their Mennonite counterparts. On the whole, the members of the Mennonite family speak a more strongly marked variety of English than the Amish.

As could be expected for native speakers of Pennsylvania German, all the sectarian informants have translation rates equal to those of the nonsectarian a-generation (between forty-three and fifty-three words). The only exception is informant 35, a six-year-old Mennonite girl. The high proportion of unreceived target words is due to her age; nevertheless, she was able to translate no fewer than thirty-five words. All the sectarian informants report that Pennsylvania German is the language they predominantly use during a normal workday.

The seven sectarians located in the middle section show between fourteen (informant 38) and twenty-two (informant 31) nonstandard variants, which is considerably less than the nonsectarians' span in the upper zone (between thirty-three [informant 8] and fifty-two [informant 3]). Clearly, the English of the nonsectarian a-generation and the majority of the b-generation is marked by more phonological interferences than the English variety spoken by the sectarian informants. The sectarians choose to separate themselves from the world, or, in their own words, from "the English," whereas the nonsectarians do not consciously attempt to dissociate themselves from mainstream American society. In the light of this information, it is quite surprising if not paradoxical that the sectarians should speak a less-accented variety of English than the older generations of their nonsectarian neighbors.

A large number of nonsectarian informants with English as their native language are found in the middle section side by side with the sectarians. Among them, there are members of the b- (informants 11, 13), c- (informants 18, 22, 23), and d-generations (informant 25). Here the distribution of the phonological variables does not clearly correlate with the three nonsectarian generations. In one case, the daughter (informant 25) has even more marked forms than her mother (informant 22). However, as would be expected, the two members of the b-generation are located in the first half of the middle section. Both of them also have markedly better translation competence than their children. While informants 11 and 13 were able to give the Pennsylvania German equivalents of fifty-two and forty-seven words, respectively, informants 18, 23, and 25 had translation rates of thirty-five, twenty-seven, and twenty-one words.

Informant 22 seems to be an exception. While her membership in the c-generation is reflected by the low number of marked variants, she has an extraordinarily high translation rate of fifty-five words. This may be due to the fact that her late father was a native speaker of Pennsylvania German, and that she was only categorized c-generation because her mother (informant 12) is a first-in-the-family native speaker of English. Moreover, informant 22 has had a lot of practice in Pennsylvania German through the conscious effort of using this language with her husband (informant 14).

Informant 13 is another good example of those cases where unexpected linguistic results can be accounted for by the social data. For a member of the b-generation, this informant has relatively few nonstandard variants in his English. Just like informant 22, who is a volunteer

114   The Influence of Pennsylvania German on English Phonology

social worker, informant 13, a high-school teacher, comes much more into contact with younger people and non-Pennsylvania Germans than other members of the b-generation.

The three oldest non-Pennsylvania German informants (42, 43, 44) are located at the end of the middle section. It is remarkable that they have between five and eight marked variants in their English and that informant 44 was able to translate three target words into Pennsylvania German. The presence of the nonstandard forms and the minimal translation competence can be assumed to result from the informants' long contact with their Pennsylvania German (specifically sectarian) neighbors in the country, outside Berwick. Especially informants 43 and 44 showed a vivid interest in the Amish, with some of whom they have become close friends.

The right-hand third of the scale, which comprises fourteen informants, begins with informant 26 on rank 32. It includes six of the nine non-Pennsylvania Germans plus the non-Pennsylvania German who married into family 1 (informant 19). In addition, there are also the sectarian informant mentioned earlier (informant 39), one member of the nonsectarian b-generation (informant 16), two of the c-generation (informants 20, 21), and three of the d-generation (informants 24, 26, 28).

The right-hand section includes all the non-Pennsylvania German informants living in Lewisburg (informants 45–50). Surprisingly enough, they do not form the very end of the scale. Four informants belonging to nonsectarian family 1 (informants 19–21, 24) have fewer ethnically marked forms. Informants 45–50 are divided into two groups. All have the feature [l] for [ɫ] before a vowel (unless preceded by a plosive), but informants 45, 47, 49, and 50 additionally have the intermediate form [ɑʴᵘ] in *south*. All these informants have a zero translation rate. Neither age nor membership in a certain generation nor gender correlates completely with the linguistic findings.

Informant 26 is the younger sister of informant 25, who is located in the center of the middle section. Not only does she have a lower translation rate (seven words vs. twenty-one), she also shows considerably fewer marked variants (six vs. seventeen). Although both sisters belong to the nonsectarian d-generation, the age difference of four years appears to play a role in these differences.

Informant 28, a nine-year-old member of the nonsectarian d-generation, has fewer ethnically marked forms than her father (informant 23) on rank 23, but one more than her mother (informant 16) on rank 38.

Unlike her parents, she is completely monolingual; her translation rate is zero.

Informant 16 is a member of the nonsectarian b-generation; both her parents were native speakers of Pennsylvania German. However, as the youngest child of her family she did not come into contact with Pennsylvania German as much as her older siblings, which is indicated by her low translation rate of twenty-four words and the low rate of marked features in her English. This unusual result for a member of the nonsectarian b-generation becomes more comprehensible if one keeps in mind that at the age of thirty-seven, informant 16 is by far the youngest member of the b-generation. Her husband (informant 23), who is the same age, belongs to the c-generation.

Informants 20 and 21 are a young married couple belonging to the nonsectarian c-generation. The woman (informant 21), who married into family 1 from another local nonsectarian family, has virtually no active competence in Pennsylvania German; her translation rate is two. Her husband, although he was able to give thirty-three of the target words in Pennsylvania German, hardly ever uses the German variety because of his insufficient active competence. Their phonological results locate the two c-generation informants next to each other almost at the end of the scale, on ranks 43 and 44.

Informant 24, a five-year-old girl belonging to the d-generation of nonsectarian family 1, can be found on the last rank in the scale. However, as no fewer than thirty-four target words were not received, this result should not be overrated. The informant's translation rate of zero reflects the fact that she is completely monolingual. Her mother (informant 19) married into family 1 from a family with Slovak-Tirolian ancestry and also has no active or passive competence in Pennsylvania German. She is found on rank 42 with just four instances of marked variants, while the girl's father (informant 18, c-generation) is located at the end of the middle zone, on rank 30.

The mother reported that after every visit of her daughter with her grandparents (informants 10 and 11, members of the b-generation) or great-grandparents (informants 1 and 2, a-generation), she could temporarily observe certain Pennsylvania German features in her child's English. Of the five ethnically marked forms found in the speech of informant 24, all are also present in her great-grandfather's, three in her great-grandmother's, four in her grandfather's, and one in her grandmother's speech. Three variants are also found in her father's, but none in her mother's variety of English.

116   The Influence of Pennsylvania German on English Phonology

All in all, the nonsectarian native speakers of Pennsylvania German cluster on the left of figure 2.29, while the non-Pennsylvania Germans are all found on the right. The sectarians occupy the middle section. This means that there is a clear-cut progression in the degrees of ethnic markedness of the English varieties spoken by these three groups. The nonsectarian a-generation is characterized by the highest degree, followed by the sectarians and the non-Pennsylvania Germans. Generally speaking, phonetic markedness correlates with membership in a certain social group.

The various generations of the nonsectarian native speakers of English are structured much less homogeneously. Although these informants are scattered all over the three sections, a certain trend in the distribution of the nonsectarian informants can be discerned.

With one exception (informant 17, c-generation), only members of the nonsectarian b-generation (informants 9, 10, 12, 14, 15) are found toward the left among the nonsectarian native speakers of Pennsylvania German. All of them are characterized by a good knowledge of Pennsylvania German. In addition, they are the firstborns in the b-generation of their respective families. The place within the b-generation is important as usually the first-born child has the most contact with parents and grandparents, the latter being native speakers of Pennsylvania German. This linguistically more conservative part of the b-generation will be called b_1-generation.

Two other members of the b-generation (informants 11, 13) are located in the middle zone; one (informant 16) is situated in the right-hand section. Not only is their competence in Pennsylvania German lower, they also have older siblings (with the exception of informant 13, who is an only child). This linguistically less conservative part of the b-generation will be termed b_2-generation. Since b_2-informants are usually not the first-born children within their generation, they tend to be younger than members of the b_1-group. However, it would be too simplistic to take age as the primary factor distinguishing the two subgroups.

With the exception of informant 16, solely members of the c- and d-generations are found toward the right, among the non-Pennsylvania German informants. Thus, on the whole, the distribution of the ethnically marked variants can be said to correlate with membership in a certain generation within the nonsectarian group. This correlation is less distinct in the sectarian and non-Pennsylvania German groups.

Generation (in the nonsectarian group) has been defined by acquisition patterns. At the same time, the differences between the generations roughly correlate with age. Therefore, if the distribution of the nonsectarians' phonological data corresponds with generation, it also, to a certain degree, correlates with age. Nonsectarian native speakers of Pennsylvania German have by far the highest degree of interference in their English. The further away a generation is from the last one to have Pennsylvania German as its native language, the fewer ethnically marked features are likely to be found. Vice versa, the younger or (to be more precise) more distant from the generation with Pennsylvania German as native language nonsectarians are, the more likely their English is to resemble the variety spoken by the non-Pennsylvania Germans, that is, a variety with few or no ethnically marked variants.

The acquisition patterns are also closely connected with the predominant use of one or the other language on an average workday. Most members of the nonsectarian a-generation on the far left of figure 2.29 use more Pennsylvania German. Immediately adjacent are the members of the b-generation, who use more English. The sectarian informants, whose predominant language is Pennsylvania German, are scattered all over the middle section. On the right-hand side, where the majority of the non-Pennsylvania German and the younger nonsectarian informants cluster, English is almost exclusively the predominant variety.

The members of the nonsectarian b_1-generation resemble the a-generation not only phonologically, but also in translation competence. Like the sectarians, they all have translation rates of around fifty words. By contrast, the translation competence of the nonsectarian c- and d-generations is significantly lower. A small number of these informants even have zero, just like the non-Pennsylvania Germans. The three members of the b_2-generation differ in their translation competence. While the two older informants 11 and 13 are on a par with the a-generation, informant 16, who is much younger, has a translation rate resembling that of the c- and d-generations.

In sum, membership in a social group, acquisition patterns, age, predominant use of one of the two varieties, and translation competence all appear to correlate with phonetic markedness to various degrees. By contrast, gender and membership in a particular one of the three nonsectarian families are not significant factors in this respect.

INTERPRETATION

In both the nonsectarian and the sectarian group, the direction of the change is from ethnically marked to unmarked. However, the two social groups differ in both the speed of the change and the distance they have covered.

In spite of their tendency toward separation, the sectarians are further on in the change toward the standard. The change started earlier and has continued more slowly and steadily. As figure 2.29 shows, even the sectarian speaker with the highest number of ethnically marked variants (informant 29 on rank 15) has less than one-third of all marked features in his speech. The last sectarian informant (39 on rank 39) comes from Ohio, which might help account for her unusual closeness to standard pronunciation. The remaining seven sectarian informants cover a relatively small area between ranks 16 and 26. They range from twenty-two (informant 31) to ten (informant 37) ethnically marked forms, with a steady decrease from left to right.

The change in nonsectarian English is happening more rapidly and unevenly. Here, the a-generation and a large portion of the b-generation have a high number of marked variants. This group reaches as far as informant 8 on rank 14. The distance to the next nonsectarian informant (11 on rank 18) is considerable (eight ethnically marked forms). This may indicate that the change in the nonsectarian group accelerates tremendously after the b_1-generation (informants 9, 10, 12, 14, 15). The English pronunciation of the b_2-generation (informants 11, 13, 16) resembles more that of the c- and d-generations. From informant 26 on rank 32 onwards, the marked variants become so sparse that even three non-Pennsylvania German informants are located further to the left in the continuum.

All this seems to be an indication of how rapidly the change gains momentum once the native language has been switched from Pennsylvania German to English. Within two generations, the ethnic marking of English has practically disappeared. This is reflected by the presence of informants 20, 21, and 24, all members of the nonsectarian c- and d-generations, at the very end of the continuum, even below all the non-Pennsylvania German monolinguals.

Particularly in the nonsectarian group a correlation between generation and linguistic change is apparent. Figure 2.29 can therefore be considered to mirror the progression of the change in correlation with time.

In connection with his *wave-model*, which includes heterogeneously structured language, the space in which it spreads, and the time in which it changes, Bailey (1973) introduces the concept of what he calls the *f-curve*.[28] This curvilinear pattern has become a standard explanatory

The Influence of Pennsylvania German on English Phonology 119

device in connection with sound change in progress, especially important in tracing the social motivation of sound change.

In some respects, the gradation line in figure 2.29 resembles Bailey's ʃ-curve. In both cases, the horizontal marks the passage of time. In figure 2.29, this is expressed by the almost perfectly chronological order of the four nonsectarian generations. However, while in Bailey's model the change decreases from top to bottom, figure 2.29 shows the opposite pattern, the words at the top being less likely to exhibit the respective regional-standard feature than those at the bottom.

For almost two centuries the nonsectarian Pennsylvania Germans had Pennsylvania German as their native language. For a very long time, the distribution of ethnically marked variants in their English resembled that of the a-generation in figure 2.29. Some speakers may even have had a few more nonstandard features not included in the present survey. This state of affairs held until a dramatic change in the acquisition pattern took place, when the present b-generation was the first to be raised in English.

As can be seen in figure 2.29, most members of the b-generation have not yet been affected in terms of the phonetic nonmarkedness of their English. Up to informant 29, changes have gone slowly. This area roughly corresponds to Bailey's first zone of slow change (between 0% and 20%).

However, two b-generation informants (11, 13) are situated in the middle section, which is equivalent to the middle area of Bailey's ʃ-curve. The fact that a large number of members of the nonsectarian c- and d-generations are located here shows that the change has accelerated. The nonsectarian group is, as it were, currently overtaking the sectarians, who are also located in the middle section, but whose process of change has been far slower.

The second area of slow change (80–100% in Bailey's diagram) begins with informant 26. Here the informants show regional-standard variants in most words though not in all. This area comprises not only non-Pennsylvania German informants, but also members of the nonsectarian c- and d-generations. Nonstandard variants are therefore quite likely to be found in the English speech of nonsectarian generations to come. The change has slowed down again in this section, until it finally goes toward zero (cf. the score of the last informant).

The observation that the speed of the change declines and does not immediately become zero is also supported by the presence of the non-Pennsylvania German informants before rank 42. This indicates that as contact phenomena the marked features can intrude into the speech of the monolinguals living in the area, which considerably decelerates the trend toward zero ethnically marked forms. Other things being equal, remnants of ethnically marked pronunciation can be predicted to persist even after the extinction of Pennsylvania German.

The more heavily the informants' English is phonetically marked, the less frequently certain sounds appear in their speech. At least on the surface, voiced and unvoiced fricatives ([s] for [z] in *zoo, houses, boys* and [ʃ] for [ʒ] in *measure*) and affricates ([tʃ] for [dʒ] in *jug, pigeon, cabbage*) are not always distinguished.

The voiced dental fricative merges with the voiced alveolar plosive in word-initial and internal positions ([d] for [ð] in *that, feather*) and with the unvoiced alveolar fricative in word-final position ([s] for [ð] in *smooth*). Similarly, the unvoiced dental fricative merges with the unvoiced alveolar fricative in word-initial and final positions ([s] for [θ] in *thistle, south*).

Word-final voiced plosives merge with unvoiced plosives (fortis consonants [p,t,k] for lenis consonants [b,d,g] in *tub, bed, egg*). The bilabial semivowel merges with the voiced labio-dental fricative ([v] for [w] in *wagon*). The differentiation between allophones is neutralized ([l] for [ɫ] not only before a vowel [unless preceded by a plosive], but also before a consonant and in word-final position as in *milk, hill*).

Diphthongs merge with monophthongs ([oː] for [oʊ] in *goat*, [eː] for [eɪ] in *gate*, and [ɑː] for [ɑʊ] in *crown*). In addition, [ʌ] is frequently substituted for [ʌ] (*cup*), [ɪ̞] for [ɪ] (*family*), [ʊ̞] for [ʊ] (*book*), [u̞ː] for [uː] (*shoe*), and [Vːə] for [Vː] (*key*).

In view of the fact, however, that isolated occurrences of the respective other variant cannot be ruled out, it would be stretching the point to speak about a reduced sound system for a certain group or even single informants.

Figure 2.31 gives a simplified overview of which social group is characterized by which phonological features on the basis of figure 2.29. "+" indicates that the majority of informants of the respective group have the feature in the majority of target words, "–" that they do not, and "±" that there is no clear distribution. Qualitatively intermediate forms were counted as ethnically marked.

The English spoken by all social groups is characterized by the feature [l] for [ɫ] before a vowel (unless preceded by a plosive), as in *lion*. Since this feature occurs almost universally in the speech of the non-Pennsylvania German speakers, it can be considered to be on its way to becoming part of the regional standard.

Both the nonsectarian c- and the d-generation do not have any general contact phenomena. However, there is a certain tendency within the

The Influence of Pennsylvania German on English Phonology 121

```
Social group
Phonological feature                                      a   b₁  b₂  S   c   d   N

[l] for [ɫ] /_V (unless /_plosive_) (lion)                +   +   +   +   +   +   +
[ɪ] for [i] /_# (family)                                  +   +   ±   ±   ±   ±   -
[s] for [ð] /_# (smooth)                                  +   +   +   -   ±   -   -
[o:] for [ou] (goat)                                      +   +   ±   ±   -   -   -
[e:] for [eɪ] (gate)                                      +   +   ±   ±   -   -   -
[tʃ] for [dʒ] (jug, pigeon, cabbage)                      +   +   ±   ±   -   -   -
[ʌ̊] for [ʌ] (cup)                                         +   +   ±   ±   -   -   -
[ÿ:] for [u:] (shoe)                                      +   ±   ±   ±   -   -   -
[ʃ] for [ʒ] (measure, pleasure)                           +   +   -   -   -   -   -
[a:] for [aʊ] (crown)                                     +   +   -   -   -   -   -
[s] for [z] (zoo, houses, boys)                           +   +   -   -   -   -   -
[p,t,k] for [b,d,g] /_# (tub, bed, egg)                   +   +   -   -   -   -   -
[d] for [ð] /#_, /V_V (that, feather)                     +   ±   -   -   -   -   -
[v] for [w] (wagon)                                       +   ±   -   -   -   -   -
[s] for [θ] /#_, /_# (thistle, south)                     +   -   -   -   -   -   -
[ʊ̈] for [ʊ] (book)                                        ±   -   -   -   -   -   -
[l] for [ɫ] /_C, /_# (milk, hill)                         -   -   -   -   -   -   -
[V:ə] for [V:] (/i:/ and /u:/) (key, shoe)                -   -   -   -   -   -   -
[w] for [v] (vegetables)                                  -   -   -   -   -   -   -
∅ for [r] /_s, /_C, /_# (stars, bird, car)                -   -   -   -   -   -   -
[f] for [v] /_# (glove)                                   -   -   -   -   -   -   -
[l] for [ɫ] /plosive_V (pleasure)                         -   -   -   -   -   -   -
[a:] for [aɪ] (mice)                                      -   -   -   -   -   -   -
```

Figure 2.31: Phonological features in social groups

a = nonsectarian a-generation   S = sectarians
b₁ = linguistically more conservative nonsectarian b-generation   N = non-Pennsylvania Germans
b₂ = linguistically less conservative nonsectarian b-generation   + = feature generally present
c = nonsectarian c-generation   - = feature generally absent
d = nonsectarian d-generation   ± = no clear majority

d-generation toward lowering of word-final /ɪ/ (*family*) and within the c-generation additionally toward [s] for [ð] (*smooth*).

The sectarians and the members of the b₂-generation have almost identical features. Both groups show a tendency toward lowering of word-final /ɪ/ (*family*), monophthongal articulation of /ou/ and /eɪ/ (*goat, gate*), unvoicing of affricates (*cabbage*), [ʌ̊] for [ʌ] (*cup*), and [ÿ:] for [u:] (*shoe*). They only differ in the feature [s] for [ð] (*smooth*), which is generally present in the English of the members of the b₂-generation, but absent in sectarian speech.

The leap to the members of the b₁-generation is the largest in the scale. Apart from [ÿ:] for [u:], all the features mentioned above tend to be present all the time. In addition, this group is generally characterized by unvoicing of alveolar and palato-alveolar fricatives (*zoo; measure*), monophthongal articulation of /aʊ/ (*crown*), and unvoicing of word-final plosives (*tub, bed, egg*). Further, there is a certain tendency toward [u̜ː] for [uː] (*shoe*), word-initial and internal [d] for [ð] (*that, feather*), and [v] for [w] (*wagon*).

The latter three features, together with all the ones mentioned so far and [s] for [θ] in word-initial and final positions (*thistle, south*), are generally present in the speech of the nonsectarian a-generation. In addition, there is a certain tendency within the a-generation to use [u̜] for [ʊ] (*book*). Only traces were found of [l] for [ɫ] before a consonant and in word-final position (*milk, hill*) and of [Vːə] for [Vː], more specifically [iːə] for [iː] and [uːə] for [uː] (*key, shoe*).

These differences, particularly between the various nonsectarian generations, can be compared to interlanguages[29] in foreign language acquisition. On their way to (theoretically) complete mastery of the target language, second-language learners proceed through a whole series of varieties which typically include elements of the first language (interferences), already acquired elements of the second language, and yet unmastered components of the second language, resulting in overgeneralizations. Sociolinguistically, incomplete acquisition is crucial to change induced by language contact.

Since the largest discrepancies among the various generations of one social group are found for the nonsectarians, the discussion will now concentrate on them.

While the linguistically more conservative part of the nonsectarian b-generation has almost the same interference system as the a-generation, the remainder of the b- as well as the c- and d-generations have far fewer ethnically marked variants.

General statements about the interference systems of the two youngest generations are difficult to make. They both include informants with very few or even no marked variants. The majority of informants have only a few isolated, unsystematically distributed contact phenomena in their English.

Figure 2.31 shows that in no case does a younger generation have any variable which an older one does not have. In this sense, one can talk about a quantitative, linear decrease of variables over the generations. As has been shown in figures 2.6–21, however, there are also qualitative differences in some variables in the course of the linguistic change. They are, within the phonological process, linear in themselves, including intermediate phonological stages. Examples are the devoiced lenis consonants [b̥,d̥,g̊] in *tub, bed, egg*, the devoiced lenis affricate [d̥ʒ̊] in *cabbage*, the devoiced alveolar lenis fricative [z̊] in *pigs*, the devoiced palato-alveolar lenis fricative [ʒ̊] in *pleasure*, the unvoiced dental fricative [θ] in *smooth*, and variants with half-length and/or off-glides ([oᵘ, oʳᵘ, oːᵘ] in *goat*, [eⁱ, eⁱⁱ, eːⁱ] in *cake*, and [ɑᵘ, ɑʳᵘ, ɑːᵘ] in *crown*.

Generally speaking, the intermediate stages are most frequent in the English varieties of the b-, c-, and d-generations. However, single features may not follow this rule. For instance, the clear-cut division postulated by Huffines (1984a, 176f.: nonsectarian native speakers of Pennsylvania German have [p,t,k] where native speakers of English have [b̥,d̥,g̥]) has not been substantiated by the present data (see figure 2.7).

As an example, figure 2.32 depicts the quantitative and qualitative change within the four generations of nonsectarian family 1. The seven informants involved are informants 1 and 2 (a-generation), their daughter (informant 11, b_2-generation) and her husband (informant 10, b_1-generation), their grandson (informant 18, c-generation) and his wife (informant 19, non-Pennsylvania German), and their great-granddaughter (informant 24, d-generation).

Figure 2.32 considers all target words. The occurrence of each feature is marked by the categories "+" (always fully marked variant), "(+)" (mainly fully marked variant), "±" (equally marked and regional-standard variants), "(–)" (mainly regional-standard variant), or "–" (always regional-standard variant). If intermediate forms are involved which are present in some words but not in others, the majority is given with the minority in parentheses; a slash indicates that two variants occur with equal frequency.

The order of the phonological features established in figure 2.30 has been retained. The informants are ordered from left to right according to their identification numbers. This method facilitates comparison with what has been said about the whole sample of informants, at the same time resulting in a quasi-implicational order.

The sums underneath the table give all occurrences of fully marked and intermediate forms, regardless of their frequency. The clearest breaks are found between the a- and b-generations on the one hand (seventeen fully marked forms for informants 1 and 2 vs. twelve for informant 10) and the b- and c-generations on the other (nine fully marked forms for informant 11 vs. four for informant 18). The three representatives of the c- and d-generations score very similar results.

There is, however, also a clear difference within the b-generation, that is, between the linguistically more conservative (b_1) and the more progressive (b_2) informants. While informant 10 has an interference system similar to that of the a-generation, the one of his wife (informant 11) differs both quantitatively and qualitatively. Informant 10 has twelve fully marked variants, whereas informant 11 has only nine. In addition, informant 10 has one regular qualitatively intermediate variant ([oːᵘ] and

124 The Influence of Pennsylvania German on English Phonology

	Informant						
	1	2	10	11	18	19	24
	Generation						
Phonological feature	a	a	b₁	b₂	c	Nc	d
[l] for [ɫ] / _V	(+)	(+)	(+)	±	(+)	(+)	–
[j] for [ɪ]	+	+	+	+	–	–	–
[s] for [ð]	+	+	–	θ	–	–	*
[oː] for [ou]	+	+	oːᵘ (+)	oᵘ (+)	–	–	–
[eː] for [eɪ]	+	+	+	+ / eːⁱ	–	–	–
[tʃ] for [dʒ]	+	+	+	±	(–)	–	+
[ʌ] for [ʌ]	(+)	(+)	(+)	(+)	(–)	–	–
[ʉː] for [uː]	+	+	(+)	+	–	–	ᴈʊ
[ʃ] for [ʒ]	+	+	–	–	–	–	*
[ɑː] for [ɑu]	+ (ɑːᵘ)	+	+	(–)	+ (ɑːᵘ, –)	–	– (ɑːᵘ)
[s] for [z]	+	+	+ (°)	– (°)	° / –	(–)	– (°)
[p,t,k] for [b,d,g]	+, ?, +	+, ?, + / °	+, +, +	–, –, – / °	–, –, –	–, –, –	–, –, °
[d] for [ð]	+	+	±	±	–	–	–
[v] for [w]	+	+	–	–	–	–	–
[s] for [θ]	+	±	(–)	–	–	–	*
[ʉ] for [ʊ]	+	±	–	–	–	–	–
[l] for [ɫ] / _C, / _#	(–)	–	–	–	–	–	–
[Vːə] for [Vː]	–	(–)	–	–	–	–	–
Fully marked	17	17	12	9	4	2	1
Intermediate	1	1	2	5	2	0	3

Figure 2.32: Quantitative and qualitative change within the four generations of nonsectarian family 1

```
a  = nonsectarian a-generation                                    +   = always fully marked variant
b₁ = linguistically more conservative nonsectarian b-generation   (+) = mainly fully marked variant
b₂ = linguistically less conservative nonsectarian b-generation   ±   = equally marked and regional-standard variants
c  = nonsectarian c-generation                                    (-) = mainly regional-standard variant
d  = nonsectarian d-generation                                    -   = always regional-standard variant
Nc = non-Pennsylvania German who married into nonsectarian generation c   ° = devoiced
                                                                  *   = no target word received
```

an occasional one ([ž]). Informant 11 has no fewer than three regular ones ([θ], [oᵘ], [eːⁱ]) and two occasional ones ([ẑ], [g̊]).

The two representatives of the a-generation (informants 1 and 2) display almost identical patterns, with seventeen fully marked variants and one intermediate form. Informant 18 is a typical representative of the c-generation, having very limited active competence in Pennsylvania German. Like his daughter (informant 24, a monolingual member of the d-generation), he shows a slight tendency toward ethnically marked forms, both quantitatively and qualitatively. By contrast, his wife (informant 19), who is a non-Pennsylvania German, has no marked variants except for the almost universal [l] before a vowel (unless preceded by a plosive) and an infrequent [s] for [z].

Whereas the fully marked variants linearly decrease in number between the a- and the d-generation, the intermediate forms are rare in the a-generation, relatively frequent in the b-generation, and not altogether unusual in the c- and d-generations. The presence of qualitatively intermediate variants may therefore be considered a sign of instability within the nonsectarian speech community. By contrast, qualitatively intermediate variants are rare in the sectarian group (see figures 2.6–21).

In some features, the transition from the ethnically marked to the regional-standard variant is characterized by the short presence of qualitatively intermediate forms in the speech of one or two informants. In others, two variants exist side by side for a while. A few prominent examples from figure 2.32 will be illustrated.

Word-final [s] for [ð] (*smooth*) is an example of qualitative transition. Between the a-generation's [s] and the c-generation's [ð] there is the [θ] of informant 11. The fact that informant 10, who on the whole is linguistically more conservative, has [ð] should not be overrated as only one target word was asked for this feature.

In nonsectarian family 1, the feature [oː] for [oʊ] (*goat*) also provides a good example of qualitative differences. While the a-generation (informants 1, 2) always has the monophthong [oː], the more conservative member of the b-generation (informant 10) has this variant only occasionally. In most words, he approaches the standard form by using an off-glide ([oːᵘ]). This form, however, is still very close to the fully marked variant. The less conservative member of the b-generation (informant 11) normally lacks the length of the first diphthongal component ([oᵘ]), thus approaching the standard diphthong even more. The standard variant is present in the speech of the members of the c- and d-generations (informants 18, 19, 24).

In the case of [eː] for [eɪ] (*cake*), the ethnically marked variant is stable in the a- and b$_1$-generations. Informant 11 (b$_2$-generation) marks the transition to the regional-standard form by using both [eː] and the intermediate variant [eːᴵ]. The member of the c-generation (informant 18), his non-Pennsylvania German wife (informant 19), and their daughter (d-generation, informant 24) have the unmarked diphthong [eɪ].

For the feature [s] for [z], informants 1, 2, and 10, who have the best competence in Pennsylvania German, use unvoiced [s]. The speech of informant 10 is characterized by the occasional presence of [z̥]. For informant 11 the converse is true, [z] being the rule and [z̥] the exception. Here the transition zone includes three more informants, namely informant 18, who uses [ž] and [z] with equal frequency, informant 19, who occasionally has [s], and even d-generation informant 24, who occasionally uses [ž].

In the features [tʃ] for [dʒ] (*cabbage*), [d] for [ð] (*feather*), [s] for [θ] (*thistle*), and [ʊ̯] for [ʊ] (*book*), the transition is marked by the simultaneous presence of the ethnically marked and unmarked variants in one or more informants. In [ʌ̞] for [ʌ] (*cup*) the transition zone consists of two informants. Informant 11 usually has [ʌ̞] and only occasionally [ʌ], whereas in the speech of informant 18 this pattern is reversed. Only the features [ɪ̯] for [ɪ] (*baby*), [ʃ] for [ʒ] (measure), and [v] for [w] (*well*) form no qualitative or quantitative transition zones at all in family 1.

COMPARISON WITH PREVIOUS STUDIES

In a study of the English variety of fifty nonsectarian Pennsylvania Germans from isolated farm valleys in southern Northumberland, northern Dauphin, and western Schuylkill Counties, an area that includes the region in which the nonsectarians of the present examination live, Huffines (1984a) isolates thirteen phonological features characteristic of her informants' speech (figure 2.33).

The first seven features are characteristic of the speech of "the Pennsylvania Germans who are nonfluent English speakers" (Huffines 1984a, 176); this group corresponds to the nonsectarian a-generation in the present study.

According to Huffines (1984a, 176), "[t]hese features seldom occur in the speech of younger Pennsylvania Germans or fluent English speakers, and it is clear that they will pass from the spoken English of the Pennsylvania German community as soon as the nonfluent English speakers die out." Of these seven features, Huffines's numbers 2, 3, and 7 are characteristic almost exclusively of the nonsectarian a-generation in the present study as well. Word-final [p,t,k] for [b,d,g] (*egg, tub, bed*) is additionally present in the speech of the nonsectarian b₁-generation. [w] for [v] (*vegetables, valentine*) was not found. The two features which proved to be much more widespread in the present sample than in Huffines's are [ʌ̞] for [ʌ] (*cup*) and [tʃ] for [dʒ] (*cabbage*). Both were found in all the nonsectarian generations. Moreover, they are present in the sectarians' English, [ʌ̞] for [ʌ] occurring even in the speech of three non-Pennsylvania German informants.

The Influence of Pennsylvania German on English Phonology 127

1. Devoicing of (j) to [č] as in *juice*[33]
2. Sibilant variant [s] of (θ) as in *thing*
3. Lack of a velarized variant of (l) as in *build*
4. Bilabial variant [w] of (v) as in *visit*
5. Fortis variants [p,t,k] of voiced morpheme-final stops (b,d,g) as in *rib*, *woods*, and *bag*
6. Backing and rounding of (ʌ) to [ʌˀ, ɔ] as in *butter*
7. Raising of (U) to [Uˆ, u] as in *butcher*
8. Lenis variants [b̥,d̥,g̥] of voiced morpheme-final stops (b,d,g)
9. Monophthongization of (ey) to [e:] as in *take*
10. Monophthongization of (ow) to [o:] as in *smoke*
11. Laxing of unstressed (i) to [I, E, ə] as in *family*
12. Monophthongization of (aw) to [a:] as in *house*
13. (V:) to [V:ə] as in *know* [noːə]

Figure 2.33: Phonological features according to Huffines 1984a

Huffines (1984a, 177) divides the features characterizing the English of the nonsectarians who are nonfluent in Pennsylvania German or monolingual speakers of English into two categories: (a) features which form a distributional pattern conditioned by a social variable; (b) features which are distributed throughout the community and appear to be stable in that they persist through the generations. The most important of the social variables is age. Huffines's phonological features 8–11 are found not only in the speech of the native Pennsylvania German speakers, but also in the English of the other nonsectarians; in the latter case the more frequently, the older the informants are.

One phonological variable (number 12) is associated with use of Pennsylvania German, though not with age (Huffines 1984a, 178). It occurs in all usage categories, but most often in the English of those speakers who use more Pennsylvania German.

Finally, epenthetic [ə] after long vowels and diphthongs in word-final position (number 13) is found in the speech of middle-aged Pennsylvania Germans and of speakers in the middle categories of Pennsylvania German usage. Its distribution suggests minimal Pennsylvania German speaking ability; it does not occur in the speech of monolingual English speakers.

Huffines's features 8–13 are in line with the present study. Of the four variables which she finds to correlate with age, three are located far at the top of figure 2.31, being not only part of the English of the nonsectarian native speakers of English, but also of the younger generations and the sectarians: word-final [ɪ] for [i] (*family*), [oː] for [oʊ] (*goat*), and [eː] for [eɪ] (*cake*).

Word-final [p,t,k] for [b,d,g] is located more toward the center of figure 2.31, as it is restricted to the speech of the a- and b₁-generations. The qualitative distinction Huffines finds for the realization of word-final /b,d,g/ as [p,t,k] by the nonsectarian native speakers of Pennsylvania German and as [b̥,d̥,g̊] by the native speakers of English is not as clear-cut in the present study. Both fortis consonants and devoiced lenis consonants occur in the English of the a- and b-generations. In the present survey, the younger generations are characterized by a quantitative deficit rather than a qualitative difference observed by Huffines.

Huffines's claim that [ɑː] for [aʊ] (*crown*) is not determined by age, but rather by use of Pennsylvania German, is only partly reflected in the present data. Although an ethnically marked variant is found for at least one representative of each nonsectarian generation, the a- and b-generations clearly prevail.[30] Huffines's explicit distinction between the factors age and language use seems to be inappropriate for the present sample. As will be shown in chapter 3, the data suggest a clear correlation between these two factors; the older a nonsectarian informant, that is, the closer he or she is to the a-generation, the more frequently he or she uses Pennsylvania German.

Huffines's observation that [Vːə] for [Vː] (*key, shoe*) is not found in the English of monolingual speakers is reflected by the present data. Her claim, however, that it is found in the speech of Pennsylvania Germans of the middle age brackets is not supported. In the present sample only two members of the nonsectarian a-generation and one d-generation informant have an epenthetic [ə].

In sum, Huffines's results of the phonological examination of her nonsectarian informants show quite a few similarities with the present findings. The remaining differences between the two surveys will be briefly summarized.

Huffines suggests a clear difference between the English of the nonsectarian native speakers of Pennsylvania German and the native speakers of English. However, of her seven phonological variables that constitute this difference (as they are almost exclusively found in the speech of native speakers of Pennsylvania German), only three can be upheld without any reservations. Instead, the data of the present sample suggest that a large number of members of the nonsectarian b-generation phonologically behave like the a-generation.

Moreover, qualitative differences are less clear-cut than in Huffines's study (e.g., word-final [p,t,k] for [b,d,g]: devoiced lenis consonants are present in all generations, including the a-generation).

Three of the four variables which according to Huffines correlate with age are found to do so in the present sample. However, her claim that [ɑː] for [ɑʊ] does not correlate with age, being the only feature that can "be expected to survive very long without the support of a segment of the community which speaks Pennsylvania German" (Huffines 1984a, 178), is not supported by the present data. Therefore, Huffines' explicit distinction between phonological features that are conditioned by a social variable (age) and those that are stable throughout the community appears to be too strict. Some features are clearly more stable than others, but all of them correlate with acquisition patterns and, therefore, with age.

Finally, epenthetic [ə], which Huffines attributes to middle-aged speakers, does not occur frequently enough to structure the informants in the present study.

Unlike Huffines, who examines the English variety of nonsectarian Pennsylvania Germans, Raith (1981) presents data of mainly sectarian informants from Lancaster County, Pennsylvania. They include three Old Order Amish, five Conservative Mennonites, six Mennonite Church Mennonites, one member of the Church of the Brethren, and one Lutheran/Reformed. Figure 2.34 shows the phonological variables found by Raith and ordered by increasing frequency from top to bottom.

initial	θ	→	s	(*thin*)
final	r	→	∅	(*floor*)
	v	→	w	(*very*)
	ɔʊ	→	oː	(*joke*)
	z	→	s	(*bells*)
	w	→	v	(*want*)
final	v	→	f	(*leave*)
	dʒ	→	tʃ	(*jug*)
	eɪ	→	eː	(*teenager*)
	ʌ	→	ɒ	(*jug*)
final	r before s	→	∅	(*teenagers*)
final	b,d,g	→	b̥,d̥,g̊	(*jug*)

Figure 2.34: Phonological features according to Raith 1981

The distribution of Raith's informants according to their scores for these phonological variables suggests three large groups: (1) the three Old Order Amish and three Conservative Mennonites, all of whom have

130   The Influence of Pennsylvania German on English Phonology

almost no Pennsylvania German interference in their English; (2) two Mennonite Church Mennonites, who show little influence of Pennsylvania German; (3) two Conservative Mennonites, four Mennonite Church Mennonites, the Lutheran/Reformed, and the member of the Church of the Brethren, whose English is heavily marked.

Raith (1981, 40) points out that this result is rather unexpected as the informants in the first group, who have the least social contact with mainstream society, have the lowest degree of Pennsylvania German influence in their pronunciation of English.

To account for this discrepancy, Raith compares the informants' language acquisition contexts (*Spracherwerbskontext*). All the informants have Pennsylvania German as their native language. The six informants of the first group did not learn English until they started school at the age of six. English was therefore acquired and first used in a formal context. Raith (1981, 44) calls the result of this planned second language acquisition after the acquisition of L_1 *bilingualism* (*Zweisprachigkeit*).

The informants belonging to the third group learned English simultaneously with Pennsylvania German, or at least from their age peers before they started school. The result of this natural acquisition process is referred to by Raith as L_1-*multilingualism* (*erstsprachige Mehrsprachigkeit*).

In the special case of the second group, language use factors (*Sprachgebrauchsfaktoren*) such as extensive contact with English speakers are responsible for the minimal interference rather than the language acquisition context.

In a second step, Raith (1981, 46ff.) describes the various types of acquisition contexts as reflections of the types of speech communities (*Sprachgemeinschaftstyp*).[31]

Unlike Huffines, Raith does not introduce the age factor into his study since age is not as significant a factor in the sectarian group as it is in the nonsectarian one.

The distribution of Raith's informants differs from that of the informants in the present study. According to Raith's results, the more distant informants are from mainstream society, the less ethnically marked their English varieties are likely to be. Although in the present study the Mennonite family is Old Order and the Amish family is New Order, the two sectarian groups are quite similar in their degrees of social and religious conservatism. Nevertheless, the slightly more conservative Mennonites are on the whole characterized by more phonetic marking than the more progressive Amish family, a result contrary to Raith's.

Four of Raith's twelve phonological variables were not found in the present data: final r → ∅ (*floor*), v → w (*very*), final v → f (*leave*), and final r before s → ∅ (*teenagers*). With the exception of the last feature, they are all located in the upper half of Raith's implicational scale, that is, they are not as frequent as others.

On the other hand, Raith did not identify the features [ɪ̯] for [ɪ] (*family*), [ɑː] for [ɑʊ] (*crown*), [ʃ] for [ʒ] (*measure*), [d] for [ð] (*feather*), [ʊ̥] for [ʊ] (*book*), [Vːə] for [Vː] (*key*), and [l] for [ɫ] before a consonant or in word-final position (*milk, hill*). Figure 2.29 shows that of these seven features, one ([Vːə] for [Vː]) does not occur at all in the speech of the sectarian informants, the other six (with the exception of [ɪ̯] for [ɪ]) being present rather infrequently. The only real discrepancy, therefore, is found in the incidence of [ɪ̯] for [ɪ], which, in two target words, occurs eight times among the sectarians in the present study.

Of the features that are present in both studies, only word-final [b̥,d̥,g̊] for [b,d,g] (*egg, tub, bed*) is quite discrepant in terms of its location in the two scales. While this variable does not at all occur in the speech of the sectarians in the present survey, it is the most common feature in Raith's. Fortis consonants instead of devoiced lenis consonants also appear only three times.

In other cases, there are clear parallels: [s] for [θ] (*thistle*), the most infrequent feature in Raith's study, occurs only once (in *smooth*) in sectarian English in the present one. Similarly, [ʌ̟] for [ʌ] (*cup*) is one of the most common features, while [s] for [z] (*zoo*) is located in the middle of the scale in both studies.

Some of the differences in results between Raith's study and the present examination could be dialectal, as Raith's informants come from southeastern Pennsylvania. Further, the discrepancies may be due partly to methodological differences. Raith used a reading text to elicit the ethnically marked variables, thus receiving a rather untypical type of speech. Because of their limited education, many of the sectarian (and older nonsectarian) informants have great difficulties reading English texts. To avoid these methodological problems, flashcards were used in the present study.

A short survey of phonological variation is included in an article by Enninger et al. (1984) on the Old Order Amish of Kent County, Delaware. Enninger and his associates used a text read by ten informants to find out which phonological variables were present in the English of the Old Order Amish as opposed to the speech of their monolingual neighbors.

The variables "loss of final /r/" and "devoicing of final stops" occur occasionally. [tʃ] for [dʒ], [eː] for [eɪ], and [ʌˀ] for [ʌ] are frequently found in the English of the Old Order Amish, and occasionally in the speech of the monolinguals. This is a rather interesting observation, as [ʌ̰] for [ʌ] (in *cup*) appears in the speech of three non-Pennsylvania Germans in the present study as well. Enninger and his associates also identify the variable "laxing of final /ɪ/," which is missing in Raith's, but present in Huffines' survey; this feature proved to be rather frequent in the present examination.

Enninger and his associates state that "the phonological deviation of the AmE of the OOA of Kent County from the AmE of their monolingual neighbors [is] hardly noticeable" (Enninger et al. 1984, 7). In contrast, the more liberal Anabaptist groups in the same area exhibit almost all the phonological interferences found by Raith (1981). With the help of a matched-guise test the authors show that the ability of monolingual English speakers to recognize Amish pronunciation is not as prevalent as might be expected on the basis of the stereotypes that exist about "Amish talk."

SYNOPSIS

The evaluation of the phonological data suggests that the three large social groups of informants—nonsectarians, sectarians, and non-Pennsylvania Germans—can be clearly distinguished by the ethnic markedness of their English. In none of these groups is gender a significant factor.

While age plays only a marginal role in both the sectarian and the non-Pennsylvania German groups, in the nonsectarian one it is significant as it generally correlates with membership in generations differing in their patterns of language acquisition.

The nonsectarian a-generation has by far the highest percentage of ethnic marking, much higher than the sectarians, who are native speakers of Pennsylvania German as well, but also higher than the nonsectarian b-generation, which is the first generation to speak English natively. The more distant a nonsectarian generation is from the a-generation, the less its English is ethnically marked. However, the speed of this decline decelerates as ethnic marking approaches zero.

Especially the speech of the nonsectarian b-, c-, and d-generations is characterized by a number of qualitatively intermediate variants. The

The Influence of Pennsylvania German on English Phonology 133

transition from ethnic markedness to the regional standard can therefore be described not only in quantitative, but also in qualitative terms.

Nonstandard forms are not only found in the English of monolingual nonsectarians, but also in the speech of non-Pennsylvania Germans who live next to the farms of Pennsylvania Germans. This allows the interpretation of the ethnically marked phonological features as contact phenomena. Thus, the contact setting—rather unsurprisingly—has led to bidirectional change, that is, despite a general tendency away from ethnically marked English the regional standard has itself been influenced by minority features.

The members of the nonsectarian a-generation and those of the b-generation who have a similar fluency in Pennsylvania German use a number of sounds, especially some voiced consonants and diphthongs, far less frequently than the sectarians and the younger nonsectarians. In the case of the bilingual informants, two separate sound inventories could be assumed for Pennsylvania German and English.[32] They are kept much more clearly distinguished by the sectarians than by the nonsectarian a-generation, although both groups consist of native speakers of Pennsylvania German. However, the fact that all the informants show interference in one way or the other proves that in no case are the two systems completely independent.

Moreover, the nonsectarian b-, c-, and d-generations, whose active competence in Pennsylvania German decreases in this order, might be assumed to use Pennsylvania German phonological interferences in their English to mark their ethnic identity. This question, however, cannot be answered without a profound knowledge of the informants' attitudes toward Pennsylvania German; it will be addressed again in chapter 4.

In sum, the phonological data collected suggest what at first glance seems paradoxical: The English variety spoken by the nonsectarian Pennsylvania Germans is characterized by considerably more phonological interference from Pennsylvania German than the English of the sectarians. Those groups that separate themselves the most from mainstream society are closer to its linguistic norms (i.e., the regional standard) than a group of Pennsylvania Germans which does not shut itself off.

The answer to the enigma lies in the language use patterns and the language attitudes of the various groups of informants. These issues will be examined in chapters 3 and 4, respectively. An explanation will be attempted in chapter 5.

3
The Effects of Language Competence, Acquisition, and Use on Maintenance and Shift

The linguistic differences among the informants described in chapter 2 can be accounted for with the aid of sociolinguistic instruments. One such tool is included in section 2.3 of the questionnaire, namely various sets of questions about the informants' language competence, language acquisition, language use, and social networks and domains.

All the data in this part are self-reported. The fieldworker read the questions to the informants and entered the answers into the questionnaire. Section 2.3 was normally filled out during the second session of the interview when the fieldworker had already become familiar with the informants.

The description will basically follow the layout of the questionnaire. The questionnaire data will be supplemented by and checked against insights gained during participant observation, the free interviews, and other conversations with the informants.

Detailed descriptions of the informants' language competence and acquisition will be followed by the central subchapter on language use. These results will allow statements on processes of language maintenance and shift in the various informant groups. Theoretical aspects of maintenance and shift will also be addressed and a synopsis will be presented.

LANGUAGE COMPETENCE

Questionnaire section 2.3.1 comprises seventeen questions dealing with the informants' linguistic competence. The four varieties explicitly mentioned are Pennsylvania German, American English, Bible High German, and Standard German. To make sure that the informants understood which variety was meant, common language labels or paraphrases

The Effects of Language Competence, Acquisition, and Use

were used, for example, "Dutch," "English," "the kind of German that's in the Bible," and "the kind of German spoken in Germany".[1]

In each case, the informants were asked whether they could understand, speak, read, and write the respective varieties. Thus, information about the informants' passive, active, reading, and written competences was gathered. In an additional question the informants were asked about other foreign languages they might know.

The first four questions deal with the informants' competence in Pennsylvania German. All the eight nonsectarian native speakers of Pennsylvania German report that they can understand and speak this variety. The seven oldest members of this group say that they are unable to write it but that they can read it with some difficulty.[2]

Only the youngest member of the a-generation (informant 8) claims that she can read and write Pennsylvania German with ease. Together with her husband (informant 15), she likes to write letters in Pennsylvania German to their friends in Germany and Austria. Both claim that they can read their friends' Standard German letters and that during their travels in Germany and Austria they were able to understand Standard German.

This pattern of language competence points to the nonsectarian b-generation. Of its eight members, three maintain that they can read Pennsylvania German with ease; two can even write it with ease.

At the same time, there is a first indication of loss of the oral competence. One b-generation informant states that he can understand Pennsylvania German only with difficulty, and one says that he can speak it only with difficulty. Thus, the old pattern among the nonsectarians of nativelike oral competence, little reading competence, and no written competence is broken up.

Nevertheless, seven of the eight b-generation informants claim to speak and understand Pennsylvania German with ease, even though, unlike their parents, they are not native speakers.

The trend toward a self-reported balance in oral and written skills is continued in the c-generation. Only two informants claim to understand and speak Pennsylvania German with ease, three say they have some difficulty, and one informant states he does not understand or speak it at all. Five c-generation informants can read Pennsylvania German with some difficulty, while no fewer than four claim to be able to write it.[3]

The results of the nonsectarian d-generation reflect the almost total loss of competence observed in the free interviews. Of the five informants, only two can understand and speak Pennsylvania German with some difficulty. Typically enough, two also claim to be able to read it, while no d-generation informant can write Pennsylvania German.

The spectrum of competence in Pennsylvania German from the native speakers of the nonsectarian a-generation to the almost monolingual informants belonging to the d-generation resembles Dorian's (1981, 107ff.) breakdown of the Gaelic speech community in East Sutherland into Gaelic-dominant bilinguals, semispeakers, and near-passive bilinguals.[4]

All the sectarian informants report that they can understand and speak Pennsylvania German with ease. Only four claim that they can also read it easily, while in the case of writing the number drops to two.

The eleven non-Pennsylvania German informants have no competence in Pennsylvania German whatsoever.

Questions 5–8 deal with the informants' competence in English. Without exception, all the informants report that they can understand, speak, read, and write English with ease.

Questions 9–12 concern the competence in Bible High German. Except for one, all the sectarian informants claim to be able to understand this variety with ease. Two members of the nonsectarian b-generation and one of the c-generation can understand it with difficulty. Two sectarians state that they can speak Bible High German, one with ease and one with difficulty. All but one sectarian informant can read it, as can one member of the nonsectarian c-generation. No informant claims to be able to write this variety.

The results of this self-report reflect the use of Bible High German in the sectarians' worship services and their use of the Luther Bible and German hymns. By comparison, the four nonsectarian informants' claims appear to be over-reports, particularly since none of these informants is a member of the linguistically most conservative a-generation.

Questions 13–16 ask about the informants' competence in Standard German. No informant claims to be able to understand, speak, read, or write it with ease. Six of the eight members of the nonsectarian a-generation can understand Standard German with difficulty, none can speak it, and one can read and write it with difficulty.

The high percentage of a-generation informants who claim to understand Standard German may be due to their experience while traveling in the German-speaking countries. To a large extent these may be overratings based on single occasions and encounters with speakers of Southern German dialects.

No fewer than nine members of the nonsectarian b-, c-, and d-generations claim to be able to understand Standard German, five to speak it, six to read it, and five to write it. These figures have to be attributed to the fact that a large number of the younger nonsectarian informants took German as a second language at Line Mountain High School, in some cases later as part of their college studies. Their knowledge of Standard German is therefore not based on their rudimentary knowledge of Pennsylvania German but constitutes second language competence. This was verified in later conversations.

Of the sectarian informants, two say they can understand Standard German and one can read it. None of the non-Pennsylvania German informants has any competence in Standard German.

Finally, question 17 asks about other languages the informants speak. Three nonsectarians, members of the a-, b-, and d-generations, report a rudimentary knowledge of Spanish.

LANGUAGE ACQUISITION

Questions 18–30 cover language acquisition. All eight nonsectarian native speakers of Pennsylvania German identify grandparents and brothers and sisters as those interlocutors who, apart from their parents, spoke Pennsylvania German to them when they were children. Two informants (3, 5) additionally name neighbors and one (6) mentions schoolmates.

All of them report that they began to learn English at the age of six when they went to school. One informant (3) also names her cousins as her source of English. No a-generation informant has ever learned Bible High German.

Apart from informant 7, who spent twelve years in school, all of them had eight years of English at school. Neither Pennsylvania German nor Bible High German nor Standard German was taught. No subject was ever taught in Pennsylvania German.

Of the nonsectarian b-generation only informant 10 reports that besides English his family also spoke Pennsylvania German to him as a child. The most common explanation why the parents of the b-generation did not teach their children Pennsylvania German as a first language is that, in their words, it would have "spoiled their English." They recognized that their children were going to live in an English-dominated society. Nevertheless, this does not necessarily mean that the nonsectarian a-generation had an exclusively negative attitude toward Pennsylvania German.[5]

All the b-generation informants have Pennsylvania German as their second language. Four (informants 10–12, 16) say that they learned it around the age of six or seven. Four informants (9, 13–15) report that when they were children, they only heard Pennsylvania German spoken in their homes and were able to understand it, but never used it themselves. Their first active use of their second language occurred much later, for instance, at school (informant 15), after marriage (informant 9), after a conscious decision to use it with his wife at the age of twenty-one (informant 14), or even not until later in life (informant 13, who reports that he was unable to have a complete conversation in Pennsylvania German until the age of forty).

All the informants say they learned Pennsylvania German from their parents and family. More infrequent sources include the neighbors (informant 11), a girlfriend (informant 12), and friends and parents' friends (informant 15).

No b-generation informant has ever been taught Bible High German, or any language other than English at school. All subjects were taught in English. Of the eight informants, four had eight years of English at school, four had twelve years.

The members of the c-generation report that they acquired passive competence in their second language before the age of twelve or fourteen, while the infrequent active use of Pennsylvania German did not usually occur until the age of eighteen or twenty.

The only exception is informant 17 (the best Pennsylvania German speaker of this group), who reports that he could understand Pennsylvania German before he went to school and started to speak it while he attended high school. Through his relatively traditional lifestyle as a farmer and family butcher as well as his infrequent contacts with monolingual English speakers, this informant's competence is better than that of some of the members of the b-generation.

In comparison with the b-generation, the sources from which the c-generation learned Pennsylvania German have changed considerably. The grandparents are now the most important source, the parents talking English to their children and even with each other. The statement of informant 22 is very revealing. She reports that she heard Pennsylvania German only among her older relatives, but nobody actually spoke it to her when she was a child. Consequently, she did not use it until she was an adult.

Institutionalized adult language learning is a strong indicator of language death. Among the nonsectarian c-generation, two informants (18, 20) report that they took classes in Pennsylvania German at Line Mountain High School. Informant 18 attended evening classes at the age of twenty-five, and in the case of informant 20 (his brother) the class was offered as an additional voluntary course while he was still attending high school.

No member of the c-generation has ever learned Bible High German. All had twelve years of English at school. Three informants (18, 20, 23) learned Standard German at high school for two or three years. Therefore, Standard German interferences are frequent in their Pennsylvania German. All subjects were taught in English.

Of the five informants of the nonsectarian d-generation, only the two older ones (informants 25 and 26), two sisters of about thirty years of age, have passive competence in Pennsylvania German. Their sources were their parents, their grandparents, and an uncle, whom they heard when they were children, but who never spoke Pennsylvania German to them directly.

Both informants received a considerable amount of instruction in Standard German (seven years in high school and in college for informant 25, four years in high school for informant 26). As is the case with those members of the c-generation who learned Standard German at school, interferences from the standard variety are very frequent in the Pennsylvania German of informants 25 and 26.

The three younger informants belonging to the d-generation, who are between five and eleven years old, are completely monolingual speakers of English.

The twelve sectarians all grew up with Pennsylvania German as their first language. They learned it from their immediate family, their relatives, and the other members of their sectarian communities. Especially those informants who had older brothers and sisters report that they learned their second language (English) very early, between the ages of three and six. At the latest the sectarians learned English when they began school, where all classes were taught in English.

Thus, the most frequent sources for the second language were the parents, brothers and sisters, and people at school. In two cases the informants also name outsiders, that is, non-Amish or non-Mennonites. Informant 32, for example, learned her first English words from non-Mennonite children for whom her mother used to baby-sit.

All the sectarian informants learned Bible High German between the ages of six and sixteen. Most often the sources were their fathers and the worship services, in which passages from the Luther Bible were read and High German hymns were sung. Only one informant (38) reports that he learned Bible High German at school, too.[6]

All the sectarian adults had either eight or nine years of schooling in English. Neither Pennsylvania German nor Standard German were taught at their schools. All subjects were taught in English.

The eleven non-Pennsylvania German informants have no competence in Pennsylvania German, Bible High German, Standard German, or any language other than English.

Even informant 19, who married into nonsectarian family 1, has never learned any Pennsylvania German since her husband is a member of the c-generation with only a rudimentary knowledge of Pennsylvania German.

On average, the non-Pennsylvania German informants had ten years of schooling in English.

LANGUAGE USE

Besides language competence and acquisition, language use[7] has an impact on maintenance and shift. The informants' language use is strongly guided by the theoretical constructs of domain[8] and role,[9] which were both used in the setup of the language use part of the questionnaire.

Another important approach is social network theory. In the present chapter this concept—in a modified form, that is, in combination with domain theory—will be applied to the description of language use.

Following the layout of the questionnaire, a brief overview of the patterns effective in the informants' childhood and adolescence will be given.

In the center of the present chapter there will be a survey of present-day language use. After some preliminaries, data will be presented that show which informants use which language with which interlocutors and in which situations. These data will be analyzed both quantitatively and qualitatively. A close examination of the use of language within the six families will follow. The final question will be whether topic influences language use.

SOCIAL NETWORK AND DOMAINS

The questionnaire includes a network part immediately before the sections dealing with language competence, acquisition, and use. In the actual interviews, the network questions were asked parallel to those on language use. For instance, the questions "Do you ever shop in the little stores in town?" and "Which of the storekeepers are Dutch?" corresponded with "Do you speak Dutch to the salespeople in the little stores in town?" and "Do you speak Dutch when you meet a Dutch-speaking friend in such a store?"

The term *social network* is used in a rather loose way here.[10] Network theory is concerned with the sum of all the people with whom a person is in contact, and works best in large coherent speech communities. The present examination of families comprises too many loose ends in that they belong to three different communities. Nevertheless, the questions were asked, but were combined with those on domain.

The network and domain part of the questionnaire is divided into eight sets of questions (N1–8), which represent eight domains. These questions cover people and typical situations whom or which the informants might encounter in their everyday lives. Apart from human and animal interlocutors, the network and domain part also accounts for other, indirect sources of language, such as books, newspapers, radio, and television. The number of domains has to be determined separately for each community.[11] Accordingly, quite a few questions within the network and domain part proved to be irrelevant for the Pennsylvania German speech communities.

The network and domain part is designed in such a way that the questions move concentrically from the informants' closest contacts ("Who are the two or three people in your present life you feel closest to?") to their contacts with people living outside the Pennsylvania German language area ("Do you ever write letters to relatives or friends living outside Pennsylvania [= outside the PG area]?"). The headings of the eight sets of questions are as follows: N1: relatives, friends and neighbors; N2: work; N3: school; N4: religion; N5: spare time; N6: shopping; N7: doctor and officials; N8: network beyond the borders of the Pennsylvania German speech area. These headings correspond with the eight domains for which the informants' language use is examined in sections 2.3.5–12 of the questionnaire.

In more theoretical terms, a person's first order network generally contains five fairly distinct zones, which can only be determined by subjective questions (Boissevain 1987, 166). At the center there is a *personal cell* consisting of a few intimate relatives and friends. The next sphere is called the *intimate zone*, which consists of slightly more distant relatives and friends who are emotionally important to a person. The *effective zone* comprises relatives and people with whom communication is maintained because they might be useful. Beyond this there is a *nominal zone* of persons who are of little importance either instrumentally or emotionally. Finally, the *extended zone* includes persons who are only partly known to the informant. These people are almost strangers, but not quite. Placement in any of these zones is subjective and continually shifting.

The following subchapters do not constitute an attempt to examine the informants' networks with a mathematical-statistical method.[12] The fact that the informants belong to six different families and at least three different ethnic groups does not allow for such an approach.[13] Instead of providing a mathematically exact description of the network of a speech community, the present study will depict sporadic observations on single informants, groups of informants, and even historical developments.

The description of the informants' networks and domains should be regarded as a tool for the better understanding of the examination of language use. As the non-Pennsylvania German informants proved to have very little contact with speakers of Pennsylvania German, the description will focus on the networks of the nonsectarian and sectarian Pennsylvania Germans.

These fairly general and descriptive remarks on the informants' contacts with one another and other people will be followed by a more theoretical interpretation in which some objective measures, including interactional (such as frequency, duration, and multiplexity) and structural criteria (such as size, density, and clusters), will support the analysis of the subjective data.

Description

The aim of the set of questions under N1 (relatives, friends, and neighbors) is to establish the core of each informant's network. The first question ("Who are the two or three people in your present life you feel closest to?") aims at the center of the network. In connection with the language use questions, it is important to know which of these people are Pennsylvania German ("Which of them are Dutch?"). The most common answers to the first question include spouses and children. Brothers and sisters, parents, daughters-in-law, and in one case a nonrelative, a work colleague, were also mentioned.

The next two questions cover relatives, friends, and neighbors. To find out how large the groups of a given informant's relatives as well as friends and neighbors were and how many of them were considered to have a Pennsylvania German cultural background, the informants were confronted with questions dealing with concrete situations, such as "How many relatives does your family usually invite to a holiday or

The Effects of Language Competence, Acquisition, and Use   143

party such as a wedding reception, a baptism, or a big birthday party? How many of them are Dutch?" and "How many friends and neighbors do you usually invite to such a holiday or party? How many of them are Dutch?"

For the relatives, numbers vary between ten and three hundred in the nonsectarian group, and between one hundred and two hundred in the sectarian group. According to the nonsectarians, 90% to 100% of these relatives are Pennsylvania German, while the sectarians say that all their relatives are plain.

While the question containing the concrete situation of a celebration appears to be quite suitable to define the range of the informants' relatives, it proved inadequate in connection with friends and neighbors. None of the nonsectarian informants was able to give the number of invited friends and neighbors, while the sectarians vaguely answered "a few." Nonrelatives do not seem to be invited to family festivities. The shares of friends and neighbors with a Pennsylvania German cultural background vary between 30% and 100%.

The questions asked under N2 (work; "What kind of people do you come into contact with at work?" and "Which of them are Dutch?") do not apply to the members of the nonsectarian a-generation as they are all retired. The network analysis was designed strictly to reflect the present state of the communities.

The members of the nonsectarian b- and c-generations, who work on farms, at the garage and school bus enterprise owned by members of family 1, or, as in the case of family 3, in the family-owned butcher shop, name coworkers and between 30% and 75% of the customers as those Pennsylvania Germans with whom they come into contact through work. The two informants teaching at Line Mountain High School (13, 14) report much less contact with Pennsylvania Germans at work.

Like their nonsectarian colleagues, the Amish and Mennonite informants working on family-owned farms have Pennsylvania German relatives as their coworkers.

The set of questions under N3 (school[14]) applies only to the six school children. They all attend different schools (informant 24: kindergarten in the Mahantango Valley; 27: Tri Valley Junior High School; 28: Mahantango Valley Elementary School; 35: Sunny Side Mennonite School; 49: Lewisburg Elementary School; 50: kindergarten in Lewisburg).

While at the Mennonite's school all the pupils including the teacher are plain and their Pennsylvania German cultural background is undisputed, the question of how many of the students and teachers at the nonsectarian schools are "Dutch" is much more difficult to answer. Even though most of the families in the Mahantango Valley have some Pennsylvania German background, intermarriages with non-Pennsylvania Germans have become more frequent than they used to be.

The two non-Pennsylvania German school-age informants (49, 50), who live in town, are not likely to come into contact with Pennsylvania German children at school.

One of the most important aspects of the informants' networks and domains is examined under N4 (religion). The first question deals with church services: "Do you have the opportunity in your area to go to church services in which Dutch and/or High German are still used?" All the informants answered affirmatively, although, as the next question reveals ("How often do these services take place?"), there is a major difference between nonsectarian and sectarian informants.

The Amish and Mennonite informants have their worship services in German, biweekly in the case of the former and weekly in the case of the latter. The only sectarian informants to worship in English are informants 38 and 39.

The nonsectarians, on the other hand, only have the chance of attending a Pennsylvania German service once a year. These services have a fairly short tradition of approximately fifteen years.[15]

With regard to the site of German-spoken services, the nonsectarian informants are divided into two groups. The majority of family 1 (informants 1, 2, 9–11, 17) name Himmel's Church in Rebuck as the church where they can worship in Pennsylvania German once a year. Two members of family 1 (informants 3, 9), six members of family 2 (informants 4–6, 12, 13, 22), and five members of family 3 (7, 8, 15, 16, 23) attend the Pennsylvania German service at Zion (Klinger's) Lutheran Church in Erdman.[16]

Thus, two networks can be established. One is formed only by members of family 1, the other one conjoins members of family 2 with members of family 3. Both networks overlap through informant 9 (figure 3.1).

One should keep in mind that the network depicted in figure 3.1 applies only once a year. The answers to the question "Where do you normally go to church?" convey a more diverse distribution.

While nine informants (1, 2, 6, 9–12, 14, 17) are regular members of the Himmel's Church congregation, only one (7) regularly attends the service at Klinger's Church. The other nonsectarian informants are scattered over a number of parishes in the area, such as St. John's (Leck Kill), Salem Church (Rough and Ready), and St. Michael's (Klingerstown), which shares its minister with Klinger's Church. Two

The Effects of Language Competence, Acquisition, and Use   145

```
 ┌─────────────────┐  ┌──────────────────────────────────────────┐
 │ Himmel's Church │  │    Zion (Klinger's) Lutheran Church      │
 │                 │  │                                          │
 │     Family 1    │  │    Family 2          Family 3            │
 │                 │  │                                          │
 │    1    2     9 │ 3│   4   5   6         7   8                │
 │                 │  │                                          │
 │   10   11   17  │  │  12  13  22        15  16  23            │
 └─────────────────┘  └──────────────────────────────────────────┘
```

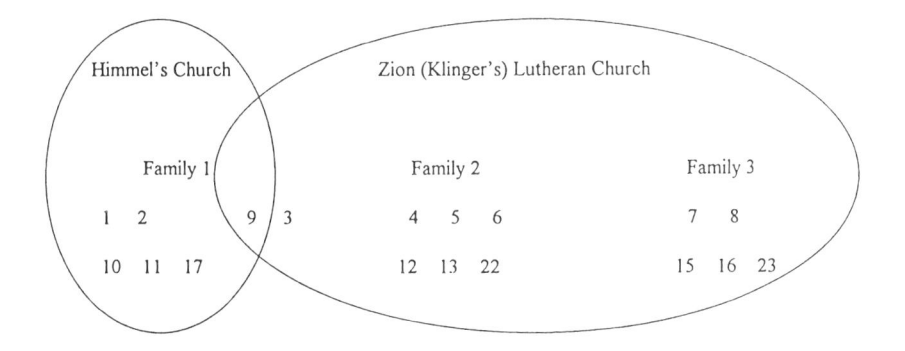

Figure 3.1: Nonsectarian informants' network constellation as determined by Pennsylvania German church services

informants (22 and 25), mother and daughter, have left their local church to join the Mormon Church.

Among the nonsectarians, there are only two informants (16 and 23), a married couple, who say that their minister is of Pennsylvania German origin, although not local to the area, but from Berks County. In all the other parishes, rural as they may be, the ministers are not locals and have no Pennsylvania German cultural background, let alone language competence.

By contrast, the congregations show high proportions of members of Pennsylvania German origin. Only two informants (10, 11) believe that 50% of the people in their congregation are Pennsylvania German, all others give an estimate of between 75% and 95%. Even the member of the Mormon Church (informant 22) estimates that 2% of the members of her local congregation are Pennsylvania Germans.

The final two questions cover the informants' contact with written texts in the field of religion. All the informants say that their household owns an English Bible. The German Bible is found in all the sectarian households as well as in those of three nonsectarian informants (7, 12, 13) and the married couples 8 and 15, 14 and 22, 16 and 23. English-German editions of the Bible are common with the sectarians. Moreover, a bilingual edition is also owned by the household of informants 8 and 15, who are collectors of old books. Thus, they are the only informants who also own the four gospels in the Pennsylvania German translation.[17]

All the church bulletins, including those of the sectarian churches, are printed in English. No regular bulletin is even partly in Pennsylvania German or Standard German. The only exceptions are the nonsectarians' annual Pennsylvania German services, for which the bulletins are printed in Pennsylvania German.

The next large set of questions (N5) deals with the people the informants come into contact with in their spare time. To get a general overview, the first questions were "What hobbies do you have?" and "In which of these activities do you meet Dutch people?"

Among the nonsectarians, quilting is named most often as a spare time activity that brings female speakers in contact, namely by informants 2, 3, 5–7, 12, and 16. Generally, these meetings are organized by the churches; sometimes relatives meet in private homes. The language used is often Pennsylvania German, but apparently less than used to be the case. Informant 5 reports that she is a member of two quilting groups. The one at Himmel's Church speaks Pennsylvania German, while the one in Herndon uses English.

Nowadays, the senior citizen centers are the places where Pennsylvania German is spoken most outside the families (informants 3, 5–7, 12). Again, the churches play a strong role in offering activities in which Pennsylvania German is used, including church suppers (informant 3), church work (informant 5), and choir practice (informant 9). One of the oldest male informants reports that playing cards is the hobby in which he speaks Pennsylvania German the most, mainly at home.[18]

The hobby named most frequently in connection with the use of Pennsylvania German among men is hunting (informants 10, 14, 17).[19] Two informants (15, 17) name the annual *Versammling* 'meeting' as an occasion when they speak Pennsylvania German in their spare time. Other activities include local toy train swap meets (informant 13) and high school basketball games, where some of the parents speak Pennsylvania German (informant 22).

While the nonsectarians can name only few activities which allow them to speak Pennsylvania German in their spare time, the sectarians use this language in practically all of their free time activities, such as quilting, baking, hiking, farm sales, and barn raisings.

Of the fifty informants, only two are members of a Pennsylvania German society. Informant 7 belongs to the Gratz Historical Society, which meets every couple of months in Gratz in Lykens Valley; informant 23 is a contributing member of the Birdsboro Pennsylvania German Society in Berks County, without ever attending their meetings. Nevertheless, no fewer than thirteen nonsectarian informants report that they occasionally attend such activities, for example, talks on the Pennsylvania German language and culture, auctions, flea markets and craft sales, theater plays, and the *Versammling*, to which only men are admitted.

All in all, seven nonsectarian men report that they have attended a *Versammling* (informants 1, 10, 13–15, 17, 23). Informant 10 is on the board of the *Yarlich Fersommling* 'annual meeting' at Lykens[20] as the

Fudermeeschter 'the food manager'. Even though native speakers are becoming rare, the *Versammlinge* thrive as annual social and folkloristic events. The Lykens *Fersommling* of 1990 voted against the future admittance of women.

From the point of view of language maintenance, events like the *Versammling* are strong indicators of ongoing language death. The same can be said about theater plays in Pennsylvania German, which are becoming more and more popular in the area, especially at family reunions and church festivals. Written by local authors, these skits are usually short and crude in language and plot. Some of the informants belonging to families 1 and 2 (informants 1, 2, 13) have taken an active part in such performances.

Five couples (informants 1 and 2, 9 and 17, 10 and 11, 29 and 30, and 31 and 32) report that they do their own home butchering and help other people with theirs. This custom is found equally among the sectarian and the nonsectarian Pennsylvania German informants. It appears to have been even more common in former times. Two informants (6, 7) say that they have given it up only recently. The set of questions about home butchering was inapplicable to the members of nonsectarian family 3, which runs a commercial butcher shop in Klingerstown.

The home butcherings take place at the informants' farms in the winter. Some informants butcher once a year (informants 10, 11), others no less than once a week during the months of January and February (informants 1, 2, 9, 17). In the case of nonsectarian family 1, the butchered meat is beef and pork, usually one cow and two pigs at a time. The Mennonite family (informants 29–32) report that they butcher beef, pork, poultry, and deer.

Since the participants in the home butcherings are usually relatives, the informants unanimously report that practically 100% are Pennsylvania German. Apart from providing the whole family with meat for a year, the home butcherings are important social events in that they bring the different generations together and help to preserve old traditions.[21]

Another aspect of the informants' spare time network is covered by the questions "Which local restaurant do you like to go to?" and "How many of the people working there are Dutch?" Most informants give names of towns in the area, such as Gratz, Pitman, Mandata, and Mifflinburg. In a number of cases, the owners and waitresses working in the restaurants are reported to be able to speak some Pennsylvania German.

The question "Do you ever go to fairs or other folk festivals?" was answered affirmatively by 75% of the informants. Most of them name the Gratz fair, some others Kutztown and the local fire company carnival in Pitman. At all these places, some of the salespeople are reported to be speakers of Pennsylvania German.

The final set of questions under the heading of spare time deals with radio, television, newspapers, and books. Except for the sectarians, all the informants say they like to listen to the radio. Almost all the informants mention a number of Pennsylvania German programs, the best-known being a fifteen-minute show at 12:15 P.M. on Sunday by C. Richard Beam of Radio WLBR Lebanon called *Die Alde Kummraade* 'the old friends'. The presenter, who is a native speaker and one of the most prominent experts on Pennsylvania German, calls himself either *der dinn Dick Beam* 'thin Dick Beam' (Pennsylvania German *dinn* 'thin' = opposite of *dick* 'fat'), or, following the tradition of many Pennsylvania German authors, uses the pseudonym *es Bischli-Gnippli* 'the little clodhopper'. In his program he covers all aspects of Pennsylvania German culture. Some informants name short clips on WBYO Boyertown, which, however, stopped being on the air in 1989 and could not be received by the majority of the informants anyway.

All the informants except for the sectarians have television. However, there are no specific Pennsylvania German programs in the area.

For the nonsectarian Pennsylvania German informants, *The Daily Item* (Sunbury), and, to a lesser extent, *The News Item* (Shamokin) are the most common dailies. Among the weekly papers, *The Citizen Standard* and, to a lesser degree, *The Upper Dauphin Sentinel* are read by the majority of the informants. The sectarians tend to subscribe to their own newspapers. Apart from dairy magazines, these include the weekly papers *Die Botschaft*,[22] *The Pathway Papers*, and *Focus on the Family*. The non-Pennsylvania German informants regularly read newspapers published near their homes such as *The Lewisburg Journal* and *The Press-Enterprise* (Bloomsburg).

Of all these newspapers, only *The Citizen Standard* and *Die Botschaft* keep alive a tradition which has existed since the Civil War, namely the Pennsylvania German columns containing poems, short prose pieces, and anecdotes.[23] *The Citizen Standard*, which is published in Valley View, regularly contains a column called *En kats Deitsch Schtick* 'a short German piece' by Bill Klouser. The column is written in Pennsylvania German with English vocabulary cues. A full English translation of the respective week's column is given once a month. In the same paper, Jesse Hepler has an English column with occasional Pennsylvania German translations. The column *Es Pennsilfaanisch Deitsch Eck* 'the Pennsylvania German corner' in *Die Botschaft*, published in Lancaster, is written wholly in Pennsylvania German. Until 1992 it was edited by C. Richard Beam.

About 75% of the informants say that they like to read books. They report that in their area it is possible to buy Pennsylvania German books, but only poetry and stories, no novels or nonfiction.

In N6 shopping is examined with regard to the informants' networks and domains. The first two questions are "Do you ever shop at the farmers' market?" and "How many of the salespeople are actually Dutch/plain?" Farmers' markets are held once a week in the larger towns such as Lewisburg, Gratz, Sunbury, and Berrisburg. About two-thirds of the informants say that they have gone shopping at such a market.

Nonsectarian family 3 has butcher stalls at the markets in Gratz and in Lewisburg. The stall in Lewisburg is run by informants 16 and 23.

Informants' estimates of how many salespeople are Pennsylvania German range from 20% to 90%. If a distinction is made, the percentage for Gratz, which is a smaller and more isolated town, is always higher than that for Lewisburg. The share of plain salespeople is estimated to be between 5% and 50%.

All the informants report that they have gone shopping in the little stores in town. As the two groups live in two different valleys, the nonsectarian informants frequent other stores than the sectarian informants.

The members of nonsectarian families 1 and 2 name Geist's at Leck Kill (informants 1, 2, 4–6, 9–11, 13, 17) and Drumheller's at Rebuck (informants 3, 9–13, 17, 22). With regard to the latter store, one informant (9) mentions that the owner understands Pennsylvania German but does not speak it, while another one (12) observes that the owners used to speak Pennsylvania German. Both these stores include a small post office, a general store, and a barroom. Mr. Geist also delivers goods to his customers' farms.[24] One informant (6) names Mrs. Snyder's store in Pitman, while another one (22) mentions a small supermarket in Dalmatia. The members of nonsectarian family 3 (informants 3, 7, 8, 15, 16, 23), most of whom live in another area of the Mahantango Valley, point to Bill Klinger's store in Klingerstown.

The sectarian informants, who live in Buffalo Valley, name completely different Pennsylvania German stores, such as Martin's in Hartleton and Hartleton County Store, whose owner is non-Pennsylvania German, but some of whose employees are Mennonites.

All the informants, including the sectarians, report that they like to go shopping at the big supermarkets and shopping malls. The vast majority say that none of the salespeople there are Pennsylvania German.

N7 concerns official contacts such as the doctor and state officials. The first question ("Is your family doctor Dutch?") was affirmed by about 50% of the informants. The vast majority of the nonsectarians name Sunbury as their nearest hospital, followed by Danville and Shamokin. For the sectarians and most non-Pennsylvania Germans, the nearest hospital is in Lewisburg. The answers to the question "How many of the doctors and nurses in the local hospital are Dutch?" range from none to few for the doctors and none to 50% for the nurses.

Unlike the sectarian informants, the nonsectarians say that the members of the town board of supervisors are Pennsylvania German. Nevertheless, the committee meetings are held in English. In the course of the interviews it turned out that there are no town halls in the small rural communities where the informants live. Thus, the question "How many of the other officials working at the town hall are Dutch?" did not apply.

N8 covers the most marginal areas of the informants' networks and domains, namely the part reaching beyond the borders of the Pennsylvania German speech area. The first question lists five large cities in Pennsylvania and asks whether the informants have ever been there. The answers suggest a surprisingly high mobility. All the informants say they have been to Lancaster, Harrisburg, and Philadelphia. Only informant 12 reports that she has never been to Reading, and informant 32, a sectarian, says that she has never visited Allentown.

With regard to the question "Where did you meet Dutch people and who were they?" the nonsectarian informants fairly consistently report that they have met strangers who were Pennsylvania Germans in Reading, Allentown, and Lancaster. Many nonsectarians have relatives there as well as in Harrisburg and Philadelphia. None of the sectarian informants has relatives or acquaintences in any of these five cities.

The next question reaches beyond Pennsylvania ("Have you ever been out of Pennsylvania?"). All the informants answered affirmatively. One informant (7) has visited every state of the Union, others have been to the West Coast or Western states (informants 1, 2, 4–6, 9, 12, 13, 22).

The journeys which informants 31 and 32 undertook before their marriage may serve as an example of the sectarians' travels. As a young man, informant 31 went on a trip to the West Coast with Mennonite friends in a van driven by a Black Bumper Mennonite. Informant 32 has been to Indiana, Montana, Ohio, and New York to visit relatives.

Whenever informants report that they met Pennsylvania Germans outside Pennsylvania, the latter were relatives (informants 9, 13, 14, 22, 32), friends (informant 9), or other people who had moved there from Pennsylvania (informants 1, 2, 7, 8, 12, 15). Nonsectarian informant 6 reports that she met Amish in Illinois.

The last step with regard to geographical distance is taken by the question "Have you ever traveled abroad, or even to Europe?" A surprisingly high number of nonsectarian informants, including some of the a-generation, answered affirmatively (informants 4–11, 13–15, 22). Even a sectarian informant (31) has traveled abroad; he went to Kitchener, Ontario, Canada, where he visited plain friends with other young Mennonites. Three of the nonsectarian informants (9, 17, 22) have also been to Canada. For informant 17 this was his only long trip; he went fishing with his high-school class.

A great number of nonsectarian informants (4–8, 13–15) have traveled to Germany, which may reflect a certain nostalgic interest in the land of their forefathers. The interviews abound with extremely positive remarks on Germany. Most informants report that their knowledge of Pennsylvania German helped them to make themselves understood in the southern parts of Germany, though not as easily in the north.

The next question, which was not applicable to the sectarians, covers the contacts the informants might have had while serving in the military. Of all the informants, only three (informants 4, 10, 14) served in the military. Informant 4 was stationed in Germany and Austria during and after World War II, where he occasionally functioned as an interpreter because of his native competence in Pennsylvania German. Informant 10 served in Korea from 1955 to 1957. Informant 14 was in the Navy from 1953 to 1957. Among other places his journeys took him to Germany, where he says his knowledge of Pennsylvania German enabled him to carry on a conversation. When asked whether they met any Pennsylvania Germans in the military, informant 4 answered no, informant 10 a few, and informant 14 met one man.

All the informants report that they like to visit Pennsylvania German speaking relatives or friends living in the Pennsylvania German area or to be visited by them. Outside the Pennsylvania German area, however, only about 50% of the informants have personal contacts with Pennsylvania German-speaking friends or relatives. Only a Mennonite woman (informant 32) says that she has a regular penfriend, another Mennonite, in Canada.

About half of the informants report that they write letters to relatives and friends living in the Pennsylvania German area. A slightly higher percentage are in correspondence with relatives and friends outside the Pennsylvania German area as the vast distances do not always allow personal visits.

INTERPRETATION

Social networks are influenced by such factors as personality, gender, community (including mobility, education, occupation, kinship), and age (Boissevain 1987, 167). In turn, the structure of people's networks influences their personalities and, quite generally, their behavior.

152   The Effects of Language Competence, Acquisition, and Use

In the present study, the effects of social network and domains on the informants' linguistic behavior will be most important.

Personality influences social networks and domains in that a person with a cheerful and friendly personality is likely to build and maintain a larger network of friends than a more reserved person. However, personality differences are found among the members of each subgroup of the present sample and do not help to structure the informants.

Sectarians are often said to be reserved and taciturn. This might apply where plain people interact with outsiders, but, as participant observation showed, inside their own community sectarians can certainly be cheerful and outgoing. The informants' personalities can be drawn upon as a network factor only in individual cases.

Similarly, the informants' gender does not appear to be particularly significant for the structure of their networks and the domains.

The results of section N2 showed that men, through their work, tend to establish more contacts than women, who are often housewives, especially in the older age groups. The informants' gender also made a difference in the question about their hobbies (N5).

The clearest line of difference is found in the sectarian communities, followed by the older nonsectarian Pennsylvania Germans. The younger and more educated the informants, the less their gender is crucial for the determination of their networks.

The most significant factor is community. Because of geographical distance and the different cultural heritage and tradition, the three large informant groups are best considered to form separate networks.

If all the fifty informants are regarded as a continuum, the three large groups will at least have to be considered to form clusters of people who are more closely linked to each other than the rest.

The presence of such clusters normally influences the informants' behavior. Clusters tend to develop behavioral norms, as becomes especially clear from the example of the sectarian Pennsylvania Germans. Members exert pressure for conformity upon each other (Boissevain 1987, 166). Some of the pressures present in the various clusters of informants might be responsible for the linguistic differences.

Contacts between these clusters exist, but they are surprisingly rare, particularly between nonsectarian and sectarian Pennsylvania Germans. Sectarians tend to consider nonsectarians to be just as much "the English" as they do non-Pennsylvania Germans. This high degree of separation both in attitude and real life is another reason for assuming three large groups with separate networks.

As the sectarians are organized in small communities of about two hundred people, they not only know a good deal about each other, but are interlinked in various ways, for instance, they participate in many activities together. In dealing with insiders they are characterized by a high degree of sociability as they consider people they meet in this setting to be friends of friends. With outsiders they are generally more introverted, partly because their isolated lifestyle has offered them little chance to practice their social skills with the nonplain, partly because of negative experiences in the past.

Life in small, stable communities is responsible for relatively dense networks, dense meaning that a large number of members of a person's network are in touch with each other. Density refers to the extent to which links that could possibly exist among persons actually do exist (Boissevain 1987, 165). The sectarians rely heavily on each other, a fact epitomized in their rejection of any kind of insurance and their mutual help in case of need (e.g., barn raisings). This network density is increased by the sectarians' minimal education and their occupation, farming, both of which hinder geographical[25] and social mobility.

The most important factor in the formation and stability of the sectarian community is religion. The religiously and ideologically motivitated rejection of modern technology such as cars, radio, and television minimizes contact with the outside world, thus contributing to the density of the inner network. Nevertheless, this does not imply that religion is unimportant for either the nonsectarian Pennsylvania German or the non-Pennsylvania German informants, as was seen in N4. The difference is that the sectarians' religious ideology has a unique isolating power.

Sectarians typically show a clear distinction between their inner network, that is, the members of their community, and their outer network, that is, the nonplain. In more theoretical terms, one can distinguish between first and second order network zones. Quite generally, people can come into contact with more people than those to whom they are directly linked. The latter form their first order network zone; those to whom they are introduced through the members of their first zone belong to their second order network zone (Boissevain 1987, 165).

As was seen in N2, most sectarians and also some nonsectarians—especially family 3—work together with family members, for example, on farms or in the butcher shop. Here the informants' networks reflect a main interactional characteristic commonly referred to as *multiplexity*. This concept describes the degree to which relations between persons consist of single or many strands (Boissevain 1987, 165). In the case of the coworkers who at the same time are an informant's relatives, the informants are connected by more than one role. Members of multiplex networks tend to be on more intimate terms with each other than people who share uniplex networks. The frequency and duration of interaction can have direct effects on multiplexity. The more contact people have and the longer their relationship has lasted, the more multiplex their relation is likely to be.

Networks that score high for multiplexity and density, such as the sectarians', are referred to as *tightly knit*; if they score low for these factors, they are called *loosely knit*. In the present sample the non-Pennsylvania Germans and the younger nonsectarians have the most loosely knit social networks.

Similar to the sectarians, the nonsectarian a-generation is characterized by minimal education and mobility and, therefore, small but dense networks. The low geographical mobility is in most cases caused by the fact that, as farmers, the informants have to be available around the clock. Much of their time is spent working alone. Low geographical mobility normally also results in low social mobility.

A good indicator for the different sizes and qualities of networks is the geographically most removed sphere in a network, namely the contacts a person has to a foreign country. While one of the sectarian informants (31) reports that he has been to Canada, none of them has ever traveled to Europe. At first glance, the nonsectarian a-generation seems to be more mobile, no fewer than five a-generation informants having traveled to Germany. However, almost all of these trips took place in the past few years, when the informants were retired. Before, their geographical mobility was much lower. In some cases it was their children who took them along on those trips.

With the non-Pennsylvania German informants, the trend to larger but, at the same time, more specialized networks already started in the oldest generation. Part of the reason was that these informants live in larger towns such as Lewisburg and Berwick. In a town, the networks are looser and the relations tend too be single-stranded. It is impossible for the informants to know everybody in their community.

In the case of the Pennsylvania German informants, nonsectarians and sectarians alike, relatives are often geographical neighbors. Kinship forms an important segment of these informants' networks. In cases where the kinship and the residential segments of a network are almost congruent, high density and a high degree of multiplexity are to be expected. The non-Pennsylvania German family, on the other hand, lives in different towns and is separated by a large geographical distance.

Age plays a decisive role for the networks and domains of one social group only, namely the nonsectarians.

In the sectarian communities, a rigid, religiously motivated system endows its members with fairly fixed rights and obligations. It is not so much age that exempts some members from certain duties, but the question of whether or not somebody is baptized and thus a full member of the community. Since the Amish and Mennonites practice adult baptism, the younger, not yet baptized community members (usually before the age of 21) enjoy more personal liberties than the older, baptized ones.

However, the social networks and domains of the unbaptized members are not considerably different from the others, apart from maybe a hidden radio or an occasional buggy ride for courtship. Their personal contacts will always remain intragroup contacts so that, in terms of language, the baptized and unbaptized group members share the same networks.

Likewise, the age factor has no strong linguistically relevant effects on the networks and domains of the members of the non-Pennsylvania German group.

Within the nonsectarian group of Pennsylvania Germans, however, age does play an important role. The networks of the very old (in the present case the native speakers of Pennsylvania German) begin to contract, as members die and are not replaced. Moreover, with failing strength the ability to get around and to communicate dwindles. This has an enormous effect on these informants' language use, as the group of people with whom they can speak Pennsylvania German is becoming smaller and smaller.

Starting with the b-generation, the nonsectarian Pennsylvania Germans' networks become larger, less dense, and less multiplex, as the informants have more schooling, show a higher geographical mobility, and thus come into contact with more people. This may be seen most clearly within the nonsectarian b- and c-generations, many of whose members temporarily left the Mahantango Valley to attend college. Today they have professions that bring them into contact with people outside their traditional network. However, these relations are often single-interest relations.

The three youngest members of the d-generation still have relatively small networks with a high degree of multiplexity and transactional and emotional content. As soon as they grow up and leave the Mahantango Valley (e.g., for college), however, they will be part of large, loosely knit networks, similar to those of the non-Pennsylvania German informants, who live in towns. They will deal with a growing number of strangers. Their dealings will become less sociable and more instrumental.

Childhood and Adolescence

General Questions

At the end of questionnaire section 2.3.3 (childhood language use) four questions (95–98) were asked about the connection between past and present language use. A brief discussion of the answers will serve as an introduction to childhood and adolescence language use.

The fact that assertive answers to these questions were received from nonsectarian informants only shows that the language use patterns in the sectarian and non-Pennsylvania German groups are more stable.

Question 95 ("When you were younger, did you use more Dutch than today?") was answered affirmatively by eight informants. Among them there are six of the eight members of the nonsectarian a-generation.

Since their childhood, the language use pattern of these informants' community has changed dramatically. The family and home domain and a few others used to be associated with Pennsylvania German. As the a-generation raised their children in English, even in their families they can speak their native Pennsylvania German only among themselves. As soon as members of one of the younger generations are present, it is not fitting to speak Pennsylvania German. Therefore, these informants do not find themselves in situations in which it is suitable to speak Pennsylvania German as often as they used to.

The two other informants who say they used to speak more Pennsylvania German (informants 10, 12) are members of the nonsectarian b-generation and have near-native competence in Pennsylvania German.

The decreasing use of Pennsylvania German in the nonsectarian a-generation gives three of its members (informants 1–3) the feeling that their language competence suffers from this lack of use (question 96: "Do you feel that you are forgetting some of your Dutch?").

The four other informants to answer this question with yes include two members of the c-generation (informants 18, 22) and two of the d-generation (informants 25, 26). They feel that the minimal competence in Pennsylvania German that they acquired in their childhood has been reduced during their adolescence and early adulthood.

In questions 97 and 98 the informants were asked to name the people with whom they used to speak Pennsylvania German but with whom they now speak English and vice versa.

The Effects of Language Competence, Acquisition, and Use 157

The shift to English was carried out by only two informants. Informant 6 (nonsectarian a-generation) reports that a former schoolmate of hers, with whom she used to speak only Pennsylvania German, insists on using English with her today, more than sixty years later. She adds that she finds this rather disturbing. In her eyes, her friend's behavior may reflect a denial of her cultural and linguistic heritage.[26]

The same shift from the use of Pennsylvania German in childhood to English in old age is reported by eighty-three-year-old informant 12 (nonsectarian b-generation) for some former schoolmates still living in the area.

The shift from English to Pennsylvania German is more common, which seems to contradict the general trend. A look at the distribution of this shift is revealing: only nonsectarian Pennsylvania Germans know interlocutors with whom they have made that particular shift.

Among them there are six of the eight members of the a-generation (informants 1, 2, 4–7). In each case, it is the informants' children who were raised in English but learned Pennsylvania German from older relatives, with whom the informants later started to speak Pennsylvania German. Now the conversations between the informants and their children are in English or Pennsylvania German. Informants 1 and 2 added that even if they address them in Pennsylvania German, their children often answer in English.

Among the informants belonging to the b-generation, four (informants 9, 14–16) confirm their parents' assessment. Other interlocutors with whom the b-generation started to speak Pennsylvania German when they were adults include relatives and friends (informant 9) as well as older local people (informant 13). Informant 14 represents a special case because of his decision to use Pennsylvania German with all the people who could speak it, including, for a while, his wife (informant 22), at the age of twenty-one. He reports that at first, because of the unfamiliar linguistic situation, his mother (informant 6) and cousins (including informant 13) resisted and answered in English.

Four members of the c-generation (informants 17, 20, 22, 23) also name interlocutors with whom they have shifted from English to Pennsylvania German. In the case of informants 17 and 22, these include their mothers (informants 9, 12) and a number of relatives and locals. Informant 20 reports that his grandfather (informant 1) sometimes starts conversations with him in Pennsylvania German, which the grandson tries to keep in the German variety until, in most cases, they switch to English because of the grandson's lack of proficiency. Informant 23 says that he sometimes uses Pennsylvania German with older customers at the family butcher shop.

Despite their number, these examples of shifts from English to Pennsylvania German are rather irrelevant for the maintenance of Pennsylvania German within the nonsectarian group. In the case of the a-generation, the use of Pennsylvania German with their children and grandchildren happens out of forgetfulness and convenience. As older members of society, they simply assume the right to speak their native language with immediate relatives. Often, however, the shift to Pennsylvania German is restricted to formalized speech acts such as greetings and saying goodbye, particularly with the c-generation as interlocutors.

The cases in which members of the b- and c-generations report shifts from English to Pennsylvania German are all restricted to single interlocutors, usually parents and grandparents, and even in these cases the shift only takes place occasionally.

The Data

Section 2.3.3 of the questionnaire represents a condensed version of the main language use part, referring to the informants' childhood and adolescence. A typical question would be asked in the past tense: "When you were a child, did you speak Dutch to your father?" Only for the six children under the age of twelve (informants 24, 27, 28, 35, 49, 50) were the questions asked in such a way that they referred to the present time.

This section of the questionnaire does not refer to a specific time in the past; instead, the information reflects the status quo in each informant's childhood. The data allow a diachronic view over a span of approximately eighty years.

In the case of the adult informants, the reported information obviously could not be checked against participant observation. Cases of presumed overrating will be discussed below. However, comparisons of reported information with participant observation in the synchronic examinations show a high degree of agreement between observed usage and questionnaire results.

In the questionnaire, one of five categories could be marked by the fieldworker according to the informant's answer to the question "Did you speak Pennsylvania German to...?": A = always, B = sometimes, C = never, even though the interlocutor understood Pennsylvania German, D = never, because the interlocutor did not understand Pennsylvania German, E = did not apply.

To facilitate the tabulation of the results, these categories are translated in the following way in figure 3.2: A is depicted as "G" ("always

The Effects of Language Competence, Acquisition, and Use   159

Pennsylvania German"), B as "B" ("both, i.e., sometimes Pennsylvania German, sometimes English"), C as "E" ("always English, even though the interlocutor understood Pennsylvania German"), D as "e" ("always English, because the interlocutor did not understand Pennsylvania German"), E as "–" ("inapplicable").

The differentiation beween "E" and "e" is necessary because of the large number of interlocutors who had no competence in Pennsylvania German. Rather than simply determining that an informant did not speak Pennsylvania German to an interlocutor, it is important to know whether this was the case even though the latter understood Pennsylvania German.

Where the interlocutor appears in the plural form (e.g., cousins, colleagues, salespeople), the informants often report that they used Pennsylvania German with those who could speak it. In these cases normally "B" was noted (sometimes also "G" if it was absolutely clear that Pennsylvania German was used in all speech events with interlocutors who could speak it). Thus "B" can have two different meanings. With interlocutors in the singular it means "sometimes Pennsylvania German, sometimes English." With interlocutors who appear in the plural form it can also mean "Pennsylvania German with some members of that group and English with others."

The broad concept of domains is here refined by the introduction of various interlocutors. However, in some cases further refining appeared to be necessary, resulting in more specific social situations such as "teacher in class" vs. "teacher in recess."

Figure 3.2 gives an overview of the fifty informants and twenty selected interlocutors and social situations (ordered as in the questionnaire). In some cases, interlocutors that appeared separately in the questionnaire have been conjoined for reasons of clarity. If different categories were assigned to an interlocutor, the "highest" one was noted in the scale. The table therefore has to be considered rather optimistic in terms of the state of maintenance of Pennsylvania German.

The interlocutors and social situations for childhood run as follows (the respective questions in the questionnaire are in square brackets): (1) parents [31, 32], (2) older brothers and sisters [33, 34], (3) younger brothers and sisters [35, 36], (4) grandparents [37–40], (5) uncles and aunts [43, 44], (6) cousins [45, 46], (7) Dutch neighbors [48], (8) the teacher in class [50], (9) the teacher during recess [51], (10) schoolmates in class [52, 53], (11) schoolmates during recess on the school playground [54, 55], (12) schoolmates on the way to or from school [56, 57], (13) when playing with friends [58, 59], (14) colleagues [60], (15) the minister [64], (16) God [72, 73], (17) salespeople [83], (18) the doctor

160 The Effects of Language Competence, Acquisition, and Use

Figure 3.2: Overview of informants' language use in childhood and adolescence

For the symbols for the social data, see figure 1.5.

G = always Pennsylvania German
B = sometimes Pennsylvania German, sometimes English
E = always English, even though the interlocutor understood Pennsylvania German
e = always English, because the interlocutor did not understand Pennsylvania German
− = inapplicable

[85], (19) the board of supervisors [86], (20) farm animals and/or pets [87–90].[27]

On the left-hand side of the table, the social data of each informant are given. The symbols are the same as in figure 1.5.

Since no non-Pennsylvania German informant reported the use of Pennsylvania German in childhood and adolescence, the following discussion of figure 3.2 will focus on the nonsectarian and sectarian informants.

It is the common characteristic of the interlocutors parents, grandparents, uncles and aunts, and Pennsylvania German neighbors (1, 4, 5, 7) that all the members of the nonsectarian a-generation and the sectarian group, that is, all the native speakers of Pennsylvania German, report the use of Pennsylvania German. Five nonsectarian informants (9–11, 15, 17) say that they spoke both Pennsylvania German and English with some of these interlocutors. All the other informants used English only.

Although not a member of the informants' families, interlocutor 7 (Pennsylvania German neighbors) may be counted into the family and home domain because of the geographical closeness and the social importance of neighbors in small rural communities, where people often live next door to each other for their whole lives.

Since the three large informant groups live geographically separated, the term *Dutch neighbors* had a different meaning for each of them. Generally, the sectarians were likely to think of plain people. Likewise, the nonsectarians thought of members of their own group. Following the common stereotype, the non-Pennsylvania Germans normally associated plain people with this term.

Within the group of brothers and sisters, a difference in language use can be observed between those who were older than the informants and those who were younger.

The difference between columns 2 (older siblings) and 3 (younger siblings) is due to discrepant language use patterns of the nonsectarian a-generation. Of the eight members of this group, five (informants 1–3, 5, 8) spoke Pennsylvania German to their younger siblings, but seven (informants 1–4, 6–8) did so when addressing their older ones. While informant 6 spoke both Pennsylvania German and English to her younger brothers and sisters, informant 4 reports that he always used English with them. Informant 5 had no older siblings, informant 7 no younger ones. The fact that nonsectarian children did not use Pennsylvania German with their younger brothers and sisters as much as with their older ones may be considered one of the most important factors in the loss of the German variety.

The use of Pennsylvania German with siblings among the members of the b-generation is minimal. Informant 11 reports that he spoke English and Pennsylvania German with both older and younger brothers; informant 10, who did not have older siblings, used both languages with his younger brothers and sisters. All the other informants spoke only English to their siblings.

Some of the nonsectarian informants say that their brothers and sisters could not speak Pennsylvania German, others report that they could but that it still was not used. One should keep in mind that the various informants are likely to have different notions of linguistic competence.

All the sectarians except for informants 38–40 (who used both Pennsylvania German and English) report that they always spoke Pennsylvania German with all their brothers and sisters. Informants 35 and 38 did not have any older siblings.

Three members of the nonsectarian a-generation (informants 1, 2, 8) always used Pennsylvania German with their cousins (interlocutor 6). Some of the nonsectarian informants (3–7, 10, 12) report that with some of their cousins, who usually lived in separate households, they spoke English, with others Pennsylvania German. As is shown by columns 2 and 3, the use of Pennsylvania German was more extensive in the case of brothers and sisters, who normally lived in the same house.

All the sectarian informants (apart from 38–40, none of whom is older than thirty) report that they only spoke Pennsylvania German with their cousins.

There are two social situations in which all the informants used English only: with the teacher in class (interlocutor 8) and with the schoolmates in class (interlocutor 10).

Similarly, in talking to the teacher during recess (interlocutor 9) English was used almost exclusively. Only informant 3 (nonsectarian a-generation) reports that she spoke German in this situation. Her teacher may have been extremely conservative and may have allowed her students to address her in Pennsylvania German during recess, although, generally speaking, English was the language of the school domain,[28] at least in interaction with the teacher at the time when informant 3 went to school.

Column 11 (speaking to the schoolmates during recess on the school playground) differs from interlocutors 8–10. The fourteen "B"-cells display a stronger tendency toward the use of Pennsylvania German. Twelve of these informants belong to the nonsectarian group, specifically the a-generation (informants 1, 2, 4–8), the b-generation (informants 9, 10, 12, 15), and the c-generation (17), while two belong to the older Mennonite generation (informants 29, 30). Once again it is informant 3 who reports that she always spoke Pennsylvania German to her schoolmates on the playground.

The school domain has been linguistically rather progressive, both in the nonsectarian and the sectarian Pennsylvania German communities. Its language changed directly from Standard German to English long before the lifetime of the present informants. Pennsylvania German has never been used in the school domain. As soon as the students entered the school grounds, the language they used was English.

Speaking to one's schoolmates on the way to or from school (interlocutor 12) is, as it were, midway between the school and play domains. The geographic distance from the school grounds is reflected by the higher score of the German variety in comparison with interlocutors 8–11.

Pennsylvania German was spoken on the way to or from school by four of the eight members of the nonsectarian a-generation (informants 3, 4, 6, 7) and by nine of the twelve sectarian informants (29–37). Another eight informants report that they sometimes used Pennsylvania German and sometimes English; they include three sectarians (informants 38–40) and, among the nonsectarians, one member of the a-generation (informant 8), three of the b-generation (informants 9, 10, 15), and one of the c-generation (informant 17).

When asked about playing with their friends (interlocutor 13), three of the eight members of the nonsectarian a-generation (informants 3, 6, 7) said that they spoke Pennsylvania German. The other five (informants 1, 2, 4, 5, 8) used both languages, as did informants 10, 15 (b-generation), and 17 (c-generation). Their friends were generally nonsectarians.

All the sectarians apart from three (informants 38–40, who used both Pennsylvania German and English), report that they always spoke Pennsylvania German. In each case, their friends were sectarians themselves.

The pattern of column 13 resembles that of 14 (work colleagues). They differ in that two sectarian informants (38, 40) report the use of Pennsylvania German with their colleagues. These colleagues were sectarians themselves, usually relatives; here multiplex relationships were taking effect.

The large number of empty cells, particularly among the sectarian and older nonsectarian informants, reflects the social reality of women being housewives and not having outside work colleagues. Exceptions are informants 6 and 8, who report the use of both English and Pennsylvania German with their colleagues, as well as informant 5, whose work colleagues could not speak Pennsylvania German.

The only other four informants to use Pennsylvania German occasionally at work were informants 9, 10, 15, and 17. As in the case of many sectarians, some of the colleagues of these four nonsectarians were at the same time their relatives.

Interlocutors 15 (minister) and 16 (God) belong to the domain of religion. More informants used Pennsylvania German when speaking to the minister than in solitary prayer. In many cases, the extended use of Pennsylvania German with the minister could be the result of a multiplex network relation: The minister was regarded as a friend, neighbor, or, particularly in the case of the sectarians, a member of the large domain sectarian speech community, rather than as a representative of the domain of religion.

Among the nonsectarians, two members of the a-generation (informants 3, 8) always spoke Pennsylvania German with the minister. Three others (informants 4–6) and one member of the b-generation (informant 10) report the use of both Pennsylvania German and English. All the sectarians say that they used Pennsylvania German.

When speaking to God, the nonsectarians used less Pennsylvania German than the sectarians. Among the former, only two members of the a-generation (informants 7, 8) report that they prayed in Pennsylvania German. One member of the nonsectarian b-generation (informant 10) used both English and Pennsylvania German.

Column 16 reveals an interesting trend within the sectarian group. While all four members of the sectarian a-generation (informants 29, 30, 36, 37) say they used to pray in Pennsylvania German, all the informants of the b- and c-generations report the use of both Pennsylvania German and English. These results hold for both Amish and Mennonites, and suggest that English is gaining ground in the sphere of religion. This trend may reflect the slow shift of some progressive sectarian groups toward English as their language of worship.

The interlocutor salespeople (17) only refers to small local stores; for the big supermarkets all the informants report the use of English.

All the members of the nonsectarian a-generation used Pennsylvania German with salespeople in small stores. Moreover, one member of the nonsectarian b-generation (informant 15) also reports to have used

Pennsylvania German, and four other informants (9, 22, 25, 26) representing all four generations say that they vacillated between English and Pennsylvania German.

All the sectarian informants, on the other hand, report they spoke English. It should be noted that they normally associated nonplain stores with this interlocutor; in plain stores they would have used Pennsylvania German because of multiplex network relations (storekeeper and member of the sectarian community).

Speaking to the family doctor (interlocutor 18) is one of the most formal social situations. Normally, in such settings, the variety carrying high social prestige tends to be preferred. It is usually characterized by a standardized grammar and orthography formally taught at school (Ferguson 1959). Although English and Pennsylvania German are not varieties of the same language, English has to be considered the H-variety and Pennsylvania German the L-variety.

With the exception of informant 8, who is the youngest of the nonsectarian a-generation, all the members of this group report their use of Pennsylvania German with the family doctor when they were children, which, of course, implies that their doctor belonged to their own speech community. Informant 8 adds that the doctor, while speaking English to the children, used Pennsylvania German with her parents, thus copying the teacher in his language use and backing the official school policy when speaking directly to the child.

All the other nonsectarian informants say they spoke English with the doctor, even though, in most cases, he reportedly could speak Pennsylvania German. Thus, the trend toward Pennsylvania German is weaker than in the case of interlocutor 17 (salespeople), which reflects the higher degree of formality.

Without exception, the sectarian informants used English with the doctor, who normally will have been nonsectarian and possibly non-Pennsylvania German.

Speaking to the members of the board of supervisors (interlocutor 19), who have the function of a mayor in most rural areas, is also an extremely formal social situation, unless the respective member happens to be a relative (multiplex network relation).

Only four informants (4–7), all of them members of the nonsectarian a-generation, report that they always used Pennsylvania German with a member of the board; one informant (3) reports speaking both English and Pennsylvania German. Twenty-two informants say that they never spoke to a township supervisor when they were children.

Column 20 (farm animals and/or pets) shows that in addition to the nonsectarian native speakers of Pennsylvania German and the sectarians, three informants (9, 15, 17) report that as children they always spoke Pennsylvania German to their farm animals. While informants 9 and 15 belong to the nonsectarian b-generation, informant 17 is a member of the c-generation.

Six nonsectarian informants say that they used both Pennsylvania German and English with their animals. Among them there are two members of the a-generation (informants 4, 5), two of the b-generation (informants 10, 11), and two of the d-generation (informants 25, 26).

QUALITATIVE ANALYSIS

As the network and domain analysis shows, the communities of sectarian and nonsectarian Pennsylvania Germans are geographically separated. Moreover, ideologically founded differences in lifestyle have resulted in large qualitative and distributional differences in the domains.

Geographical distance is responsible for the fact that interlocutors such as neighbors, work colleagues, the teacher, and the minister are not the same for the two goups and, therefore, hardly comparable.

Differences in domain can lead to differences in language use, even if the two groups share the same interlocutors. Salespeople and doctor (interlocutors 17, 18) are a case in point. As they regarded these interlocutors as outsiders, the sectarian informants naturally used English with them, even though the interlocutors might have been able to speak Pennsylvania German (cf. informants 29, 30, 36, 37). Nonsectarian informants, on the other hand, felt free to use Pennsylvania German with these interlocutors, who belonged to their own group.

In view of these facts, it appeared advisable to establish separate implicational scales for the two groups of informants (figure 3.3). This allows a comparison of the orders of interlocutors within each speech community.

The top scale in figure 3.3 orders sectarian informants and interlocutors implicationally. The homogeneity of this group is reflected by the fact that gradation lines are found between "G" and "B" as well as between "B" and "E."[29]

The order of the informants reflects correlations with age as well as community (Amish or Mennonite). The most important dividing line is between informants 35 and 38 (ranks 9 and 10). Below it, only young

The Effects of Language Competence, Acquisition, and Use   167

Sectarians

```
                                    Interlocutors/Social situations
                              1  4  5  7 15 20 14  3  6 12 13  2 16 11  8  9 10 17 18 19
                              P  G  U  P  M  F  C  Y  C  S  P  O  G  S  T  T  S  S  D  B
                              A  R  N  I  I  A  O  O  O  C  L  L  O  C  E  E  C  A  O  O
                              R  A  C  N  R  R  U  U  U  H  A  D  D  H  A  A  H  L  C  A
                              E  N  L  I  M  M  N  N  S  O  Y  D  E  O  C  C  O  E  T  R
                              N  D  E  S     L  T  G  I  O  I     R  O  H  H  O  S  O  D
                              T  P  S  T     E  E  E  N  L  N     S  L  E  E  L  P  R  O
                              S  A     E     R  R  R  S  M  G     I  M  R  R  M  E     F
                                 R     R        S              S     A        A  P     S
                                 E                             W     T  I  I  T  L     U
                                 N                             I     E  N  N  E  E     P
                                 T                             T     S        S        E
                                 S                             H                       R
                                       A                             C  R        I     V
                                       N                             L  E        N     I
                                       D                             A  C              S
                                       A                             S  E        C     O
                                       U                             S  S        L     R
                                       N                                S        A     S
                                       T                                         S
                                       S                                         S
                                       
                    Social data
        Rnk Inf  Fam Gen Age Sex Var
         1   29   M  (a)  57  m  PG    G  G  G  G  G  G  G  G  G  G  G  G  B  E  E  E  E  E  E  E
         2   30   M  (a)  55  f  PG    G  G  G  G  G  -  G  G  G  G  G  G  B  E  E  E  E  E  E  E
         3   36   A  (a)  52  m  PG    G  G  G  G  G  -  G  G  G  G  G  G  E  E  E  E  E  E  E  E
         4   37   A  (a)  51  f  PG    G  G  G  G  G  G  G  G  G  G  G  G  E  E  E  E  E  E  E  -
         5   31   M  (b)  37  m  PG    G  G  G  G  G  G  G  G  G  G  G  G  B  E  E  E  E  e  e  -
         6   33   M  (b)  13  m  PG    G  G  G  G  G  -  G  G  G  G  G  G  B  E  E  E  E  e  e  -
         7   32   M  (b)  27  f  PG    G  G  G  G  G  -  G  G  G  G  G  G  B  E  E  E  E  e  e  -
         8   34   M  (b)  22  f  PG    G  G  G  G  G  -  G  G  G  G  G  G  B  E  E  E  E  e  e  -
         9   35   M  (c)   6  f  PG    G  G  G  G  G  -  G  G  G  G  G  G  B  E  E  E  E  e  e  -
        10   38   A  (b)  29  m  PG    G  G  G  G  G  G  G  B  B  B  B  -  B  E  E  E  E  e  e  -
        11   40   A  (b)  17  m  PG    G  G  G  G  G  G  B  B  B  B  B  B  E  E  E  E  'E e  e  -
        12   39   A  (b)  30  f  PG    G  G  G  G  G  f  B  B  B  B  B  B  E  E  E  E  'e e  e  -
```

Nonsectarians

```
                                        Interlocutors/Social situations
                              17 20 11  1 13 12 14  4  2  5  3  7  6 18 19 15 16  9  8 10
                              S  F  S  P  P  S  C  G  U  Y  C  D  B  M  G  T  T  S
                              A  A  C  A  L  C  O  R  N  O  O  O  O  O  I  E  E  C
                              L  R  H  R  A  H  L  L  C  U  U  N  O  I  R  A  A  H
                              E  M  O  E  Y  O  L  A  L  N  N  S  R  N  L  C  C  O
                              S     O  N  I  O  A  N  E  G  S  T  D  I  S  H  H  O
                              P  A  L  T  N  L  G  D  S  E  I  I  E  S  P  E  E  L
                              E  N  M  S  L  M  U  P  I     N     R  T  E  R  R  M
                              O  I  A     A  A  E  A  B     S     S  E  R     M  A
                              P  M  T     T  T  S  R  L     A     F     V  I  I  T
                              L  A  E     E  E     E  I     U     U     I  N  N  E
                              E  L  S     S  S     N  N     N     P     S        S
                                 S           I        T  G        E     O     R  C
                                 /         I  N        S          R     R  E  L  I
                                 P           R                    V        C  A  N
                                 E           E                    I        E  S
                                 T           C                    S        S  S  C
                                 S           E                    O        S     L
                                             S                    R              A
                                             S                                   S
                                                                                 S
                    Social data
        Rnk Inf  Fam Gen Age Sex Var
         1    3   1   a   77  f   E    G  G  G  G  G  -  G  G  G  G  G  B  G  B  G  G  G  E  E  E
         2    8   3   a   60  f   E    G  G  B  G  B  B  B  G  B  G  B  B  G  E  -  G  G  B  E  E
         3   10   1   b   54  m  E    G  B  B  B  B  B  B  -  B  B  B  B  B  G  G  B  E  -  E  E
         4    6   2   a   74  f   PG   G  B  B  G  G  B  G  G  G  B  G  B  B  G  G  B  E  -  E  E
         5    4   2   a   71  m   PG   G  B  B  G  G  B  E  e  -  G  -  G  G  B  G  G  B  E  E  E
         6    5   2   a   68  f   PG   G  B  B  G  B  E  -  G  G  -  -  G  B  B  G  G  B  E  E  E
         7    7   3   a   79  f   PG   G  G  B  G  G  -  G  -  G  G  G  G  B  B  G  G  B  E  E  E
         8    1   1   a   77  m   PG   G  B  B  G  B  -  G  G  G  G  G  G  G  G  G  G  E  E  E  E
         9    2   1   a   77  f   PG   G  G  B  G  B  E  B  G  G  G  G  B  G  G  -  E  E  E  E  E
        10   11   1   b   53  f   E    B  G  B  B  B  -  E  E  B  B  B  E  E  -  E  E  E  E  E  E
        11    9   1   b   57  f  PG/E  B  G  G  B  B  B  B  -  E  E  E  -  e  E  E  E  E  E
        12   15   3   b   61  m   E    G  G  B  E  B  B  B  E  -  E  E  -  e  E  E  E  E  E
        13   17   1   c   35  m   E    E  G  B  B  B  B  E  -  E  E  e  -  e  E  E  E  E  E
        14   25   2   d   31  f   E    B  B  E  E  E  e  E  E  E  E  e  -  e  E  E  E  E  E
        15   26   2   d   27  f   E    B  B  E  E  E  E  E  E  E  E  e  -  e  E  E  E  E  E
        16   22   2   c   54  f   E    B  E  E  E  E  E  E  E  -  E  E  -  E  E  E  E  E  E
        17   12   2   b   83  f   E    E  E  E  E  E  E  -  E  E  E  E  -  E  E  E  E  E  E
        18   16   3   b   37  f   E    E  E  E  E  E  E  E  E  E  -  E  E  -  E  E  E  E  E  E
        19   14   3   b   54  m   E    E  E  E  E  E  E  E  -  E  E  e  -  e  E  E  E  E  E
        20   21   1   c   23  f   E    E  E  E  E  E  E  E  -  E  E  e  -  e  E  E  E  E  E
        21   13   2   b   49  f   E    E  E  E  E  E  E  E  E  -  E  E  -  e  E  E  E  E  E
        22   20   1   c   26  m   E    E  E  E  E  E  E  E  -  E  E  E  -  e  E  E  E  E  E
        23   23   3   c   37  m   E    E  E  E  E  E  E  -  E  -  E  E  -  E  E  E  E  E  E
        24   18   1   c   30  m   E    E  E  E  E  E  e  -  E  -  E  e  -  e  E  E  E  E  E
        25   24   1   d    5  f   E    E  E  E  E  e  E  E  -  E  -  E  -  e  E  E  E  E  e
        26   27   3   d   11  m   E    E  E  e  E  e  e  -  E  -  E  e  -  E  E  E  E  E  e
        27   28   3   d    9  f   E    E  E  E  E  e  e  -  E  -  E  e  -  E  E  E  E  e  e
        28   19  1/N  (c) 30  f   E    e  E  e  e  e  e  e  e  -  e  e  -  e  e  E  e  e  e
```

Figure 3.3: Sectarian and nonsectarian language use in childhood and adolescence

For the symbols for the social data, *see* figure 1.5.

G = always Pennsylvania German
B = sometimes Pennsylvania German, sometimes English
E = always English, even though the interlocutor understood Pennsylvania German
e = always English, because the interlocutor did not understand Pennsylvania German
- = inapplicable

Amish informants are found. While informant 35 has "G" ten times and "B" once, informant 38 is characterized by only seven "G"- and five "B"-cells. This shows that with four interlocutors (younger siblings, cousins, schoolmates on the way to and from school, while playing with friends), with whom the informants above this line always spoke Pennsylvania German, those below used both German and English.

All the three b-generation Amish (informants 38–40) are located at the end of the scale, which reflects the slightly lesser linguistic conservatism of the Amish family.

The b-generation Mennonites (informants 31–35) occupy the center of the scale. The five informants show hardly any difference in their language use patterns.

The Amish a-generation (informants 36, 37) is located above the young Mennonites. These groups of informants differ in that the latter always prayed in Pennsylvania German, while the Mennonites used both languages.

The Mennonite a-generation is most conservative with respect to language use. Unlike any other informant, they report that conversations with schoolmates during recess were not exclusively in English but in both languages.

Gender is not a significant factor for the distribution of the sectarian informants.

Three large groups of interlocutors can be distinguished. When speaking to parents, grandparents, uncles and aunts, in-group neighbors, the minister, farm animals, and work colleagues, all the informants used Pennsylvania German at all times. As the first six interlocutors score exactly the same result, their order in the scale is arbitrary and follows that of the questionnaire.

In the middle group, also English was possible in the case of the younger Amish, the interlocutors including younger and older siblings, cousins, schoolmates on the way to or from school, and friends at play. In praying to God, Pennsylvania German and English were used alternatively by the younger Mennonites as well.

The third group of interlocutors includes both schoolmates and teacher during recess and in class, as well as salespeople, doctor, and members of the board of supervisors. Here the language was always English (with the exception of the two oldest Mennonites, who used either language with their schoolmates during recess). Typically, the three last interlocutors (salespeople, doctor, township supervisors) belong to the outside world.

By contrast, the continuum of the nonsectarians (bottom scale of figure 3.3) is less homogeneous.[30] There are two important dividing lines, the first one between informants 2 and 11 (ranks 9 and 10) with eleven vs. six "G"/"B"-cells, the second one between informants 17 and 25 (ranks 13 and 14) with six vs. two "G"/"B"-cells.

All eight a-generation informants are located between ranks 1 and 9. Although informant 10 is found on rank 3, his membership in the b-generation is reflected by the fact that he shows no "G"-cells but thirteen "B"-cells.

The intermediate zone (ranks 10–13) is occupied by informants 9, 11, 15, and 17. Roughly speaking, these informants form a transition zone between the native speakers of Pennsylvania German and the English monolinguals. Three of them belong to the b-generation, while one (informant 17) is a member of the c-generation.

As the network and domain analysis has shown, informant 17 has a rather traditional lifestyle. Even though his age and acquisition pattern make him a member of the c-generation, his language use pattern is similar to that of the more conservative members of the b-generation.

Four members of the b-generation (informants 12–14, 16), the rest of the c-generation, and all the d-generation informants are located on ranks 14–28. The non-Pennsylvania German who married into family 1 (informant 19) is also included in this group. From rank 18 onward, English was used with all the interlocutors at all times.

Informants 25 and 26 stand out through their alternative use of English and Pennsylvania German with salespeople and farm animals. These informants, who are sisters, belong to the nonsectarian d-generation, but are almost the same age as c-generation informant 17 (all around thirty years old). As their present competence in Pennsylvania German is very limited, informants 25 and 26 are likely to have overreported on their language use patterns. Particularly in the case of the salespeople, the interlocutor may have spoken Pennsylvania German at times while the children answered in English.

In the case of informant 18, such overratings became very obvious through his remarks in the course of the interview ("a few words," "we tried," "jokingly," "talked to Johnny once when I got drunk," "fooling around" as answers to the question whether he used Pennsylvania German with certain interlocutors). This kind of wishful thinking is characteristic of a number of informants belonging to the nonsectarian b-, c-, and d-generations and will play an important role in the discussion of language attitudes.

Although she is older than any of the members of the nonsectarian a-generation, informant 12 is a member of the first generation in her family to have English as the native language. In figure 3.3 she is found on rank 17, far below many of her younger relatives and acquaintances, which reflects her more progressive pattern of language use. She is even located below her two granddaughters (informants 25, 26). This means that her language use pattern as a child resembles that of her granddaughters more than that of her age peers.

All six informants who use Pennsylvania German predominantly today are found in the upper zone: only three informants (3, 8, 10) who speak more English today are among those informants marked as conservative by their childhood language use. Accordingly, the one informant (9) who reported that today she uses Pennsylvania German and English to the same extent is found in the transition zone. Thus, it becomes clear that there is a strong connection between the language use patterns the informants had as children and those they have today.

Unlike language acquisition, gender is not a significant factor for the distribution of the informants in figure 3.3. On the basis of the scale, it is also hard to distinguish between families 1, 2, and 3.

The salespeople form the beginning of the interlocutors' continuum. The owners of the small country stores were usually elderly native speakers of Pennsylvania German, so their stores offered an opportunity to both older and younger informants to use Pennsylvania German outside the family domain.

Farm animals and household pets are the second interlocutor from the left. However, particularly with the youngest informants the use of Pennsylvania German was often restricted to a few standardized phrases or calls.[31]

Interlocutors 11 (schoolmates during recess), 13 (playing with friends), and 12 (schoolmates on the way to or from school) can be regarded as forming a block. Especially with schoolmates during recess, however, almost all the cells containing Pennsylvania German are "B," only one being a pure "G."

Since many of the work colleagues (interlocutor 14) were at the same time relatives, they appear on the left of the scale.

The left and the center of the continuum are occupied by a large block formed by home domain interlocutors (parents, grandparents, older and younger siblings, uncles and aunts, in-group neighbors, cousins). These interlocutors are characterized by a high number of "G"-cells, particularly among the a-generation informants. The family and home domain can therefore be regarded as the last bastion of Pennsylvania German. To put it more bluntly, as soon as Pennsylvania German is not spoken at the dinner table any more, there is no other area of life where it is used in all situations.[32]

The seven interlocutors on the right of the continuum represent a block of official settings. The doctor, the township supervisors, and the minister are outstanding public figures.

The three interlocutors on the far right (teacher during recess, teacher in class, schoolmates in class) all belong to the school domain. Unlike interlocutors 11 (schoolmates during recess) and 12 (schoolmates on the way to or from school), they describe such formal situations as speaking in class and/or speaking with the teacher.

Finally, a comparison of the orders of the interlocutors in the sectarians' and the nonsectarians' scales shows that for the sectarians the salespeople, who offered a good opportunity to speak Pennsylvania German to the nonsectarians, were part of the outside world and, therefore, dealt with in English, just like the doctor and the supervisors. By contrast, the minister was always spoken to in Pennsylvania German by the sectarians, but, for lack of competence, mostly in English by the nonsectarians.

In both groups, the language of the school, at least in its official settings, was English. Likewise, in both groups, Pennsylvania German was used most consistently in the home domain.

The use of Pennsylvania German in childhood was more extensive in the sectarian group. Only the members of the nonsectarian a-generation report a similar degree of Pennsylvania German.

PRESENT-DAY LANGUAGE USE

GENERAL QUESTIONS

Questionnaire section 2.3.4 served to elicit some general information on present spoken and written language use patterns.

All the sectarian informants answered "Pennsylvania German" to question 99 ("What language do you usually talk in when you speak during the day?").

Of the eight nonsectarian native speakers of Pennsylvania German, six (informants 1, 2, 4–7) still use their native language more often than their second language. Only informants 3 and 8 are exceptions in using more English.

Informant 3 blames her neighbors and children, who speak only English, for her language use. This remark is a good example of the a-generation's negative assessment of their children's proficiency in Pennsylvania German. It should be noted that with his near-native competence the son of informant 3, informant 10, is one of the best speakers of the b-generation.

Informant 8 is married to informant 15, a native speaker of English; they use English with one another.

With one exception, all the members of the nonsectarian generations b through d identify English as their predominant language. Informant 9 (b-generation) reports, however, that she uses the two languages equally, English more at work in the chicken house and Pennsylvania German with a number of family members. Her son, informant 17 (c-generation), says that he uses a lot of Pennsylvania German during the butchering season.

With the help of question 100 ("With whom and how long did you speak Dutch during the last two days?"), the informants were prompted to name concrete interlocutors so that their more unspecified answers to question 99 could be checked against reality.

In the case of the sectarian informants, family and community members were mentioned. Some informants (e.g., 30) said that they had not spoken any English over the past two days. Informant 29 had spoken English only with the (non-Pennsylvania German) woman for whom his wife babysat and with a farm supply dealer.

The members of the nonsectarian a-generation typically name their spouses, children, brothers and sisters, storekeepers, and church friends. Answers from members of the b-generation include parents, aunts and uncles, brothers and sisters, friends, colleagues, customers, and storekeepers. The members of the c-generation mainly name grandparents and great-aunts and great-uncles, adding, however, that only a few sentences are spoken. One informant (18) reports that he sang the song "Schnitzelbank" at his grandparents' wedding anniversary. None of the members of the d-generation could name any recent concrete Pennsylvania German interlocutor.

Questions 101–128 deal with the written medium. Pennsylvania German is read by all the informants except for the non-Pennsylvania Germans, four members of the nonsectarian a-generation (informants 1, 2, 4, 7) and informant 9 (b-generation). All the informants read English, but only the sectarians say they read Bible High German. Informants 8 and 15, who have traveled to Germany a lot, say they also read Standard German, particularly letters from German friends.

Types of Pennsylvania German texts read by the informants include prose, poetry, plays, notes, and, most importantly, the small articles in the weekly Pennsylvania German corners of the local newspapers.

Considerably fewer informants state that they also write Pennsylvania German. This statement was made by all groups except for the non-Pennsylvania Germans (informants 8, 13–15, 22, 25, 32). While all the informants report that they write English, none writes Bible High German or Standard German.

Among the written texts in Pennsylvania German are notes (informants 13, 14, 22, 25, who all belong to nonsectarian family 2), diary entries (informant 32, a Mennonite) and letters (informants 8, 14, 22, 32). In the letters, however, mostly short phrases are used such as on a Christmas greeting card, or phrases are quoted that "might have been used by the children," as informant 32 explained.

INTERLOCUTORS AND SOCIAL SITUATIONS

Language Use within the Community

Figure 3.4 shows the patterns of present-day language use within the community. The table is based on the data received for questionnaire sections 2.3.5–13. Apart from the last one, which examines miscellaneous situations, these sections cover the domains introduced in connection with the network and domain survey.

The phrasing of the questions strictly refers to the present. Thus, figure 3.4 gives purely synchronic data. A typical question runs as follows: "Do you speak Dutch to your father?" The informants were asked to answer in the same manner as in the childhood section: A = always, B = sometimes, C = never, even though the interlocutor understands Pennsylvania German, D = never, because the interlocutor does not understand Pennsylvania German, E = does not apply. The answers are translated into symbols in the same way as in figure 3.2.

To facilitate an overview, twenty central interlocutors representing each domain (N1–8) at least once were selected. In some cases, interlocutors were conjoined again. Frequently, differentiations made by the questionnaire were not reflected in the data. For instance, none of the informants reported a discrepancy in language use when speaking to the doctor or members of the board of supervisors either privately or in official business.

174 The Effects of Language Competence, Acquisition, and Use

Figure 3.4: Overview of informants' present-day language use

```
                                    Interlocutors/Social situations
                                    1  2  3  4  5  6  7  8  9 10 11 12 13 14 15 16 17 18 19 20

                                    P  S  S  C  G  G  U  N  C  P  P  P  C  T  M  G  S  D  S  A  O
                                    A  I  P  H  R  R  N  E  O  G  G  O  E  I  O  A  O  U  N  N
                                    R  B  O  I  A  A  C  P  U        L  A  N  D  L  C  P  I  E
                                    E  L  U  L  N  N  L  H  S  N  F  L  C  I     E  T  E  M  S
                                    N  I  S  D  D  D  E  E  I  E  R  E  H  S     S  O  R  A  E
                                    T  N  D  R  P  C  S  W  N  I  I  A  E  T     P  R  V  L  L
                                    S  G  E  E  A  H  /  S  S  G  E  G  R  E     E     I  S  F
                                       S     N  R  I  A     /  H  N  U  S  R     O     S  /
                                             N  E  L  U  N  B  D     S           P     O  P
                                                T  R  T  E  I  O  S              L     R  E
                                                D  E  E  C  S  R                 E     E  T
                                                S  E  S     S                           S
                                                N

              Social data
Inf  Fam Gen Age Sex Var                                                                       G   B   E   e   -

1    1   a   77  m   PG    -  G  G  B  -  e  G  B  B  e  G  -  -  -  e  -  G  e  G  E  G     7   3   1   4   5
2    1   a   77  f   PG    -  G  G  B  -  e  -  B  B  B  e  G  -  -  -  e  -  G  e  B  E  E   4   4   2   4   6
3    1   a   77  f   E     -  G  -  B  -  E  B  B  B  B  B  -  -  -  e  E  B  E  -  -  B     1   8   3   1   7
4    2   a   71  m   PG    -  G  G  B  -  e  G  E  G  G  G  -  -  -  e  E  G  E  G  B  G     9   2   3   2   4
5    2   a   68  f   PG    -  G  G  B  -  e  G  E  E  G  G  -  -  -  e  E  G  E  G  B  G     8   2   4   2   4
6    2   a   74  f   PG    -  G  -  B  -  e  G  G  G  G  G  -  -  -  e  E  G  e  E  B  G     8   2   2   3   5
7    3   a   79  f   PG    -  G  -  B  -  e  -  B  G  E  G  -  -  -  e  E  B  E  e  -  G  G  5   3   2   3   7
8    3   a   60  f   E     -  G  E  E  -  e  e  G  E  B  B  B  -  -  e  E  G  E  E  E  G     4   3   7   2   4
9    1   b   57  f   PG/E  B  B  B  -  B  -  e  B  B  B  B  B  -  -  e  E  B  E  B  B  G     1  12   2   2   3
10   1   b   54  m   E     B  B  B  -  e  -  e  B  B  B  B  B  -  -  e  E  E  E  B  E  G     1   9   4   3   3
11   1   b   53  f   E     E  E  B  e  -  e  E  E  E  E  E  -  -  e  E  E  E  E  E  G        1   1  12   3   3
12   2   b   83  f   E     -  B  -  B  -  e  -  B  B  B  -  -  -  e  E  E  e  e  E  -  B     0   6   2   5   7
13   2   b   49  m   E     B  B  -  -  -  -  B  e  G  B  B  B  -  -  e  E  G  E  B  b  B     2   9   2   2   5
14   2   b   54  m   E     G  B  B  -  -  -  G  e  B  G  G  B  -  -  e  B  e  e  B  G  G     6   6   0   5   3
15   3   b   61  m   E     B  E  E  -  e  -  B  E  E  B  B  B  -  -  e  E  E  E  E  B  B     0   7   9   2   2
16   3   b   37  f   E     E  E  E  e  -  -  -  E  e  E  E  E  -  -  e  E  E  E  E  E  E     0   0  15   2   3
17   1   c   35  m   E     B  B  -  -  -  B  -  B  e  B  B  B  -  -  e  E  B  e  B  G  B     1  10   1   3   5
18   1   c   30  m   E     E  E  e  e  -  -  -  e  e  E  E  -  -  e  E  E  E  E  E  B        0   2  13   3   2
19   1/N (c)  30  f   E     e  e  e  -  -  -  -  -  e  e  E  E  -  -  e  E  E  E  E  E  e     0   0   7  10   3
20   1   c   26  m   E     E  E  -  e  -  -  -  E  e  E  E  E  -  -  e  E  E  E  E  E  B     0   2  11   4   3
21   1   c   23  f   E     E  e  e  -  E  -  E  e  e  E  E  -  -  e  E  E  e  E  E  e        0   0   9   8   3
22   2   c   54  f   E     B  B  B  e  -  -  B  e  B  E  B  e  -  -  e  E  B  e  -  G  B     1   8   2   5   4
23   3   c   37  m   E     E  E  E  e  e  -  B  e  E  E  E  E  -  -  E  E  E  E  E  B        0   2  14   2   2
24   1   d    5  f   E     E  -  -  -  -  E  -  -  -  E  e  -  -  e  e  E  E  -  E  e        0   0   7   6   7
25   2   d   31  f   E     E  E  -  -  B  -  E  -  e  -  E  e  e  e  E  E  e  B  E           0   2   7   6   5
26   2   d   27  f   E     E  E  -  -  B  -  E  -  E  e  e  e  E  E  E  e  B  E              0   2   7   6   5
27   3   d   11  m   E     E  e  -  -  E  -  E  -  e  E  e  -  e  E  E  E  E  -  E  e        0   0   9   5   6
28   3   d    9  f   E     E  e  -  -  E  -  E  -  E  e  -  e  E  E  E  -  E  e              0   0   9   5   6
29   M   (a) 57  m   PG    G  G  G  G  -  G  G  G  G  G  G  -  -  G  G  e  e  G  G           14   0   0   3   4
30   M   (a) 55  f   PG    -  G  G  G  -  G  G  G  G  G  -  -  G  G  e  e  G  G             13   0   0   3   4
31   M   (b) 37  m   PG    G  G  G  G  -  G  G  G  G  G  -  -  G  B  e  e  G  G             13   1   0   3   3
32   M   (b) 27  f   PG    G  G  G  G  -  G  G  G  G  G  -  -  G  B  e  e  G  G             13   1   0   3   3
33   M   (b) 13  m   PG    G  G  -  -  G  -  G  G  G  G  -  E  G  G  e  e  G  G             11   1   1   3   4
34   M   (b) 22  f   PG    G  G  G  G  -  G  G  G  G  G  -  -  G  B  e  e  G  G             13   1   0   3   3
35   M   (c)  6  f   PG    G  G  -  -  G  -  G  -  G  G  G  -  E  G  e  e  -  G  G          10   1   1   2   6
36   A   (a) 52  m   PG    G  G  G  G  -  B  G  G  G  G  -  -  G  G  e  e  G  G             13   1   0   3   3
37   A   (a) 51  f   PG    G  G  G  G  -  B  G  G  G  G  -  -  G  G  e  e  G  G             13   1   0   3   3
38   A   (b) 29  m   PG    G  G  B  E  G  -  G  G  G  G  -  -  G  E  e  e  G  G             11   1   2   3   3
39   A   (b) 30  f   PG    G  G  B  E  G  -  G  G  G  G  -  -  G  E  e  e  G  G             11   1   2   3   3
40   A   (b) 17  m   PG    G  G  -  -  G  -  G  B  G  G  -  -  G  G  e  e  G  G             11   1   0   3   5
41   N   (a) 81  f   E     -  E  -  e  -  e  -  E  -  -  -  -  e  E  e  e  e  E  E           0   0   5   7   8
42   N   (b) 63  m   E     -  e  e  e  -  e  e  e  E  -  -  -  e  E  e  e  E  e             0   0   2  12   6
43   N   (b) 50  m   E     e  e  e  -  e  e  e  E  E  -  -  e  E  e  e  E  e                0   0   4  13   3
44   N   (b) 52  f   E     E  e  e  -  e  e  e  E  E  -  -  e  E  e  e  E  e                0   0   5  12   3
45   N   (b) 54  m   E     -  e  e  e  -  e  -  E  -  -  e  E  e  e  E  e                   0   0   3  12   5
46   N   (b) 52  f   E     -  -  e  e  -  e  e  -  E  -  -  e  E  e  e  E  e                0   0   3  11   6
47   N   (c) 31  m   E     e  e  e  E  -  e  e  -  -  e  -  E  e  e  E  e                   0   0   3  13   4
48   N   (c) 30  f   E     e  -  e  e  -  e  e  -  -  e  E  e  e  E  e                      0   0   2  11   7
49   N   (d)  8  m   E     e  e  -  e  -  e  -  -  e  E  e  e  -  E  e                      0   0   2  10   8
50   N   (d)  5  f   E     e  e  -  e  -  e  -  -  e  E  e  e  -  E  e                      0   0   2  10   8

                  G    12 20 11  7  8  2 18 11 15 17 19  0  0 12  5  7  0  3 16 22
                  B     6  7  6  9  5  2  8  7 11  7  9  4  0  0  6  5  0  6  8  9
                  E    12  9  4  4  6  1  9  5 10 14 11  4  2  5 37 14 16 11 24  5
                  e     6 11 11 16  2 18 11 19 14  4  5  6  5 33  0 24 34  9  0 14
                  -    14  3 18 14 29 27  4  8  0  8  6 36 43  0  2  0  0 21  2  0
```

For the symbols for the social data, see figure 1.5.

G = always Pennsylvania German
B = sometimes Pennsylvania German, sometimes English
E = always English, even though the interlocutor understands Pennsylvania German
e = always English, because the interlocutor does not understand Pennsylvania German
- = inapplicable

The Effects of Language Competence, Acquisition, and Use   175

The guidelines for the evaluation are the same as those presented above, in the section on childhood and adolescence. Therefore, figure 3.4 gives a rather optimistic impression of the state of maintenance of Pennsylvania German. Cases in which the fieldworker had the feeling that informants overrated their use of Pennsylvania German will be discussed later.

The interlocutors are (question numbers in brackets): (1) parents [133, 134], (2) brothers and sisters [135–38], (3) spouse [139, 140], (4) children [141, 142], (5) grandparents [143–46], (6) grandchildren [147, 148], (7) uncles and aunts [153], (8) nephews and nieces [154], (9) cousins [155, 156], (10) Dutch neighbors [160–63], (11) Dutch friends [164–67], (12) colleagues [168, 169], (13) teachers [186, 187], (14) the minister [209], (15) God [211–16], (16) salespeople [264], (17) the doctor [270–71], (18) the board of supervisors [276, 278], (19) farm animals and/or pets [301, 302; 317, 318], (20) oneself [319].

As all the non-Pennsylvania German informants are monolingual, the discussion of figure 3.4 will center on the nonsectarians' and sectarians' language use patterns.

The interlocutor parents is depicted in column 1. None of the nonsectarian a-generation informants has parents still living. However, there is one informant belonging to the b-generation (14) who always uses Pennsylvania German with his mother (informant 6).

Otherwise, there are only four members of the b-generation (9, 10, 13, 15) and two of the c-generation (17, 22) who use both languages with their parents in the nonsectarian group. The present-day use of Pennsylvania German is a secondary development, which in most cases did not start until late adolescence. All these informants were raised in English.

All the sectarians whose parents are still alive report the exclusive use of Pennsylvania German.

Brothers and sisters (interlocutor 2) are always addressed in Pennsylvania German by all the members of the nonsectarian a-generation and all the sectarian informants. While the b-generation uses both languages (exceptions: informants 11, 15, 16), most members of the c- and d-generations use English exclusively (exceptions: informants 17, 22).

As to the language use with one's spouse (interlocutor 3), four informants (1, 2, 4, 5) of the nonsectarian a-generation report the exclusive use of Pennsylvania German, while informant 8 always speaks English with her husband (informant 15), who is a native speaker of English. The other informants belonging to the a-generation are widows.

Both Pennsylvania German and English are only used by two couples (informants 14 and 22, 10 and 11). In both cases the use of English clearly predominates.

Not all the sectarians use Pennsylvania German exclusively. The two Beachy Amish (informants 38, 39) address each other in either language.

With children (interlocutor 4), Pennsylvania German is less prevalent. Within the nonsectarian a-generation both languages are used (informants 1–7). Only the youngest member of this group (informant 8) always speaks English to her children. Informants 4 and 5 report that they speak both languages with their son (informant 13), but exclusively English with their daughters. This is one of the few cases of discrepant language use between the genders. However, since the two daughters, who are seven and nine years younger than their brother, both have left the Pennsylvania German area, the difference in gender may not even be at the heart of this split.

Two older members of the b-generation (informants 9, 12) also report the use of both languages.

With the exception of the two Beachy Amish (informants 38, 39), all the sectarian informants who have children (29–32, 34, 36, 37) always speak Pennsylvania German to them.

Of the nonsectarians, informants 17, 18, 20, 25, and 26 report the use of both languages with their grandparents (interlocutor 5). Participant observation showed, however, that, with the exception of informant 17, the use of Pennsylvania German is restricted to occasional phrases, such as "hello," "goodbye," and "thank you." Longer conversations involving only the informants and their grandparents are normally conducted in English. This is reflected by the a-generation's almost unanimous report of "e" (no competence in Pennsylvania German) for their grandchildren in column 6.

All the sectarian informants who still have grandparents always speak Pennsylvania German to them.

Nonsectarian informants who have grandchildren (interlocutor 6) usually cannot speak Pennsylvania German to them as the latter are monolingual.

Both members of the Mennonite a-generation (informants 29, 30) always use Pennsylvania German with their grandchildren. The two informants belonging to the Amish a-generation (36, 37) speak Pennsylvania German to most of their grandchildren, but English at least sometimes to some of them, for example, the children of informants 38 and 39, who are raised in English by their parents. None of the other sectarian informants has grandchildren yet.

Apart from informant 3 ("B"), all the members of the nonsectarian a-generation who still have uncles and aunts (informants 1, 4–6, 8) always speak Pennsylvania German with them (interlocutor 7). Informant 14 (b-generation) also follows this practice.

The two languages are used by most of the other b-generation informants (9, 10, 13, 15) and the older members of the c-generation (informants 17, 22, 23).

The columns for interlocutors 7 (uncles and aunts) and 1 (parents) would be practically identical if it were not for the latter's large number of inapplicable cells for the members of the nonsectarian a-generation.

All the sectarians use exclusively Pennsylvania German with their uncles and aunts.

Among the nonsectarians, only informant 6 says she uses exclusively Pennsylvania German with her nephews and nieces (interlocutor 8). This pattern, however, refers to only one nephew (informant 13) as the others cannot speak Pennsylvania German.

Six other nonsectarians (informants 1–3, 7, 9, 10) say they use both languages.

All the sectarians except for one young Amish (informant 40) always address their nephews and nieces (interlocutor 8) in Pennsylvania German.

Three informants belonging to the nonsectarian a-generation (4, 6, 7) always speak Pennsylvania German to their cousins (interlocutor 9). Four others (informants 1–3, 8) use both languages, and only one (informant 5) uses English exclusively.

Beyond the a-generation, both languages are used by informants 9, 10, 12–14 (b-generation) as well as by informants 17 and 22 (c-generation). Participant observation has shown that in most cases the language competence of the cousins varies and that the language use patterns depend on the interlocutors' competence.

All the sectarian informants use Pennsylvania German exclusively.

In the nonsectarian group, informants 4–6 (a-generation) as well as 13 and 14 (b-generation) always speak Pennsylvania German to their neighbors (interlocutor 10). Two members of the a-generation (informants 1, 2) say they have no Pennsylvania German neighbors, while one (informant 7) always speaks English even though her interlocutors know Pennsylvania German. The other two a-generation informants (3, 8) along with informants 9, 10, 12, 15 (b-generation) and 17 (c-generation) use the two languages.

All the sectarians report the exclusive use of Pennsylvania German. Of the non-Pennsylvania Germans, only informants 43 and 44 have Pennsylvania German neighbors (a number of Amish families living near Berwick).

Even though they do not belong to the family domain, Pennsylvania German friends (interlocutor 11) seem to carry a similar degree of intimacy as family members. All the sectarians and almost all the members of the nonsectarian a-generation (with the exception of informants 3 and 8) use exclusively Pennsylvania German when speaking to an intragroup friend.

Most b-generation informants (except for 11 and 16) use Pennsylvania German at least sometimes. However, participant observation has shown that the language competence of the interlocutor plays a decisive role and that, on the whole, English prevails.

Below the b-generation, only informants 17 and 22 (c-generation) sometimes use Pennsylvania German when speaking to their friends.

Four members of the nonsectarian b-generation (informants 9, 13–15) speak both Pennsylvania German and English to their work colleagues (interlocutor 12), but no informant uses Pennsylvania German exclusively.

The large number of inapplicable cells in column 12 is due to the fact that retired people, housewives, children, and farmers normally have no colleagues.

Interlocutor 13 (teachers) is only applicable to the school age informants. No child speaks Pennsylvania German to the teachers at school, even though, as in the case of the two Mennonite students (informants 33, 35), their teacher is able to speak it.

Interlocutor 14 (minister) divides the nonsectarians from the sectarians most clearly. While the latter always speak Pennsylvania German to their spiritual leaders, the language used with the minister in the nonsectarian (as well as in the non-Pennsylvania German) group is always English. In most cases (exceptions: informants 16, 18, 23, 27, 28), the ministers are reported to have no competence in Pennsylvania German.

Column 15 gives the results for praying. Of all the nonsectarians, informant 14, who fervently supports the maintenance of Pennsylvania German, is the only one to pray in Pennsylvania German at least sometimes.

Of the twelve sectarian informants, five (informants 29, 30, 36, 37, 40) report that they always address God in Pennsylvania German. The majority of them belongs to the older generation. The younger Mennonites (informants 31–35) pray in both languages, the two Beachy Amish (informants 38, 39) in English.

Column 16 (salespeople) is characterized by seven cases of exclusive use of Pennsylvania German (informants 1, 2, 4–6, 8, 13).[33]

Five nonsectarian informants (3, 7, 9, 17, 22), who belong to the a-, b-, and c-generations, report that they use both Pennsylvania German and English in local stores.

All the sectarians report the use of English as none of the storekeepers can speak Pennsylvania German. Obviously, they thought of nonplain stores when asked what language they use with the storekeepers in town.

No informant ever speaks Pennsylvania German to the family doctor (interlocutor 17). While about half the nonsectarians say that their physician can speak some Pennsylvania German, the sectarian informants unanimously deny such competence.

Column 18 (board of supervisors) resembles column 16 (salespeople). Exclusive use of Pennsylvania German is reported by informants 1, 4, and 5 (all members of the nonsectarian a-generation). Both Pennsylvania German and English are used by informants 2 (a-generation), 9, 10, 13, 14 (b-generation), and 17 (c-generation).

In the case of the nonsectarians, the multiplexity of relationships may be responsible for the use of the L-variety (Pennsylvania German) with an interlocutor usually associated with a fairly formal setting. As the member of the board of supervisors is often at the same time a relative, friend, or neighbor, the use of Pennsylvania German is normal.

Nevertheless, the informants' age (or generation) and competence plays a role, too. The younger nonsectarians simply do not have enough competence in Pennsylvania German allowing them to use it. Likewise, the interlocutors' language competence is important. Informants 25 and 26 (d-generation) report that the members of their board of supervisors cannot speak Pennsylvania German.

The same is unanimously reported by the sectarian informants. Nevertheless, the latter would not speak Pennsylvania German to a township supervisor even if he or she had the competence simply because the supervisor is a representative of the outside world, and indeed of the government.

The structure of column 19 (farm animals and/or pets) is quite surprising. Among the nonsectarians, it is not so much the members of the a-generation (only informant 7) who use Pennsylvania German exclusively, but younger informants such as informant 14 (b-generation) as well as informants 17 and 22 (c-generation).

In addressing farm animals or pets, both languages are used by informants 4–6 (a-generation), 9, 13, 15 (b-generation), and 25, 26 (d-generation).

Five informants forming a small family within family 2, including informant 6 (a-generation), her son (informant 14: b-generation) and his wife (informant 22: c-generation) as well as their daughters (informants 25, 26: d-generation), all report that they use at least some Pennsylvania German with their farm animals.

All the sectarians speak Pennsylvania German to their animals.

The situation with the most extensive use of Pennsylvania German is that of the informants talking to themselves (interlocutor 20). However, the data in this column refer to a very specific situation as described to the informants in question 319 ("Imagine you stub your toe and say something, will it be in Dutch?"). Thus, "speaking to oneself" is narrowed down to exclamations of pain or curses.

Pennsylvania German is used exclusively by all the sectarians, almost all the members of the nonsectarian a-generation (except for informants 2, 3) and four members of the b-generation (informants 9–11, 14). It is used occasionally by the rest of the b-generation (except for informant 16) and the c-generation (except for informant 21).[34]

Quantitative Analysis

The qualitative analysis of the data will be preceded by a brief quantitative one. Various diagrams will show which varieties are used by selected groups of informants with the twenty interlocutors specified in figure 3.4. The groups under examination will be differentiated by community and, within the nonsectarian group, by generation.

Figure 3.4 showed that the non-Pennsylvania German informants, for lack of competence, never use any Pennsylvania German. They will

The Effects of Language Competence, Acquisition, and Use   181

therefore be included neither in the quantitative nor in the qualitative analysis.

Figure 3.5 gives the percentages of language use of the sectarian and nonsectarian groups.

	Nonsectarians Number	%	Sectarians Number	%
G	59	14.0	147	74.2
B	105	24.9	10	5.1
E	159	37.8	6	3.0
e	98	23.3	35	17.7

Figure 3.5: Percentages of language use of nonsectarians and sectarians with the twenty interlocutors specified in figure 3.4

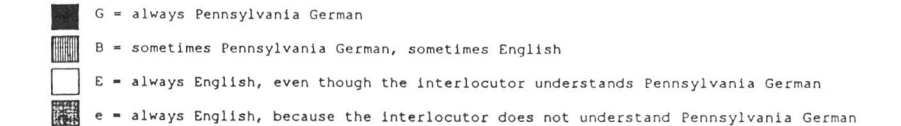

G = always Pennsylvania German
B = sometimes Pennsylvania German, sometimes English
E = always English, even though the interlocutor understands Pennsylvania German
e = always English, because the interlocutor does not understand Pennsylvania German

The share of exclusive use of Pennsylvania German is more than five times higher in the sectarian group than it is in the nonsectarian group (74.2% vs. 14.0%). By contrast, the use of both English and Pennsylvania German is almost five times higher in the nonsectarian than in the sectarian group (24.9% vs. 5.1%). While the use of English despite the interlocutors' competence in Pennsylvania German is only 3.0% for the sectarians, it is 37.8% for the nonsectarians. On the other hand, use of English because of the interlocutors' lack of competence is more similar in both groups (nonsectarians: 23.3% vs. sectarians: 17.7%).

These results document the stable diglossia[35] existing within the sectarian community. On the whole, more situations are handled exclusively in Pennsylvania German than in Pennsylvania German and English. If interlocutors know Pennsylvania German, it is most often used, as this linguistic competence characterizes them as group members.

182   The Effects of Language Competence, Acquisition, and Use

The relation between "G" and "B" is reversed in the nonsectarian group, which documents its current involvement in a shift from Pennsylvania German to English. Situations in which Pennsylvania German is always used are rare, not only in comparison with the sectarians, but also with the number of situations which are handled in both languages.

Figure 3.6 shows the percentages of language use of the four nonsectarian generations.

	a-generation		b-generation		c-generation		d-generation	
	Number	%	Number	%	Number	%	Number	%
G	46	39.0	11	8.4	2	2.0	0	0.0
B	27	22.9	50	38.2	24	23.8	4	5.6
E	24	20.3	46	35.1	50	49.5	39	54.9
e	21	17.8	24	18.3	25	24.7	28	39.5

Figure 3.6: Percentages of language use of the four nonsectarian generations with the twenty interlocutors specified in figure 3.4

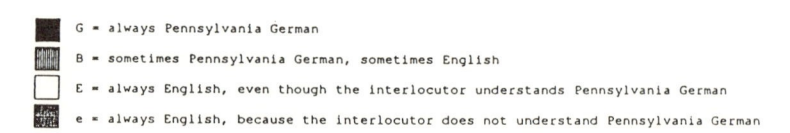

G = always Pennsylvania German
B = sometimes Pennsylvania German, sometimes English
E = always English, even though the interlocutor understands Pennsylvania German
e = always English, because the interlocutor does not understand Pennsylvania German

The share of exclusive use of Pennsylvania German decreases from 39.0% for the a-generation via 8.4% for the b-generation and 2.0% for the c-generation to 0% for the d-generation. At the same time, the pattern of the percentages of the alternative use of both languages is rather irregular. While for the a-generation it is 22.9%, it reaches its maximum of 38.2% in the b-generation. The rate for the c-generation (23.8%) is still higher than the one for the a-generation. In the d-generation, it drops to 5.6%. Accordingly, the use of English (both "E" and "e") rises steadily from the a- to the d-generation.

Altogether, the decisive point in the change is between the a- and the b-generation. Thus, differences in language use patterns reflect the differences in language acquisition, more specifically in native languages.

Only the pattern of the nonsectarian a-generation resembles that of the sectarian group. In both cases, more situations are handled exclusively in Pennsylvania German than in the two languages. However, while the ratio is 74 to 5 for the sectarians, it is reduced to 39 to 23 for the nonsectarian a-generation. This is evidence that even the oldest nonsectarian generation in the survey does not show the same stable diglossia as the sectarian group.

The shift from Pennsylvania German to English, which is extremely accelerated between the a- and b-generations, almost reaches its final stage in the d-generation. While there are no cases of exclusive use of Pennsylvania German, even the alternative use of both languages is only 5.6%. It seems safe to predict that in the next generation it will be zero.

In sum, the sectarians use far more Pennsylvania German than the nonsectarians. While for the sectarians the use of Pennsylvania German prevails in all age groups, the exclusive use of Pennsylvania German among the nonsectarians is only found in the oldest generations and with a limited number of interlocutors. Generally speaking, the younger the nonsectarian informants are, the less Pennsylvania German they use.

Qualitative Analysis

As was the case for the data for childhood and adolescence language use, the qualitative analysis of the synchronic data will be based on two separate implicational scales (figure 3.7).

The top scale of figure 3.7 orders the sectarian informants and their interlocutors implicationally. Interlocutor 12 (colleagues) has been disregarded: the column contained only inapplicable cells as the sectarian informants are all farmers, housewives, or schoolchildren. Gradation lines are between "G" and "B" as well as between "B" and "E"/"e."[36]

The interlocutors are divided into two major groups. The one on the left consists of interlocutors belonging to intra-community domains. From left to right, they are brothers and sisters (interlocutor 2), uncles and aunts (7), cousins (9), sectarian neighbors (10), sectarian friends (11), spiritual leaders (14), farm animals (19), the informants themselves (20), parents (1), grandparents (5), and nephews and nieces (8). Except for one case within the column of interlocutor 8 (nephews and nieces), where informant 40 reports the use of both languages, all the sectarian informants always use Pennsylvania German with these interlocutors. In fact, the first eight columns do not even differ through the presence of

184   The Effects of Language Competence, Acquisition, and Use

Sectarians

```
                              Interlocutors/Social situations
                        2  7  9 10 11 14 19 20  1  5  8  3  4 15  6 13 16 17 18
                        S  U  C  P  P  M  A  O  P  G  N  S  C  G  T  S  D  S
                        I  N  O  G  G  I  N  N  A  R  E  C  H  A  E  A  O  U
                        B  C  U  I  F  N  N  N  R  A  P  H  I  R  A  L  C  P
                        L  L  S  N  I  I  I  I  E  N  H  O  L  D  C  E  T  E
                        I  E  I  E  R  M  S  E  N  D  E  O  D  E  H  S  O  R
                        N  S  N  I  S  A  T  L  T  P  W  L  R  N  E  P  R  V
                        G  /  S  G  T  L  E  F  S  A  E     E     R  E     I
                           A     H  E  E  S  /     R           N        O  S
                           U     B  N  S     P     E                    P  O
                           N     O  D        E     N                    L  R
                           T     R           T     T                    E  S
                           S     S                 S
                                                   /
                                                   N
                                                   I
                                                   E
                                                   C
                                                   E
                                                   S
      Social data
 Rnk Inf Fam Gen Age Sex Var
  1  29   M  (a)  57  m  PG    G  G  G  G  G  G  G  G  -  G  G  G  G  |- e  e  e  e
  2  30   M  (a)  55  f  PG    G  G  G  G  G  G  G  G  -  -  G  G  G  G| - e  e  e  e
  3  36   A  (a)  52  m  PG    G  G  G  G  G  G  G  G  -  -  G  G  G  G| B - e  e  e
  4  37   A  (a)  51  f  PG    G  G  G  G  G  G  G  G  -  G  G  G  G| B  - e  e  e
  5  40   A  (b)  17  m  PG    G  G  G  G  G  G  G  G  G  B  -  -  G| -  - e  e  e
  6  31   M  (b)  37  m  PG    G  G  G  G  G  G  G  G  G  G  G  G| B  -  - e  e  e
  7  32   M  (b)  27  f  PG    G  G  G  G  G  G  G  G  G  G  G  G| B  -  - e  e  e
  8  34   M  (b)  22  f  PG    G  G  G  G  G  G  G  G  G  G  G  G| B  -  - e  e  e
  9  33   M  (b)  13  m  PG    G  G  G  G  G  G  G  G  G  G  G| -  -  B  - e  e  e
 10  35   M  (c)   6  f  PG    G  G  G  G  G  G  G  G  G  -  -  -  B  E  e  e  e
 11  38   A  (b)  29  m  PG    G  G  G  G  G  G  G  G  G  B  E  E  -  -  e  e  e
 12  39   A  (b)  30  f  PG    G  G  G  G  G  G  G  G  G  B  E  E  -  -  e  e  e
```

Nonsectarians

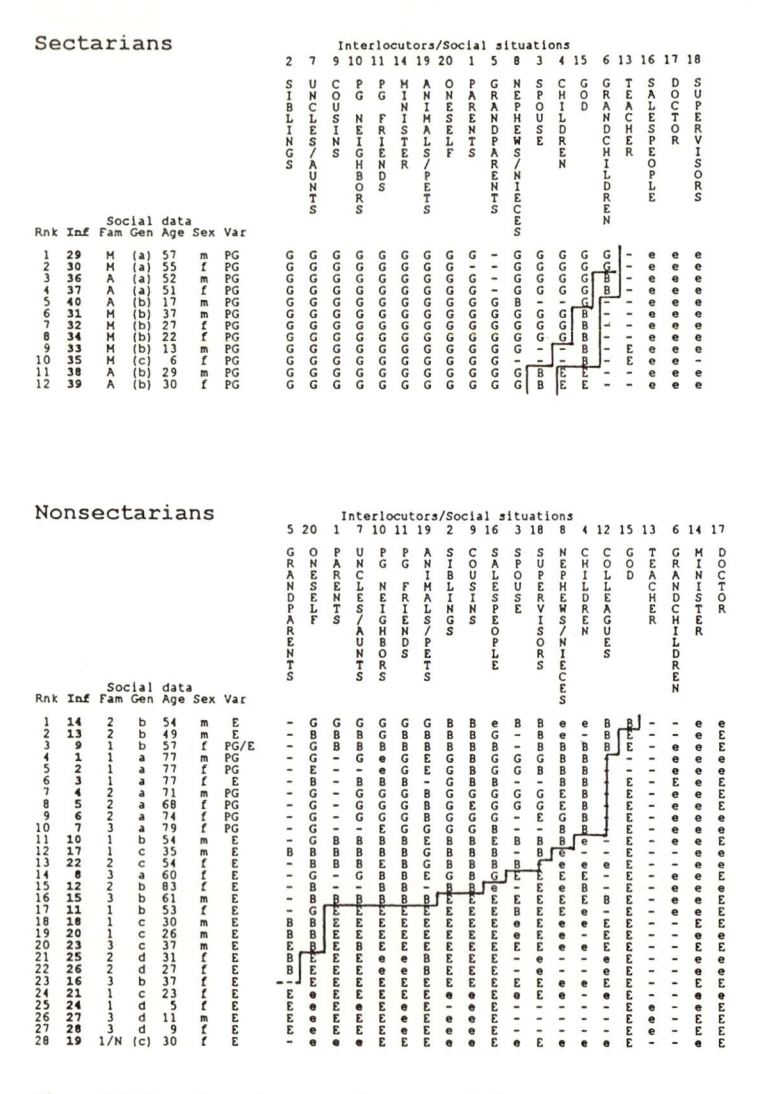

```
                              Interlocutors/Social situations
                      5 20  1  7 10 11 19  2  9 16  3 18  8  4 12 15 13  6 14 17
                      G  O  P  U  P  P  A  S  C  S  S  P  S  C  C  G  T  G  M  D
                      R  N  A  N  G  G  N  I  O  A  U  O  U  H  O  R  E  R  O  O
                      A  N  R  C  I  F  N  B  U  L  P  P  P  I  L  A  A  A  I  C
                      N  E  E  L  N  I  I  L  S  I  E  E  E  L  L  N  C  N  N  T
                      D  S  N  E  E  R  M  I  I  E  R  W  R  D  E  D  H  D  I  O
                      P  /  T  S  R  S  A  N  N  S  V  E  V  R  A  C  E  P  S  R
                      A  A  S  /  T  T  L  G  S  /  I  N  I  E  G  H  R  A  T
                      R  U     A  H  E  E  S     P  S  T  S  N  U  I     R  E
                      E  N     U  N  S  S  /     E  O  S  O     E  L     E  R
                      N  T     N  D     /  P     O  R     R        D     N
                      T  S     T  O        E     P  S     I        R     T
                      S        S  R        T     L        E        E     S
                               /           S     E        S        N
                               A
      Social data
 Rnk Inf Fam Gen Age Sex Var
  1  14   2  b  54  m  E        -  G  G  G  G  B  B  e  B  B  e  e  B  B| -  -  e  e
  2  13   2  b  49  m  E        -  B  B  B  G  B  B  B  G  -  B  e  -  B  |E -  -  e  e
  3   9   1  b  57  f  PG/E     -  G  B  B  B  B  B  B  B  B  -  B  B  B| B  -  e  e  E
  4   1   1  a  77  m  PG       -  E  -  G  e  G  E  B  B  G  G  G  B  G  B| -  -  e  e  E
  5   2   1  a  77  f  PG       -  E  -  -  e  G  E  G  B  B  -  G  B  B  B| -  -  e  e  E
  6   3   1  a  77  f  E        -  B  -  B  B  B  -  B  B  -  B  B  -  -  B  E  -  E  e  E
  7   4   2  a  71  m  PG       -  G  -  G  G  G  B  G  G  G  G  G  G  E  B  |E -  e  e  E
  8   5   2  a  68  f  PG       -  G  -  G  G  G  B  G  G  G  G  G  G  E  B  |E -  e  e  E
  9   6   2  a  74  f  PG       -  G  -  G  G  G  B  G  G  G  G  G  B  E  B  |E -  e  e  E
 10   7   3  a  79  f  PG       -  G  -  -  G  G  E  B  G  B  G  B  -  E  B  |E -  e  e  E
 11  10   1  b  54  m  E        -  G  B  B  B  G  E  E  B  B  B  B  e  -  E  |- -  e  e  E
 12  17   1  c  35  m  E        B  B  B  B  B  B  G  B  B  -  B  B  |E e  e  e  E  -  e  E
 13  22   2  c  54  f  E        -  B  B  B  E  B  G  B  B  B  B  B| e  e  e  E  -  -  e  E
 14   8   3  a  60  f  E        -  G  -  B  B  E  G  B  G  E| E  E  E  -  e  e  e  -  e  E
 15  12   2  b  83  f  E        -  B  -  B  B  -  B  B| B  |e  -  E  B  -  E  e  e  e  e  E
 16  15   3  b  61  m  E        -  B  B  B  B  B  E  |E  E  E  E  E  B  E  E  e  e  -  e  E
 17  11   1  b  53  m  E        -  G  |E E  E  E  E  E  E  E  E  E  B  B  e  -  E  -  e  E
 18  18   1  c  30  m  E        B  |B E  E  E  E  E  E  E  E  E  e  E  e  E  -  -  E  E
 19  20   1  c  26  m  E        B  |B E  E  E  E  E  E  E  E  E  e  e  E  E  -  -  E  E
 20  23   3  c  37  m  E        E  |E B  E  E  E  E  E  E  E  E  E  e  e  E  E  -  -  E  E
 21  25   2  d  31  f  E        B  |E E  e  e  B  E  E  E  -  e  -  -  e  E  -  -  E  E
 22  26   2  d  27  f  E        B  |E E  E  e  B  E  E  E  E  e  E  e  -  e  E  -  e  E  E
 23  16   3  b  37  f  E        -  |- E  E  E  E  E  E  E  E  E  E  E  -  E  -  -  E  E
 24  21   1  c  23  f  E        E  e  E  E  E  E  E  e  e  E  e  E  e  -  e  E  -  -  e  E
 25  24   1  d   5  f  E        E  e  E  e  e  E  E  -  e  -  E  -  -  -  -  E  e  -  e  E
 26  27   3  d  11  m  E        E  e  E  E  E  e  E  e  e  E  -  -  -  -  -  E  e  -  E  E
 27  28   3  d   9  f  E        -  e  E  E  E  e  E  e  e  E  -  -  -  -  -  E  e  -  E  E
 28  19  1/N (c) 30  f  E        -  e  e  e  E  E  E  e  e  E  e  E  e  e  E  -  -  e  E
```

Figure 3.7: Sectarian and nonsectarian present-day language use

```
For the symbols for the social data, see figure 1.5.

G = always Pennsylvania German
B = sometimes Pennsylvania German, sometimes English
E = always English, even though the interlocutor understands Pennsylvania German
e = always English, because the interlocutor does not understand Pennsylvania German
- = inapplicable
```

empty cells. Their order is therefore arbitrary, following the one used in the questionnaire.

The extreme right-hand side of the continuum includes three interlocutors belonging to the outside world. From right to left, they are the board of supervisors (18), the doctor (17), and salespeople (16). All communication with these interlocutors is in English, because they cannot speak Pennsylvania German.

Interlocutor 13 (teachers) presents a special case. As the sectarian school is almost totally a domain of English, the two schoolchildren in the sample (informants 33, 35) report the use of English at school, even though the teacher knows Pennsylvania German.[37]

The four interlocutors in between are not addressed in the same language by all the sectarian informants. From a sociolinguistic point of view, they are the most interesting in that they may indicate shift in progress. From left to right, this group includes the interlocutors spouse (3), children (4), God (15), and grandchildren (6). They all belong to the most personal sphere, either as immediate family members or in the special situation of praying.

Despite this intermediate area of slow and orderly shift from Pennsylvania German via Pennsylvania German and English to English, the pattern of interlocutors in the sectarian scale reflects a relatively stable, diglossic situation.

The further down informants are in the continuum, the more English they use. The continuum is roughly ordered according to generations, with the members of the a-generation on top and the b- and c-generations toward the bottom. Even within a given generation, language use orders the informants almost perfectly according to their age, with the oldest informants on top and the youngest at the bottom. The only exceptions are informant 40, who should be a little further down for his age, and informants 38 and 39, the Beachy Amish.

The Beachy Amish are mainly responsible for both the generational order of the informants and the intermediate area of interlocutors described above. They are the ones who speak both languages to each other (interlocutor 3: spouse), and English to their children (interlocutor 4) and to God (interlocutor 15). At the same time, they are responsible for their parents' (informants 36, 37) "B"-cells for interlocutor 6 (grandchildren). The old couple speaks Pennsylvania German to most of their grandparents, but has to speak English with the (monolingual) children of informants 38 and 39. The same explanation holds for the "B"-cell found for informant 40 (the brother of informant 38) in column 8. While he speaks Pennsylvania German with most of his nephews and nieces, this informant has to use English with the children of the Beachy Amish couple.

Thus, only interlocutor 15 (God) shows indications of a shift independent of the two Beachy Amish. Unlike their elders, the five members of the Mennonite b- and c-generations pray for themselves sometimes in Pennsylvania German and sometimes in English. However, this pattern indicates the split of a single domain rather than linguistic progressiveness. Rather than simply meaning "sometimes Pennsylvania German, sometimes English," "B" indicates that some newer, prephrased prayers are in English, while free praying is in Pennsylvania German.[38]

Since the conversion of younger members of conservative sectarian groups to more progressive denominations is the exception rather than the rule,[39] the scale suggests a higher degree of language shift than should normally be assumed for sectarian Pennsylvania Germans. Nevertheless, the fact that such breaks do occur occasionally as well as the young Mennonites' use of English in prayers indicate that the sectarian diglossic situation is not totally unaffected by certain tendencies toward shift. In this respect, the scale reflects a very slow historical process. Over the centuries, the sectarian community has been shifting from German monolingualism to growing bilingualism in Pennsylvania German and English.

In sum, the sectarians' outlook on society is reflected by their language use patterns. The split into two large groups of interlocutors mirrors the fairly strict division of their world into the plain community, with Pennsylvania German as the predominant code, and the outside world, with which they deal in English, the zone of cells marked "B" being relatively small.

Over the generations, very little shift in language use patterns can be seen. There is a tendency for younger informants to use slightly less Pennsylvania German. However, the shift to English has affected comparatively few interlocutors and informants. The high scalability reflects this relative stability.

In the specific case of this survey, the Mennonite family has a more conservative language use pattern than the Amish family. This reflects the fact that the Mennonite family is Old Order while the Amish family is New Order. Accordingly, the most progressive language use is shown by the young Amish couple who converted to the more progressive branch of the Beachy Amish (informants 38, 39).

Only in the Beachy Amish part of the Amish family can the use of Pennsylvania German be expected to decrease rapidly. In the rest of the Amish family and in the Mennonite family, Pennsylvania German is quite stable in the home domain.

As the bottom scale of figure 3.7 shows, the nonsectarian group is far more irregular in terms of its language use patterns.[40] As the exclusive use of Pennsylvania German is frequent only among some older informants, the gradation line is drawn between "B" and "E." If the occasional use of Pennsylvania German is included on the left (with the "G"-cells), the informants are structured more clearly. Only one "G"-cell is found in direct contact with an "E"-cell along the gradation line. The intermediate belt of "B" shows that the shift from Pennsylvania German to English[41] within the nonsectarian group is not completely abrupt, but still rapid.

Similar to the sectarians' scale, there is a general trend for the less formal interlocutors and situations to be located on the left and the more formal ones on the right. The lower the level of formality, the more prevalent the use of Pennsylvania German; the more formal a situation, the more English is used.

The most important vertical dividing line separates interlocutor 4 (children) from 15 (God), partly running through a stretch of empty cells for the a-generation informants and interlocutor 12 (colleagues).[42] While nine informants use Pennsylvania German at least sometimes when talking to their children, only one does the same when praying to God. To the left of this line only informal and intimate interlocutors are found, including relatives, other members of the nonsectarian group, and the farm animals. The group on its right includes more formal situations, in which the interlocutors are often no group members (teacher, minister, doctor).

However, one interlocutor from the family domain does appear on the formal side of the continuum, namely the grandchildren (interlocutor 6). Apparently, formality is not the only factor for the predominant use of English; the interlocutors' lack of competence must also be taken into account.

Those interlocutors in the family and home domain who belong to an older or at least the same generation as the respective informant are the ones that evoke the most conservative language use patterns, that is, a strong use of Pennsylvania German. The younger the interlocutors, the more English is used.

Both present-day and childhood language use (*see* figure 3.3: interlocutor 4) suggest that if the older nonsectarian informants still had grandparents, they would use Pennsylvania German with them. Therefore, interlocutor 5 appears on the far left of the continuum despite a large number of inapplicable cells.

Interlocutor 20 (oneself) may not be entirely free from overreporting. This accounts for the fact that the column is located to the left of interlocutors older than the informants themselves, such as parents (1) and uncles and aunts (7).

The order of the informants roughly follows membership in generation, with the a-generation at the top and the d-generation at the bottom. The nonsectarians' language use pattern found for interlocutor 2 (brothers and sisters) reflects the acquisition situation best. The a-generation uses Pennsylvania German exclusively, the majority of the b-generation uses both languages, the c-generation is split between the use of the two languages and exclusively English, and the d-generation always uses English.

Three b-generation informants (9, 13, 14) are located even above the a-generation. The main reason is that they sometimes speak Pennsylvania German with their work colleagues, while the a-generation does not have any work colleagues.[43]

However, informants 9 and 13 in particular show a qualitative difference from the a-generation, with only one and two "G"-cells. By speaking Pennsylvania German to as many speakers as possible, informant 14 tries to encourage others. For all these reasons, the three b-generation informants at the top of the scale have to be regarded as special cases.

Of the a-generation, only informant 8 is located below rank 10. The fact that her spouse is a native speaker of English may have contributed to her relatively progressive language use patterns. She is the only a-generation informant to speak exclusively English with her children.

While the (slight and slow) shift within the sectarian group was found to correlate with age, this factor can only be regarded as a rough indicator in the case of the nonsectarians. Instead, as was the case with phonetic marking, membership in a certain generation as determined by language acquisition is important. This accounts for the fact that informant 12 (rank 15), who is the oldest informant in the survey, does not use as much Pennsylvania German as most of the nonsectarians who are the same age. The latter are native speakers of Pennsylvania German, while informant 12 belongs to the first generation in her family to speak English natively.[44]

Two other outstanding informants are 17 and 22, members of the c-generation. For their generation and age, both show an extensive use of Pennsylvania German. Informant 22 even surpasses her mother (informant 12). The reason is that she is married to informant 14 and, to a certain degree, shares his positive attitude toward Pennsylvania German. Informant 17 works as a farmer and has very limited contact with outsiders.

The largest gap between two consecutive informants is found between informants 15 and 11 (ranks 16 and 17). While informant 15 uses Pennsylvania German at least partly with seven interlocutors, informant 11 has only one "G"-cell and one "B"-cell. The fact that both these informants belong to the b-generation is another indication of the necessity of distinguishing between a progressive and a conservative branch within this generation.

In the case of informant 11, even the family and home domain is largely English. Reasons could be her rather indifferent attitude toward Pennsylvania German and her relatively limited competence. Feeling uncomfortable and insecure in Pennsylvania German, this informant avoids using it even at home. Her language use pattern stands in sharp contrast with her sister's (informant 9, rank 3), who is only four years older. While informant 9 led a relatively secluded life as a farmer's wife, informant 11 runs a gas station and school bus enterprise with her husband, so she has more contact with outsiders and young people, most of whom are monolingual English speakers.

Informants 18, 20, 23 (c-generation) and 25, 26 (d-generation) are typical representatives of the younger generations, who like to use a few Pennsylvania German phrases with their grandparents or know some swearwords.

One step below, in the very youngest age group within the d-generation (informants 24, 27, 28), no Pennsylvania German whatsoever is used.

In sum, the relatively large number of deviations from a perfect scale on the one hand and of cells marked "B" on the other suggests that the nonsectarian group is in the process of changing its language use patterns dramatically. These patterns reflect the division into generational groups as determined by language acquisition.

The language use pattern for interlocutor 2 (brothers and sisters) is the one that reflects the division of the nonsectarian generations a through d most clearly. With their siblings, the a-generation uses Pennsylvania German, the more conservative members of the b-generation speak both languages, and some less conservative ones only English. All the members of the c-generation (except for informant 17) and the d-generation also use English exclusively, the former despite the interlocutors' competence in Pennsylvania German, the latter because of its lack.

With the two interlocutors with whom the a-generation predominantly uses both languages (4: children, 8: nephews and nieces) the younger generations use only English. It is the grandparents, that is, the oldest interlocutors, with whom the youngest informants use some Pennsylvania German. Parents (interlocutor 1), spouse (3), children (4), and grandchildren (6) follow, ordered by age, from left to right. This shows that the shift from Pennsylvania German to English is irreversible even within the family. Four interlocutors outside the home domain on the far right are addressed in English by all the nonsectarian informants. Here, the shift is complete.

One of the most obvious differences between the two scales is the shape of the gradation lines. In the sectarian scale, the two lines are equally steep, while the one in the nonsectarian continuum is relatively flat.

Because of their strict diglossia, the use of Pennsylvania German decreases, if at all, only slowly among the sectarians. The only countermovement against their high birthrates (and, subsequently, high number of additional native speakers of Pennsylvania German) is the occasional dropout of individual family members joining more progressive denominations (such as the Beachy Amish). The steep gradation line may therefore be taken to indicate a breakup of the group. While the large majority of sectarians preserves the traditional diglossic situation, a few younger group members undermine the stable diglossia by raising their children in English. Thus, the only factor harmful to the preservation of Pennsylvania German in the sectarian group is the decision of a minority not to follow the traditional language use patterns and the subsequent development of two groups. Figure 3.7 shows that at the beginning of the split no more than four interlocutors are affected.

Among the nonsectarians, Pennsylvania German is dying very rapidly. The scale represents a continuum which includes all the informants evenly, the gradation line being relatively flat. The loss of Pennsylvania German is progressing through all generations with increasing speed. All the interlocutors are affected; there is no column containing only "G"-cells. Pennsylvania German is dying because it is used in fewer and fewer domains—the sign of an instable situation. The decisive factor in this shift is the loss of Pennsylvania German within the family.

Another major difference betweeen the two scales is the higher number of "B"-cells in the nonsectarian continuum, reaching from interlocutor 5 on the far left to interlocutor 15 toward the right. Especially for interlocutor 5 (grandparents) it reaches far down in the informants' continuum, even including two members of the d-generation (informants 25, 26). For many of the younger informants the grandparents are those speakers with whom they occasionally try their rudimentary knowledge of Pennsylvania German. The large number of "B"-cells reflects the instability of the nonsectarian bilingual situation.

The Effects of Language Competence, Acquisition, and Use 191

Further, the nonsectarians' continuum of interlocutors is not characterized by the same strict division into two groups. Most strikingly, although it belongs to the family domain, interlocutor 6 (grandchildren) is located among the formal interlocutors through the exclusive use of English. On the one hand, this reflects the fact that the nonsectarians' society is less strictly structured. At the same time, it is an indication that it has progressed further in the linguistic shift.

Of the four interlocutors at the formal end of the continuum in the sectarians' scale (13: teacher, 16: salespeople, 17: doctor, and 18: board of supervisors) two, salespeople and supervisors, are found among the interlocutors associated with family and home in the nonsectarians' scale. Both salespeople and township supervisors are group members for the nonsectarians, but not for the sectarians.

Accordingly, the block of interlocutors associated with formal situations is smaller in the nonsectarians' scale where only the teacher (13) and the doctor (17) are left as interlocutors. The minister (interlocutor 14), who is not located at the formal end in the sectarians' scale, is only addressed in English by the nonsectarians, mainly for his lack of Pennsylvania German competence.

All this shows that through the network differences the formality of a number of domains is defined differently in the two groups. However, there is a second important factor responsible for those differences, namely some interlocutors' lack of competence in Pennsylvania German.

In all, the nonsectarians are the more interesting group with respect to language use. Unlike the sectarian group, in which the patterns of language acquisition are the same for all generations, the nonsectarian informants differ in terms of native language, access, and exposure to Pennsylvania German.

More direct conclusions about the nature of the shift can be drawn from a comparison between the informants' present-day and childhood language use, despite a small number of discrepant interlocutors[45] (cf. figures 3.2 and 3.3 as against figures 3.4 and 3.7).

A comparison of the order of informants and interlocutors and the rough appearance of the gradations in figures 3.3 and 3.7 shows that the language use patterns for childhood and for the present are very similar. In both cases, the two informant groups are generally structured according to age or, in the case of the nonsectarians, according to the patterns of language acquisition, while the interlocutors are ordered from more informal ones on the left to more formal ones on the right of the continuum.

Both the present-day language use patterns of the various generations and the comparison of childhood with present-day language use suggest that the shift runs in the direction from Pennsylvania German to English. Within the nonsectarian group, the interlocutor doctor is a case in point. While seven members of the a-generation spoke exclusively Pennsylvania German to the doctor when they were children (figure 3.2: interlocutor 18), all the nonsectarian informants report the present-day use of English (figure 3.4: interlocutor 17). During the childhood of the oldest informants, the nonsectarians' doctors were usually members of their group; nowadays the doctors in the towns and hospitals of the area are mostly outsiders, with no competence in Pennsylvania German.

Similarly, five members of the nonsectarian a-generation spoke Pennsylvania German to the minister in their childhood (figure 3.2: interlocutor 15), while today they all use English exclusively (figure 3.4: interlocutor 14). The young ministers assigned to parishes in the Pennsylvania German area usually come from outside the region and do not speak the language of their older parishioners.

However, the shift from Pennsylvania German to English is not only visible in the case of interlocutors commonly associated with formal speech situations. For the interlocutor Pennsylvania German neighbors, all eight nonsectarian a-generation informants report the exclusive use of Pennsylvania German in their childhood (figure 3.2: interlocutor 7), while now only three of them use Pennsylvania German exclusively and two occasionally (figure 3.4: interlocutor 10). Even in the home domain interlocutors with competence in Pennsylvania German are becoming rare.

Nevertheless, not only the lack of competence on the interlocutors' part is responsible for the shift. The farm animals and pets are a case in point. Of the whole nonsectarian group, no fewer than nine informants always used Pennsylvania German and six both Pennsylvania German and English as children (figure 3.2: interlocutor 20). Today four informants are left who use Pennsylvania German exclusively and eight who use both languages (figure 3.4: interlocutor 19).

In the nonsectarian group, the informants' order for childhood differs slightly from the one for present-day language use. In figure 3.7 three b-generation informants (9, 13, 14) are located at the top of the scale, even before all the members of the a-generation. The former are characterized by far less use of Pennsylvania German in childhood (figure 3.3); informants 13 and 14 did not use this variety at all. At first glance, this change in structure runs contrary to the shift from Pennsylvania German to English.

These informants represent a group of Pennsylvania Germans who nostalgically but futilely attempt to maintain their linguistic and cultural

The Effects of Language Competence, Acquisition, and Use   193

heritage. Now that they are older, some native speakers of English (mostly members of the b-generation) use Pennsylvania German with the older native speakers of Pennsylvania German (grandparents, parents, neighbors, salespeople, etc.), with whom they always used English as children. However, the use of Pennsylvania German is normally only possible with a-generation interlocutors, and it is most often sporadic. For lack of competence, it is rather untypical with age peers and particularly with younger group members. The short renaissance of Pennsylvania German will by no means prevent its imminent death in the nonsectarian group.[46]

By contrast, there are hardly any differences in the sectarians' order between figures 3.3 (childhood) and 3.7 (present-day language use). As the Beachy Amish couple did not convert (and, subsequently, adopt a more progressive language use pattern) until they were adults, their childhood language behavior is practically identical with that of the youngest Amish (informant 40). In the present-day scale, however, informant 40 remained much more conservative and is therefore located higher than his older (now Beachy Amish) brother (informant 38) and the latter's wife (informant 39).

Altogether, the sectarian community is characterized by fairly stable diglossia, while the nonsectarians are in the middle of a language shift. In an originally monolingual Pennsylvania German society English was necessary for the nonsectarians only to deal with outsiders. Later, it became the code of a number of formal domains, such as school, religion, and, more recently, the doctor. With the shift from Pennsylvania German to English as the first language between the a- and b-generations, English entered the family and home domain. From this point, the shift gained in speed and ultimately became irreversible. As competent interlocutors are dying out, Pennsylvania German is dying as well.

Language Use within the Family

The data for both childhood and present-day language use suggest that Pennsylvania German is most extensively used with the interlocutors belonging to the family domain. Therefore, the question of who speaks which language to whom within the family deserves special attention.

The following survey examines all six informant families separately, the emphasis being on the three nonsectarian ones. For the latter,

194   The Effects of Language Competence, Acquisition, and Use

implicational scales illustrating the prevailing patterns of language use within the families will be given.

In figures 3.8–10, the informants ordered along the vertical (together with their social data) report their language use with the interlocutors on the horizontal. For each pair of informant and interlocutor, two reports are given, that is, one from each perspective. The one is located in the lower left of each scale, the other one in the upper right. In figures 3.8 and 3.9, discrepant reports are marked in bold type. In figure 3.10, where no discrepancies occurred, the area to the right of and above the diagonal line is left out.

Figure 3.8 gives a comprehensive overview of which language each member of nonsectarian family 1 speaks to each informant also belonging to this family.

					Informant											
Inf	Gen	Age	Sex	Var	1	2	3	10	9	17	11	18	20	19	21	24
1	a	77	m	PG	-	G	G	B	B	B	B	**E**	**E**	e	e	e
2	a	77	f	PG	G	-	G	B	B	B	B	**E**	**E**	e	e	e
3	a	77	f	E	G	G	-	B	B	B	E	E	E	e	e	e
10	b	54	m	E	B	B	B	-	B	B	B	E	E	e	e	e
9	b	57	f	PG/E	B	B	B	B	-	B	B	E	E	e	e	e
17	c	35	m	E	B	B	B	B	B	-	E	E	E	e	e	e
11	b	53	f	E	**E**	**E**	E	B	**E**	E	-	E	E	e	e	e
18	c	30	m	E	B	B	E	E	E	E	E	-	E	e	e	e
20	c	26	m	E	B	B	E	E	E	E	E	E	-	e	e	e
19	(c)	30	f	E	E	E	E	E	E	E	E	E	E	-	e	e
21	c	23	f	E	E	E	E	E	E	E	E	E	E	e	-	e
24	d	5	f	E	E	E	E	E	E	E	E	E	E	e	e	-

Figure 3.8: Language use within nonsectarian family 1

For the symbols for the social data, see figure 1.5. Discrepant reports are in bold type.

G = always Pennsylvania German
B = sometimes Pennsylvania German, sometimes English
E = always English, even though the interlocutor understands Pennsylvania German
e = always English, because the interlocutor does not understand Pennsylvania German

Informants 1–3, all members of the a-generation, use their German variety when speaking to each other, no matter whether they use more Pennsylvania German (informants 1, 2) or more English (informant 3) during a normal workday. With all three members of the b-generation (informants 9–11) and the fairly tradition-oriented informant 17 (c-generation) they speak Pennsylvania German or English. The only exception is informant 3. When speaking to her daughter-in-law (informant

11), she always uses English. The three a-generation informants unanimously report that in conversations with the other four members of the c-generation (informants 18–21) and with the one d-generation informant (24) they always use English, partly despite their interlocutors' competence in Pensylvania German ("E"), partly because of their lack of it ("e").

In conversations among each other and with informant 17, the members of the b-generation normally use both Pennsylvania German and English. Informant 11 is an exception in that she always uses English with those mentioned above apart from her husband (informant 10). Her relatively poor command of Pennsylvania German forces her to speak more English than other members of her generation. When talking to members of the c- and d-generations, the b-generation informants always use English. The only exception is informant 17, with whom informants 9 and 10 (his mother and his uncle) sometimes speak Pennsylvania German.

The language used by the c- and d-generations in both intra- and intergroup contacts is English. Informant 19 is listed as a member of the c-generation of Pennsylvania German family 1, although in terms of her cultural origin this informant, who married into the family, would have to be regarded as a non-Pennsylvania German.

Figure 3.8 includes several discrepant reports. While informants 18 and 20 report that they sometimes speak English and sometimes Pennsylvania German with their grandparents (informants 1, 2), their grandparents say they always speak English. This discrepancy does not mean that two different codes are used by the interlocutors during a given conversation, but that the informants simply rated their language use differently. The simultaneous use of separate codes over an extended period of time is not a significant or common characteristic of the Pennsylvania German speech community. In all those infrequent cases during participant observation in which, for some reason, a conversation started out in separate codes, the code was immediately changed by one of the interlocutors, virtually with the next sentence. In the above example of discrepant report of language use, the two grandsons tend to overrate their use of Pennsylvania German. A short greeting or phrase given to their grandparents in Pennsylvania German is enough for them to rate their language use as "B."

Other discrepancies are found between informant 11 and her father (informant 1), her mother (informant 2), and her older sister (informant 9). Here the situation is reversed. Informant 11, who claims that she does not like to speak Pennsylvania German, reports the use of English; her older relatives report the same use as with all the other members of the b-generation, that is, sometimes English and sometimes Pennsylva-

196   The Effects of Language Competence, Acquisition, and Use

nia German. Although raised in English, an occasional switch to Pennsylvania German later in life is not uncommon within the b-generation.

Figure 3.9 gives an overview of the language use pattern of nonsectarian family 2. As in family 1, the members of the a-generation (informants 4–6) always use Pennsylvania German when speaking with one another. With the three members of the b-generation (informants 12–14) and with one representative of the c-generation (informant 22), they report the use of both Pennsylvania German and English. The only exception is informant 6, who says that she always uses Pennsylvania German when speaking with her nephew (informant 13) and her son (informant 14). When communicating with the members of the d-generation (informants 25, 26), the a-generation always uses English.

Inf	Gen	Age	Sex	Var	6	4	5	14	13	12	22	25	26
6	a	74	f	PG	-	G	G	G	G	B	B	E	E
4	a	71	m	PG	G	-	G	B	B	B	B	E	E
5	a	68	f	PG	G	G	-	B	B	B	B	E	E
14	b	54	m	E	G	G	G	-	B	B	B	E	E
13	b	49	m	E	B	B	B	B	-	B	B	E	E
12	b	83	f	E	B	B	B	B	B	-	B	E	E
22	c	54	f	E	B	B	B	B	B	B	-	E	E
25	d	31	f	E	E	E	E	E	E	E	E	-	E
26	d	27	f	E	E	E	E	E	E	E	E	E	-

Figure 3.9: Language use within nonsectarian family 2

For the symbols for the social data, see figure 1.5. Discrepant reports are in bold type.

G = always Pennsylvania German
B = sometimes Pennsylvania German, sometimes English
E = always English, even though the interlocutor understands Pennsylvania German

Two members of the b-generation (informants 12, 13) report the use of both Pennsylvania German and English with the a-, b-, and c-generations.

Three cases of discrepant reports are found in the communication between the a- and the b-generation. While informant 13 (b-generation) does not confirm the exclusive use of Pennsylvania German claimed by informant 6 (a-generation) in conversations among each other, the other two cases are reversed. Informant 14 reports the exclusive use of Pennsylvania German with his uncle (informant 4) and his aunt (informant

The Effects of Language Competence, Acquisition, and Use 197

5); on the other hand, informants 4 and 5 say that they use both Pennsylvania German and English when speaking with their nephew. Several times during the interviews informant 14 claimed that he always uses Pennsylvania German with all three members of the a-generation in his family. Participant observation has confirmed his claim.

His wife (informant 22), although a member of the c-generation (since her mother, informant 12, is not a native speaker of Pennsylvania German), shows the same language use pattern as informants 12 and 13 (b-generation). The daughters of informants 14 and 22 (informants 25, 26), however, have the typical pattern of the c- and d-generations. All their intrafamily communication is in English.

Figure 3.10 shows all the intragroup language use patterns of nonsectarian family 3. Unlike in families 1 and 2, Pennsylvania German is never used as the only variety. Even the informants belonging to the a-generation (7, 8), mother-in-law and daughter-in-law, say that they use the two languages among each other.

					Informant						
Inf	Gen	Age	Sex	Var	7	8	15	16	23	27	28
7	a	79	f	PG	-						
8	a	60	f	E	B	-					
15	b	61	m	E	B	E	-				
16	b	37	f	E	E	E	E	-			
23	c	37	m	E	E	E	E	E	-		
27	d	11	m	E	E	E	E	E	E	-	
28	d	9	f	E	E	E	E	E	E	E	-

Figure 3.10: Language use within nonsectarian family 3

For the symbols for the social data, see figure 1.5.

B = sometimes Pennsylvania German, sometimes English
E = always English, even though the interlocutor understands Pennsylvania German

Of all the other informants, only one member of the b-generation (informant 15) reports using both varieties with his mother (informant 7). In all other communication English is used exclusively. No discrepancies are found in the self-reports.

Within family 3, age and spouse's generation are important factors in addition to one's own generation in terms of language use. Although informants 15 and 16 both belong to the b-generation, they have different language use patterns. While that for informant 15 is shared by a member of the a-generation, the pattern of informant 16 is typical of the c- and d-generations. The difference in age (informant 15: sixty-one; informant 16: thirty-seven) and the fact that informant 15 is married to a member of the a-generation, while the husband of informant 16 belongs to the c-generation, account for the differences.

In sum, nonsectarian families 1 and 2 use more Pennsylvania German within the family than family 3. This may be due to the fact that the latter includes only two a-generation informants, one of whom is married to a member of the b-generation, with whom she has always used English.

Exclusive use of Pennsylvania German is found for no informant belonging to family 3, but is common among the members of the a-generation of families 1 and 2. While there is no use of Pennsylvania German whatsoever beyond the b-generation in family 3, the frequent use of both Pennsylvania German and English is documented for at least one member each of the c-generation of families 1 and 2.

Altogether, Pennsylvania German as well as English are often used in conversations between the a- and the b-generation and within the b-generation. The use of both Pennsylvania German and English is rare for members of the c-generation and not found for any member of the d-generation. No member of generations c and d in any of the three nonsectarian families uses only Pennsylvania German with any intrafamily interlocutor.

As the informants in figures 3.8–10 are ordered almost perfectly by generations, deviations in the transition from "G" via "B" to "E"/"e" are indicative of heterogeneity. As the number of deviant cells decreases from family 1 to family 3, the former appears to be the most heterogeneous and the latter the most homogeneous. Family 3 has progressed the furthest in the shift to English.

All the sectarian informants report the exclusive use of Pennsylvania German among each other. Thus, the family domain can readily be claimed to be occupied by Pennsylvania German.[47]

All communication between members of the non-Pennsylvania German family is in English, as the informants have neither active nor passive competence in Pennsylvania German.

The Effects of Language Competence, Acquisition, and Use 199

Language Use and Gender

The correlation between language use and gender will be approached from two sides. It will be examined how both the informant's and the interlocutor's gender influences language use.

The self-reported data in figure 3.11 were collected with the help of those questions in questionnaire sections 2.3.5 (family and home) and 2.3.7 (school) that distinguish between male and female interlocutors.

| | Male informant speaking to a . . . || Female informant speaking to a . . . ||
	male interlocutor	female interlocutor	male interlocutor	female interlocutor
	Number %	Number %	Number %	Number %
G	47 29.9	52 30.0	54 26.4	55 26.1
B	29 18.5	32 18.5	40 19.5	44 20.8
E/e	81 51.6	89 51.5	111 54.1	112 53.1

Figure 3.11: Language use and gender

G = always Pennsylvania German
B = sometimes Pennsylvania German, sometimes English
E/e = always English

Interlocutors:
father - mother
older brother(s) - older sister(s)
younger brother(s) - younger sister(s)
son(s) - daughter(s)
paternal grandfather - grandmother
maternal grandfather - grandmother
grandson(s) - granddaughter(s)
male - female cousin(s)
father-in-law - mother-in-law

male - female Pennsylvania German neighbors
male - female Pennsylvania German friends
male - female schoolmates in class
male - female schoolmates during recess on the school playground
male - female schoolmates on the way to or from school
male - female schoolmates about homework one does not understand
male - female schoolmates when playing

These pairs of interlocutors include (in parentheses the number of the questions in the questionnaire): father (133)–mother (134), older brother(s) (135)–older sister(s) (136), younger brother(s) (137)–younger sister(s) (138), son(s) (141)–daughter(s) (142), paternal grandfather (143)–paternal grandmother (144), maternal grandfather (145)–maternal grandmother (146), grandson(s) (147)–granddaughter(s) (148), male cousin(s) (155)–female cousin(s) (156), father-in-law (157)–mother-in-law (158), male Pennsylvania German neighbors (162)–female Pennsylvania German neighbors (163), male Pennsylvania German friends (166)–female Pennsylvania German friends (167), male schoolmates in class (188)–female schoolmates in class (189), male schoolmates during recess on the school playground (190)–female schoolmates during recess on the school playground (191), male schoolmates on the way to or from school (192)–female schoolmates on the way to or from school (193), male schoolmates about homework one does not understand (194)–female schoolmates about homework one does not understand (195), male schoolmates when playing (197)–female schoolmates when playing (198).

All sixteen pairs differentiating the interlocutors according to gender are associated with either the family and home domain or with school. For an examination of the factor gender in language use, a small section of the language use spectrum suffices. No distinction will be made between using English although the interlocutors can speak Pennsylvania German ("E") and using it because they cannot speak it ("e"). As this survey is strictly synchronic, the questions concerning the school domain were applicable only to the six school children among the informants.

Of the fifty informants, twenty-two are male and twenty-eight female. The imbalance is especially strong in the nonsectarian a-generation (two males vs. six females) because of the higher life expectancy of women. The ratio between male and female informants is 11:17 for the nonsectarians, 6:6 for the sectarians, and 5:5 for the non-Pennsylvania Germans. The percentages given in figure 3.11 take this imbalance into account.

In an attempt to find out whether the informants' gender is significant for their use of language, the differences between male and female informants when speaking to a male interlocutor will be examined first (figure 3.11). Pennsylvania German is always used by 29.9% of the male informants as compared to 26.4% of the females (difference: +3.5%). The shares for both Pennsylvania German and English are even more similar, that is, 18.5% for men and 19.5% for women (difference: –1%). English is always used by 51.6% of the male and by 54.1% of the female informants (difference: –2.5%).

The same comparisons can be made for male and female informants speaking to a female interlocutor. In this case, 30% of the men always use Pennsylvania German as compared to 26.1% of the women (difference: +3.9%). Both languages are used by 18.5% of the male informants and by 20.8% of the females (difference: –2.3%). The shares for the exclusive use of English are 51.5% for the male as compared to 53.1% for the female informants (difference: −1.6%).

Both with male and female interlocutors, male informants tend to use exclusively Pennsylvania German more often than female informants, while female informants score a higher percentage of the two languages and exclusive use of English than their male counterparts. As far as it goes, this result would be in line with earlier surveys on the impact of gender on language use, showing that men tend to use the L-variety more often than women.[48]

However, even impressionistically the differences in numbers between male and female informants are rather small. A chi-square test reveals that they are not statistically significant at the $p \leq 0.05$ level. Thus, the informants' gender does not really have an impact on their use of language.

In a second step, the significance of the interlocutors' gender will be examined. Figure 3.11 shows that 29.9% of the male informants always use Pennsylvania German when speaking with the sixteen male interlocutors; with the female interlocutors the share is 30% (difference: −0.1%). The two languages are used by 18.5% of the male informants with both the male and the female interlocutors. 51.6% of the male informants use only English with the male interlocutors as compared to 51.5% with the female interlocutors (difference: +0.1%).

Of the female informants, 26.4% always use Pennsylvania German when speaking to the male interlocutors. In conversations with the female interlocutors the share is 26.1% (difference: +0.3%). English or Pennsylvania German are used by 19.5% of the female informants when addressing the male interlocutors, and by 20.8% when speaking to the female interlocutors (difference: −1.3%). 54.1% of the female informants use only English with the male interlocutors vs. 53.1% with the female interlocutors (difference: +1%).

As compared to the male informants, the differences in percentages for the females are somewhat higher. Nevertheless, the differences are even smaller than those found in the examination of the informants' gender. Therefore, the interlocutors' gender does not significantly influence language use either.

In conclusion, the data for language use suggest that the differences between the scores of the two sexes are so minimal that gender cannot be considered a significant factor for language use. This is true for both the informant's and the interlocutor's gender. For the present sample of informants, community and generation are a much more important social factor determining language use than gender.

Topic

In addition to interlocutors and situation, topic of conversation, or subject matter, will be considered the third major factor in the concept of domain. Questionnaire section 2.3.14 (questions 336–48) was designed to find out whether the topic plays a role in the use of Pennsylvania German or English.

To help the informants with their decisions, a concrete setting was given ("Imagine you are talking with a Dutch-speaking neighbor over the fence."). This made it clear that the interlocutor was supposed to be able to speak Pennsylvania German and that the situation was part of the home domain.

Figure 3.12 orders the data implicationally. The fifty informants along with their social data run from top to bottom. Thirteen topics are ordered along the horizontal. Following the order in the questionnaire, they run as follows: family matters (question 336), local affairs (337), farming (338), weather (339), religion (340), sports (341), health (342), fashion (343), cars (344), business (345), finances (346), national affairs (347), international politics (348).

The symbols ("G," "B," "E," and "–") are used in the same way as in figure 3.4. Since the setting made it clear that the interlocutor was supposed to be a speaker of Pennsylvania German, the symbol "e" was not necessary.[49]

The implicational scale has a relatively uniform shape with a large upper area in which all the informants use Pennsylvania German for all the topics and a lower area of approximately the same size in which only English is used. In the center of the continuum there is a cluster of "B"-cells. The gradation line (between "B" and "E") forms a relatively flat curve.

International politics, found at the right edge of the chart, is the subject matter that elicits most readily the use of English. Even two members of the sectarian a-generation (informants 29, 30) report that they do not always discuss this topic in Pennsylvania German.

For finances, the use of the two languages reaches one informant further (informant 10 on rank 23).

While all the sectarian informants use Pennsylvania German when they discuss sports, only four of the nonsectarians report the same behavior, among them only one member of the a-generation (informant 6). Altogether eight informants (1–3, 7–9, 12, 15), six of whom are female, say they never discuss sports in any language.

Empty cells are also found in the columns representing international politics (four), finances (three), business (four), fashion (four),

The Effects of Language Competence, Acquisition, and Use 203

		Social data				Topic FAMILY	LOCAL	FARMING	WEATHER	NATIONAL	CARS	HEALTH	FAITH	BUSINESS	RELIGION	SPORTS	FINANCES	INTERNATIONAL
Rnk	Inf	Fam	Gen	Age	Sex	Var												
1	31	M	(b)	37	m	PG	G	G	G	G	G	G	G	G	G	G	G	G	G
2	32	M	(b)	27	f	PG	G	G	G	G	G	G	G	G	G	G	G	G	G
3	33	M	(b)	13	m	PG	G	G	G	G	G	G	G	G	G	G	G	G	G
4	34	M	(b)	22	f	PG	G	G	G	G	G	G	G	G	G	G	G	G	G
5	35	M	(c)	6	f	PG	G	G	G	G	G	G	G	G	G	G	G	G	G
6	36	A	(a)	52	m	PG	G	G	G	G	G	G	G	G	G	G	G	G	G
7	37	A	(a)	51	f	PG	G	G	G	G	G	G	G	G	G	G	G	G	G
8	38	A	(b)	29	m	PG	G	G	G	G	G	G	G	G	G	G	G	G	G
9	39	A	(b)	30	f	PG	G	G	G	G	G	G	G	G	G	G	G	G	G
10	40	A	(b)	17	m	PG	G	G	G	G	G	G	G	G	G	G	G	G	G
11	6	2	a	74	f	PG	G	G	G	G	G	G	G	G	G	G	G	G	G
12	13	2	b	49	m	E	G	G	G	G	G	G	G	G	G	G	G	G	G
13	14	2	b	54	m	E	G	G	G	G	G	G	G	G	G	G	G	G	G
14	22	2	c	54	f	E	G	G	G	G	G	G	G	G	G	G	G	G	G
15	8	3	a	60	f	E	G	G	G	G	G	–	G	E	–	G	–	G	G
16	12	2	b	83	f	E	G	G	G	G	G	G	G	G	G	–	G	–
17	29	M	(a)	57	m	PG	G	G	G	G	B	G	G	G	G	G	G	G	B
18	30	M	(a)	55	f	PG	G	G	G	G	B	G	G	G	G	G	G	G	B
19	4	2	a	71	m	PG	G	G	G	G	G	G	G	G	B	B	B	B	G
20	5	2	a	68	f	PG	G	G	G	G	G	G	G	G	B	B	B	B	G
21	17	1	c	35	m	E	B	B	B	B	B	B	B	–	B	B	B	B	B
22	3	1	a	77	f	E	B	B	B	B	B	–	B	B	B	B	–	B	B
23	10	1	b	54	m	E	B	B	B	B	B	B	B	B	B	B	B	B	E
24	9	1	b	57	f	PG/E	B	B	B	B	E	–	B	B	B	B	–	–	E
25	7	3	a	79	f	PG	G	G	G	G	G	–	G	G	E	–	–	–
26	15	3	b	61	m	E	B	B	B	B	B	B	B	E	B	–	E	E
27	1	1	a	77	m	PG	G	G	G	G	G	E	–	–	E	–	–	–
28	2	1	a	77	m	PG	G	G	G	G	G	E	–	–	E	–	–	–
29	11	1	b	53	f	E	E	E	E	E	E	E	E	E	E	E	E	E
30	16	3	b	37	f	E	E	E	E	E	E	E	E	E	E	E	E	E
31	18	1	c	30	m	E	E	E	E	E	E	E	E	E	E	E	E	E
32	19	1/N	(c)	30	f	E	E	E	E	E	E	E	E	E	E	E	E	E
33	20	1	c	26	m	E	E	E	E	E	E	E	E	E	E	E	E	E
34	21	1	c	23	f	E	E	E	E	E	E	E	E	E	E	E	E	E
35	23	3	c	37	m	E	E	E	E	E	E	E	E	E	E	E	E	E
36	24	1	d	5	f	E	E	E	E	E	E	E	E	E	E	E	E	E
37	25	2	d	31	f	E	E	E	E	E	E	E	E	E	E	E	E	E
38	26	2	d	27	f	E	E	E	E	E	E	E	E	E	E	E	E	E
39	27	3	d	11	m	E	E	E	E	E	E	E	E	E	E	E	E	E
40	28	3	d	9	f	E	E	E	E	E	E	E	E	E	E	E	E	E
41	41	N	(a)	81	f	E	E	E	E	E	E	E	E	E	E	E	E	E
42	42	N	(b)	63	m	E	E	E	E	E	E	E	E	E	E	E	E	E
43	43	N	(b)	50	m	E	E	E	E	E	E	E	E	E	E	E	E	E
44	44	N	(b)	52	f	E	E	E	E	E	E	E	E	E	E	E	E	E
45	45	N	(b)	54	m	E	E	E	E	E	E	E	E	E	E	E	E	E
46	46	N	(b)	52	f	E	E	E	E	E	E	E	E	E	E	E	E	E
47	47	N	(c)	31	m	E	E	E	E	E	E	E	E	E	E	E	E	E
48	48	N	(c)	30	f	E	E	E	E	E	E	E	E	E	E	E	E	E
49	49	N	(d)	8	m	E	E	E	E	E	E	E	E	E	E	E	E	E
50	50	N	(d)	5	f	E	E	E	E	E	E	E	E	E	E	E	E	E

Figure 3.12: Informants' language use as guided by topic of conversation

Situation: "Imagine you are talking with a Dutch-speaking neighbor over the fence. In which language do you discuss . . . ?"

For the symbols for the social data, see figure 1.5.

G = always Pennsylvania German
B = sometimes Pennsylvania German, sometimes English
E = always English, even though the interlocutor understands Pennsylvania German

and cars (six). The majority of these inapplicable cells is caused by the answers of informants 1–3, 7, and 8, all of whom are members of the nonsectarian a-generation.[50]

With respect to religion, three otherwise linguistically conservative members of the nonsectarian a-generation (informants 1, 2, 7) differ from their peers by reporting the exclusive use of English. This individual linguistic behavior may be influenced by the general use of English in nonsectarian worship services and in conversations with the minister.

The column for business is very similar to that for finances. A slight difference is caused by informant 9, who reports "B" for the former, but "E" for the latter.

The next three topics to the left include fashion, health, and cars. Once again, informants 1 and 2 stand out through their use of English for health.

The remaining five subject matters (national affairs, weather, farming, local affairs, family matters) form a block on the extreme left of the continuum. Here Pennsylvania German is always used by all the informants down to informant 2 on rank 28 (informants 3, 9, 10, 15, 17 using English as well). Minor exceptions are found only for national affairs, which are discussed in either Pennsylvania German or English by the two older Mennonite informants (29, 30), and always in English by informant 9 (nonsectarian b-generation).

In all, the subject matters for which the use of Pennsylvania German is most extensive include family matters, local affairs, farming, and the weather. The close affinity of these topics with the family and home domain is striking. By contrast, finances and international politics, subject matters remote from the center of the family, are more often discussed in English. The order from left to right of the topics family matters, local affairs, national affairs, and international politics reflects an increasing distance from the core of the family.

The first ten ranks of the informants' continuum are occupied by sectarians. Only the two oldest Mennonite informants (29, 30) prove to be somewhat less consistent in their use of Pennsylvania German; they sometimes use English discussing national affairs and international politics.

Below rank 10, an absolutely consistent use of Pennsylvania German for all topics is reported by only one member of the nonsectarian a-generation (informant 6), two members of the b-generation (informants 13, 14), and one of the c-generation (informant 22). All of them belong to family 2, which, at least in connection with subject matter, exhibits the most conservative language use of all the nonsectarian families. In the three older generations, family behavior appears to precede generational behavior, family 2 being the most and family 3 the least conservative.

The Effects of Language Competence, Acquisition, and Use 205

Accordingly, the distribution of the nonsectarian a-generation is relatively heterogeneous. Besides informant 6, six informants (1, 2, 4, 5, 7, 8) show a clear tendency toward Pennsylvania German; however, there are a number of inconsistencies in the form of empty cells or cells marked "B" or even "E." Only informant 3 does not exclusively use Pennsylvania German (or English) for any of the thirteen topics.

This informant, together with three members of the nonsectarian b-generation (informants 9, 10, 15) and one member of the c-generation (informant 17), forms the group which reports the predominant use of both Pennsylvania German and English. They form a transition zone in the center of the continuum between the areas of "G" and "E."

All the informants below rank 28 use exclusively English for all topics. Apart from two members of the nonsectarian b-generation (informants 11, 16) and four informants belonging to the c-generation (informants 18, 20, 21, 23), all the five members of the d-generation (informants 24–28) as well as all the non-Pennsylvania Germans are found in this group.

Gender does not seem to group the informants with respect to language use as determined by subject matter. The variety the informants predominantly use during a normal workday is more indicative. Of the fourteen informants who use Pennsylvania German for all topics, eleven also say that on a given day they use more Pennsylvania German than English.

The fact that the other three informants say they use Pennsylvania German in all given subject matters but at the same time claim that English is their predominant language is only an apparent contradiction. It is caused by the setting given in the question, which assumes that the interlocutor belongs to the home domain and is fluent in Pennsylvania German.

This example shows that the interlocutor is more important for the informants' language use than the topic. Quite generally, in the middle section of figure 3.12 (between ranks 12 and 28), there is no consistency in the variety the informants use on a normal workday. Of seventeen informants, seven (informants 1, 2, 4, 5, 7, 29, 30) use Pennsylvania German, eight (informants 3, 8, 10, 13–15, 17, 22) English, and one (informant 9) the two languages.

At the poles of the scale, the relationship between the variety used normally and the variety used in certain subject matters is perfectly uniform. Those informants (in the upper third) who use Pennsylvania German for all topics normally speak Pennsylvania German, those (in the bottom third) who use English for all subject matters speak more English on a normal workday.

In sum, the pattern of language use as determined by topic shows striking similarities with that governed by interlocutors and situations. It seems that the connection of the topics with certain domains plays a significant role. The informants' membership in a social group and their competence in Pennsylvania German are of equal importance.

All in all, however, there are indications that the interlocutor is more important for language use than topic. The relative flatness of the gradation line in figure 3.12 suggests that it is not so much subject matter that governs language use but the interlocutors' and informants' competence. Competent interlocutors can discuss any topic in Pennsylvania German.[51]

LANGUAGE MAINTENANCE AND SHIFT[52]

The term *language maintenance* refers to the collective retention of a language, even though it is threatened by the existence of one or more languages in the community (bilingualism or multilingualism).

Language maintenance in a bilingual community usually coincides with diglossia. A case in point is the sectarian group, which quite consistently uses Pennsylvania German and English in certain domains, thus maintaining Pennsylvania German.

Language maintenance typically occurs in communities which distinguish between "us" and "them" (Fasold 1984, 240). In the case of the sectarian Pennsylvania Germans, the presence of this "us-them concept" becomes evident through the fact that they refer to their nonplain neighbors as "the English."

Language shift is the collective abandonment of one language in favor of another. Its ultimate stage is language death. A prerequisite for both language shift and language death is societal bilingualism.

With regard to language shift, the nonsectarians are the most interesting group. Here Pennsylvania German shows the typical symptoms of a receding language. It is spoken in very few private domains, with English, the majority language, advancing into the domains of the minority language. While the family and home domain is the last in which Pennsylvania German survives,[53] this variety is seldom used in public. Even within the family, Pennsylvania German is mostly used by the elderly and with the elderly.

The high speed of the language shift in the nonsectarian group is reflected by the fact that both in the c- and d-generations monolingual informants are found. The data show that new babies are highly unlikely to become bilinguals. The consequence will be language death.

Beside the sociolinguistic approach, Dressler (1988, 1556ff.) identifies sociopolitical, socioeconomic, sociocultural, and sociopsychological aspects as being important in a discussion of language maintenance and shift. The latter two deal with the prestige of the languages and the speakers' attitudes toward their languages.

The sociopolitical aspect plays a minor role in the case of Pennsylvania German, since the United States government does not actively regulate the use of Pennsylvania German. The school conflict between the Amish and the state of Pennsylvania lasting from the late 1930s until the 1950s (*see* Hostetler 1993, 261–64) was not about language but rather about the consolidation of schools and the length of schooling. The American mainstream society's negative feelings toward everything German during the two world wars, however, certainly had a negative impact on the maintenance of Pennsylvania German.

Socioeconomic reasons play a much greater role today. Urbanization and industrialization are detrimental to the maintenance of minority languages. They are part of the reason for Pennsylvania German not being spoken in larger towns any more.

In the case of the nonsectarian group examined in the present study, mechanization, modernization, and particularly traffic development have changed the community's lifestyle dramatically. Higher education, greater geographical mobility, and the end of the almost complete isolation of the Mahantango Valley are decisive factors for the shift to English.

It does not come as a surprise that the sectarians, who managed to prevent automobiles, radio, television, and sometimes telephones from determining their lives, have maintained Pennsylvania German to a much larger extent.

In the present study, the main interest is on the question of shift or maintenance of a language (here Pennsylvania German) within a community as a whole. The results of chapter 3, therefore, are about societal language shift.

Another type of switching, the unreciprocal use of the minority language,[54] turned out to be extremely rare. The constellation that the older person uses the L-variety and the younger the H-variety did not occur in a single case of participant observation in any group examined. If, for some reason, one person switched from one code to the other, the interlocutor usually switched as well.[55]

The translation task in section 1.2 of the questionnaire made it clear that the informants know at all times which code they are using. As the switchings do not happen very frequently during a conversation and both interlocutors normally use the same code, it is usually quite easy for the informants to state which language they use with which interlocutor.

Up to a point, language maintenance or shift is predictable.[56] Language shift occurs if a community either desires to or is forced to give up its identity as an identifiable sociocultural group, usually a minority group, in favor of an identity as a part of some other community. Especially in the former case, the attitudes the members of a minority hold toward their culture and their language play a decisive role.

SYNOPSIS

In essence, the data for language competence show that Pennsylvania German is nonexistent in the non-Pennsylvania German community, thriving in the sectarian group, and dying in the nonsectarian population. In the latter, the competence spectrum reaches from native command (a-generation) to zero competence (d-generation). All the informants have active and passive competence in English. In addition, most sectarians have passive competence in Bible High German.

While the sectarians are all native speakers of Pennsylvania German who acquired English at school and from older siblings, the nonsectarians are characterized by heterogeneous acquisition patterns. The a-generation is the last one to have Pennsylvania German as its native language. The b-generation is the first one to be raised in English, learning Pennsylvania German from their grandparents. The c- and d-generations are another one and two generations, respectively, away from the last native speaker in their families, with the result that a decreasing number of informants acquires Pennsylvania German.

The network and domain analysis carried out in conjunction with the examination of language use shed light on two facts. First, the three groups of informants (nonsectarians, sectarians, non-Pennsylvania Germans) form separate social networks. Second, the concept of domains is a better tool for the description of the language use of the six families than social network.

Data collected about the informants' childhood allowed for a diachronic comparison. For both the nonsectarians and the sectarians, very similar patterns were found for childhood and present-day language use.

Within the examination of present-day language use, interlocutors and situations proved to be the most important factors. Topic does not have the same impact on language choice.

As all qualitative analyses showed, the domains to which the interlocutors and topics belong are critical for language use. The closer an interlocutor or subject matter is affiliated with the home and family domain, the more readily Pennsylvania German is used; the more official and distant from the center of the family a domain is, the more English is spoken. This general pattern holds for both the sectarians and the nonsectarians.

An examination of language use within the families showed that in the nonsectarian group Pennsylvania German is used extensively only among the members of the a-generation. Other informants speak it sporadically only with the a-generation, never among themselves. Thus, even in the last domain in which the minority language survives, the family and home, its exclusive use can be predicted to cease as soon as the a-generation dies.

Both the informants' and the interlocutors' gender plays only a minor role for language use. Instead, membership in a certain ethnic group on the one hand, and in a certain generation as determined by the native language on the other, proved to be the most significant social variables.

While the diglossic society of the sectarians allows for a high degree of language maintenance, the nonsectarians' lack of diglossia is responsible for this group's rapid shift from Pennsylvania German to English.

The decisive step happened approximately fifty years ago, when the a-generation unanimously broke with a two-century-old tradition by raising their children in English.[57] The reasons for this development will be discussed in chapter 4, which deals with language attitudes.

4
Language Attitudes: A Matched-Guise Test

The informants' attitudes toward Pennsylvania German, ethnically marked English, and the regional standard of English were tested with the help of a matched-guise test, in which the informants rated short pieces of language.[1] The basic assumption was that the informants' reactions toward the speaker of a certain variety reflect their attitude toward that variety itself, and that, by the same token, their general attitude toward certain varieties guides their judgment of the speakers of these varieties. After a brief introduction to the method and an overview of the data, various diagrams will be presented which, by showing ever more detailed aspects of the data, facilitate specific statements about the informants' attitudes.

The matched-guise test cannot be separated from the larger context of the present study; together with the language use analysis presented earlier, it aims at accounting for the linguistic differences found among the informants. Not only will this test give insight into the effects these varieties have on the informants when they hear them, it will also structure the informants with respect to their attitudes toward the varieties. To do this, a number of questions will have to be answered. The subchapters entitled "First Perspective: Questions" and "Second Perspective: Voices" will deal with whether or not the presence of any negative and/or positive stereotypes in connection with the Pennsylvania Germans is reflected in the data. More specifically, it will be examined which of the guises, if any, are perceived to carry the stereotype of the "dumb Dutchman" (to name only the one which appears to be most prevalent). "Third Perspective: Informants" constitutes an attempt to state which informants hold those putative stereotypes. It will have to be seen whether certain social groups among the informants can be identified as sharing common language attitudes. Only if this is the case can one speak about language stereotyping in its true sense. A synopsis will summarize the examination of the informants' language attitudes.

METHOD

The first matched-guise test in linguistics was designed and applied by Lambert and his associates in 1960. In their study as well as in another pioneering study by Lambert (1967), English Canadian and French Canadian listeners rated English and French speakers on fourteen personal characteristics such as intelligence, likeability, and good looks. The same method was applied, among others, by MacKinnon in his study of Scottish Gaelic and English in 1977.[2]

The matched-guise technique has become the most widely used indirect method for the testing of language attitudes.[3] In an ideal matched-guise test, the same bilingual speakers vocalize the same text in their different varieties, usually on audiotape. The informants' reactions are then totally based on their attitudes toward the varieties they hear and are not influenced by extralinguistic factors such as a preference for one speaker's voice over another's.

Most matched-guise tests are combined with semantic differential scales, tools used to enable the informants to express their attitudes toward the varieties (Osgood, Suci, and Tannenbaum 1957). The poles of each scale are formed by adjectives standing in opposition to one another. The informants have a choice of marking one of several grades between the poles. Judgments about language varieties do not simply constitute a unidimensional differentiation of social stratification. To account for the multidimensionality of attitudes, the informants are given a broad set of semantic differential scales helping them to rate the speakers.

TEST DESIGN

The matched-guise test lasted about forty-five minutes. Informants listened to nine pieces of spoken language of approximately sixty seconds each from a tape recorder. The samples came from three pilot interviews carried out with four Pennsylvania German speakers before the actual collection of data.

The speakers were a nonsectarian couple in their sixties from the Mahantango Valley, a sixty-six-year-old New Order Mennonite farmer from Snyder County, and a sixty-three-year-old Lutheran minister from Lehigh County. All the speakers had acquired Pennsylvania German natively. The contents of the samples centered on the daily chores on the farm, school life, hunting, and growing up in "Pennsylvania Dutch country."

The nine samples were arranged randomly so that the informants did not notice that the guises had been collected from only four speakers, all of whom could be heard once in Pennsylvania German (PG) and once in more or less strongly accented Pennsylvania German English (PGE). In addition, one of the speakers, the minister (speaker D, voice 9), spoke practically unaccented American English (AmE), a variety he had acquired during his extended service outside the Pennsylvania German area.

The order of the guises along with additional information, such as the respective speaker, the variety used, the theme, a short description of the way of speaking, and the length of each sample, can be seen in figure 4.1.

Voice	Speaker	Variety	Theme	Characteristics	Length
1	D	PG	his hobby: writing PG texts	nonsectarian, male, little English interference, Lehigh County	54 seconds
2	C	PG	interior of a one-room schoolhouse	New Order Mennonite, male, quiet, little PG interference, Snyder County	56 seconds
3	B	PG	recipe for potpie	nonsectarian, female, energetic, little English interference, Mahantango Valley	52 seconds
4	A	PGE	hunting	nonsectarian, male, strong PG interference, Mahantango Valley	55 seconds
5	D	PGE	growing up in rural Pennsylvania	nonsectarian, male, extremely strong PG interference, Lehigh County	59 seconds
6	C	PG	how to churn butter	New Order Mennonite, male, strong English interference, Snyder County	44 seconds
7	B	PGE	children's daily chores on the farm	nonsectarian, female, fast, very strong English interference, Mahantango Valley	70 seconds
8	A	PG	the various jobs he held in his life	nonsectarian, male, little English interference, Mahantango Valley	65 seconds
9	D	AmE	school life in rural Pennsylvania	male, regional standard, acquired in professional life as a minister	37 seconds

Figure 4.1: Guises played to the informants

Language Attitudes: A Matched-Guise Test 213

The exact wording of the nine samples, together with a translation of the four Pennsylvania German samples and a brief description of their linguistic quality, is given below. In the transcriptions, both silent and voiced pauses are indicated (cf. Crystal and Davy 1969, 34f.; Crystal and Davy 1975, 16; and Quirk et al. 1985, 1605). A period (.) marks a brief pause, a dash (–) a unit pause, and two dashes (—) a double pause. Voiced pauses are marked by *uh* (representing [ɜː(m)]). False starts and hesitations are represented according to normal orthographic practices.

Voice 1:

hab ich eeniche hobbies . well – ich uh gleich fer Deitsch zu schreiwe . sell kannscht uh – aaseehne – un – ich hott ich wott yuscht ich hett viel meh Zeit fer sell zu duh – ich muss uh ich muss plenty Zeit hawwe . ich muss uh fer sell zu duh ich muss an ee Ding denke . uh uh – gudi Weil – no was ich duh uh – ich duh Sache hieschreiwe – Gedanke as ich hab vun . vun dem Ding as ich schreiwe will duh ich . Sache hieschreiwe – un . uh – ich denk an wo wie . is es bescht . fer sell zu sage – un no . schreiw ich sell hie un – no mol . wann ich . lang driwwer gedenkt hab . un ich bin . ich fiehl gut davun . duhn ichs aafange zammehenge

Do I have any hobbies? Well, I like to write in Dutch, you can see that. And I just wish I had more time to do that. I must have plenty of time, to do that I must think of one thing for quite a while. Then what I do, I write down things. I write down thoughts I have of the thing I want to write. And I think what's the best way to say that, and then I write it down; and then when I've thought about it for a long time and I feel good about it, I start putting it together.

Characteristics: Nonsectarian Pennsylvania German with little English interference. Fluent, native command. Two direct lexical borrowings (*hobbies, plenty*) from English. Retroflex /r/ in *schreiwe, hieschreiwe*. Dark /l/ in *will, sell*.

Voice 2:

well – no he would have the classes reciting in front – they were up in front – see there was a desk – there is the old desk – where the teacher stood back of – and where those drawers are – there was books . lined up in front there – and uh – then uh . usually . there were four rows of seats – two on the boys' side and two . rows on the . girls' side probably eight – eight in a row – maybe only six . six or eight of them in a row – and that's the way —that's the way it was and then . when we recited we would go up on each front – there was . it was a folding contraption – there was a desk part on the back here – where you had your books in and . where you studied on top of and then here was a seat – and this could be . could be – when you were finished you would . put it back . and when you wanted to use it you'd push it down

Characteristics: Sectarian Pennsylvania German English. Less marked than nonsectarian English. Final [ɪ] in *usually* and *probably*. Monophthongs [eː] in *eight, way* and [oː] in *row, folding*. Monophthong [ɑː] in *down*.

Voice 3:

no duhn ich uh ich deet sage vielleicht drei vier koppche voll Mehl rausmesse – no duhn ich uh – uh now . ich bin net supposed fer die Oier zu yuuse wechem Cholesterol awwer – ich duh alsemols die . die Oier nei – vier fimf Oier . uffkleppere un un . ins Mehl mixe – un no . Millich uh – fer – s nassmache weescht so desds ausrolle kannscht – no duhschts yuscht . recht dinn ausrolle . un den schneide – un no duhscht uh wann dei Brieh kochich is – en layer potpie in dei . Kessel . no . en layer uh – gschleisde . Grummbeere – now mir . duhne Grummbeere nei – no en layer potpie – no Grummbeere no potpie no Grummbeere – seller Weg bisd all dei potpie im Kessel hoscht — no kochschts bisds weech is

Then I measure out, I'd say maybe three or four cups of flour. Then I— now, I'm not supposed to use eggs because of the cholesterol, but I sometimes put eggs in, beat four or five eggs and mix them into the flour; and then milk, to moisten it, you know, so that you can roll it out. Then you just roll it out quite thinly and then cut it. And then, when your broth is boiling, you put a layer of potpie into your pot, then a layer of sliced potatoes—now we put potatoes in—then a layer of potpie, then potatoes, then potpie, then potatoes. That way until you have all your potpie in the pot. Now you cook it until it's soft.

Characteristics: Nonsectarian Pennsylvania German with little English interference. Fluent, native command. The lexical borrowings from English (*cholesterol, potpie, layer, gschleist* [from *sliced*]) are *termini technici* from cooking. Trilled /r/ in all Pennsylvania German words (*Brieh, Grummbeere, ausrolle, uffkleppere*), retroflex /r/ in English loan words (*cholesterol, layer*).

Voice 4:

one summer . during the Fourth of July – me and her went for a ride and went up in the mountains upstate – and we saw a bear — and beaver . it has beaver upstate then too we — passed a place where there was three beaver in one dam one time – and when I was a little fellow I used to do a lot of trapping — skunks . possum . coon . muskrats – my sister has a picture . where I'm holding a skunk here on my arm like this – a little one – that one I had pretty tame – but one time I had . I forget how many I had penned up – a skunk really isn't much of a scared animal they . they can't run fast – for trapping every time you'd catch one, we used to shoot them with a twenty-two rifle — but . they'd spray every time you'd shoot one — well then you had to carry them home – oh . we smelled

Characteristics: Nonsectarian Pennsylvania German English with strong interference from German. Syntactic feature: *it has beaver upstate*. Phonological features: [ʌ] in *one, up, skunks, run*; monophthongs [eː] in *upstate, place, tame, spray* and [oː] in *holding, home*; monophthong [ɑː] in *mountains*; [s] in *three*; [v] in *one, went, we*.

Voice 5:

no . I grew up in a little town it was down there in Lehigh County – and . the town . near the town was East Texas – that's a dumb name for Pennsylvania but that was it . East Texas – it was six miles west of Allentown . a town of three hundred people – and uh – uh that's where I went to school – now my father w was not a farmer we had a little place maybe three quarters of an acre we grew vegetables – such as beans and peas – lots of raspberries — and uh . early in the springtime we would go hunting dandelion and clean that and lots of Easter clothes . were bought with the money that we used to s . sell from the dandelion early in the spring

Characteristics: Nonsectarian Pennsylvania German English with extremely strong interference from German. Phonological features: [ʌ] in up, *dumb, hunting*; [tʃ] in *vegetables*; [s] in *beans, peas, raspberries*; monophthongs [eː] in *place, acre* and [oː] in *no*; monophthong [ɑː] in *town, down, County*; [s] in *three, Easter clothes, with the*; [v] in *was, west, where, went, we, would*; [ṳː] in *school*; [w] in *vegetables*; trilled /r/ in *grew*.

Voice 6:

aus die Raahm vun die Millich – vun die Kieh — ja des uh des hot Millich unne drin ghatt un owwe druff war die Raahm – die Fett vun die Millich – un mir hen sell sell ab . genumme – un uh . in en Haffe geduh – bis uh die neegscht Woch vun ee Woch to die anner zu die anner – now – mir hen ken refrigerator ghatt . wie ich erscht meind – un no hen mers in die schpringhouse ghalde . die Brunnehaus wu die . Brunne war – un des hot Saches k kalt ghalde un mir hen s uh gemeent . sell war wunderbar kalt – awwer no wie die . frigeration rumkumme is no wars annerschder

From the cream from the milk of the cows—yes, the milk was at the bottom and on top was the cream, the fat of the milk. And we skimmed it off and put it into a crock until the following week, from one week to the other. Now, we didn't have a refrigerator as I remember just now. And so we kept it in the springhouse, the *Brunnehaus*, where the spring was. And that kept the things cool, and we thought that that was very cold. But then when refrigeration came up, then it was different.

Characteristics: Sectarian Pennsylvania German with strong English interference. Fluent, native command. No dative case (*aus die Raahm vun die Millich vun die Kieh*). English loan words (*refrigerator, frigeration*), sometimes even where Pennsylvania German terms exist (*schpringhouse* for *Brunnehaus*). Phonological interferences from English: retroflex /r/ in English loan words (*refrigerator*) as well as in Pennsylvania German words (*drin, druff, Brunnehaus, Brunne*); dark /l/ in *sell, ghalde, kalt*.

Voice 7:

and . we had our chores that we had to do in the morning before we went to school – like uh the girls – uh – we had to s sometimes sweep the kitchen – we had to do the dishes – in the morning – we had to fix our beds – now this was all before we went to school and if we fooled around – and made that we got late – then of course sometimes we got punished you know . for fooling around – and . we also in the evening we had work that we had to do then . after we came home from school . we had to . bring in in the wood we had the old cook stoves – and the ashes had to be taken out in the evening and wood had to be brought in so it would last over night . and also coal had to be brought in – we had a a coal stove in the living room . and a and a . wood burning stove in the kitchen – and then uh coal had to be brought in and the ashes taken out – we had to . f feed the chickens in the evening – we had to milk the cows – and uh – s bed the . put straw down for the cows – and . all that kind of things you know – it was all our work that we had to do

Characteristics: Nonsectarian Pennsylvania German English with very strong interference from German. Syntactic feature: *made that we got late*. Phonological features: [s] in *chores, girls, dishes, beds, stoves, chickens, cows*; monophthongs [eː] in *made, came* and [oː] in *old, coal, stove*; monophthong [ɑː] in *around, out, cows*; [v] in *we, sweep, went, wood*; [u̞ː] in *do*.

Voice 8:

well . zuerscht hab ich gebauert ich hab ich . hab gebauert uff die Bauerei nooch as my daadi gschtarewe is – un – ich hab gebauert no fer elf Yaahr . ich war achzeh Yaahr wu . mei daadi gschtarewe is – no hab ich gebauert — mer hen Kieh ghatt un Hinkel ghatt – mer hen en hunnert Acker ghatt . as mer gebauert hen — no mein neegschter job hab ich im Busch gschafft ich hab Beem umgemacht . Holz ghackt – un a lot vun sellem is noch die mines gange fer – die mines – was sie in die mine gyuust hen fer – drowwe hewe — datt haw ich siwwe Yaahr gschafft – no – vun datt haw ich uffm Weg gschafft – ich hab helfe . Darrwege mache – des uh – die Darrwege – blacktop – datt haw ich noch gschafft – well . ich hab ich schaff now noch park . partzeit now noch – ich hab dreissich Yaahr an sellem gschafft — un sell bringt mich uff zu now

Well, first I was a farmer. I farmed on the farm after my dad had died. And I was then a farmer for eleven years. I was eighteen years old when my dad died. Then I was the farmer. We had cows and we had chickens. We had a hundred acres which we farmed. Then for my next job I worked in the woods. I cut trees and chopped wood. And a lot of that went to the mines, for the mines, what they used in the mine to hold it up. There I worked seven years. Then, after that, I worked on the road. I helped to build tar roads, the tar roads, blacktop. There I still worked, well, I'm still working there part time now. I've been working there for thirty years. And that brings me up to now.

Characteristics: Nonsectarian Pennsylvania German with little English interference. Fluent, native command. Few lexical borrowings from English (*well, mines, part* in *partzeit*). Trilled /r/ in all Pennsylvania German words (*Bauerei, gschtarewe, drowwe, dreissich*), retroflex /r/ in English loan word only (*part*).

Voice 9:

it was a two-room school see – there were grades one – two three and four were — Mrs. Snyder was our teacher she's a married woman – and then — the other side was five six seven and eight . and that was uh Mr. Yohe was our teacher – and so I went . for eight years in the same building but two different rooms – and that school was run by the Lower Macungie Township system – and uh at . the end of eight grades . you took the township examination

Characteristics: Regional-standard English.

After the informants had heard one speaker, they were asked to fill out one sheet of the matched-guise test. Each sheet comprised twenty-nine questions, the first twenty-one of which were to be answered on a five-grade semantic differential scale.[4] In question 1, for example, the poles of the scale were formed by the expressions "well educated" and "poorly educated."

The informants had a choice of five grades to rate each speaker, the center cell indicating an indifferent attitude. The two cells forming the poles represent the notion "extremely." Accordingly, in question 1 the informants had the choice between the five grades "extremely well educated," "well educated," "neutral," "poorly educated," and "extremely poorly educated."

The ratings were fed into the computer in such a way that the left-hand pole was counted as 1, the next circle as 2, the neutral cell as 3, the following circle as 4, and the right-hand pole as 5 (figure 4.2). Through the odd number of cells, the informants were given the possibility of expressing indifference. Such a "soft" test device seemed to be more in

Language Attitudes: A Matched-Guise Test 219

```
        well educated              poorly educated
o───────────o───────────o───────────o───────────o
1           2           3           4           5
extremely               neutral                 extremely
```

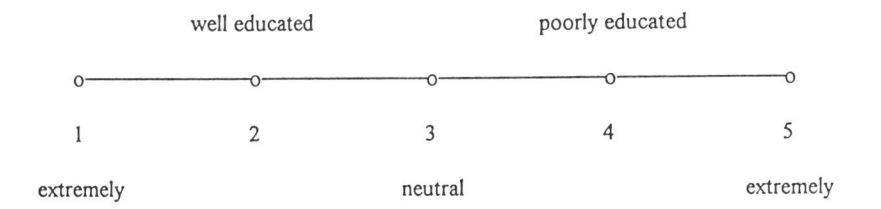

Figure 4.2: Example of a five-grade semantic differential scale

line with reality than an even number of cells, which disallows neutral answers and may at times force the informants to make artificial decisions. The presence of a neutral cell did not produce an excessive amount of undecided answers. The five-grade semantic scale was preferred over a seven- or even nine-grade scale for practical reasons; on the one hand, it gives the informant enough possibilities to choose from, and, on the other, keeps the scale short enough to be clear.[5]

The questions were carefully chosen according to the sociolinguistic situation of the Pennsylvania German speech community encountered during the pilot interviews and in numerous preparatory conversations. The answer to each question constitutes one informant's connotative association in connection with a speaker.

The questions were selected in such a way that the sum of all associations results in a fairly comprehensive description of the informant's attitude toward the speakers and their varieties. They reached from education (question 1), intellectual ability (question 2), professional status (question 3), power (question 4), and wealth (question 5) via a variety of character traits (questions 6–15), origin (question 16), religion (question 17), and lifestyle (question 18) to intellegibility (question 19), identification with the speaker (question 20), and the informants' familiarity with the variety they heard (question 21).

In detail, the opposites given in the first twenty-one questions were as follows: (1) well educated–poorly educated, (2) intelligent–dumb, (3) professional–laborer, (4) is in charge of things–has little authority, (5) has a lot of money–has little money, (6) honest–insincere, (7) dependable–not dependable, (8) generous–stingy, (9) friendly and likeable–unfriendly and unlikeable, (10) good sense of humor–no sense of humor, (11) self-confident–unsure of self, (12) hard-working–lazy, (13) reserved–flashy, (14) modest–boastful, (15) stubborn–easy-going, (16) comes from a city–comes from a rural area, (17) nonreligious–religious,

(18) progressive/open-minded–traditional/conservative, (19) easy to understand–difficult to understand, (20) I'd like to speak like this speaker myself–I wouldn't like to speak like this speaker myself, (21) I meet such speakers often–I meet such speakers rarely.

The majority of questions 22–29 did not consist of polar adjectives and were therefore not scalable. They served as external evidence supplementing the data from questions 1–21.

In some instances the test was administered to more than one informant at a time. After the instructions were given, the first of nine voices was played. The informants were then asked to answer the twenty-nine questions before this procedure was repeated for voices 2–9. Group administration did not detrimentally affect the results. In general, the informants were very enthusiastic about this part of the interview. The non-Pennsylvania German informants listened to the four Pennsylvania German samples with great interest, even though they could not understand what was being said.

CHOICE OF TEXTS AND SPEAKERS

In most matched-guise tests the reading texts have exactly the same contents in all the language varieties. Although this is the only way to provide entirely comparable samples, it would have produced extremely artificial language for two reasons. First, Pennsylvania German is, at least for the average speaker, merely a spoken variety without a standardized orthography and, therefore, hard to read. Secondly, a number of informants would have found it as difficult to read the English text fluently.

Therefore, during the preliminary stages of the study, the speakers were asked to retell a short Aesopian fable in their respective varieties. It became clear, however, that for a number of them the contents of the fable was difficult to relate. Informants listening to the guises might have rated the speakers' success or failure in getting across the right plot rather than the different language varieties. Moreover, the result of those reproductions would have been fairly artificial pieces of text, almost as artificial as texts read aloud.

To avoid these difficulties, clippings from actual interviews were selected as guises. Thus, absolute naturalness of speech was obtained at the relatively small cost of slight deviations in contents. As the themes of all the clippings center on the Pennsylvania German world, the differences in contents are felt to be negligible. The disadvantage of relative inequality is compensated by complete naturalness.

At first glance, the selection of the speakers may appear to be problematic. The objection could be raised that a broader variety should have been added. For example, younger voices could have been included in the test, not only complete bilinguals from the sectarian group, but also nonfluent speakers of Pennsylvania German from the nonsectarian group. In addition, a speech sample of pure regional standard by a non-Pennsylvania German speaker could have been given.

For a number of practical reasons, however, all such ideas were dismissed. First, the informants would have had too many guises to rate. Secondly, the design of an authentic matched-guise test with corresponding pairs or triplets of guises would have been destroyed. Thirdly, young nonsectarians are native speakers of English; their Pennsylvania German pieces would have been the only nonfluent samples in the test. Finally, as all the speakers selected are Pennsylvania Germans and belong into the same age group, they may be regarded as a fairly homogeneous group. Therefore, not only single guises are comparable, but also the sums of ratings within each group, that is, the German voices and the English voices.

STRENGTHS AND WEAKNESSES OF THE MATCHED-GUISE TECHNIQUE

One of the advantages of the matched-guise technique is that it represents a relatively objective device for measuring language attitudes. Unlike in direct questioning, the fieldworkers avoid guiding their informants' responses by the manner in which their questions are phrased. Not knowing that they are listening to the same voices twice or three times, the informants provide relatively unprejudiced data. Moreover, it is more exciting for them to listen to short pieces of language from a tape, and afterwards rate them, than to be asked a list of rather abstract questions.

The most common criticism is that this technique is artificial and too far removed from a genuine language situation (Giles and Bourhis 1976, Bourhis and Giles 1976). People do not normally judge their interlocutors by their voices only. Other general weaknesses, such as tiresome repetition and unnatural reading style (Fasold 1984, 153), were avoided in this particular test. The technique turned out to be unsuitable for the youngest informants, that is, children under the age of nine (informants 24, 35, 49, 50). However, the same is true for the overt questions as a means to investigate attitudes (questionnaire section 3.1).

Another problem was that informant 27 filled out the nine evaluation sheets rather mechanically, using the same pattern for all the speakers. For this reason, his results had to be disregarded. No informant found out that the nine samples came from only four speakers. One listener, however, recognized a grandfather clock ticking in the background on two samples. Fortunately, the informant merely asked whether both men had been interviewed in the same room.

THE DATA: AN OVERVIEW

Figure 4.3 gives an overview of the data. It has a three-dimensional layout, with the voices arranged on the horizontal, the informants on the vertical, and the questions along the third dimension.[6] Each piece of data is, as it were, attached to these three dimensions. This model allows for the examination of the data under the three perspectives of "questions," "voices," and "informants," the data for a certain question, voice, or informant (or groups of them) forming layers of the cube.

Voices, informants, and questions are all ordered from top to bottom or left to right by the average of points. If question 6 shows an average of 1.59, this means that for this question the informants on average assigned 1.59 points to all the voices taken together. Likewise, if informant 6 shows an average of 1.71, this means that she, on average, assigned 1.71 points to all the questions and voices taken together. If voice 9 has an average of 2.21, this means that all the informants in all the questions assigned 2.21 points to voice 9.

In each case, the total numbers of points and answers are given. In the few instances where the number of answers does not match with the number given in parentheses, the informants had not answered one or more questions. In calculating the averages, the totals were divided by the number of questions actually answered.

In the upper part of the figure, the identification numbers of the questions are given together with their poles.

The column "Inf" gives the informants' identification numbers. The social data on the right is the same as in figure 1.5. Of the fifty informants, forty-three successfully participated in the matched-guise test. Of the seven for whom no or no valid data were collected, two were physically unable to undergo this demanding part of the interview (informants 41, 42), four were considered too young (informants 24, 35, 49, 50), and one rated all the voices the same (informant 27).

In the row marked "Voice," the numbers 1–9 indicate the nine voices played to the informants. The four speakers are marked by letters, "A" standing for the nonsectarian husband from the Mahantango Valley, "B" for his wife, "C" for the New Order Mennonite, and "D" for the

Language Attitudes: A Matched-Guise Test

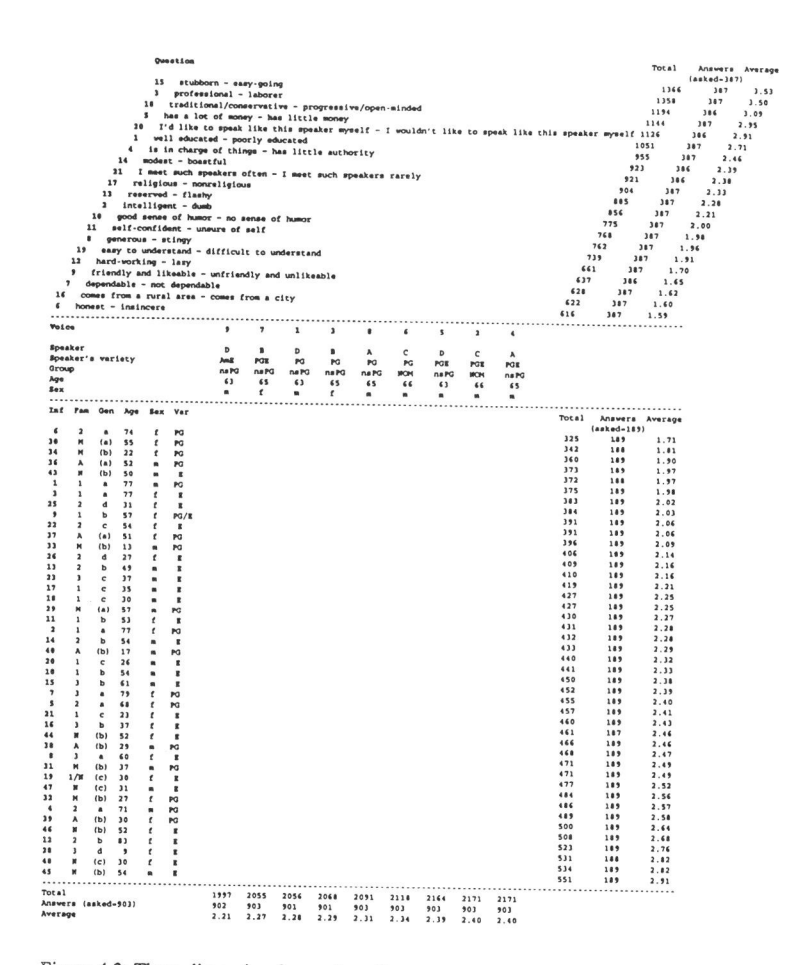

Figure 4.3: Three-dimensional overview diagram

PGE = Pennsylvania German English   nsPG = nonsectarian Pennsylvania German   NOM = New Order Mennonite
For the other abbreviations and symbols, see figure 1.5.

Lutheran minister. The speakers' varieties are indicated by "PG" (Pennsylvania German), "AmE" (unaccented American English), and "PGE" (American English with a distinct Pennsylvania German accent, syntax, lexicon and intonation). In the row designated "Group," "nsPG" means "nonsectarian Pennsylvania German" and "NOM" means "New Order Mennonite." The last two rows of this block give the speakers' age and gender.

The spans of averages in the fields of questions, voices, and informants reveal a number of differences. The voices show the smallest range (0.19), with the lowest value for voice 9 (2.21) and the highest for voices 2 and 4 (2.40). For the nine voices this results in an average gap of 0.021. The range of averages for the informants is wider (1.20), informant 6 having an average of 1.71 and informant 45 one of 2.91. Converted to the forty-three informants, however, the average gap (0.028) is very similar to that for the voices. The twenty-one questions present the widest range (1.94). Question 6, which received the smallest average, has 1.59, while question 15, at the other extreme, has 3.53. The average gap of 0.092 is more than three times greater than that of the informants and voices.

All in all, the questions were perceived as being more diverse than the voices, which is not altogether surprising. Eight of the nine voices were marked as Pennsylvania Germans, either through the use of Pennsylvania German itself or through Pennsylvania German interference in their English. Since all the informants live in the Pennsylvania German area, it can be assumed that they readily detected those features.

The scores for the questions are given in the upper part of figure 4.3. The lower an average for a question (and the further to the front a question is situated in the diagram), the more the informants associated the first characteristic given in each line with all the voices taken together.

A comparison of the wordings of the questions with the list given above shows that in three cases (questions 16–18) the poles are reversed. When the data base was established, the positive pole was taken to be on the left and its negative equivalent on the right. This pattern had not been kept consistent in the questionnaire in order to prevent mechanical rating (or at least aid in its detection).

The decision of which pole was positive and which negative was generally based on the set of values held by mainstream American society. In some cases, however, the decision was difficult to make, so that the general perspective of the people living in the area under examination was taken to be the decisive factor. In question 16 "comes from a rural area" was considered to be the positive pole over "comes from a city," in 17 "religious" over "nonreligious," and in 18 "traditional/conservative" over "progressive/open-minded." For the same reason, "stubborn" rather than "easy-going" was taken to be the positive adjective in question 15. Pilot interviews had shown that especially for sectarian Pennsylvania Germans and conservative nonsectarian Pennsylvania Germans "easy-going" is not a positive characteristic.

Even in a relatively undifferentiated listing of data such as figure 4.3, preliminary groupings of questions are discernible. Questions 1 and 3–5, which cover the speakers' education and status, cluster in the top third of the continuum. They are joined by question 20, which asks about the informants' identification with the speakers.

The voices are depicted in the middle and at the bottom of figure 4.3. The lower the average, the more favorably a voice was rated. According to their averages, the nine voices can be provisionally divided into three groups, separated from one another by averages of 0.06 and 0.05.

Voice 9, which received the lowest average rating, is the only standard American English sample. The second group comprises voices 1, 3, and 6–8. In this group, all but voice 7, which is a Pennsylvania German English guise, are Pennsylvania German samples. The third group (voices 2, 4, 5) is formed by three Pennsylvania German English samples.

Overall, the regional standard sample that forms group 1 was most favorably rated. In group 2, the presence of voice 7 is rather surprising, especially since it received the lowest average in this group and, therefore, stands quite isolated from the Pennsylvania German English samples forming group 3. The latter group was rated the least favorably, so that, generally speaking, all the informants taken together reveal a more positive attitude toward Pennsylvania German than toward the Pennsylvania German English variety. However, voice 7 shows that there are exceptions to this rule.

Strictly speaking, the idea of the matched-guise test is to compare those pairs (and the triplet) of voices that belong to the same speaker. When this procedure is applied, the material clearly structures itself as well.

The three varieties of speaker D are found to be divided in all three major groups, his regional-standard sample forming group 1, his Pennsylvania German sample belonging to group 2, and his Pennsylvania German English sample being a part of group 3. Likewise, speakers A and C appear in group 2 with their Pennsylvania German sample and in group 3 with their Pennsylvania German English sample.

Speaker B represents an exception; both her samples are found with almost identical ratings in group 2. In fact, speaker B presents the only case where Pennsylvania German English receives a slightly more favorable rating than Pennsylvania German. Speaker B is the only female speaker in the study and has a very energetic and fast speaking style. In both her varieties, she was rated rather favorably. Her husband, speaker A, received less favorable ratings in both his samples. Similarly, speaker

C, the only sectarian speaker, was rated more negatively in both varieties.

The informants' continuum is depicted between the two blocks for the voices. The higher the informants appear on the scale, the more favorably they rated the nine voices.

The largest differences between averages are found at the upper and lower ends of the scale, whereas the large group of informants in the middle shows relatively small differences in averages, clear groupings being difficult to discern.

The majority of the non-Pennsylvania Germans are found toward the end of the scale, which reflects their rather negative attitude toward all nine voices taken together. The various generations of the nonsectarians and the sectarians are more or less widely scattered over the continuum.

First Perspective: Questions

To gain access to the data, it is necessary to determine which of the twenty-one questions cluster. As a first step, the purely statistical instrument of factor analysis will be used. It will be supplemented by a less formalized way of grouping the questions.

Factor Analysis

Factor analysis is a method of data reduction. With respect to the twenty-one questions in this study, one could argue that certain scales correlate in their results, that is, measure very much the same thing. For instance, a speaker who receives positive ratings for education (question 1) may also score high on intelligence (question 2). The present factor analysis tries to identify such clusters of questions, reducing the twenty-one single items or variables to a smaller number of underlying dimensions of meaning, referred to as *factors*. The loadings of the factors determine with which weight the single variables contribute to the constitution of the factors or latent dimensions.

The following factor analysis was computed at the Universitätsrechenzentrum Heidelberg, Germany, with the 6.04 version of the

Language Attitudes: A Matched-Guise Test 227

SAS computer program. In a first step, a correlation matrix was established (figure 4.4). The basic assumption is that correlations may exist between any of the twenty-one questions. Although, theoretically, there could be as many as twenty-one factors, the goal is to reduce the number of factors on the one hand and to obtain a representation of the variables by qualitatively interpretable factors on the other. The questions with a high correlation coefficient are suspected to contain the same factor.

Figure 4.4: Correlation matrix

The more the coefficients in figure 4.4 approximate the value 1.00000, the higher the positive correlation between the two respective questions. Coefficients below 0.4 have been neglected. According to the correlation matrix, the following questions correlate: question 1 with 2–5 and 20; question 2 with 4, 5, and 11; question 4 with 5 and 11; question 6 with 7–9 and 12; question 7 with 8, 9, 11, and 12; question 8 with 9, 10, and 12; question 9 with 10 and 12; question 13 with 14. By contrast, questions 15–19 and 21 do not appear to correlate with any other question. On the basis of these preliminary results, the following two major correlations can be established, which are likely to constitute the two primary factors: questions 1–5, 11, 20 and questions 6–14.

This analysis can be further refined through factor extraction, that is, a principal component analysis. In a first approach, all twenty-one questions are assumed to represent significant factors. Figure 4.5 shows the twenty-one variables with their *eigenvalues*. If only one factor was responsible for the results of all twenty-one variables, its eigenvalue would be 21. Figure 4.5 also gives the percentage of the total mean variation for each factor and the cumulated percentage of variance from factors 1–21.

Factor	Eigenvalue	Percentage of total mean variation	Cumulated percentage of variance
1	4.807460	53.32	53.32
2	2.992559	33.19	86.51
3	0.893879	9.91	96.43
4	0.691233	7.67	104.09
5	0.406046	4.50	108.60
6	0.344633	3.82	112.42
7	0.207237	2.30	114.72
8	0.161766	1.79	116.51
9	0.061900	0.69	117.20
10	0.007406	0.08	117.28
11	−0.027115	−0.30	116.98
12	−0.060274	−0.67	116.31
13	−0.070431	−0.78	115.53
14	−0.092502	−1.03	114.50
15	−0.120341	−1.33	113.17
16	−0.140109	−1.55	111.61
17	−0.165706	−1.84	109.78
18	−0.192359	−2.13	107.64
19	−0.211127	−2.34	105.30
20	−0.222486	−2.47	102.83
21	−0.255506	−2.83	100.00

Figure 4.5: Factor extraction

Factor 1 has an eigenvalue of 4.807460 and accounts for 53.32% of the total mean variation. Factor 2 (eigenvalue: 2.992559) covers 33.19%. As the column on the far right shows, these two factors together are responsible for 86.51% of the variance. Starting with factor 3, the eigenvalues and, therefore, the percentages accounted for by each additional factor decrease rapidly. Starting with factor 11, they even become negative, which means that they go against the general tendency and are, therefore, detrimental. Altogether, only the first two factors are significant.

Figure 4.6 gives a scree plot of the eigenvalues of the twenty-one variables. The variables are ordered along the horizontal and the eigenvalues along the vertical. The *Kaiser criterion* specifies that the number of factors to be extracted equals the number of factors with eigenvalues greater than 1. Accordingly, in the present examination, the number of significant factors is two.

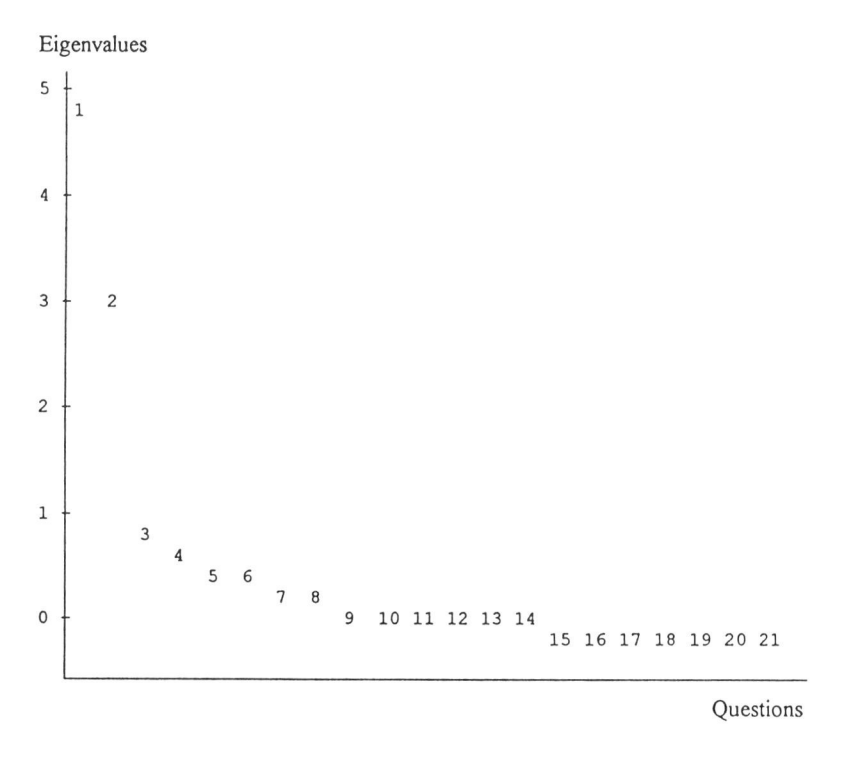

Figure 4.6: Scree plot of eigenvalues

In the next step, the relation of the two significant factors to the individual variables is established. Figure 4.7 shows a factor matrix indicating the factor loadings, that is, the correlation coefficients of factors 1 and 2 for each of the twenty-one questions. For a maximum of interpretability, the factor matrix was rotated with the help of the varimax method.

When rotating, the axes of the coordinate system on which the factors are plotted are turned. In this process the coefficients change, but the eigenvalues do not. After rotation, the variance explained by factor 1 is 4.050273, the eigenvalue of factor 2 is 3.749746.

The values range from 0.86092 (question 1, factor 2) to –0.63610 (question 18, factor 2). Values larger than 0.430946 are in bold type in figure 4.7. Indicating high factor loadings, these values allow the grouping together of questions. The results are quite similar to the tenta-

	Question	Factor 1	Factor 2
1	well educated–poorly educated	–0.00122	**0.86092**
2	intelligent–dumb	0.26521	**0.76421**
3	professional–laborer	–0.32247	**0.69933**
4	is in charge of things–has little authority	0.11841	**0.68406**
5	has a lot of money–has little money	–0.01706	**0.62182**
6	honest–insincere	**0.79049**	0.17583
7	dependable–not dependable	**0.76847**	0.19108
8	generous–stingy	**0.75075**	0.17282
9	friendly and likeable–unfriendly and unlikeable	**0.76105**	0.25933
10	good sense of humor–no sense of humor	**0.56551**	0.24569
11	self-confident–unsure of self	0.34338	**0.48014**
12	hard-working–lazy	**0.67853**	0.05267
13	reserved–flashy	0.35637	–0.05730
14	modest–boastful	**0.48732**	–0.09906
15	stubborn–easy-going	–0.35566	–0.32164
16	comes from a rural area–comes from a city	0.39364	–0.30903
17	religious–nonreligious	**0.53238**	–0.19150
18	traditional/conservative–progressive/open-minded	0.10977	–0.63610
19	easy to understand–difficult to understand	0.28302	0.42586
20	I would–I wouldn't like to speak like this speaker myself	0.21246	**0.55647**
21	I meet such speakers often–I meet such speakers rarely	0.24967	0.10539

Figure 4.7: Rotated factor matrix: Correlation coefficients

tive statements made on the basis of the correlation matrix (figure 4.4): Factor 1 has high loadings for questions 6–9, 10, 12, 14, and 17; factor 2 groups questions 1–5, 11, and 20 together.

Figure 4.8 shows the distribution of the questions with the help of a plot diagram, with factor 1 on the vertical and factor 2 on the horizontal. Two clusters of questions emerge: questions 6–10, 12, and 13–18 around the vertical axis of factor 1, and questions 1–5, 11, and 19–20 around the horizontal axis of factor 2. Only question 21 appears to be located right in the middle between the first and the second cluster. The interpretation of the factors and a discussion of the two groups of questions will follow.

Factor 1

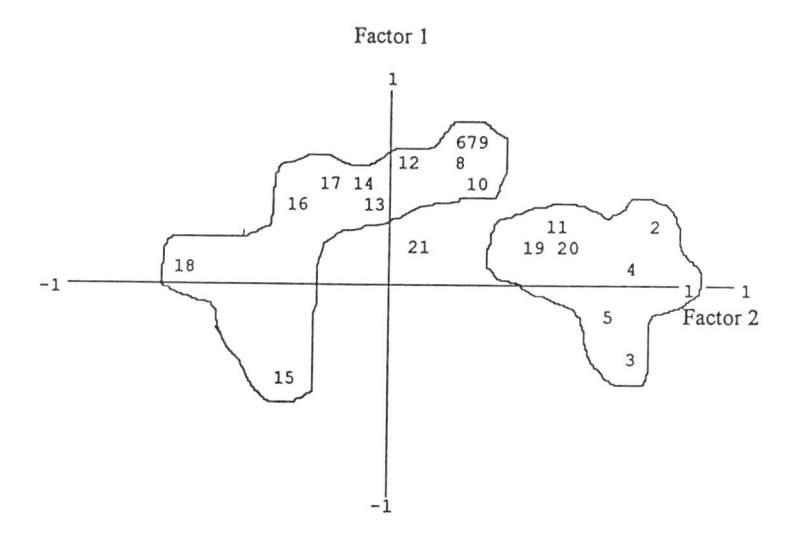

Figure 4.8: Plot of factor pattern

NONSTATISTICAL APPROACH

A second, somewhat less formalized approach produces identical clusters of questions. The underlying assumption is that the nine voices can be divided into two groups, one comprising the ethnically marked voices, that is, all the voices speaking either Pennsylvania German or Pennsylvania German English (voices 1–8), the other one being formed by the regional standard of English (voice 9).

In figure 4.9 the questions are ordered according to the differences between the ethnically marked voices and the regional standard. The greater the difference, the more the characteristic mentioned first in each pair is attributed to the speaker of the unmarked variety only.

A broken line separates positive difference values from negative ones. Above this line, the first characteristic of each pair is associated more with the unmarked variety, below more with the ethnically marked varieties. However, the continuum around this line is so dense and the gaps in this area are so small (e.g., +0.01 vs. –0.01) that the line cannot be regarded as a significant instrument to structure the questions. Instead, large gaps between the difference values are more revealing.

232 Language Attitudes: A Matched-Guise Test

Question	Contents	Voices 1-8	Voice 9	Difference
3	professional – laborer	3.60	2.74	+0.86
19	easy to understand – difficult to understand	1.98	1.32	+0.66
1	well educated – poorly educated	2.78	2.16	+0.62
4	is in charge of things – has little authority	2.52	2.00	+0.52
5	has a lot of money – has little money	3.00	2.53	+0.47
2	intelligent – dumb	2.26	1.81	+0.45
20	I would – wouldn't like to speak like this myself	2.96	2.51	+0.45
11	self-confident – unsure of self	2.02	1.62	+0.40
21	I meet such speakers often – rarely	2.42	2.07	+0.35
6	honest – insincere	1.60	1.46	+0.14
7	dependable – not dependable	1.63	1.53	+0.10
15	stubborn – easy-going	3.53	3.46	+0.07
13	reserved – flashy	2.28	2.27	+0.01
14	modest – boastful	2.39	2.40	-0.01
8	generous – stingy	1.96	2.00	-0.04
12	hard-working – lazy	1.69	1.79	-0.10
9	friendly and likeable – unfriendly and unlikeable	1.63	1.74	-0.11
10	good sense of humor – no sense of humor	1.98	2.14	-0.16
17	religious – nonreligious	2.29	2.67	-0.62
18	traditional – progressive	3.01	3.74	-0.73
16	comes from a rural area – comes from a city	1.50	2.46	-0.96

Figure 4.9: Continuum of questions ordered according to differences between the ethnically marked voices (1–8) and the regional standard of English (voice 9)

```
────────  =  largest differences between two consecutive difference values
- - - - -  =  dividing line between positive and negative difference values
```

The four largest differences between two consecutive difference values are marked by continuous lines. Of these, the three widest gaps are found at the poles of the continuum, namely in the upper part between questions 3 and 19 (0.20) and in the lower part between questions 10 and 17 (0.46) as well as 18 and 16 (0.29). Only one gap of approximately the same size (0.19) is found in the center of the continuum, separating question 21 (+0.35) from question 6 (+0.14). As large gaps are more to be expected at the poles of a continuum than in its center, the line in the center appears to be the most significant. Therefore, the questions may be divided into two large groups.

Figure 4.10 facilitates an overview of the data given in figure 4.9 in the form of a diagram. The values the questions scored for voices 1–8

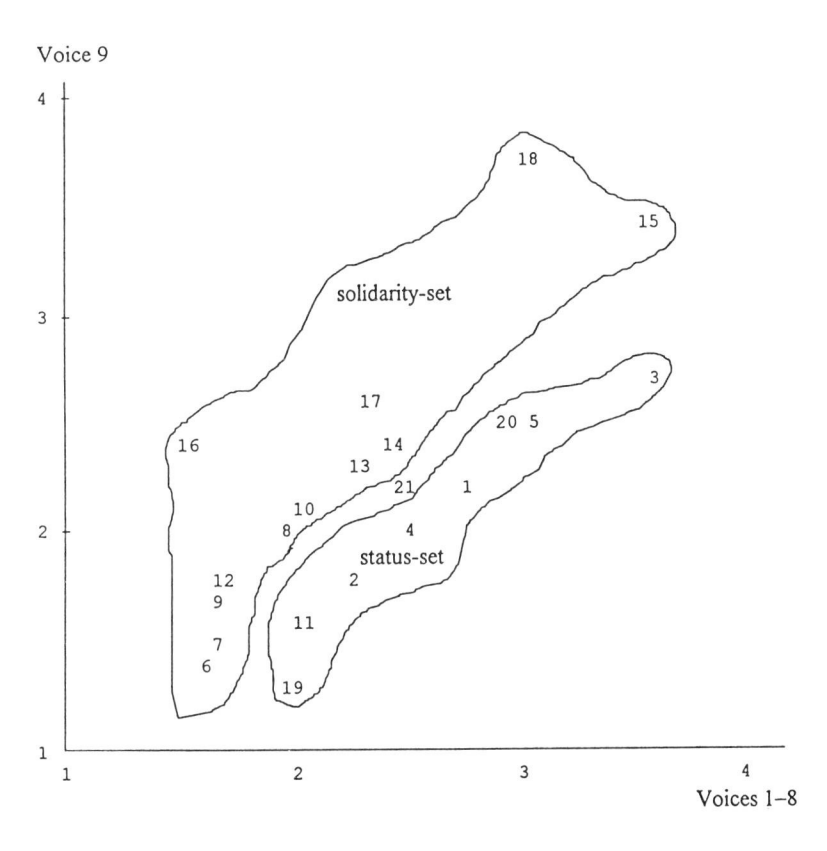

Figure 4.10: Continuum of questions according to their scores for the ethnically marked voices (1–8) and the regional standard of English (voice 9)

are given on the horizontal, those for voice 9 on the vertical. The numbers indicate the questions. The advantage of the diagram over the table lies in the fact that the variances leading to each difference value become significant. Circles mark the clusters of questions. Even though the border between the two clusters may be less clear than in figure 4.8, the groups in the two diagrams are identical. The factor analysis and the less formalized method identify the same clusters of questions.[7]

The first group comprises the first eight questions listed in figure 4.9. They deal with education (1), intellectual ability (2), professional status (3), power (4), wealth (5), self-confidence (11), intellegibility (19), and identification with the speaker (20). Following Carranza and Ryan (1975, 91), this group will be referred to as a *status-stressing* set of questions; their guiding theme is social success.

The second group comprises the last twelve questions. They concern emotional issues such as honesty (6), dependability (7), generosity (8), friendliness (9), humor (10), diligence (12), reserve (13), modesty (14), stubbornness (15), rural origin (16), religiousness (17), and conservatism (18). This group of questions will be termed the *solidarity-stressing* set.

In both diagrams, question 21 is located right in between the two large clusters. In view of the contents of the question, this result is not surprising. Since familiarity with a certain variety is neither a question of status nor of solidarity, question 21 will be excluded from all subsequent calculations.

In figures 4.9 and 4.10 a positive difference value indicates that the informants associated the positive characterization with voice 9 (the voice speaking an ethnically unmarked variety) more than with voices 1–8 (the ethnically marked voices).

In the opinion of all the informants taken together, the left poles of the questions on the first thirteen ranks, down to the dividing line between positive and negative difference values, characterize a speaker of the regional standard more than an ethnically marked speaker. The most important characteristics associated with the regional standard are the positive poles of the status-set questions described earlier. Among these, being a professional as opposed to a laborer stands out by far with respect to its difference value.

In addition, speakers of the regional standard are on the whole believed to be better educated, to have more authority and money, and to be more self-confident than speakers of ethnically marked English. Further, all the informants taken together say that the regional-standard variety is easier to understand and that they are more familiar with it. Moreover, the majority of the informants would prefer speaking regional standard to speaking an ethnically marked variety. To a far lesser extent, standard speakers are also perceived to be more honest, dependable, stubborn, and reserved than speakers who reveal their affiliation with the Pennsylvania Germans through their speech.

The status set also includes question 2 (intelligence). It was found that higher intelligence is attributed to speakers of unmarked English. Thus, the material reflects the presence of the stereotype of the "dumb Dutchman." This stereotype, however, is composed of a wider variety of negative characteristics than simply that of being unintelligent. The order of the question scales at the top of figure 4.9 shows how large a share each single negative trait is likely to have. Being a laborer seems to be the most important component, followed by poor education, little authority, and little money. Lack of intelligence and self-confidence, however, do not appear to be the strongest, let alone the only, components of the stereotype of the "dumb Dutchman."

Starting with question 14, the adjectives and statements on the left are taken to be more characteristic of ethnically marked speakers than of regional-standard speakers. All these questions belong to the solidarity set. The characteristics attributed to the Pennsylvania Germans include modesty, generosity, diligence, likeability, and a good sense of humor. Whereas for these questions the gaps between the difference values are extremely small, the three final questions (16–18) are clearly separated from the rest. It can be stated, therefore, that besides the negative stereotype discussed above, religiousness, conservatism, and the fact that they live in a rural area are perceived to be the main characteristics of the Pennsylvania Germans.

SECOND PERSPECTIVE: VOICES

The two large groups of questions isolated in the previous chapter will be used to show which character traits were associated with which voices. In addition, question 2 (intelligent–dumb) will serve as an indicator of the reflection of the wide-spread sterotype of the "dumb Dutchman" in the data.

Further information will be presented from outside the actual matched-guise test. In questions 22–29, each voice was characterized with the help of supplementary questions which were not part of the computed material. The answers give further evidence of how the informants perceived the guises.

STATUS DIMENSION

The table at the bottom of figure 4.11 shows the scores of the nine voices for the status set of questions, that is, on the socially evaluative dimension. The lower the value, the more favorable the score.

By far the largest gap separates voice 9 (2.08) from voice 2 (2.38). This result is an indication that the division of the voices into ethnically marked (voices 1–8) and regional-standard English (voice 9) was justified. While the gap between voice 2 and voice 1 (2.50) is also relatively large, the six voices toward the end of the continuum share almost the same values (between 2.65 and 2.71).

Language Attitudes: A Matched-Guise Test

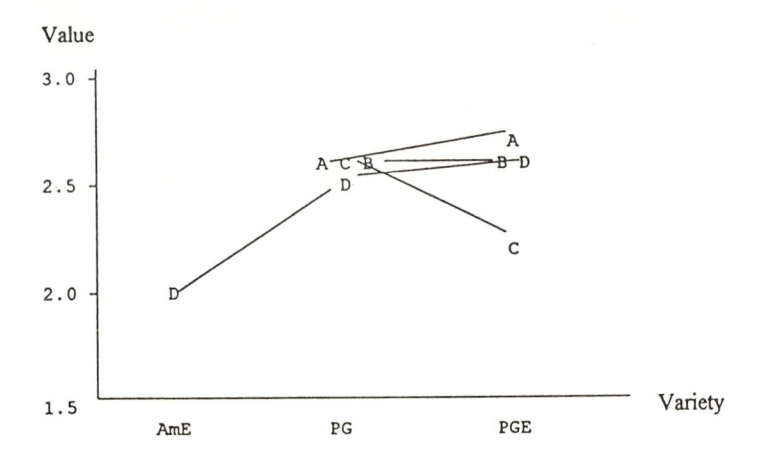

Voice	Speaker	Variety	Value
9	D	AmE	2.08
2	C	PGE	2.38
1	D	PG	2.50
7	B	PGE	2.65
3	B	PG	2.67
6	C	PG	2.67
5	D	PGE	2.67
8	A	PG	2.68
4	A	PGE	2.71

Figure 4.11: Continuum of voices based on status-set questions (1–5, 11, 19, 20)

The fact that the regional standard of English (voice 9) and the Mennonite's English sample (voice 2) received the most favorable ratings for status fully corresponds with the findings of the phonological examinations of the informants' English varieties. Sectarian English is considerably less marked by interferences from Pennsylvania German than the English variety spoken by the nonsectarians. In its degree of markedness, it is comparable to the regional standard.

The results also show that on the whole there is no clear-cut difference in status ratings between the Pennsylvania German samples and their Pennsylvania German English counterparts.

The top part of figure 4.11 presents the data in the form of a diagram. Pairs and a triplet of voices belonging to the same speaker are graphically connected to facilitate comparison.

Speaker A received the most negative ratings for both his varieties, with a slight preference for Pennsylvania German (voice 8: 2.68) over Pennsylvania German English (voice 4: 2.71). Although speaker B's two varieties are located in the same area, this time Pennsylvania German English (voice 3: 2.67) is slightly favored over Pennsylvania German (voice 7: 2.65). The same pattern, only much more distinctive, is found for speaker C, whose Pennsylvania German is rated almost like that of the other three speakers (voice 6: 2.67), but whose Pennsylvania German English is attributed by far higher social status (voice 2: 2.38). It is only surpassed by speaker D's regional standard of English (voice 9: 2.08). The latter's ethnically marked variety of English (voice 5: 2.67) received rates similar to the other ethnic guises, while his Pennsylvania German (voice 1: 2.50) was rated rather favorably.

Even though question 2 (intelligent–dumb) is included in the status set of questions, it will be examined separately for further evidence of how important intelligence is in the formation of the stereotype of the "dumb Dutchman." As was indicated in figure 4.9, the epithet does not necessarily constitute the most significant, let alone the sole, component of this notion.

In figure 4.12, the nine voices are ordered from top to bottom according to the values they scored for intelligence. Voice 9, the only guise using the regional standard of English, was considered to belong to the most intelligent person in the continuum. The gap between the value of voice 9 and the next voice (1) is the largest in the table (0.19). The next four ranks are occupied by the four Pennsylvania German guises (voices 1, 3, 6, 8), followed by the four voices using Pennsylvania German English (voices 2, 5, 7, 4). The large gap at the top and the unusually clear clustering show that the stereotype is present among the informants.

Within the ethnically marked varieties themselves, the voices using Pennsylvania German received better ratings for intelligence than those using Pennsylvania German English. This indicates that the stereotype of the "dumb Dutchman" is not a uniform, undifferentiated phenomenon. An interesting aspect of this notion emerges from the fact that the characterization "dumb" is attributed more to Pennsylvania Germans speaking accented English than to those speaking Pennsylvania German. In other words, "dumb" seems to denote the inability to speak "proper" English.

A look at the respective guises (*see* top of figure 4.12) shows that in each case the Pennsylvania German voice received a higher rating for intelligence than the Pennsylvania German English guise. Speaker D scored the largest differences, followed by speakers A and B, whose dif-

238   Language Attitudes: A Matched-Guise Test

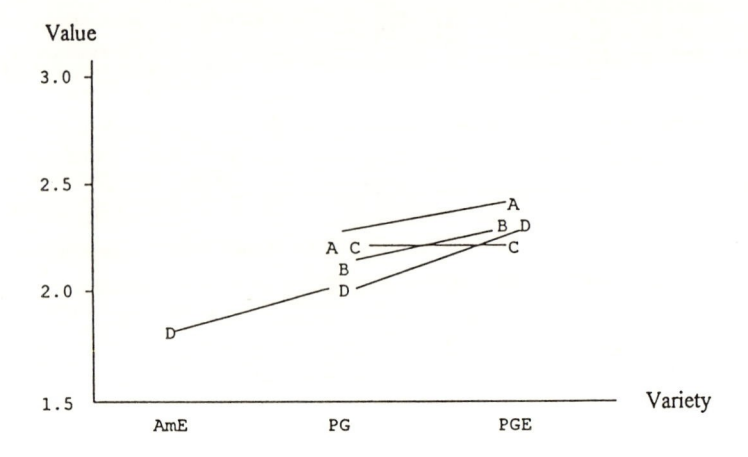

[Figure: line graph with Value axis (1.5 to 3.0) and Variety axis (AmE, PG, PGE)]

Voice	Speaker	Variety	Value
9	D	AmE	1.81
1	D	PG	2.00
3	B	PG	2.16
6	C	PG	2.20
8	A	PG	2.25
2	C	PGE	2.25
5	D	PGE	2.34
7	B	PGE	2.37
4	A	PGE	2.48

Figure 4.12: Continuum of voices based on intelligence (question 2)

ference values are almost identical. The Mennonite speaker C shows hardly any difference in the ratings for his two guises. His Pennsylvania German English sample scored the best rating for intelligence of all the ethnically marked English guises in the test.

In both figures 4.11 and 4.12, speaker A's guises are located at the top of the scale in the area of least favorable ratings. Speaker D's curves for his triplet of guises are practically identical. The rating patterns for speakers B and C, however, differ in the two diagrams. With respect to status, both speakers' Pennsylvania German English guises were preferred to their Pennsylvania German guises. As far as intelligence is concerned, however, the scores are reversed.

In all, the scores for intelligence (figure 4.12: between 1.81 and 2.48) are better than those for general status (figure 4.11: between 2.08 and 2.71). Apparently, the "dumb Dutchman" is not primarily characterized by lack of intelligence, but other factors are more important. Figure 4.9 showed that being a laborer, being poorly educated, and having little authority and money are stronger traits. Another important characteristic is being difficult to understand (question 19), which is congruent with the earlier observation that the marked variety of English many Pennsylvania Germans speak contributes to the stereotype.

SOLIDARITY DIMENSION

Figure 4.13 shows the continuum of voices based on the solidarity set of questions. Again, small values indicate favorable ratings.

The same two voices (9 and 2) that scored the highest ratings in status are assigned by far the lowest ratings on the solidarity scales (2.30 and 2.41). Sectarian English (voice 2) is rated even lower than the regional standard (voice 9). Once again, the ethnically marked voices cluster very closely (between 1.98 and 2.18), all scoring considerably more favorable results than voices 2 and 9.[8]

The top part of figure 4.13 gives an overview of the relations between the pairs and the triplet. The patterns for speakers A and C and voices 1 and 5 of speaker D are very similar. In each case, Pennsylvania German is rated more favorably than Pennsylvania German English. This relation is reversed for speaker B. In the latter case, however, both guises are very close together and rated rather positively.

In comparison with figure 4.11 (status), the relations for speakers C and D are reversed. Whereas for status speaker C scored higher with Pennsylvania German English, his Pennsylvania German is rated more positively for solidarity. The difference in the patterning of speaker D's voices 1 and 9 is even more striking. For status, the regional standard (voice 9) scores high, whereas on the solidarity dimension Pennsylvania German is rated more positively.

240   Language Attitudes: A Matched-Guise Test

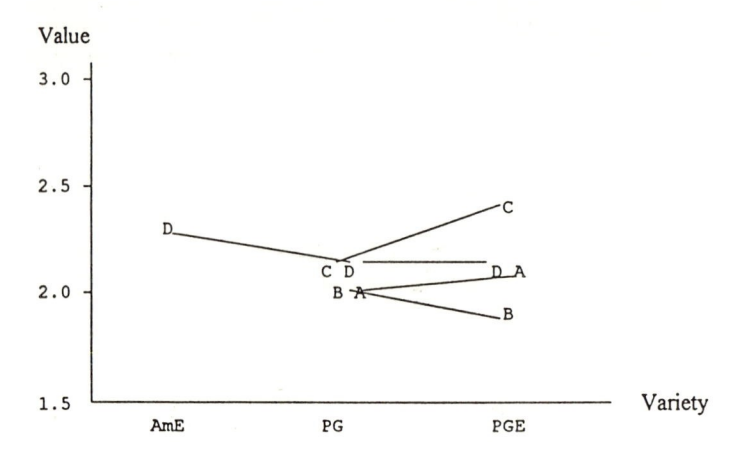

Voice	Speaker	Variety	Value
7	B	PGE	1.98
3	B	PG	2.01
8	A	PG	2.03
6	C	PG	2.10
1	D	PG	2.11
4	A	PGE	2.16
5	D	PGE	2.18
9	D	AmE	2.30
2	C	PGE	2.41

Figure 4.13: Continuum of voices based on solidarity-set questions (6–10, 12–18)

Figure 4.14 sums up the scores for the varieties on the status and solidarity dimensions. The two ethnically marked guises score almost identical values if all the informants are taken together. Both received by far better ratings on the solidarity dimension than on the status dimension. The difference is larger for Pennsylvania German (2.06 vs. 2.63) than for Pennsylvania German English (2.18 vs. 2.60).

The scores for the regional standard contrast sharply. This variety received more positive ratings on the status dimension than on the solidarity dimension.

In sum, the informants attribute high social status, such as education, intelligence, wealth, and authority, to the regional standard; if they had the choice, ethnically unmarked English would be the variety they

Language Attitudes: A Matched-Guise Test   241

```
            2   AmE              2.5   PGE PG              3
Status      I—I—I—I—I—I—I—I—I—I—I




Solidarity  I—I—I—I—I—I—I—I—I—I—I
            2   PG  PGE  AmE     2.5                       3
```

――――――― = Pennsylvania German (voices 1,3,6,8)
----------- = Pennsylvania German English (voices 2,4,5,7)
.... = regional standard of English (voice 9)

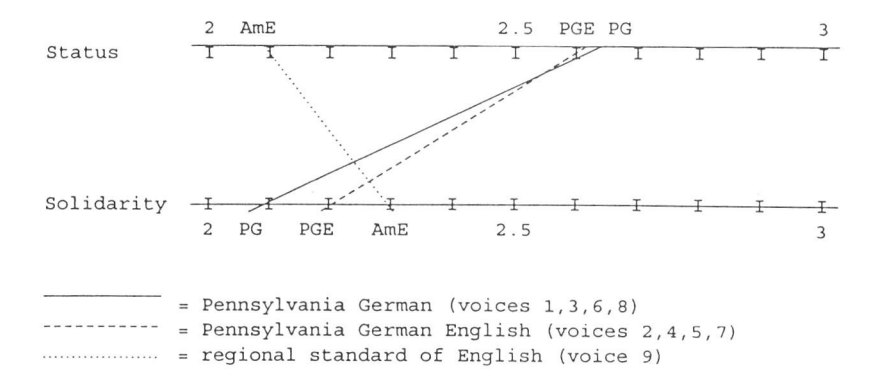

Dimension	PG	PGE	AmE
Status	2.63	2.60	2.08
Solidarity	2.06	2.18	2.30

Figure 4.14: Average ratings of varieties on the two judgmental dimensions of status and solidarity

would like to speak themselves. The same informants associate characteristics on the solidarity dimension, such as honesty, dependability, generosity, friendliness, modesty, and religiousness, with speakers of both Pennsylvania German and Pennsylvania German English.

EXTERNAL EVIDENCE

To receive further information about how the informants perceived the nine voices, eight questions were set up in an appendix to the matched-guise questions. Their exact wording can be found in the appendix (questionnaire section 3.2, questions 22–29).

Of the eight questions, three (questions 24–26) were chosen to show how the informants perceived voices 2, 5, and 9. Voice 2 has been selected because it is the New Order Mennonite's guise of Pennsylvania German English, which has considerably less interference from Pennsylvania German than the other (nonsectarian) samples. It is one purpose of figure 4.15 to confirm that the informants were actually aware of this difference.

242   Language Attitudes: A Matched-Guise Test

	Question		
Voice	24 (dutchified?) Average	25 (Dutch?) Dutch : non-Dutch	26 (plain?) Plain : non-plain
2 (Sectarian PGE)	2.76	26:17 (60.5%:39.5%)	2:24 (4.7%:55.8%)
5 (Nonsectarian PGE)	1.62	40:3 (93.0%:7.0%)	10:30 (23.3%:69.8%)
9 (AmE)	3.62	22:20 (51.2%:46.6%)	1:20 (2.3%:46.5%)

Figure 4.15: Scores of voices 2, 5, and 9 for selected questions (24–26) from the appendix of the matched-guise evaluation sheet

```
Question 24: Does this speaker speak dutchified English or nondutchified
             English (on a scale from 1-5)?
Question 25: Is this speaker Dutch or non-Dutch?
Question 26: (If he/she is Dutch:) Is this speaker a member of the plain
             group or the nonplain group?
```

The major goal, however, is to show that voices 5 and 9, which are two varieties of English spoken by the same speaker (D), were perceived to be different. If this were not the case, a large part of the matched-guise comparisons for the various groups of informants, namely those which show how the informants rate ethnically marked English (voice 5) as opposed to the regional standard of English (voice 9), would be invalid.

The three additional questions selected in figure 4.15 run as follows: question 24: "Does this speaker speak dutchified English or nondutchified English?," question 25: "Is this speaker Dutch or non-Dutch?," and question 26: "(If he/she is Dutch:) Is this speaker a member of the plain group or the non-plain group?" Questions 25 and 26 each gave two possibilities for an answer. In question 24, as in the calculated questions before, the informants' answers were based on a five-grade semantic differential scale.

In question 24, voice 5 was clearly identified as featuring Pennsylvania German interferences (average: 1.62), while its counterpart, voice 9, was perceived as representing (or at least approaching) the regional standard of English (average: 3.62). In no case did voice 9 score lower than voice 5.

Voice 2, which lies between voices 5 and 9 (average: 2.76), was a very difficult guise to rate, since a relatively unmarked variety of English is not typically associated with speakers of Pennsylvania German, let alone with sectarian speakers. It is due to this nonassociation that the answers to question 25 for voice 2 are quite varied. Twenty-six of the forty-three informants (60.5%) thought they were listening to a speaker of Pennsylvania German (Dutch) origin; seventeen informants (39.5%) considered voice 2 to belong to a non-Pennsylvania German speaker. Of those who thought the speaker was Pennsylvania German, only two (4.7%) guessed correctly that he was a sectarian. By contrast, voice 5 received no fewer than ten "P" ratings (23.3%). Sectarian Pennsylvania German English is stereotypically associated with heavy interference from Pennsylvania German, a view contradicted by all linguistic findings.

In answering question 25, only three informants (7.0%) said that voice 5 was not Pennsylvania German. By contrast, no fewer than twenty informants (46.5%) assumed wrongly that voice 9 belonged to a non-Pennsylvania German speaker. Speaker D has indeed acquired the regional standard of English so well that approximately half of the informants, all of whom are native to the area and know the Pennsylvania German culture well, thought he was not Pennsylvania German. In question 26 only one informant (2.3%) thought that voice 9 belonged to a plain speaker. A comparison of voices 5 and 9 suggests that voice 9 did sound more like the regional standard of English, even though some of the informants were still skeptical and obviously noticed slight remnants of Pennsylvania German interferences.

The results of questions 22, 23, and 27–29 may be summarized very briefly. Question 22 ("Did this speaker speak Dutch or English?") was answered correctly without exception, showing that all the informants can clearly distinguish between the different varieties. Question 23 ("Does this speaker speak a pure Dutch [= a Dutch that is close to High German]?") was difficult to answer for the non-Pennsylvania Germans and the younger generations of the nonsectarians and has therefore been neglected here. Question 27 ("Which part of the Pennsylvania German area does this speaker come from?") often remained unanswered, indicating that it is difficult to perceive dialectal differences in both Pennsylvania German and Pennsylvania German English. Question 28 ("Which religious group [Amish, Mennonite, etc.] does this speaker belong to?") often did not apply or remained unanswered. Those informants who did attempt to reply were mostly members of the sectarian or the non-Pennsylvania German group, which shows that these groups associate Pennsylvania German more with Amish and Mennonite than the nonsectarian Pennsylvania Germans. With respect to question 29 ("Could you make a guess about the speaker's age?") most informants assumed correctly that all four speakers belonged into the age group between sixty and seventy.

THIRD PERSPECTIVE: INFORMANTS

The various groups of questions and voices established in the previous chapters will serve as tools in answering the most important question this matched-guise test was designed to solve, namely how the attitude data structure the informants.

One of the goals will be to determine which informants hold the stereotype of the "dumb Dutchman". To this end, the status set of questions and a comparison between the ethnically marked voices and the regional-standard voice will be important instruments.

The second major question is which informants perceive which of the two ethnically marked varieties as the stronger ethnicity marker. Here, the main tools will be the solidarity set of questions and a comparison between the Pennsylvania German and the Pennsylvania German English voices.

The subdivision into groups of informants as determined by the social variables (language acquisition patterns, generation, age, gender, religion, etc.) will be used as a starting point of the discussion. Overview diagrams will be supported by tables showing the continua of informants in a more detailed fashion.

THE STEREOTYPE OF THE "DUMB DUTCHMAN": ETHNICALLY MARKED VARIETIES VERSUS THE REGIONAL STANDARD

FORMATION AND MANIFESTATION OF THE STEREOTYPE

With both insiders and outsiders, Pennsylvania German has enjoyed little overt prestige. It is commonly held that it is no "real" language, has "no grammar," and is "neither German nor English." The reason for this is its deviation from Standard German. Sooner or later, this alleged degeneracy of the language becomes a reflection of its speakers. They are "the dumb Dutch," ignorant country bumpkins who cannot speak English correctly and have no education (Louden 1988, 107–10).

Negative attitudes toward the Pennsylvania Germans reach back into the very beginning of the formation of their language and culture. The Pennsylvania Germans' complete or partial lack of competence in English occasionally led even such distinguished scholars as Benjamin Franklin into making derogatory remarks about their intelligence.[9] Based on this tradition, the stereotype of the "dumb Dutchman" has become widespread, not only among the Pennsylvania Germans themselves, but also among outsiders.[10] Today, it is encountered all over southeastern and central Pennsylvania.

The origin of the ridicule of the Pennsylvania Germans by outsiders may partly be due to the nonsectarians' negative self-image. In connection with questionnaire section 3.1, in which the informants were asked a number of questions concerning their language attitudes, and in numerous conversations before and after the formal interviews, the fieldworker received many revealing comments. Asked why from the 1930s parents chose not to speak Pennsylvania German to their children, informant 23, a member of the nonsectarian c-generation, stated, "Our parents didn't want us to have a Pennsylvania German accent in our English. They didn't want us to have a hard time at school as they did." This statement reflects the negative implications associated with a knowledge of Pennsylvania German. Needless to say, many local schoolteachers stigmatized children who spoke English with a Pennsylvania German accent or the dialect itself.

The public afterlife of the dying variety of Pennsylvania German is twofold (Huffines 1990b, 119). On the one hand, a small group of supporters attempts to maintain Pennsylvania German by using it in local newspaper columns, radio broadcasts, annual church services, and annual entertainment programs. On the other hand, there is a large number of commercial settings in which Pennsylvania German English is used to attract attention and to achieve humor. In such cases, authenticity is sacrificed for entertainment.

It is in these latter instances that the stereotype of the "dumb Dutchman" is exploited commercially and, at the same time, disseminated. Examples of assumed Pennsylvania German expressions, most of which turn out to be grossly exaggerated and cannot be validated, are found not only in numerous commercial publications about the variety of English used by the Pennsylvania Germans,[11] but also on diner placemats, hot pads, cutting boards, and other items of daily use. In many cases, the accompanying illustrations reveal which subgroup of the Pennsylvania Germans is alluded to. In some cases, the authors refer to the sectarians (as in *Ferhoodled English*), in others to the nonsectarians (as in Gates 1987). Most often, however, the symbols of certain groups are mixed indiscriminately, and even "Dutch" windmills are used to symbolize the Pennsylvania Germans.

A small group of local entertainers use Pennsylvania German English to make puns and reinforce ethnic jokes about the Pennsylvania Germans. While older nonsectarians, who speak both Pennsylvania German and Pennsylvania German English themselves, enjoy the humor and the exaggeration of the "dumb Dutch" stories in connection with the phonological interference, outsiders generally understand neither the humor nor the culture from which it derives (Huffines 1990b, 123).

Nevertheless, the stereotype of the naive and ignorant Pennsylvania German persists. Among the non-Pennsylvania Germans, it is fostered by the affected use of Pennsylvania German English for commercial purposes. It can only achieve its desired effect because mainstream society views the Pennsylvania German culture and language as nonthreatening to the Anglo-American culture.

Altogether, among the nonsectarians and in the surrounding mainstream society, Pennsylvania German ethnicity has a predominantly negative image. The few positive assets nonsectarians attribute to their ethnic language include its establishing familiarity, its usefulness as a secret language within the family, its role as a medium to relive childhood memories, and its vehicle of expression of ethnic pride. However, unlike the sectarians, the nonsectarian group is characterized by its lack of ethnic self-identity.

The historical conditions of the sectarian group contrast sharply. While the nonsectarian Pennsylvania Germans identified with mainstream society, the plain people strove for separation from the world. In sectarian communities, both Pennsylvania German and English became associated with high prestige. Most importantly, the German dialect enjoys an overt prestige as a group identifier. At the same time, English has a covert prestige in two respects. Since the plain groups see themselves as Americans with a different lifestyle, they need English for the practical reason of dealing with monolingual outsiders. This rather neutral attitude is supplemented by a positive one toward English as the sole medium of school and writing (Louden 1988, 118–20).

The inside perspective sharply contrasts with the more negative outsiders' view of sectarian culture. Plain people are generally viewed to reject mainstream society and its language (English) and are consequently overly exoticized. This gave rise to the fallacious assumption that English plays a minimal role in sectarian society. Louden (1991, 117, based on Hostetler 1980, 372ff. and Kraybill 1989, 250ff.) shows that the separation from mainstream society is really a strategy of making well-thought-out selections and compromises. Likewise, there is not really a distance to English in the sense that plain people use it only when forced to, for instance, with outsiders. Instead, English is used in certain intrafamily domains (e.g., motherese, numbers, first names), thus having a covert prestige (*see* Louden 1991, 126ff.).

It will now have to be seen whether the data reflect these rather general remarks on the attitudes of the various subgroups toward their cultures and language varieties.

STATUS

Figure 4.16 shows how the informants rated the voices in connection with the status set of questions. It discriminates between non-Pennsylvania Germans, sectarians, and nonsectarians, and within the latter group between generations a through d. It also gives the results for both sexes and all the informants together. The lower the values for the three groups of voices, the higher they were perceived in status.

For the evaluation of the results, the interrelationship of the three guises seems to be more important than the scores one guise received from various groups. For instance, the regional standard received the best ratings in the nonsectarian a-generation, followed, in this order, by the b-, c-, and d-generations.

However, one has to be careful not to jump to the conclusion that the regional standard enjoys the highest status within the a-generation and the lowest within the d-generation. The a-generation informants quite generally assigned better ratings, not only to the regional standard, but to all three guises, whereas the d-generation informants were much stricter with all the voices they heard. Therefore, comparisons of the scores of the three guises within each group will be at the center of the following discussion.

Overall, the standard speaker is assigned by far the highest status (2.08), while the speakers of Pennsylvania German and Pennsylvania German English score almost identical values (2.63 and 2.60, respectively). The same basic pattern holds for all the nonsectarians taken together. They clearly attribute the highest status to the standard speaker (2.01), while the values for the two ethnic varieties are almost the same, this time slightly more in favor of the Pennsylvania German voices (2.54 vs. 2.57).

The nonsectarian a-generation differs in that it more clearly assigns higher status to the Pennsylvania German speakers than to the Pennsylvania German English speakers (2.19 vs. 2.33).

248 Language Attitudes: A Matched-Guise Test

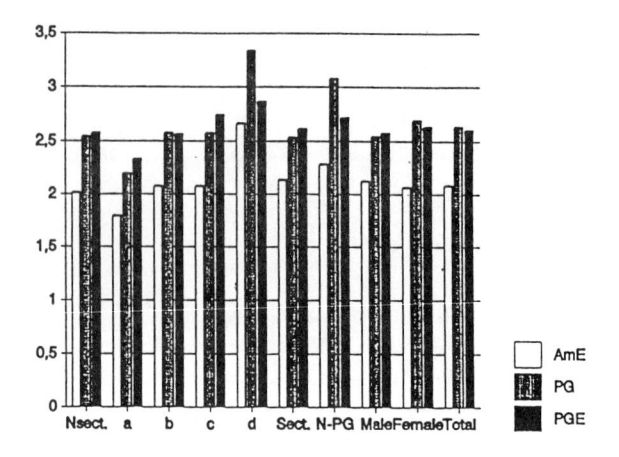

	AmE (voice 9)	PG (voices 1,3,6,9)	PGE (voices 2,4,5,7)
Nonsectarians	2.01	2.54	2.57
Nonsectarian a-generation	1.79	2.19	2.33
Nonsectarian b-generation	1.94	2.57	2.56
Nonsectarian c-generation	2.07	2.57	2.74
Nonsectarian d-generation	2.66	3.33	2.86
Sectarians	2.13	2.53	2.61
Non-Pennsylvania Germans	2.28	3.07	2.71
Male	2.12	2.54	2.57
Female	2.06	2.69	2.63
Total	2.08	2.63	2.60

Figure 4.16: Ratings of selected groups of informants for three groups of voices and the status-set questions (1–5, 11, 19, 20)

Their children (b-generation) favor the Pennsylvania German English speakers over the Pennsylvania German speakers although the difference is minimal (2.56 vs. 2.57). The b-generation's rather remarkable deviation in attitude from the a- and c-generations reflects the phonological differences described in chapter 2. A minority of the nonsectarian b-generation uses a relatively unmarked pronunciation of English, similar to that of the c-generation. The larger part, however, retains a relatively high percentage of Pennsylvania German features in their English, which is only slightly surpassed by the nonsectarian native speakers of Pennsylvania German.

The c-generation shows the same attitudinal pattern as the a-generation. Generally, within the c-generation, the competence in Pennsylvania German and the degree of phonological interference have both decreased to a minimum. Again, these linguistic realities are mirrored in the attitude patterns. Pennsylvania German English (2.74) is assigned lower status than Pennsylvania German (2.57).

By contrast, the d-generation's attitudinal pattern resembles that of the non-Pennsylvania Germans. The d-generation informants assign remarkably low status (3.33) to the Pennsylvania German voices, which reflects their almost complete monolingualism.

Like all the nonsectarians, the sectarians as well as the non-Pennsylvania Germans assign the highest status to the regional-standard voice. However, the latter two groups differ in their assessments of the ethnically marked voices. While the sectarians slightly favor the speakers of their native language (Pennsylvania German), the non-Pennsylvania Germans assign by far higher status to the Pennsylvania German English speakers.

The differences in ratings between the sexes are negligible. Both male and female informants associate the highest status with the standard speaker (2.12 and 2.06, respectively). The ethnically marked varieties are given almost identical ratings. While the male informants attribute slightly higher status to Pennsylvania German (2.54 vs. 2.57), the female informants prefer Pennsylvania German English (2.63 vs. 2.69).

To find out more details about the manner in which the informants cluster through their language attitudes, the discussion has to be narrowed down further. In connection with status, it appears to be most appropriate to compare the informants' reactions to those voices which represent Pennsylvania German ethnicity (voices 1–8) with their reactions to the regional standard of English (voice 9).[12]

Figure 4.17 provides the results of such a comparison on the basis of the status set of questions. The first two columns give each informant's identification number and rank in the continuum. The block in the center gives the social data in the same way as in figure 1.5. The value given in the column labeled "Voices 1–8" is the average each informant assigned with regard to status to all the voices associated with Pennsylvania German ethnicity. The column designated as "Voice 9" lists the average each informant gave to the only Standard English voice in the test. On the extreme right the difference between the two respective averages is given.

The informants are ordered from top to bottom according to their difference values. Those thirty-six informants who show a positive difference assigned higher averages to voices 1–8 than to voice 9, thereby attributing higher status to the regional-standard voice. Seven informants

250 Language Attitudes: A Matched-Guise Test

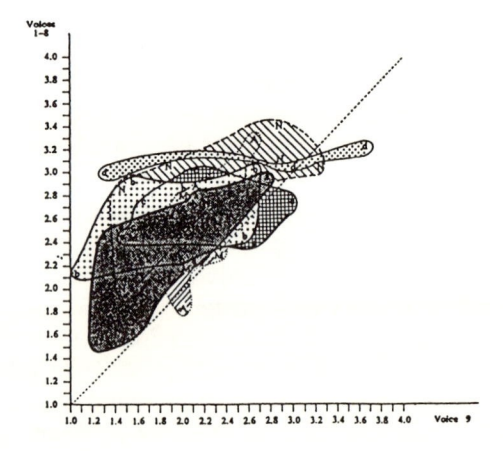

Rank	Informant	Fam	Gen	Age	Sex	Var	Voices 1-8	Voice 9	Difference
1	25	2	d	31	f	E	3.00	1.33	+1.67
2	46	N	(b)	52	f	E	2.87	1.44	+1.43
3	14	2	b	54	m	E	2.91	1.55	+1.36
4	19	1/N	(c)	30	f	E	3.05	1.88	+1.17
5	11	1	b	53	f	E	2.13	1.00	+1.13
6	5	2	a	68	f	PG	2.43	1.33	+1.10
7	18	1	a	30	m	E	2.76	1.66	+1.10
8	7	3	a	79	f	PG	2.51	1.44	+1.07
9	23	3	c	37	m	E	2.48	1.44	+1.04
10	22	2	c	54	f	E	2.54	1.55	+0.99
11	21	1	c	23	f	E	3.02	2.11	+0.91
12	29	M	(a)	57	m	PG	2.45	1.55	+0.90
13	15	3	b	61	m	E	2.86	2.00	+0.86
14	32	M	(b)	27	f	PG	2.84	2.00	+0.84
15	31	M	(b)	37	m	PG	2.65	1.88	+0.77
16	38	A	(b)	29	m	PG	2.88	2.11	+0.77
17	8	3	a	60	f	E	2.83	2.11	+0.72
18	40	A	(b)	17	m	PG	2.69	2.00	+0.69
19	39	A	(b)	30	f	E	3.30	2.66	+0.64
20	16	3	b	37	f	E	2.72	2.11	+0.61
21	9	1	b	57	f	PG/E	2.23	1.66	+0.57
22	43	N	(b)	50	m	E	2.01	1.44	+0.57
23	44	N	(b)	52	f	E	2.75	2.22	+0.53
24	48	N	(c)	30	f	E	3.41	2.88	+0.53
25	12	2	b	83	m	E	3.02	2.66	+0.36
26	1	1	a	77	m	PG	1.54	1.22	+0.32
27	33	M	(b)	13	m	PG	2.59	2.33	+0.26
28	13	2	b	49	m	E	2.25	2.00	+0.25
29	2	1	a	77	f	PG	2.00	1.77	+0.23
30	45	N	(b)	54	m	E	3.11	2.88	+0.23
31	4	2	a	71	m	PG	2.97	2.77	+0.20
32	37	A	(a)	51	f	PG	2.61	2.44	+0.17
33	3	1	a	77	f	E	2.23	2.11	+0.12
34	26	2	d	27	f	E	3.08	3.00	+0.08
35	34	M	(b)	22	f	PG	2.19	2.11	+0.08
36	6	2	a	74	f	PG	1.59	1.55	+0.04
37	30	M	(a)	55	f	E	2.30	2.33	-0.03
38	10	1	b	54	m	E	2.45	2.55	-0.10
39	36	A	(a)	52	m	PG	1.84	2.00	-0.16
40	47	N	(c)	31	m	E	3.06	3.22	-0.16
41	20	1	c	26	m	E	2.75	3.00	-0.25
42	17	1	c	35	m	E	2.40	2.66	-0.26
43	28	3	d	9	f	E	3.22	3.66	-0.44

Figure 4.17: Informants' reactions to voices 1–8 (PG ethnicity) as compared to voice 9 (AmE) as reflected by their answers to the status-set questions (1–5, 11, 19, 20)

For abbreviations and symbols, see figure 1.5.

at the end of the continuum show negative differences, thus rating the ethnically marked voices more favorably.

In the diagram at the bottom of figure 4.17 the results for voices 1–8 are mapped on the vertical and those for voice 9 on the horizontal. The straight line through the middle of the graph represents zero difference, expressing identical evaluation of the two varieties. The informants to its left attribute higher status to voice 9; those to the right prefer the ethnically marked voices. The closer informants are to the straight line, the less extreme their vote one way or the other.

The maximum difference value is far higher when voice 9 is preferred (+1.67) than in the case of voices 1–8 (–0.44). In the diagram this is indicated by the fact that the seven informants to the right of the straight line cluster much more closely around it than do the thirty-six informants to its left.

Although the majority of the members of the nonsectarian a-generation are located around the straight line, none of them is found to associate higher status with the ethnically marked voices.

Of the eight members of the b-generation, only informant 10 prefers the ethnically marked varieties in status. The rest are scattered over the area of positive difference values.

Within the nonsectarian c- and d-generations, the percentage of informants preferring voices 1–8 is slightly higher. Of the six members of the c-generation, two (informants 17, 20) have negative difference values. The rest cluster around the +1.00 mark. Of the three informants belonging to the d-generation, one (informant 28) is in the negative zone. The heterogeneity of this small group of three is reflected by the fact that d-generation informants have both the overall highest (informant 25) and lowest (informant 28) difference values.

The sectarians roughly form two groups, one around the +0.80 mark and the other near the zero line. There is no pattern distinguishing between either Mennonites and Amish or men and women.

Finally, the non-Pennsylvania Germans are scattered over the whole continuum. A cluster of three informants (34, 44, 48) is located on ranks 22–24 with difference values around +0.55.

Quite generally, the tendency appears to be the younger the informants belonging to the nonsectarian group, the more strictly they rate. The a-generation assigns the best rates in status, the d-generation the worst. This trend is also apparent in the non-Pennsylvania German group, with the c-generation informants 47 and 48 assigning high, that is, negative ratings. The same is true for the sectarians, where the b-generation informants 31–33 and 38–40 are the strictest. However, this tendency applies to both the ethnically marked voices and the regional-standard voice. The role of generation with respect to preference for one or the other of the two guises will be discussed later, after the presentation of the data for intelligence and identification.

INTELLIGENCE

Figure 4.18 is based on one specific question included in the status set of questions, namely question 2 (intelligent–dumb). It reduces the stereotype of the "dumb Dutchman" to one of its major aspects, intelligence.

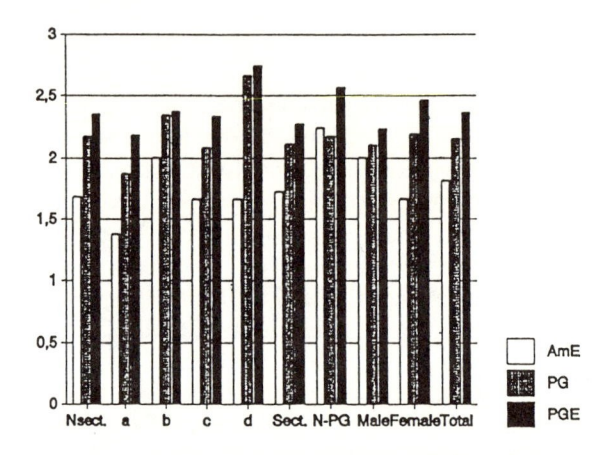

	AmE (voice 9)	PG (voices 1,3,6,9)	PGE (voices 2,4,5,7)
Nonsectarians	1.68	2.17	2.35
Nonsectarian a-generation	1.37	1.87	2.18
Nonsectarian b-generation	2.00	2.34	2.37
Nonsectarian c-generation	1.66	2.08	2.33
Nonsectarian d-generation	1.66	2.66	2.74
Sectarians	1.72	2.11	2.27
Non-Pennsylvania Germans	2.24	2.17	2.56
Male	2.00	2.10	2.23
Female	1.66	2.19	2.46
Total	**1.81**	**2.15**	**2.36**

Figure 4.18: Ratings of selected groups of informants for three groups of voices and intelligence (question 2)

All the informants taken together rated the standard speaker to be the most intelligent one (1.81), followed by the speakers of Pennsylvania German (2.15) and those of Pennsylvania German English (2.36). This order holds for the sectarians, all the nonsectarians taken together, the nonsectarian a-, b-, c-, and d-generations, and both male and female informants.

In the case of both the nonsectarian b- and the d-generation, however, the difference between the ratings for the Pennsylvania German voices and those for the Pennsylvania German English voices is extremely small (2.34 vs. 2.37 and 2.66 vs. 2.74, respectively).

A comparison between male and female informants reveals that although the overall pattern is identical, the women discriminate more clearly between the three voice groups than the men.

The fact that the ethnic informants assign the greatest intelligence to the speaker of standard English reflects the presence of the stereotype of the "dumb Dutchman" in the Pennsylvania German area. Only the non-Pennsylvania Germans display a different attitude pattern. They consider the Pennsylvania German speakers to be the most intelligent ones (2.17), closely followed by the standard speaker (2.24) and, with a large gap, by the Pennsylvania German English speakers (2.56). This pattern may be attributed to this monolingual group's slightly naive concept that speakers of Pennsylvania German, who they know can also speak English, are intelligent because they speak a second language.

With the exception of the non-Pennsylvania Germans, the informants believe that standard speakers are the most intelligent ones. Speakers of Pennsylvania German are rated second best. Thus, purity in language use is a sign of high intelligence, whereas speakers of marked English are rated most negatively. Knowing the ethnic language is less damaging to intelligence than speaking ethnically marked English. All in all, the regional standard provides positive evidence of intelligence, Pennsylvania German English negative evidence, and Pennsylvania German the benefit of doubt.

The largest differences as compared to the ratings for general status (*see* figure 4.16) are found in the nonsectarian d-generation and in the non-Pennsylvania German group. In these groups, Pennsylvania German scored the worst results for status, but not for intelligence. In addition, there is a slight difference for all the informants taken together. For intelligence, the order is regional standard, Pennsylvania German, Pennsylvania German English, whereas for general status, marked English is rated slightly better than the ethnic variety.

Figure 4.19 gives more details about the informants' attitude continuum based on the question about intelligence. The span of difference values is more than one point wider than that for status (*see* figure 4.17), reaching from +1.87 to –1.50. The results are somewhat less differentiated, as all the values for voice 9 are whole numbers. In the diagram this is reflected by the informants' ordering along the horizontal in columns over the integers 1–4.

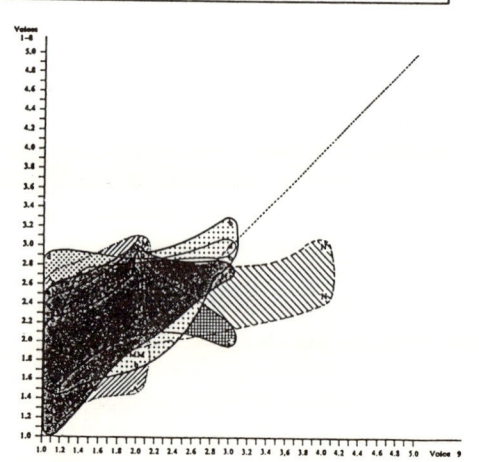

Rank	Informant	Fam	Gen	Age	Sex	Var	Voices 1-8	Voice 9	Difference
1	28	3	d	9	f	E	2.87	1.00	+1.87
2	40	A	(b)	17	m	PG	2.62	1.00	+1.62
3	5	2	a	68	f	PG	2.50	1.00	+1.50
4	19	1/N	(c)	30	f	E	2.50	1.00	+1.50
5	18	1	c	30	m	E	2.37	1.00	+1.37
6	7	3	a	79	f	PG	2.25	1.00	+1.25
7	25	2	d	31	f	E	2.25	1.00	+1.25
8	11	1	b	53	f	E	2.12	1.00	+1.12
9	23	3	c	37	m	E	2.12	1.00	+1.12
10	39	A	(b)	30	f	PG	3.12	2.00	+1.12
11	3	1	a	77	f	E	2.00	1.00	+1.00
12	8	3	a	60	f	E	3.00	2.00	+1.00
13	21	1	c	23	f	E	3.00	2.00	+1.00
14	14	2	b	54	m	E	2.87	2.00	+0.87
15	32	M	(b)	27	f	PG	2.87	2.00	+0.87
16	16	3	b	37	f	E	2.75	2.00	+0.75
17	33	M	(b)	13	m	PG	1.75	1.00	+0.75
18	38	A	(b)	29	m	PG	2.62	2.00	+0.62
19	9	1	b	57	f	PG/E	1.50	1.00	+0.50
20	22	2	c	54	m	E	1.50	1.00	+0.50
21	43	N	(b)	50	f	E	1.50	1.00	+0.50
22	2	1	a	77	f	PG	1.37	1.00	+0.37
23	6	2	a	74	f	PG	1.37	1.00	+0.37
24	31	M	(b)	37	m	PG	2.37	2.00	+0.37
25	12	2	b	83	f	E	3.25	3.00	+0.25
26	20	1	c	26	m	E	2.25	2.00	+0.25
27	30	M	(a)	55	f	PG	1.25	1.00	+0.25
28	37	A	(a)	52	f	PG	2.25	2.00	+0.25
29	44	N	(b)	52	f	E	2.25	2.00	+0.25
30	1	1	a	77	m	PG	1.00	1.00	0.00
31	26	2	d	27	f	E	3.00	3.00	0.00
32	46	N	(b)	52	f	E	2.00	2.00	0.00
33	10	1	b	54	m	E	2.87	3.00	-0.13
34	29	M	(a)	57	m	PG	1.87	2.00	-0.13
35	34	M	(b)	22	f	PG	1.87	2.00	-0.13
36	4	2	a	71	m	PG	2.75	3.00	-0.25
37	13	2	b	49	m	E	1.75	2.00	-0.25
38	15	3	b	61	m	E	1.75	2.00	-0.25
39	45	N	(b)	54	m	E	2.75	3.00	-0.25
40	36	A	(a)	52	m	PG	1.50	2.00	-0.50
41	48	N	(c)	30	f	E	3.12	4.00	-0.88
42	17	1	c	35	m	E	2.00	3.00	-1.00
43	47	N	(c)	31	m	E	2.50	4.00	-1.50

Figure 4.19: Informants' reactions to voices 1-8 (PG ethnicity) as compared to voice 9 (AmE) as reflected by their answers to question 2 (intelligence)

For abbreviations and symbols, see figure 1.5.

Nevertheless, the basic structure remains the same as that for the status set of questions. The majority of informants assign higher intelligence to the regional-standard voice. However, the minority group preferring the ethnically marked varieties is now larger, and some of its members articulate their preference more decisively. Therefore, in figure 4.19, some informants are found much further below the straight line than in figure 4.17.

As before, the members of the nonsectarian a-generation are almost exclusively located above the straight line. The only exception is informant 4, who speaks heavily marked English himself.

The tendency of the b-generation to prefer the ethnically marked voices more than their elders becomes clearer in connection with intelligence than with overall status. Three informants (10, 13, 15) are below the straight line, although still fairly close to it.

The distribution of the nonsectarian c-generation is quite similar to that for status. The majority of this group attributes higher intelligence to voice 9; informant 17, who has the best knowledge of Pennsylvania German in his generation, is the only one preferring the ethnically marked voices.

The d-generation is too small a group to allow valid generalizations. While informants 25 and 26 show the same attitude pattern as before, informant 28 is found on rank 43 in figure 4.17 and on rank 1 in figure 4.19. This instability in attitude may be attributed to the fact that informant 28 is nine years old and her attitude patterns are not as set as the adults'.

The sectarian informants show virtually the same distribution in the continuum as they did in connection with the status set of questions. The only exceptions are informant 40 on rank 2, who attributes higher intelligence than overall status to voice 9, and informant 29 on rank 34, who prefers voice 9 with regard to status but voices 1–8 in terms of intelligence.

The most striking differences are found for the non-Pennsylvania German informants. While the majority of this group attributed higher status to the regional standard, the ratio is equal with respect to intelligence. Three informants (19, 43, 44) prefer voice 9, one (informant 46) is undecided, and three (informants 45, 47, 48) prefer voices 1–8. Thus, the non-Pennsylvania Germans are the group to assign highest intelligence to the ethnically marked speakers. Low intelligence, it can be concluded, is attributed to the ethnically marked voices more by people from within their own group than by outsiders.

IDENTIFICATION

In figure 4.20 a second important aspect included in the status set of questions has been isolated, namely identification. The two poles of

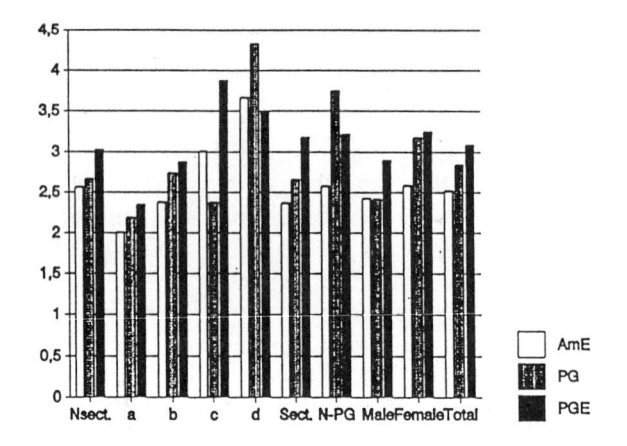

	AmE (voice 9)	PG (voices 1,3,6,9)	PGE (voices 2,4,5,7)
Nonsectarians	2.56	2.66	3.02
Nonsectarian a-generation	2.00	2.18	2.34
Nonsectarian b-generation	2.37	2.73	2.87
Nonsectarian c-generation	3.00	2.37	3.87
Nonsectarian d-generation	3.66	4.32	3.49
Sectarians	2.36	2.65	3.17
Non-Pennsylvania Germans	2.57	3.74	3.21
Male	2.42	2.41	2.89
Female	2.58	3.17	3.24
Total	2.51	2.83	3.08

Figure 4.20: Ratings of selected groups of informants for three groups of voices and identification (question 20)

question 20 in the questionnaire are formed by "I'd like to speak like this speaker myself" and "I wouldn't like to speak like this speaker myself." This question is of particular importance as it forces the informants to commit themselves overtly.

All the informants taken together identify themselves most with the regional standard (2.51), followed by Pennsylvania German (2.83) and, with a similarly large distance, by ethnically marked English (3.08). This pattern is also found for all the sectarians and all the nonsectarians taken together, and for the nonsectarian a- and b-generations.

Interestingly enough, both the nonsectarian c- and the d-generation deviate from this attitude pattern. The c-generation identifies most with the speakers of Pennsylvania German (2.37), followed by the regional standard (3.00) and the ethnically marked varieties of English (3.87). The d-generation does not show a high identification rate for any of the three groups of voices. Ethnically marked English (3.49) is slightly favored over the regional standard (3.66), while Pennsylvania German (4.32) receives the least favorable result. In its downright rejection of the German dialect, the d-generation resembles the non-Pennsylvania German group.

In connection with intelligence (*see* figure 4.18), the members of the two youngest nonsectarian generations hold the same attitudes as their elders, favoring the regional standard over the ethnically marked varieties and Pennsylvania German over ethnically marked English. However, when it comes down to the existential question of how they would like to speak themselves, this pattern is unstable. In both generations, the regional standard is not the desired goal any more. Here, the nostalgic wish of keeping one's ethnic identity may come to the fore in the attitude patterns. One generation (c) would seem to choose Pennsylvania German as an instrument, the other, which is further away in time from the last native speakers (d), ethnically marked English.

The non-Pennsylvania Germans, as so often before, do not follow the pattern of the majority either. They identify most with their own variety, the regional standard (2.57), followed by ethnically marked English (3.21) and Pennsylvania German (3.74), which is a foreign language to them. Although in figure 4.18 they attributed high intelligence to the speakers of Pennsylvania German, the non-Pennsylvania German informants do not seem to be prepared to take the next step of wishing to speak this language themselves.

The sexes reveal a difference in their attitudinal patterns with regard to identification. While the female informants show the majority's attitude pattern, their male counterparts identify just slightly more with Pennsylvania German (2.41) than with the regional standard (2.42), followed by ethnically marked English (2.89). Thus, whereas the male informants strive for purity (no matter if in the form of unmarked English or Pennsylvania German), the female ones prefer only the regional standard. This reflects the findings of chapters 2 and 3, which showed that men have slightly more ethnically marked features in their English and that a slightly higher percentage of men uses exclusively Pennsylvania German with certain interlocutors.

Figure 4.21 shows the informants' distribution for identification with the ethnically marked voices and the regional standard. The span of difference values is extremely wide, ranging from +3.87 to −1.88. Approximately two-thirds of the informants identify more with the regional standard, while the remaining third favors the ethnically marked varie-

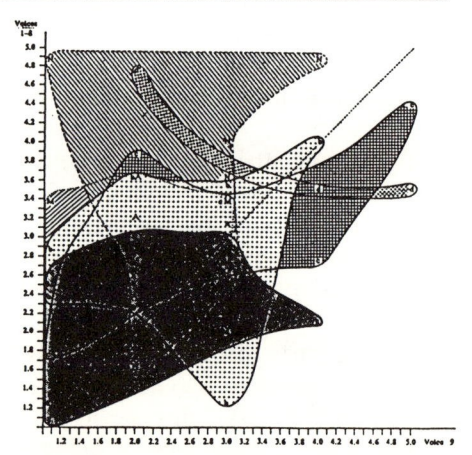

Rank	Informant	Fam	Gen	Age	Sex	Var	Voices 1-8	Voice 9	Difference
1	46	N	(b)	52	f	E	4.87	1.00	+3.87
2	25	2	d	31	f	E	4.75	2.00	+2.75
3	14	2	b	54	m	E	2.87	1.00	+1.87
4	22	2	c	54	f	PG	3.87	2.00	+1.87
5	7	3	a	79	f	E	2.62	1.00	+1.62
6	12	2	b	83	f	E	3.62	2.00	+1.62
7	38	A	(b)	29	m	PG	3.62	2.00	+1.62
8	29	M	(a)	57	m	PG	2.50	1.00	+1.50
9	39	A	(b)	30	f	PG	3.50	2.00	+1.50
10	11	1	b	53	f	E	2.37	1.00	+1.37
11	32	M	(b)	27	f	PG	3.37	2.00	+1.37
12	8	3	a	60	f	E	3.00	2.00	+1.00
13	48	N	(c)	30	f	E	4.00	3.00	+1.00
14	19	1/N	(c)	30	f	E	4.87	4.00	+0.87
15	23	3	c	37	m	E	1.75	1.00	+0.75
16	31	M	(b)	37	m	PG	2.75	2.00	+0.75
17	45	N	(b)	54	m	E	3.62	3.00	+0.62
18	47	N	(c)	31	m	E	2.62	2.00	+0.62
19	2	1	a	77	f	PG	2.60	2.00	+0.60
20	16	3	b	37	f	E	3.57	3.00	+0.57
21	5	2	a	68	f	PG	2.50	2.00	+0.50
22	18	1	c	30	m	E	3.37	3.00	+0.37
23	33	M	(b)	13	m	PG	3.37	3.00	+0.37
24	40	A	(b)	17	m	PG	2.37	2.00	+0.37
25	6	2	a	74	f	PG	1.25	1.00	+0.25
26	9	1	b	57	f	PG/E	2.25	2.00	+0.25
27	37	A	(a)	51	f	PG	3.12	3.00	+0.12
28	1	1	a	77	m	PG	1.00	1.00	0.00
29	4	2	a	71	m	PG	4.00	4.00	0.00
30	15	3	b	61	f	E	2.75	3.00	-0.25
31	30	M	(a)	55	f	PG	2.75	3.00	-0.25
32	36	A	(a)	52	m	PG	2.75	3.00	-0.25
33	44	N	(b)	52	f	E	2.62	3.00	-0.38
34	13	2	b	49	m	E	2.62	3.00	-0.38
35	17	1	c	35	m	E	1.62	2.00	-0.38
36	43	N	(b)	50	m	E	3.50	4.00	-0.50
37	26	2	d	27	f	E	4.37	5.00	-0.63
38	21	1	c	23	f	PG	2.00	3.00	-1.00
39	34	M	(b)	22	f	E	2.75	4.00	-1.25
40	20	1	c	26	m	E	3.50	5.00	-1.50
41	28	3	d	9	f	E	1.25	3.00	-1.75
42	10	1	b	54	m	E	2.12	4.00	-1.88
43	3			77	f				

Figure 4.21: Informants' reactions to voices 1-8 (PG ethnicity) as compared to voice 9 (AmE) as reflected by their answers to question 20 (identification)

For abbreviations and symbols, see figure 1.5.

ties. As in the case of intelligence (*see* figure 4.19), three informants are undecided.

Apart from informant 3 at the very end of the continuum, all the members of the nonsectarian a-generation either express higher identification with voice 9 or are undecided. In the diagram, these informants are all fairly close to the straight line, which means that they generally do not have any extreme attitudes one way or the other.

The range of the b-generation is wider. Of the eight informants, two (informants 10, 13) identify more with the ethnically marked varieties. Informant 10 was also found to favor voices 1–8 with respect to status and intelligence, informant 13 with regard to intelligence. They are both excellent speakers of Pennsylvania German and expressed a strong interest in the preservation of the Pennsylvania German language and culture.

Of the six members of the c-generation, three (informants 18, 22, 23) favor the regional standard of English, whereas the others (informants 17, 20, 21) prefer the ethnically marked varieties in terms of identification. In addition, informant 20 was found to favor voices 1–8 for status; informant 17 favored these voices for both status and intelligence. In connection with identification, the c-generation's distribution is characterized by a fairly balanced and moderate attitude.

The same is true for the sectarian informants. Although no fewer than eight of eleven identify more with the regional standard, all the sectarian informants cluster closely around the straight line.

The three informants belonging to the nonsectarian d-generation gave more extreme opinions. As was the case for status and intelligence, informant 25 clearly favors the regional standard with respect to identification. She assigns an average of 4.75 to the eight ethnically marked voices, which reflects her consistently negative rating of these varieties. Her sister, informant 26, and informant 28 both would rather speak an ethnically marked variety. Informant 26 was undecided with respect to intelligence and only slightly preferred the regional standard of English in overall status. Informant 28, the nine-year-old girl, continues her extreme rating pattern. She assigns the most negative rating (5) to voice 9, thus identifying more with the ethnically marked varieties. Whereas she also favored voices 1–8 for status, she preferred voice 9 with respect to intelligence.

Favoring the regional standard, five of the seven non-Pennsylvania German informants are found above the straight line. A cluster of four is located between ranks 13 and 18. Informant 46 is found at the top of the continuum. She assigns a value of 4.87 to voices 1–8 and a value of 1 to voice 9, thus expressing a close-to-maximum identification with the latter. Informant 19 has the same negative rating for the ethnically marked voices, but rates the regional standard less positively than informant 46. Of all the non-Pennsylvania German informants, only informants 43 and 44 express higher identification with voices 1–8 than with voice 9. With regard to both status and intelligence, these two informants were found to prefer the regional-standard variety. This is another indication for the high degree of commitment elicited with the help of question 20.

INTERPRETATION

With respect to social status, intelligence, and identification, all groups of informants share a clear preference for unmarked American English over ethnically marked English. It is only in the degree of this preference that they differ. In other words, the stereotype of the "dumb Dutchman" is present in all subgroups, but it is stronger in some groups than in others.

The group with the most consistent negative attitude toward ethnically marked varieties on the status dimension is the nonsectarian a-generation. Here, informants 3 (for identification) and 4 (for intelligence) are the only ones to show sporadic deviations from the general stereotype. Altogether, the group with the heaviest Pennsylvania German interference in their English and the only nonsectarian generation with native competence in Pennsylvania German shows the strongest reservations against their own culture with respect to social status. This attitude reflects this generation's historical decision to spare their children stigmatization by raising them in English.

Their children, the nonsectarian b-generation, exhibit a somewhat stronger tendency toward preferring the ethnically marked varieties; however, the regional-standard variety of English still enjoys by far higher social status. The three informants who deviate in their attitude patterns by giving higher credit to the ethnically marked varieties are informants 10, 13, and 15, all of whom have near-native competence in Pennsylvania German. Their attitudinal data reflects a feeling of impending loss of the Pennsylvania German language and culture. Many informants of the b-generation expressed regret about not being able to pass on their parents' language to their children for lack of competence and because of the irrevocable change of acquisition patterns within their society. Their last resort is the active support of language revival attempts, for example as a member of the board of the *Versammling* (informant 10), as an interpreter in Pennsylvania German skits (informant 13), or as an occasional author of historical articles for the local paper (informant 15).

The nonsectarian c-generation also assigns clearly higher status to the regional standard of English; however, like the b-generation, it exhibits a stronger tendency to favor the ethnically marked varieties occasionally. With respect to identification, the regional standard even loses its first rank in the order of preferences to Pennsylvania German, a variety in which most of the members of the c-generation have only rudimentary competence. Very good speakers of Pennsylvania German (informant 17) as well as speakers whose high school knowledge of Standard German is better than their command of Pennsylvania German (informants 20, 21) are most outstanding in this tendency. All these informants, however, share a fervent interest in their linguistic and cultural heritage and repeatedly expressed regret about its decline.

The nonsectarian d-generation also prefers the regional-standard variety with respect to social status. The small number of three informants, however, and their rather extreme opinions make valid statements difficult. Informant 28, the nine-year-old girl, shows a rather unstable attitude pattern. Informant 25 clearly favors American English, while her sister, informant 26, is less decided. While with respect to status and intelligence the regional standard is preferred, Pennsylvania German English holds the first rank with respect to identification. Here, the trend set by the c-generation continues. Regional-standard speakers may enjoy high social status; however, in connection with the very personal question of identification, the informants of both the c- and the d-generation prefer one of the two ethnically marked varieties. This finding may point toward the issue of strategic ethnic marking to show one's ethnic identity. The members of the d-generation lack both active and passive competence in Pennsylvania German, either fully (informant 28) or to a very large extent (informants 25, 26).

The overall preference of the regional standard shows that the stereotype of the "dumb Dutchman" is also present among the sectarians. However, although they are native speakers of Pennsylvania German like the nonsectarian a-generation, the sectarians display a stronger tendency toward favoring the ethnically marked varieties. Those informants who tend to be affected the least by the stereotype are informants 30 and 36, and to a certain extent 29 and 34. Three of them are members of the sectarian a-generation. This finding may be taken as evidence that the stereotype is especially strong among the younger sectarians. All in all, the sectarians' attitude patterns are rather moderate, with little tendency toward extreme opinions. Most informants cluster around the straight line in figures 4.17, 4.19, and 4.21.

The non-Pennsylvania Germans favor the regional standard with regard to social status and identification. Only with respect to intelligence are the ratings more balanced, with a slight preference for the Pennsylvania German voices. With this rating the monolingual informants may honor the Pennsylvania Germans' competence in a second language. As low intelligence is an important aspect of the stereotype of the "dumb Dutchman," this conception can be concluded to be stronger within the Pennsylvania German community (both sectarian and nonsectarian) itself than outside. However, the more negative identification rating for Pennsylvania German English as compared to the regional standard shows that the non-Pennsylvania Germans would not want to speak an ethnically marked variety of English themselves.

Both the pilot interviews and the evaluation of the matched-guise test have made it clear that the stereotype of the "dumb Dutchman" consists of more than just lack of intelligence. With general status, intelligence, and identification, three major contributing factors have been examined. The selection of these aspects facilitated an outline of the general trends within the groups of informants. Apart from other negative characteristics, even a certain number of positive traits may contribute to the image. However, it has to be assumed that the precise idea expressed by the stereotype varies from subgroup to subgroup, possibly even from individual to individual.

MARKING ONE'S ETHNIC IDENTITY: PENNSYLVANIA GERMAN VERSUS PENNSYLVANIA GERMAN ENGLISH

SOLIDARITY

The data given in figure 4.22 reveal rather different facets of the informants' attitudes. Here the solidarity set of questions is used to establish ratings for the three groups of voices. The differences in values are very small compared to those in figures 4.16, 4.18, and 4.20.

Most strikingly, in the emotional sphere the standard speaker is rated least favorably by all groups of informants. Overall, the Pennsylvania German speakers are assigned the highest solidarity ratings (2.06), followed by the Pennsylvania German English voices (2.18) and the speaker using the regional standard (2.30).

The only two groups to deviate from this pattern are the nonsectarian d-generation and the non-Pennsylvania Germans. In both cases, the regional standard is still rated the most unfavorably, while the voices speaking ethnically marked English are rated the highest, even higher than Pennsylvania German itself.

As in figure 4.16 (status), the d-generation, whose members are practically monolingual English speakers, shows an attitude pattern similar to that of the non-Pennsylvania Germans. As to the members of the latter group, it is hardly surprising that their language attitudes differ

Language Attitudes: A Matched-Guise Test

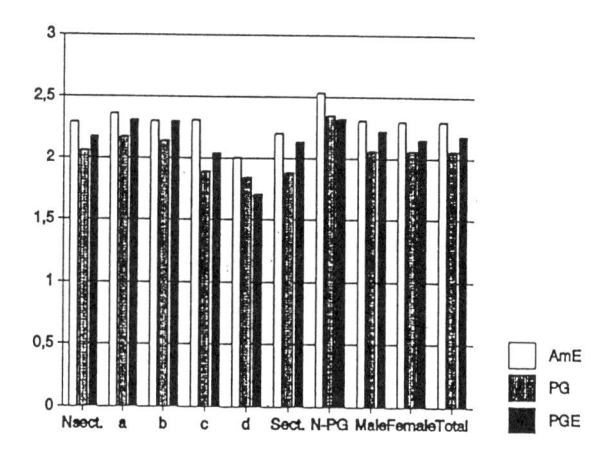

	AmE (voice 9)	PG (voices 1,3,6,9)	PGE (voices 2,4,5,7)
Nonsectarians	2.29	2.06	2.17
Nonsectarian a-generation	2.36	2.17	2.31
Nonsectarian b-generation	2.30	2.14	2.30
Nonsectarian c-generation	2.31	1.89	2.04
Nonsectarian d-generation	2.00	1.84	1.70
Sectarians	2.20	1.88	2.13
Non-Pennsylvania Germans	2.53	2.35	2.32
Male	2.31	2.06	2.22
Female	2.30	2.06	2.15
Total	2.30	2.06	2.18

Figure 4.22: Ratings of selected groups of informants for three groups of voices and the solidarity-set questions (6–10, 12–18)

from those of their ethnic neighbors if one keeps their monolingual heritage in mind.

Both male and female informants reflect the overall rating patterns. The numerical differences between the two groups are negligible.

Figure 4.23 gives a detailed breakdown of how the informants are structured by their reactions to the Pennsylvania German and the Pennsylvania German English voices on the basis of the solidarity set of questions. The span of difference values is extremely small (between +0.44 and −0.68), which is illustrated by the fact that all the informants cluster closely along the straight line.

264 Language Attitudes: A Matched-Guise Test

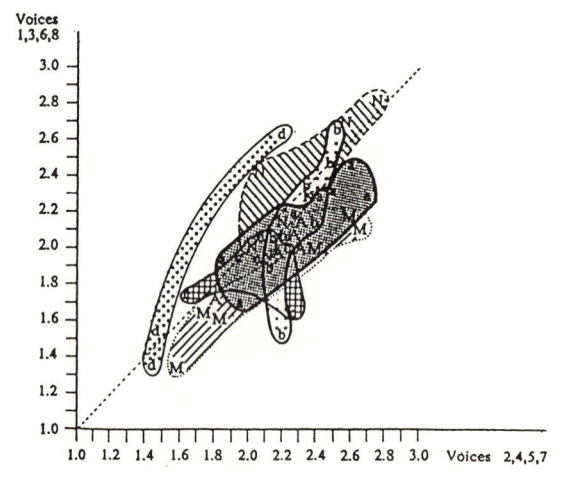

Rank	Inform-ant	Fam	Gen	Age	Sex	Var	Voices 1,3,6,8	Voices 2,4,5,7	Difference
1	28	3	d	9	f	E	2.64	2.20	+0.44
2	44	N	(b)	52	f	E	2.43	2.08	+0.35
3	12	2	b	83	f	E	2.66	2.52	+0.14
4	46	N	(b)	52	f	E	2.68	2.56	+0.12
5	22	2	c	54	f	E	1.75	1.64	+0.11
6	3	1	a	77	f	E	1.93	1.85	+0.08
7	26	2	d	27	f	E	1.54	1.47	+0.07
8	45	N	(b)	54	m	E	2.81	2.75	+0.06
9	8	3	a	60	f	E	2.22	2.20	+0.02
10	10	1	b	54	m	E	2.35	2.33	+0.02
11	18	1	c	30	m	E	1.95	1.97	-0.02
12	11	1	b	53	f	E	2.47	2.50	-0.03
13	17	1	c	35	m	E	2.06	2.10	-0.04
14	19	1/N	(c)	30	f	E	2.18	2.22	-0.04
15	47	N	(c)	31	m	E	2.14	2.20	-0.06
16	4	2	a	71	m	PG	2.20	2.27	-0.07
17	13	2	b	49	m	E	2.06	2.14	-0.08
18	25	2	d	31	f	E	1.35	1.43	-0.08
19	37	A	(a)	51	f	PG	1.72	1.81	-0.09
20	1	1	a	77	f	PG	2.29	2.39	-0.10
21	48	N	(c)	30	f	E	2.29	2.39	-0.10
22	34	M	(b)	22	f	PG	1.64	1.75	-0.11
23	2	1	a	77	f	PG	2.47	2.60	-0.13
24	20	1	c	26	m	E	1.93	2.06	-0.13
25	43	N	(b)	50	m	E	1.95	2.08	-0.13
26	15	3	b	61	m	E	2.06	2.20	-0.14
27	40	A	(b)	17	m	PG	2.02	2.16	-0.14
28	36	A	(a)	52	m	PG	1.97	2.14	-0.17
29	38	A	(b)	29	m	PG	2.14	2.31	-0.17
30	7	3	a	79	f	PG	2.31	2.50	-0.19
31	33	M	(b)	13	m	PG	1.62	1.81	-0.19
32	23	3	c	37	m	E	2.02	2.22	-0.20
33	9	1	b	57	f	PG/E	1.91	2.12	-0.21
34	30	M	(a)	55	f	PG	1.34	1.58	-0.24
35	6	2	a	74	f	PG	1.70	1.95	-0.25
36	16	3	b	37	f	E	2.14	2.39	-0.25
37	29	M	(a)	57	m	PG	2.00	2.33	-0.33
38	39	A	(b)	30	f	PG	2.00	2.33	-0.33
39	5	2	a	68	f	PG	2.29	2.70	-0.41
40	32	M	(b)	27	f	PG	2.18	2.60	-0.42
41	31	M	(b)	37	m	PG	2.10	2.66	-0.56
42	21	1	c	23	f	E	1.64	2.27	-0.63
43	14	2	b	54	m	E	1.52	2.20	-0.68

Figure 4.23: Informants' reactions to voices 1, 3, 6, 8 (PG) as compared to voices 2, 4, 5, 7 (PGE) as reflected by their answers to the solidarity-set questions (6–10, 12–18)

For abbreviations and symbols, see figure 1.5.

Less than one quarter of the informants express higher solidarity with Pennsylvania German English. Between ranks 11 and 43, a large majority of thirty-three informants feel more solidarity with the speakers of Pennsylvania German.

Of the nonsectarian a-generation, only two informants (3, 8) prefer Pennsylvania German English speakers with regard to solidarity. Two informants of the b-generation (10, 12) and one of the c-generation (22) are found in the upper quarter of the table, which constitutes approximately the same share of the overall number of each of the three subgroups.

By contrast, two members of the nonsectarian d-generation (informants 26, 28) are located in the upper quarter, but only one (informant 25) in the lower part. Here, the preference with regard to solidarity is shifted toward Pennsylvania German English.

The by far clearest vote in favor of Pennsylvania German is expressed by the sectarians. None of the eleven informants of this group prefers Pennsylvania German English with regard to solidarity.

The non-Pennsylvania Germans' reaction is quite different. Of the seven informants, no fewer than three (informants 44–46) express higher solidarity with the Pennsylvania German English voices, just as the majority of the nonsectarian d-generation did. This result is not surprising; it is hard to feel solidarity with someone whose language one cannot understand.

STATUS

In connection with the results based on the solidarity set of questions, it is instructive to see how the informants are structured by their reactions to the status set of questions. The scores of selected groups of informants for three groups of voices and the status-set questions were depicted in figure 4.16. Figure 4.24 compares the informants' reactions to the Pennsylvania German voices with those to the Pennsylvania German English ones.

The span of difference values is approximately twice as large in figure 4.24 as in 4.23 (between +1.03 and −1.00). Accordingly, the informants are clustered more widely around the straight line. While only one quarter of the informants expressed higher solidarity with speakers of Pennsylvania German English, exactly half of them assign higher status to the ethnically marked variety of English than to Pennsylvania German. One informant (25) is undecided.

Of the eight members of the nonsectarian a-generation, only one (informant 3) assigns higher status to Pennsylvania German English.

The next generation (b) is split on this issue. Four informants (9, 10, 14, 15) prefer the ethnically marked variety of English, the others (11–13, 16) Pennsylvania German.

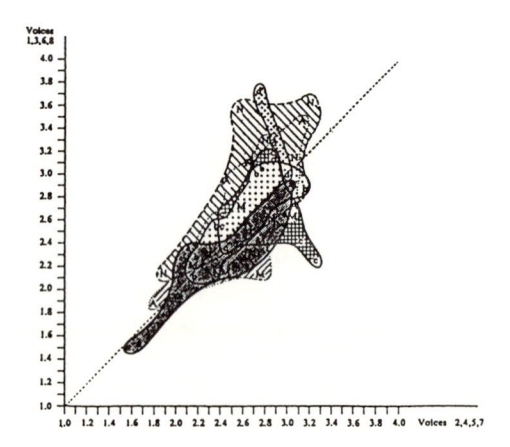

Rank	Informant	Fam	Gen	Age	Sex	Var	Voices 1,3,6,8	Voices 2,4,5,7	Difference
1	47	N	(c)	31	m	E	3.58	2.55	+1.03
2	28	3	d	9	f	E	3.72	2.72	+1.00
3	19	1/N	(c)	30	f	E	3.30	2.80	+0.50
4	40	A	(b)	17	m	PG	2.94	2.44	+0.50
5	48	N	(c)	30	f	E	3.63	3.19	+0.44
6	46	N	(b)	52	f	E	3.08	2.66	+0.42
7	26	2	d	27	f	E	3.27	2.88	+0.39
8	39	A	(b)	30	f	PG	3.47	3.13	+0.34
9	21	1	c	23	f	E	3.19	2.86	+0.33
10	14	2	b	54	m	E	3.05	2.77	+0.28
11	15	3	b	61	m	E	3.00	2.72	+0.28
12	3	1	a	77	f	E	2.36	2.11	+0.25
13	22	2	c	54	f	E	2.66	2.41	+0.25
14	43	N	(b)	50	m	E	2.13	1.88	+0.25
15	10	1	b	54	m	E	2.55	2.36	+0.19
16	23	3	c	37	m	E	2.55	2.41	+0.14
17	31	M	(b)	37	m	PG	2.72	2.58	+0.14
18	45	N	(b)	54	m	E	3.16	3.05	+0.11
19	9	1	b	57	f	PG/E	2.27	2.19	+0.08
20	36	A	(a)	52	m	PG	1.88	1.80	+0.08
21	34	M	(b)	22	f	PG	2.22	2.16	+0.06
22	25	2	d	31	f	E	3.00	3.00	0.00
23	11	1	b	53	f	E	3.11	2.16	-0.05
24	37	A	(a)	51	f	PG	2.58	2.63	-0.05
25	1	1	a	77	m	PG	1.50	1.58	-0.08
26	7	3	a	79	f	PG	2.47	2.55	-0.08
27	17	1	c	35	m	E	2.36	2.44	-0.08
28	2	1	a	77	f	PG	1.94	2.05	-0.11
29	4	2	a	71	m	PG	2.91	3.02	-0.11
30	6	3	a	74	f	PG	1.52	1.66	-0.14
31	16	1	b	37	f	E	2.64	2.80	-0.16
32	13	2	b	49	m	E	2.13	2.36	-0.23
33	44	N	(b)	52	f	E	2.63	2.86	-0.26
34	12	2	b	83	f	E	2.88	3.16	-0.28
35	30	M	(a)	55	f	PG	2.16	2.44	-0.28
36	38	A	(b)	29	m	PG	2.72	3.05	-0.33
37	8	3	a	60	f	E	2.66	3.00	-0.34
38	32	M	(b)	27	f	PG	2.66	3.02	-0.36
39	33	M	(b)	13	m	PG	2.41	2.77	-0.36
40	5	2	a	68	f	PG	2.19	2.66	-0.47
41	29	M	(a)	57	m	PG	2.13	2.77	-0.64
42	18	1	c	30	m	E	2.41	3.11	-0.70
43	20	1	c	26	m	E	2.25	3.25	-1.00

Figure 4.24: Informants' reactions to voices 1, 3, 6, 8 (PG) as compared to voices 2, 4, 5, 7 (PGE) as reflected by their answers to the status-set questions (1–5, 11, 19, 20)

For abbreviations and symbols, see figure 1.5.

This incongruity continues in the nonsectarian c-generation. Here the ratio is 3:3; however, the two informants who most distinctly assign higher status to Pennsylvania German are two members of the c-generation (informants 18 and 20, two brothers).

As before, the nonsectarian d-generation does not follow the attitude pattern of their elders. Of the three informants, two (informants 26, 28) strongly prefer Pennsylvania German English, while one (informant 25) is undecided.

Once again, the d-generation's pattern is reflected by that of the non-Pennsylvania Germans. Of the seven members, six are located in the upper half; only informant 44 is found to assign higher status to Pennsylvania German, a language she neither speaks nor understands.

The sectarian group is split on this isssue. Five of its members prefer Pennsylvania German English, the other five favor Pennsylvania German with regard to status.

INTERPRETATION

Figure 4.25 gives an overview of how selected groups of informants rate the three guises with respect to status and solidarity. The values are extracted from figures 4.16 and 4.22. All the guises to the left of the straight line are rated better for solidarity than for status. The closer a guise is located to the straight line, the more equal its status and solidarity ratings. Only guises to the right of the straight lines scored better results for status.

The nonsectarian generations a through c and the sectarians share the same pattern. They all assign higher status to the regional standard and higher solidarity rates to the two ethnic varieties. The younger the nonsectarians, the more the patterns are shifted to the upper left, that is, the less status and the more solidarity are assigned overall. However, the distances between the varieties remain virtually the same. Pennsylvania German enjoys both higher status and higher solidarity than Pennsylvania German English in all these groups but the b-generation.

The nonsectarian d-generation and the non-Pennsylvania Germans share a rating pattern that differs from that of the other subgroups. The regional standard scores highest in status; however, in the d-generation it is located to the left of the straight line, that is, it scores better for solidarity than for status. It is a common characteristic of the two monolingual groups to prefer Pennsylvania German English to Pennsylvania German in both status and solidarity.

Language Attitudes: A Matched-Guise Test

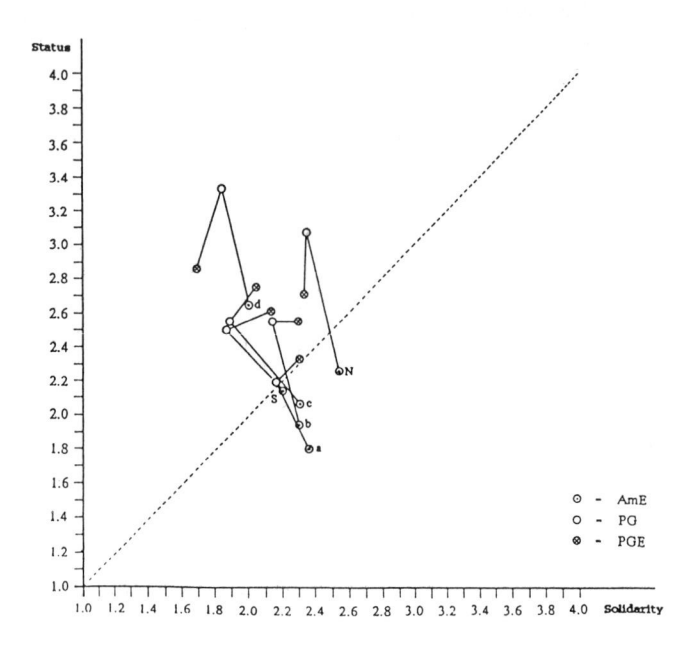

	AmE (voice 9)		PG (voices 1,3,6,9)		PGE (voices 2,4,5,7)	
	Status	Solidarity	Status	Solidarity	Status	Solidarity
a-generation	1.79	2.36	2.19	2.17	2.33	2.31
b-generation	1.94	2.30	2.57	2.14	2.56	2.30
c-generation	2.07	2.31	2.57	1.89	2.74	2.04
d-generation	2.66	2.00	3.33	1.84	2.86	1.70
Sectarians	2.13	2.20	2.53	1.88	2.61	2.13
Non-PG	2.28	2.53	3.07	2.35	2.71	2.32

Figure 4.25: Ratings of selected groups of informants for three groups of voices with regard to status and solidarity

A comparison between figures 4.23 and 4.24 narrows the discussion down to the two ethnic varieties. Overall, the informants assign higher status to Pennsylvania German English more readily than they express their solidarity with speakers of this variety. With respect to both solidarity and status, it is the monolingual subgroups of the nonsectarian d-generation and the non-Pennsylvania Germans who most consistently prefer the ethnically marked variety of English to Pennsylvania German.

More than any other group, the nonsectarian a-generation favors Pennsylvania German, its native language, with regard to status and follows the majority in its basic preference for this variety as far as solidarity is concerned. The nonsectarian b- and c-generations do not stand out from the majority in their attitude patterns. Pennsylvania German is preferred with regard to solidarity, while the informants are undecided with respect to status.

The same pattern is found for the sectarian informants; they clearly express higher solidarity with speakers of their native language, Pennsylvania German.

The above comparison of attitudes toward Pennsylvania German and Pennsylvania German English is necessary in order to answer the question whether those groups of nonsectarians who only have a rudimentary command of Pennsylvania German use an ethnically marked variety of English to express ethnic affiliation.[13] In other words, the present attitude test facilitates an answer to the question whether those phonological features found in the English of the b- and c-generations are strategic ethnic markers.[14]

The attitude patterns found for the nonsectarian b- and c-generations only partially suggest a deliberate ethnic marking of their English variety. As figure 4.16 showed, the regional standard of English is rated far higher in status than the ethnically marked variety of English. Therefore, with regard to status, the b- and c-generations have no reason to turn to Pennsylvania German English rather than to the regional standard when speaking English.

However, figure 4.22 has made it clear that, with respect to solidarity, at least in the c-generation, the regional standard is regarded most unfavorably and that Pennsylvania German is rated more positively than Pennsylvania German English. The latter observation has been clarified in the comparison of figures 4.23 and 4.24. It could, therefore, be argued that the c-generation, since their command of Pennsylvania German is limited, turns to Pennsylvania German English in order to express ethnic identity. This statement, however, requires immediate qualification; deliberate ethnic marking is only reflected in that area of the attitude sphere that refers to solidarity, not in that referring to status.

A look at the other subgroups illustrates how problematic a wholesale assumption of strategic ethnic marking in the b- and c-generations is. The nonsectarian a-generation's variety of English has been shown to have the most phonological interferences from Pennsylvania German. Since this generation also prefers the regional standard with regard to status and Pennsylvania German with regard to solidarity, these ethnic markings can by no means be strategic expressions of linguistic and cultural attitudes. Moreover, this group has Pennsylvania German as their native language to mark ethnic affiliation, at least among each other.

The nonsectarian d-generation and the non-Pennsylvania Germans present a different case. Although they also rate the regional standard the highest with regard to status, they are the only two groups to prefer Pennsylvania German English to Pennsylvania German with respect to solidarity. In view of their attitude patterns, these informants would have good reason to mark their English. However, as was shown in chapter 2, these two groups have a minimal degree of interference in their English.

Some of the sectarian informants showed a small number of ethnically marked features; however, their attitude patterns reveal a preference for the regional standard with regard to status and a preference for their native language, Pennsylvania German, with regard to solidarity. Since, like the a-generation, all the sectarians have Pennsylvania German at their disposal to mark ethnic identity within their group, it is not plausible to explain the few interference features found in their English by their attitudinal patterns. Rather, the results from the attitude test, along with the language use patterns, offer an explanation why sectarian English is relatively unmarked.

In sum, the nonsectarian b- and c-generations are the most interesting subgroups as far as ethnic marking of their English is concerned. Within their generations, the regional standard turned out to be preferred to Pennsylvania German English (and Pennsylvania German) with regard to status. Thus, at first glance, there appears to be no reason for these groups to mark their English. However, to express ethnic identity, emotional solidarity is a more important dimension than social status. With respect to solidarity, the regional standard receives the most negative rates. Here, both groups take Pennsylvania German to be the best carrier.

The b-generation, many of whose members have a near-native command of Pennsylvania German, considers Pennsylvania German English and the regional standard of English to be equally unsuitable to express solidarity if compared to Pennsylvania German. Thus, their phonological interferences may be said to depend on their active competence in Pennsylvania German rather than on their language attitudes.

By contrast, the members of the c-generation have been shown to have a fairly poor command of Pennsylvania German. Although they also show fewer phonological interferences, those that remain could be said to depend, at least partially, on a strategic marking of their English. This allows the c-generation to show its ethnic identity, which it cannot express by using Pennsylvania German itself.[15]

In the next generation, the attitude patterns have changed; at the same time, the amount of phonological interference is even more negligible.

SYNOPSIS

The matched-guise test was designed to bring to light the nature of people's attitudes toward Pennsylvania German, Pennsylvania German English, and regional-standard English. Moreover, it served to clarify how the various subgroups differ in their attitudinal patterns.

With respect to the twenty-one questions forming the categories in which the informants' attitudes were described, the data suggest a division into a status and a solidarity set of questions. Among other parameters, the former includes education, intellectual ability, professional status, power, and wealth, all of which help to measure social success. The latter group consists of emotional parameters such as honesty, generosity, friendliness, humor, and modesty.

On the basis of these two dimensions, statements about the informants' attitudes toward the voices can be made. For status, the regional standard and the Mennonite's sample of English, that is, the unmarked varieties of English, received by far higher rates than Pennsylvania German English and Pennsylvania German. For intelligence alone, the regional standard of English received the best ratings as well. The speakers using Pennsylvania German were rated slightly more intelligent than those using Pennsylvania German English. The two voices with the highest rates for status score the lowest on the solidarity dimension. Here, the ethnically marked varieties were clearly preferred. Thus, speakers of the regional standard are attributed high social status, but the informants do not feel particularly close to them on the emotional scale. For speakers of both Pennsylvania German and Pennsylvania German English, the results suggest a reversed attitude pattern.

The results of the analysis of the questions and the voices serve as instruments to determine structural differences in the attitude patterns characteristic of the various groups of informants. In this respect, it appears to be important to notice that each group of informants has a different group of people in mind when speaking about the "typical Pennsylvania German." It has become clear from the interviews and personal conversations with the informants that while the nonsectarians generally first think of their own group, sectarians and non-Pennsylvania Germans typically associate the Amish and Mennonites with being the prototype.[16]

As was shown in the analysis of questions and voices, there can be little doubt about the presence of the stereotype of the "dumb Dutchman" among the informants. Rather than including just lack of intelligence, this stereotype consists of a large number of facets. The negative poles of the status set of questions probably comprise the most significant characteristics. Moreover, different subgroups may have different notions of the "dumb Dutchman."

The data made it clear that it is the Pennsylvania Germans themselves who foster the stereotype, looking down upon their own culture. It should be borne in mind that age, or rather acquisition patterns, are very important within this group. The older the nonsectarians are (i.e., the closer they are to the last generation with Pennsylvania German as native language), the less status they attribute to their own people. Future generations, however, will have a more positive attitude, as the results of the d-generation indicate.

Within the sectarian and the non-Pennsylvania German groups, age plays a less significant role, as there is no correlation with acquisition patterns. Still, there is a certain tendency of the stereotype to be more prevalent among the younger sectarians than among their elders. This may be a reflection of the common revolt of the younger generation against tradition; if so, it will disappear as they become older. Quite generally, the non-Pennsylvania Germans foster the negative stereotype the least. This attitude may reflect a reverence toward the bilingualism of many Pennsylvania Germans.

The negative ratings that the two ethnic varieties received with respect to social status reflect the historical development within the nonsectarian group. The a-generation, the first one to raise their children in English, gave in to the stereotype of the "dumb Dutchman" in an attempt to spare them the social pressure caused by speaking with a "Dutch" accent. The data show that to the present day the stereotype is strongest among the nonsectarian a-generation, the very group whose English shows the highest degree of Pennsylvania German interference.

Quite generally, the nonsectarians' language attitudes constitute the reversal of the phonological findings. While a general decrease in Pennsylvania German phonological interference was found between the nonsectarian generations a through d, the data from the matched-guise study revealed a general decrease of absolute favor of the regional standard over the ethnically marked varieties from the a- to the d-generation.

Therefore, strong phonological interference from Pennsylvania German goes hand in hand with a relatively negative attitude toward such contact phenomena. Vice versa, the less Pennsylvania German interference nonsectarian informants have in their own variety of English, the less negative their attitude toward the ethnically marked varieties.

This form of self-hatred with regard to one's own culture, or at least to what others think about it, has been less strongly developed among the sectarians. It should be noted that this group also shows less phonological interference. This may be one of the reasons why most of the sectarians have not shifted from Pennsylvania German to English as their native language.

Being outsiders, it is easy for the non-Pennsylvania Germans not to reject Pennsylvania German ethnicity as clearly as the members of the culture themselves, stigmatized as they are by a low-prestige accent.

Altogether, the attitudinal patterns found in and around the Pennsylvania German speech community reflect at least two important general tendencies. First, negative images people might have of a minority can become associated with its language varieties. Second, ethnic stigmatization and low evaluation of linguistic varieties are especially strong within the minority itself. In some subgroups, stigmatized self-images may turn into linguistic self-hatred, which ultimately leads to language shift.

Apart from the stereotype of the "dumb Dutchman," the question was tackled whether the attitudinal patterns of any of the subgroups suggest that they might identify themselves with the Pennsylvania German culture and language in a positive way.

Numerous remarks during the interviews and the discussion of the attitude questions in questionnaire section 3.1 suggest that many informants are proud to be Pennsylvania Germans, regretting the impending loss of the language. The existence of Pennsylvania German language classes and other attempts at language revival (annual Pennsylvania German church services, *Versammlinge,* Pennsylvania German skits) are expressions of positive feelings toward this culture. The matched-guise test offers objective and systematic data for exploring these attitudes. Based on these results, one can ask which of the subgroups turn to their English variety to express this form of ethnic identification.

A comparison of all three varieties shows that among the majority of informants the regional standard enjoys the highest status but scores lowest for solidarity. With respect to the latter, the ethnically marked varieties are generally preferred. To examine the issue of ethnic marking, the discussion was narrowed down to a comparison of the two ethnic varieties. The question was whether a positive ethnic identity is transported more by Pennsylvania German or by Pennsylvania German English, and whether there are differences between the various groups of informants.

With respect to status, there is, on the whole, almost no difference in rating between the two ethnic varieties. The nonsectarian a- and c-generations and the sectarians slightly favor Pennsylvania German, which is the native language of two of these groups. The nonsectarian b- and d-generations and the non-Pennsylvania Germans prefer Pennsylvania German English, the latter two groups quite clearly.

With regard to solidarity, Pennsylvania German is generally preferred to Pennsylvania German English. The only two groups to deviate from this pattern are the nonsectarian d-generation and the non-Pennsylvania Germans. As monolingual speakers of English, they prefer the English variety in terms of both status and solidarity.

All in all, the better a group's command of Pennsylvania German, the more positive its attitude toward this variety appears to be. Those groups that have neither an active nor a passive command of Pennsylvania German tend to prefer Pennsylvania German English.

Altogether, it can be observed that besides the negative attitudes toward the Pennsylvania German culture manifested in the stereotype of the "dumb Dutchman," there are also positive attitudes toward it. These, however, focus on the solidarity dimension. The majority of informants feel higher solidarity with a speaker of an ethnic variety. While those informants who have at least rudimentary competence in Pennsylvania German (nonsectarian generations a through c, sectarians) prefer Pennsylvania German to Pennsylvania German English, the monolinguals (nonsectarian d-generation and non-Pennsylvania Germans) favor the ethnically marked variety of the language they speak themselves.

This positive attitude toward a dying culture accounts for the numerous revival attempts and the general regret about the impending loss, especially among the nonsectarian Pennsylvania Germans. Linguistically, a certain degree of ethnic marking to express one's cultural identity might be accounted for by this feeling of solidarity.

Such marking of the English variety is necessary only for those groups that do not have the original ethnic language, Pennsylvania German, at their disposal. Phonological and attitudinal results suggest that particularly the members of the nonsectarian c-generation may use their variety of English to mark their ethnic identity.

How half-hearted such positive attitudes toward the ethnically marked variety of English are, can be seen from the ratings it received with respect to identification. When it came to stating which of the three varieties the informants would like to speak themselves, not only the a- and b-generations, but also the c-generation put Pennsylvania German English on the last rank. This shows that deep inside the informants' acceptance of ethnically marked English is lower than the results with respect to solidarity might suggest. Eventually, all revival attempts are doomed to failure not only because of changing acquisition patterns, but also because of these negative language attitudes. In fact, the former are only a consequence of the latter.

In conclusion, the various subgroups show a number of remarkable differences with respect to their language attitudes. In many cases the nonsectarian a- and c-generations and the sectarians show similar attitude patterns. The nonsectarian b-generation seems to stand out at times, while the nonsectarian d-generation often resembles the non-Pennsylvania German group in its attitude patterns. The latter's quite separate sociolinguistic heritage accounts for many of the attitudinal differences.

Age is a relevant factor only insofar as it parallels different acquisition patterns. The various nonsectarian generations are a case in point. Among the sectarian and the non-Pennsylvania German informants, age is a less significant determiner of attitude patterns. There is a certain tendency within the sectarian group for the older informants to disfavor the ethnically marked varieties less strongly than the younger informants. In other words, the younger the sectarians, the more they favor the regional standard. By contrast, membership in the Mennonite or Amish subgroups did not prove to be a significant factor.

Age plays an even smaller role within the non-Pennsylvania German group. Unlike their sectarian counterparts, the younger non-Pennsylvania Germans show a slightly higher acceptance of the ethnically marked varieties than their elders. Gender did not prove to be a significant factor for differences in attitudes in any subgroup.

5
Synthesis and Conclusion

The final chapter shows how, based on the historical background information, the language use analysis and the attitude test can be used to account for the phonological differences found in the informants' varieties of English.

First, the two most significant social factors, community and generation, will be discussed in summary. A comprehensive attempt to solve the "Pennsylvania German paradox" will be followed by an assessment of the role of language use and attitudes in the formation of linguistic differences. Some remarks on the Pennsylvania German contact situation and possible future trends will round off the conclusion.

SOCIAL FACTORS

COMMUNITY

As was to be expected from the historical differences, the three main social groups (nonsectarians, sectarians, and non-Pennsylvania Germans) form clear clusters in all three areas of examination. The nonsectarians' English phonology is most heavily marked, followed by the sectarians' and the non-Pennsylvania Germans'. The fact that certain features are found in the latter's speech shows that the pressure of convergence not only affects the minority language (Pennsylvania German), but also, to a certain extent, the language of the surrounding majority (English).

Chapter 3 demonstrated that the three groups do not share common networks. If one wanted to apply the term *Sprachinsel* ('speech island'), one would have to assume two or even three separate Pennsylvania German speech islands (one including the nonsectarian families and one the Mennonite and Amish informants) within the surrounding mainstream society.

The groups also differ in their acquisition patterns. Two of them are homogeneous in this respect. While all the sectarian informants learned Pennsylvania German natively and English at school, all the non-Pennsylvania Germans are monolingual speakers of English. In the case of the nonsectarians, the generation factor complicates this matter even further.

Differences in network and acquisition result in different language use patterns. Among the nonsectarians, Pennsylvania German does not serve any unique function. The bilingualism still present among the older speakers is unstable. By contrast, the sectarians' bilingualism is supported by diglossia. Both Pennsylvania German and English are used in certain domains, fulfilling non-overlapping functions. This constellation ensures the maintenance of Pennsylvania German in the sectarian informant families.

Chapter 4 showed that the informants are also structured by their attitudinal patterns. The non-Pennsylvania Germans and the youngest nonsectarian informants generally display the least negative prejudice against ethnic speakers. Compared to the older nonsectarians, the sectarians have a stronger positive attitude toward their own ethnicity, their identity being mainly based on their religion. To maintain their religious rigor, their lifestyle has to be traditional. Unlike the nonsectarians, the sectarians are content with their past and present situation. This attitude might be expressed by the words "If it ain't broken, don't fix it." Among the older nonsectarians, the stereotype of the "dumb Dutchman" is far more widely disseminated. As they wanted their children to have it easier at school and later in life, they tried to spare them the stigma of dutchified English by teaching them English natively.

In all, the nonsectarians are characterized by the widest diversity in their English phonology, their language use patterns, and their language attitudes. Linguistically and sociolinguistically, they are the most interesting group.

GENERATION

The nonsectarians' linguistic diversity is caused by vast differences between young and old. Since the differences in acquisition patterns are clearly generational, it is more appropriate to regard generation rather than age as a significant social factor.

In chapter 2 the strongest interference was found to be present in the English of the a-generation and the linguistically conservative part of the b-generation. The less conservative section of the b-generation and the c-generation show far less interference, a trend which becomes even stronger among the d-generation.

Within the nonsectarian group, a dramatic acceleration of change is taking place. Heavy ethnic marking, as it was the rule among the native speakers of Pennsylvania German for roughly two centuries, stops almost immediately after the acquisition pattern changes to English as first language. The following generation (b) is split, which is due to differences in language use and attitude patterns. The conservative part of the b-generation and the c-generation represent the stage of highest speed in the change. Within a generation and a half, the amount of interference declines dramatically. The d-generation already represents a phase of deceleration and restabilization. This interpretation is supported by the fact that the non-Pennsylvania German monolinguals display a similar degree of phonological interference.

Part of this development can be accounted for by the informants' language use patterns, which in turn are strongly influenced by their acquisition patterns. The nonsectarian a-generation are the last speakers to use Pennsylvania German extensively inside and, to a certain degree, outside the family. The number of potential interlocutors is, however, steadily declining as the members of their own group are dying. Chapter 3 showed that even intra-family use of Pennsylvania German is minimal when members of the b-generation or younger talk to each other. The family is the last bastion of the minority language. As soon as Pennsylvania German stops being used at home, it will die.

It would be too simplistic to attribute the steady decrease of interference from generations a through d to the acquisition and language use patterns only. The questions why the b-generation is linguistically split and why almost monolingual members of the c-generation should have a certain amount of phonological ethnic marking in their English would remain unexplained. The answers were found in chapter 4: The informants differ in their attitude patterns.

Those members of the b-generation who show heavy phonological interference do not foster the stereotype of the "dumb Dutchman" to the same extent as the linguistically less conservative part of their generation. Instead, they almost exclusively take a strong interest in the preservation of the Pennsylvania German language and culture. By contrast, those b-generation informants with little interference typically have a more negative attitude toward their ethnic background and, at the same time, less competence in the German dialect.

A positive attitude toward Pennsylvania German appears to be responsible for the relatively high degree of interference in the speech of the c-generation, most of whose members have very little competence in Pennsylvania German. These informants, who on the whole are better educated and have more contacts beyond the Pennsylvania German area, exhibit regret about the impending loss of their elders' language and culture. Since they do not have the medium of Pennsylvania German at their disposal, they may be said to show their ethnic identity through strategic ethnic marking of their English phonology, although only in a limited number of features.

The fact that in the next generation (d) the trend toward a more positive attitude toward ethnicity continues but is not mirrored in the linguistic results shows that acquisition and language use patterns are of prime importance as explanatory instruments as compared to attitudes.

THE PENNSYLVANIA GERMAN PARADOX

The data of chapter 2 reflect a paradox that has occupied researchers for a long time. Both culturally and linguistically, the Pennsylvania Germans form several separate speech communities. The most visible differences are the ones between the sectarian and the nonsectarian Pennsylvania Germans.

Contrary to all expectations, the sectarians, who live in strictly regulated religious communities and strive to keep apart from the surrounding mainstream society, are characterized by comparatively little Pennsylvania German interference in their phonology of English. At the same time, their variety of Pennsylvania German has been found to show a high degree of interference from English.[1] By contrast, the English phonology of the nonsectarians, who are fully integrated into American mainstream society, is marked to a far greater extent, at least in the older generations. Those nonsectarians, however, who have a good active command of Pennsylvania German show comparatively little English interference (figure 5.1).

This apparent paradox can be partly explained with the help of the results from the language use analysis. The sectarians are characterized by di- or even triglossia, that is, they use their three varieties (Pennsylvania German, English, and Bible High German) in fixed domains. Code switching during discourse is not appropriate. The strict use of Pennsylvania German in most domains within the community necessitates the elaboration of the German dialect by borrowing from English. The strong lexical interference in sectarian Pennsylvania German is nec-

Degree of interference	Sectarians	Nonsectarians
in English	low	high
in Pennsylvania German	high	low

Figure 5.1: The Pennsylvania German paradox

essary in order to maintain discourse. Moreover, sectarian speakers are constantly forced to "translate" information and experiences (communication with outsiders, written material, new topics) from English into Pennsylvania German—another factor contributing to lexical and syntactical convergence (Huffines 1992, 179). Thus, sectarian Pennsylvania German is an example of a language variety reaching functional stability through structural instability (*see* Enninger and Wandt 1982).

English is the sectarians' medium at school. The plain communities are extremely careful to teach their children "good" English, that is, English with little lexical, syntactical, and phonological interference from Pennsylvania German. This strict prescriptivism only applies to English, not to Pennsylvania German. Cases of slips of the tongue, where "dutchified English" is used, are often pointed at in a humorous way. Marked English is taken as a characteristic of the nonsectarian Pennsylvania Germans. English is used in all interaction with outsiders and is the only written medium outside the religious domain. Altogether, the sectarians' use of English is norm-oriented and prevalent in transactional as well as formal situations.

In the nonsectarian families the domain patterns are less strict. For instance, it is possible to switch completely from Pennsylvania German to English if the German dialect does not supply the necessary terms. Moreover, speaking English rather than Pennsylvania German is more and more becoming the norm, as most younger speakers are monolinguals. This protects nonsectarian Pennsylvania German from many intrusions from English that would be necessary if all conversation in certain domains had to be in the German dialect.

As code switching is frequent, nonsectarian native speakers have little need to translate. Consequently, they exhibit far less translation skill from English into Pennsylvania German than the sectarians (Huffines 1991, 190). If they translate at all, the direction is from their

Synthesis and Conclusion

native Pennsylvania German to English, the result being "dutchified English." The most direct influences are in syntax and the lexicon, but chapter 2 showed that there is also strong interference from Pennsylvania German in the English phonology. Among the nonsectarians the degree of interference decreases with age, or rather, the changes in acquisition patterns. Nevertheless, remnants of interference are found in the English of the members of the youngest generations, who are monolinguals, and even of the surrounding non-Pennsylvania Germans. Part of the explanation of this phenomenon can be found in the attitudinal patterns of the various subgroups.

The matched-guise test of chapter 4 revealed that the informants' attitude toward the Pennsylvania German language and culture is double-edged.

On the one hand, there is the stereotype of the "dumb Dutchman," a negative attitude found in all subgroups of the Pennsylvania Germans and the surrounding non-Pennsylvania Germans. The data showed that the one group affected the most by this stereotype is the nonsectarian a-generation. These findings correlate with dramatic historical changes in the nonsectarians' acquisition patterns, that is, the a-generation's shift from Pennsylvania German to English as their children's native language. The reason most often given in the interviews was that the latter should not have a German accent in their English.

The data revealed that in each case the status dimension is responsible for the negative attitudes. In other words, Pennsylvania German ethnicity is considered to be damaging in connection with such factors as education, intelligence, and power. More specifically, speaking English with a Pennsylvania German accent is most heavily stigmatized. Pennsylvania German itself is generally rated more positively, though not to the same extent as the regional standard. Only the non-Pennsylvania Germans tend to envy the bilinguals' competence in Pennsylvania German.

On the other hand, there is also a positive attitude toward the Pennsylvania German language and culture. Among the nonsectarians this manifests itself in their pride of their heritage, their unanimous regret of the loss of the German dialect, and the numerous folkloristic and linguistic revival attempts. In the sectarian group the positive ethnic identity expresses itself in their religiousness and separation from mainstream society. The non-Pennsylvania German informants also show positive traits of attitude toward their neighbors' ethnicity.

In the matched-guise data the positive attitude is expressed on the solidarity dimension, in connection with character traits such as generosity, friendliness, and industry. The positive attitude may account for some of the Pennsylvania German phonological interference in the English of the nonsectarian c-generation. Its members have such minimal competence in Pennsylvania German that they resort to English to express their ethnic identity.[2]

LANGUAGE, USE, AND ATTITUDE

Figure 5.2 gives an overview of the various subgroups' degree of phonological interference, language use, and attitude patterns, thus putting the results of chapters 2–4 into relation.

The fact that the nonsectarian a-generation has the highest degree of phonological interference is accounted for by its members having Pennsylvania German as their native language and their broad use of it. These factors are more significant than their fairly negative attitude. In other words, because of their linguistic situation the informants are normally unable to hide their accent even if so desired. Moreover, if the a-generation informants wanted to show their ethnicity, they would do so by using Pennsylvania German itself.

As is indicated by the double notation in figure 5.2, the b-generation is split. The linguistically more conservative part (b_1) uses Pennsylvania German more frequently and has a more positive attitude toward its ethnicity. Still, it is doubtful that its high degree of phonological interference marks ethnic identity, as Pennsylvania German is at these informants' disposal.

Group	Pennsylvania German interference in English	Use of Pennsylvania German	Attitude
a	very high	broad	negative
b_1	high	broad	more positive
b_2	medium	medium	negative
c	low	minimal	more positive
d	very low	none	more positive
Sectarians	low	extensive (diglossia)	more positive
Non-PG	very low	none	more positive

Figure 5.2: Interaction of degree of phonological interference, language use, and attitude patterns in various subgroups

The smaller amount of interference in the speech of the less conservative section (b_2) can be attributed to their less extensive use of Pennsylvania German and a more negative attitude. The latter prevents these informants from deliberately marking their ethnic affiliation.

Although the degree of interference in the speech of the nonsectarian c-generation is lower, it cannot be totally accounted for by their minimal use of Pennsylvania German. In fact, most c-generation informants have no more than rudimentary passive competence. The more positive attitude toward ethnicity seems to result in a strategic marking of English to express ethnic identity.

The almost negligible amount of interference in the d-generation's English correlates with the virtually zero degree of use of Pennsylvania German in this group, which mostly consists of complete monolinguals. The language use pattern outweighs the effects of the somewhat more positive language attitudes and the fact that Pennsylvania German itself is not available as an ethnicity marker.

In the case of the sectarians, the attitude is split. On the one hand, their Pennsylvania German identity is closely connected with the positive concepts of religion and tradition. On the other hand, they are extremely norm-oriented when they teach their children English, which shows that the "dumb Dutchman" stereotype is present as well. Both Pennsylvania German and English enjoy a certain degree of prestige, the former more overtly, the latter more covertly. In the light of these facts, it would be too simplistic to say that because of their positive attitude toward Pennsylvania German the sectarians' bilingualism is stable, while the nonsectarians are losing the German dialect because of their negative language attitudes.

Rather, as was also the case with the nonsectarians, attitude is not the prime force, language competence, or repertoire, being more important. Since the sectarians have Pennsylvania German at their disposal to express ethnic identity, there is no need for them to mark their English. Linguistically, sectarians express their ethnic identity through diglossia, not through accented English.

The non-Pennsylvania Germans' pattern equals that of the nonsectarian d-generation. In spite of a relatively positive attitude toward Pennsylvania German ethnicity, their English is hardly accented because of their own monolingualism and little exposure to speakers of Pennsylvania German.

An unbiased observer might expect attitudes to guide both language use and language behavior. One should think that informants with a positive attitude toward Pennsylvania German ethnicity are likely to speak Pennsylvania German more often (if they have active competence) and to have more interference in their English. Figure 5.2 shows that this is not the case. Generally speaking, positive attitudes coincide with low degrees of interference rather than vice versa.

Thus, language use patterns appear to have a certain priority over attitude patterns with respect to their effect on the informants' linguistic behavior. All in all, the informants' language attitudes proved to be mixed and, therefore, less distinct. It can be seen in almost all the tables and diagrams showing the informants' distribution that phonology and language use structure them far more clearly than the attitudes. Although ascertained and evaluated with formalized methods, attitude seems to be less tangible.

The whole sample contains only one informant whose attitude patterns are stronger than any other factor. As a fervent supporter of his ethnic heritage, informant 14 tries to express his positive attitude through his conscious language choice by using Pennsylvania German "with as many people as possible." Accordingly, his English shows a high degree of interference.

Only in the case of the members of the linguistically less conservative section of the b-generation are attitude and language use fully in line with respect to their effects on language. Two typical representatives of this group may serve as illustrations.

Informants 11 and 16 both showed a comparatively negative attitude toward Pennsylvania German language and culture. In addition, as the coowner of a gas station, informant 11 comes into daily contact with monolinguals. Informant 16 is married to a member of the c-generation and has practically no active competence in Pennsylvania German. Thus, their low degree of interference does not come as a surprise.

An exception is found even in this section of the b-generation, which only goes to show how important individual differences are. In chapter 2, informant 13 was also identified as having less phonological interference in his English than most other b-generation informants. Considering his acquisition, use, and attitude patterns, the phonological result is rather surprising. Informant 13 has very good active competence in Pennsylvania German, uses Pennsylvania German in far more situations than informants 11 and 16, and shows a relatively positive attitude toward Pennsylvania German ethnicity. The explanation for the low degree of interference lies in the fact that, as a school teacher, informant 13 has a fairly high education and frequently comes into contact with non-Pennsylvania Germans.

CONCLUDING REMARKS AND OUTLOOK

In a contact situation, the law of inertia seems to play an important role. It is easier to stick with a language than shift to another, unless there are social reasons for change.

Having lacked the delaying factor of religious separatism, the non-sectarian families have felt more pressure for change than the sectarians. As a result, they have assimilated to mainstream society in their lifestyle, and, consequently, in their language. Once the assimilation process began, the higher prestige of the surrounding culture gathered momentum and has kept the process going. Socially, the result will be full assimilation to mainstream society; linguistically, it will be language death.

To the present day, the three distinctive features of sectarian identity have been language, horse-and-buggy transportation, and dress. In the earliest period of settlement, the difference between the sectarians and the surrounding society was small with regard to all three features. However, while mainstream society developed, the sectarians continued their traditional lifestyle. Their present distinctive identity is based on religion, that of the nonsectarians on economic values.

The sectarians fulfill the three factors of stable bilingualism: early acquisition of both languages, neutral or positive attitudes toward both languages, and functional need for both languages in well-defined, non-overlapping domains (Louden 1987, 20–29; 1988, 16–24; 1989, 30; and 1993, 170). By contrast, the nonsectarians fulfill none of these prerogatives; their bilingualism is therefore unstable.

Depending on which language motivates it, two types of linguistic transfer can be distinguished (Van Coetsem 1988, 3 and 7ff.). In *sl-agentivity* the source language is the agent, in *rl-agentivity* the agent is the recipient language.[3] The main characteristic of sl-agentivity is *interference* (in Weinreich's term) or *imposition* (in Van Coetsem's term) of features of the source language onto the recipient language. The result of rl-agentivity is the *borrowing* of features of the source language into the recipient language.

Whether sl- or rl-agentivity occurs depends on which language a speaker knows better. If the source language is linguistically dominant, sl-agentivity and imposition result; if the speaker has better competence in the recipient language, the result is rl-agentivity and borrowing.

Certain components of language are more susceptible to transfer than others. At the more stable extreme is phonology; syntax lies somewhere in the middle, while the lexicon is the least stable component. Van Coetsem (1988, 25ff.) calls the difference between these language domains in stablity and resistance to change the *stability gradient of language*.

In contact situations, the stable components of language are preserved longer than the less stable ones. The high stability of phonology is the reason for its selection as the area of investigation in the present study, which concentrated on the results of instable bilingualism among the nonsectarians.

Following Van Coetsem (1988), Louden (1988, 12f.) relates the concept of stability to the types of transfer:

> When correlated with the two transfer types, stability can be understood as impeding change in situations of borrowing, while promoting change in imposition. Thus sl-agentivity tends to affect phonology more than rl-agentivity, which would affect lexicon more significantly. In other words, in cases of sl-agentivity, speakers will generally impose phonological features from their linguistically dominant language onto the rl. In cases of of rl-agentivity, speakers will tend to borrow features from less stable components of language, such as vocabulary, from the sl into their linguistically dominant rl.

In other words, the two types of transfer affect different components of language. While imposition (sl-agentivity) tends to affect the more stable component of phonology, borrowing affects the lexicon. This point is borne out by the results of the nonsectarian informants interviewed for the present study.

When members of the nonsectarian a-generation speak English, English is their recipient language and Pennsylvania German is their source language. Since Pennsylvania German is their native (and thus linguistically dominant) language, sl-agentivity and therefore imposition of stable components occurs: These speakers impose Pennsylvania German phonological features onto their English and produce "accented English."

The question remains how this model accounts for the relatively smaller, but nevertheless perceptible, amount of ethnically marked phonological variants in the English of members of the nonsectarian generations b through d. As for these speakers Pennsylvania German is not linguistically dominant, sl-agentivity and imposition of stable phonological variables cannot readily be expected.

However, there is another factor that determines the type of transfer, namely social dominance. Chapter 4 showed that all the nonsectarians rate Pennsylvania German so high on the solidarity dimension that they regard it as the socially dominant language. This makes the phonological impositions from Pennsylvania German onto the English of the younger nonsectarians plausible.[4]

In sum, the linguistic differences between the English varieties spoken by the sectarians and the nonsectarians can be attributed to different dominance patterns. For the nonsectarian a-generation, Pennsylvania German is the linguistically and socially dominant language, whereas for the members of the nonsectarian generations b through d a social (although not linguistic) dominance of Pennsylvania German can be suspected.

Such an imbalance is not present in the case of the sectarian Pennsylvania Germans. The transfer types are neutralized; although movement of linguistic material still occurs, it is not clear whether imposition (sl-agentivity) or borrowing (rl-agentivity) is present. Instead of these two types of transfer, which are characteristic of substratal and superstratal relations, convergence happens in a contact situation of stable (diglossic) bilingualism.

Convergence is found between two languages in an adstratal relation (i.e., one that is coexistent over an extended period of time), and means the transfer of linguistic features from these languages to a common system.[5]

The neutralization of the imbalance in linguistic and social dominance accounts for the fact that the sectarian Pennsylvania Germans' English is characterized by less phonological imposition than that of the nonsectarian a-generation and part of the b-generation. By the same token, this process helps to explain why plain Pennsylvania German shows so much more borrowing from English than the Pennsylvania German spoken by the nonsectarians.

At the end of the outline in chapter 1, reference was made to the wider goal of the present study, which was defined as the description of language maintenance and shift among several subgroups of the Pennsylvania Germans. The term *shift* has been preferred to *loss*, as the latter would put too much emphasis on the death of Pennsylvania German. Because of significant changes in language use and attitude patterns, nonsectarian Pennsylvania German has reached the final stage before extinction. However, as has been shown throughout the present study, the death of nonsectarian Pennsylvania German is not the only result of the Pennsylvania German–English language contact. Another one is change within the system, for instance, convergence as seen in plain Pennsylvania German, or (forming the center of the present study) imposition of Pennsylvania German features on the English of the various subgroups.

The close study of several multigenerational families belonging to different subgroups (including the surrounding majority culture) facilitates a certain degree of generalization of the concrete results and predictions of future developments. If two languages are in contact over a considerable period of time, the expected result is assimilation of some kind. In an unstable bilingual situation, the eventual loss of the minority language can be expected. This may be seen in the steady decline of Pennsylvania German from nonsectarian generations a through d. The opposite development, namely language maintenance, demands an explanation; in the present case, the question is what the impetus of the maintenance of sectarian Pennsylvania German is. The answer is the stable bilingualism, in connection with diglossia, prevalent in this group. The price to be paid is system-internal convergence to the majority language (English).

The "normal" process in a language contact situation is the general shift away from the minority language to the language of the majority. If the minority language leaves its traces on the majority language before it dies out (cf. phonological Pennsylvania German interference in English), this is merely a by-product. It is a way for the minority language, as it were, to survive its own death. This only happens in a situation of instable bilingualism (in the present examination among the nonsectarian informants). If the minority language survives, there is no need for imposition (as in the sectarians' case).

What future developments seem likely in the three large groups? The survival of Pennsylvania German over the next generations is secured through its use as a native language in the conservative sectarian communities. Because of the high birthrate in this group, the number of native speakers of Pennsylvania German is growing. However, there are a number of progressive sectarian communities in which English has taken the place of Pennsylvania German as the language of the worship service. This shift is detrimental to the maintenance of Pennsylvania German among the sectarians at large.

In the nonsectarian group the process of shift is in full swing. Pennsylvania German will be extinct as a native language with the death of the present grandparent generation. The loss of any active competence in this group can be expected within the next couple of decades. Time is therefore pressing for any linguistic examination of the nonsectarian group while all stages of language competence from native Pennsylvania German to monolingual English may still be found. Nevertheless, even after its death, Pennsylvania German will leave its traces in the English spoken in the area, in the speech of both the younger nonsectarians and the surrounding non-Pennsylvania Germans.

Appendix: Questionnaire

The appendix gives only those sections of the questionnaire which have been evaluated in detail. The original numbering has been retained. Some parts have been somewhat condensed in space.

Appendix: Questionnaire

1 language

1.2 Pennsylvania German English phonology (flashcards)

1.2.1 PGE [ʃ] for AmE [dʒ]
1. jug
2. pigeon
3. cabbage

1.2.2 PGE [t̥,d̥,g̥]/[p,t,k] for AmE final [b,d,g]
4. tub
5. bed
6. egg

1.2.3 PGE [s] for AmE [z]
7. zoo
8. houses
9. boys
10. girls
11. pigs

1.2.4 PGE [v] for AmE [w]
12. well
13. wagon
14. wheel

1.2.5 PGE [w] for AmE [v]
15. vegetables
16. valentine

1.2.6 PGE [s] for AmE [θ]
17. thistle
18. author
19. south

1.2.7 PGE [d] for AmE [ð]
20. that
21. feather
22. smooth

1.2.8 PGE ∅ for AmE final [r]
23. car
24. bear

1.2.9 PGE ∅ for AmE [r] before consonant or /s/
25. bird
26. stars

1.2.10 PGE [ʃ] for AmE [ʒ]
27. measure
28. pleasure

1.2.11 PGE [f] for AmE final [v]
29. glove
30. hive

1.2.12 PGE [l] for AmE [ɫ]
31. ladder
32. milk
33. hill

1.2.13 PGE [oː]/[ɔː] for AmE [oʊ]
34. goat
35. soap

1.2.14 PGE [eː]/[ɛː] for AmE [eɪ]
36. cake
37. gate

1.2.15 PGE [ʌ] for AmE [ʌ]
38. cup
39. sun

1.2.16 PGE [ɑʊ]/[ɑː] for AmE [aʊ]
40. mouse
41. crown

1.2.17 PGE [ɑɪ]/[ɑː] for AmE [aɪ]
42. mice
43. lion

1.2.18 PGE [y] or [u] for AmE [ʊ]
44. book
45. wolf

Appendix: Questionnaire

1.2.19 PGE [j]/[aɪ]/[e] for AmE unstressed [ɪ]

    46. family
    47. baby

1.2.20 PGE [Və] or [V+off-glide+ə] for AmE [V:] or [V+off-glide]

    48. key
    49. saw
    50. shoe
    51. pie
    52. tray
    53. boy
    54. cow
    55. crow

2 Language use and network

2.1. Personal data

Name: ....

Address: ....

Phone: ....

Sex: ○ male   ○ female

Date of birth: .... age: ....

Place of birth: ....

Are you Dutch?   ○ yes   ○ no

How long have you lived in this area? ....

Other places you have lived: .... how long? .....

Profession(s)/Occupation(s) (also former): .... from .... to ....

Where do/did you work?: ....

Schools and colleges: ....

Religion: ....

Number of brothers and sisters: ....

Are you   ○ single?   ○ married?   ○ widowed?

If married or widowed: Your spouse's name: ....

Number of children: ....

Number of grandchildren: ....

Number of great-grandchildren: ....

2.2 Family structure

2.2.1 Please state for each of your grandparents:

  1) their name
  2) Are/Were they Dutch?
  3) Can/Could they a) understand
             and b) speak Dutch?
    (Please make any comment on their language (Dutch, English, Bible German) you feel is important.)

Appendix: Questionnaire

4) a) When and
   b) where was he/she born?
5) a) places where he/she lived and
   b) how long? ....
6) Where do they live now?
7) their a) former and
   b) present profession(s)/occupation(s)
8) their religion
   the grade when he/she left school, high school or college

2.2.2 Please state for your father and mother:

1) their name
2) Can/Could they a) understand and
   b) speak Dutch? (any comments?)
3) a) When and
   b) where were they born?
4) a) places where they lived and
   b) how long
5) Where do they live now?
6) the grade when they left school, high school or college
7) their a) former and
   b) present profession(s)/occupation(s)
8) their religion
9) a) names and
   b) places of residence of brothers and sisters

2.2.3 Please state for each of your brothers and sisters:

1) their name
2) Can/Could they a) understand and
   b) speak Dutch? (any comments?)
3) a) When and
   b) where were they born?
4) a) places where they lived and
   b) how long
5) Where do they live now?
6) the grade when they left school, high school or college
7) their a) former and
   b) present profession(s)/occupation(s)
8) their religion

2.2.4 Please state for your spouse:

his/her name: ....
Is/Was he/she Dutch?   o yes   o no
Can/Could he/she a) understand and
                 b) speak Dutch? (any comments?)
   a) o yes   o no   b) o yes   o no

When and where was he/she born?
   a) .... b) ....
places where he/she lived:
   .... how long? ....
the grade when he/she left school, high school or college:
....
his/her a) former and
       b) present profession(s)/occupation(s):
   a)
   b)
his/her religion:
a) names and
b) places of residence of brothers and sisters:
   a) .... b) ....
the date of your marriage:

2.2.5 Please state for each of your children:

1) their name
2) Can they a) understand and
            b) speak Dutch? (any comments?)
3) a) When and
   b) where were they born?
4) a) places where they lived and
   b) how long
5) Where do they live now?
6) the grade when they left school, high school or college
7) their a) former and
   b) present profession(s)/occupation(s)
8) their religion

2.2.6 Please state for each of your grandchildren:

1) their name
2) Can they a) understand and
            b) speak Dutch? (any comments?)
3) a) When and
   b) where were they born?
4) a) places where they lived and
   b) how long
5) Where do they live now?

Appendix: Questionnaire

6) the grade when they left school, high school or college
7) their a) former and
    b) present profession(s)/occupation(s)
8) their religion

2.2.7 Please state for other members of your family who live/lived in your house or in the area:

1) their a) name and
         b) degree of relationship
2) Are/Were they Dutch?
3) Can/Could they a) understand and
                  b) speak Dutch? (any comments?)
4) a) When and
   b) where were they born?
5) a) places where they lived and
   b) how long
6) Where do they live now?
7) the grade when they left school, high school or college
8) their a) former and
         b) present profession(s)/occupation(s)
9) their religion

2.3 Network and language use

Network part (to be asked parallel to the language use part)

N1: Relatives, friends, and neighbors

Who are the two or three people in your present life you feel closest to? Which of them are Dutch?

a. ....
b. ....
c. ....
d. ....

How many relatives does your family usually invite to a holiday or party such as a wedding reception, a baptism, or a big birthday party?
....

How many of them are Dutch?
....

How many friends and neighbors do you usually invite to such a holiday or party?
....

How many of them are Dutch?
....

N2: Work

What kind of people do you come into contact with at work? Which of them are Dutch?
....

N3: School

How many students and teachers are at your school?

- students ....
- teachers ....

How many of them are Dutch?

- students ....
- teachers ....

N4: Religion

Do you have the opportunity in your area to go to church services in which Dutch and/or High German are still used?

o yes   o no

How often do these services take place?
....

Where do you normally go to church?
....

How often do you go to the Dutch or High German services?
....

Is the minister Dutch?   o yes   o no

How many people in the congregation are Dutch?   ....

Appendix: Questionnaire 295

Does your household own

- an English Bible? ○ yes ○ no
- a German Bible? ○ yes ○ no
- an English/German Bible? ○ yes ○ no
- a Dutch Bible? ○ yes ○ no

In your community, are there church bulletins written

- in Dutch? ○ yes ○ no
- in English? ○ yes ○ no
- in High German? ○ yes ○ no
- in English with a Dutch column? ○ yes ○ no
- in English with a HG column? ○ yes ○ no

N5: Spare time

What hobbies do you have? ....
In which of these activities do you meet Dutch people?
....

Are you a member of a PG club or society?
○ yes ○ no
What's its name? ....
Where do you meet? ....
How often do you meet? ....
How many members are Dutch? ....
Do you ever go to activities organized by a PG club or a PG society?
○ yes ○ no
Which events do you go to/actively participate in?

- *Versammling* ○ passive ○ active
- talks on Dutch language and culture ○
- the Grundsowlodge ○
- auctions ○
- flea markets / craft sales ○
- theater plays ○
- other: .... ○

Do you do your own butchering? ○ yes ○ no
Do you go to help people with their own butchering?
○ yes ○ no

Where do you butcher? ....
What kind of animals? ....
How often? ....
How many of the participants are Dutch? ......

Which local restaurants do you like to go to?
How many of the people working there are Dutch?
....

Do you ever go to fairs or other folk festivals?
○ yes ○ no
Which are they and where do they take place?
How many of the salespeople and visitors are Dutch?

Do you ever listen to the radio? ○ yes ○ no
What kind of programs do you listen to?
....
Are there Dutch radio programs in your area? ○ yes ○ no
What kind of programs are these?
....

Do you ever watch TV? ○ yes ○ no
What kind of programs do you watch?
....
Are there Dutch TV programs in your area? ○ yes ○ no
What kind of programs are these?
....

Which newspapers and magazines do you usually read?
....

In your area, are there newspapers, magazines, or bulletins
- written wholly in Dutch? ○ yes ○ no
- with a Dutch column? ○ yes ○ no

Appendix: Questionnaire

What are the names of these publications and what do they deal with?
....

What kind of articles do you find in the Dutch columns?
....

Do you like reading books?   o yes   o no

What kind of books do you read?
....

Do you have the opportunity in your area to buy books written in Dutch?

o yes   o no

What kind of books are these?

- novels   o yes   o no
- stories   o yes   o no
- poetry   o yes   o no
- non-fiction   o yes   o no
- other: ....

N6: Shopping

Do you ever shop at the farmers' market?   o yes   o no

How many of the salespeople are actually

- Dutch? ....§
- plain? ....§

Do you ever shop in the little stores in town?

o yes   o no

Which of the storekeepers are Dutch?
....

Do you ever shop

- at the big supermarkets?   o yes   o no
- at the shopping malls?   o yes   o no

How many of the salespeople are Dutch

- at the big supermarkets? ....§
- at the shopping malls?   ....§

N7: Doctor and officials

Is your family doctor Dutch?   o yes   o no

Where is the nearest hospital? ....

How many of the doctors and nurses in the local hospital are Dutch?

- doctors ....§
- nurses ....§

Is the mayor/Are the members of the board of supervisors of your town Dutch?

o yes   o no

How many of the other officials working at the town hall are Dutch?

........§

N8: Network beyond the borders of the Pennsylvania German speech area

Have you ever been

- to Reading?   o yes   o no
- to Allentown?   o yes   o no
- to Lancaster?   o yes   o no
- to Harrisburg?   o yes   o no
- to Philadelphia?   o yes   o no
- to other big cities in Pennsylvania? o yes   o no

When? ....

Where did you meet Dutch people and who were they?
....

Have you ever been out of Pennsylvania?

o yes   o no

Where and when? ....

Where did you meet Dutch people and who were they?
....

Have you ever traveled abroad, or even to Europe?

o yes   o no

Where to and when? Who did you travel with?
....

Appendix: Questionnaire

Where did you meet Dutch people and who were they?
....

FOR NONSECTARIANS ONLY:

Do/Did you serve in the army?   o yes   o no

When? ....

Where are/were you stationed? ....

How long? ....

Do/Did you meet any Dutch people in the army?

o yes   o no

Do you ever visit Dutch-speaking relatives or friends living nearby (=inside the PG area), or do they ever visit you?

o yes   o no

Who are they, and where do they live?
....

Do you ever visit Dutch-speaking relatives or friends living outside Pennsylvania (=outside the PG area), or do they ever visit you?

o yes   o no

Who are they, and where do they live?
....

Do you have a regular penpal?   o yes   o no

Is he/she Dutch?   o yes   o no

Where does he/she live? ....

Do you ever write letters to relatives or friends living nearby (=inside the PG area)?

o yes   o no

Are they Dutch? Where do they live?
....

Do you ever write letters to relatives or friends living outside Pennsylvania (=outside the PG area)?

o yes   o no

Are they Dutch? Where do they live?
....

Language use part (to be asked parallel to the network part)

2.3.1 Language competence

a = no
b = with difficulty
c = with ease

	a	b	c
1. Can you understand Dutch (=Pennsylvania German)?			
2. Can you speak Dutch?			
3. Can you read Dutch?			
4. Can you write Dutch?			
5. Can you understand English?			
6. Can you speak English?			
7. Can you read English?			
8. Can you write English?			
9. Can you understand the kind of German that's in the Bible (Bible German)?			
10. Can you speak Bible German?			
11. Can you read Bible German?			
12. Can you write Bible German?			
13. Can you understand the kind of German that's spoken in Germany (Standard German)?			

Appendix: Questionnaire

14. Can you speak Standard German?
15. Can you read Standard German?
16. Can you write Standard German?
17. Which other languages do you speak? ....

2.3.2 Language acquisition

18. Which was your first language? ....
19. Who, apart from your parents, did you speak your first language to when you were a child?
    ....
20. Which was your second language? ....
21. At what age did you learn your second language? ....
22. Where did you learn your second language? (parents, grandparents, school, trade, other?)
    ....
23. At what age did you learn High German? ....
24. Who taught you High German? .... did you have at school?

How many years of

25. - Dutch   ....
26. - English   ....
27. - High German ....
28. - Standard German ....

Which subjects were taught in

29. - English? ....
30. - Dutch? ....

2.3.3 Childhood and adolescence

A = always
B = sometimes
C = never, even though interlocutor understood PG
D = never, because interlocutor didn't understand PG
E = didn't apply

	A	B	C	D	E

When you were a child, did you speak Dutch...

31. to your father?
32. to your mother?
33. to your brother(s) older than you?
34. to your sister(s) older than you?
35. to your brother(s) younger than you?
36. to your sister(s) younger than you?
37. to your paternal grandfather?
38. to your paternal grandmother?
39. to your maternal grandfather?
40. to your maternal grandmother?
41. to your godfather?
42. to your godmother?
43. to your uncles?
44. to your aunts?
45. to your male cousins?
46. to your female cousins?
47. to other members of your family and other relatives?
    ....
    to your neighbors

Appendix: Questionnaire

48. - who are Dutch?
49. - who are not Dutch?
50. to your teacher in class?
51. to your teacher during recess?
52. to your male schoolmates in class?
53. to your female schoolmates in class?
54. to your male schoolmates during recess on the school playground?
55. to your female schoolmates during recess on the school playground?
56. to your male schoolmates on your way to or from school?
57. to your female schoolmates on your way to or from school?
58. when playing with your male friends?
59. when playing with your female friends?

When you were younger,....
60. did you speak Dutch to your work colleagues?
61. did you speak Dutch to your boss?
62. did you speak Dutch to your clients or customers?
63. did you speak Dutch to other people at work?
....
64. did you speak Dutch to the minister?
65. were certain parts of the church service in Dutch or Bible German?

If yes, which parts were in |D |BG|E?|
66. - liturgy
67. - hymns
68. - prayers
69. - sermon
70. - announcements
71. - other: ....
   did you pray for yourself in
72. - Dutch?
73. - Bible German?
   did you read the Bible or was it read to you in
74. - Dutch?
75. - English?
76. - High German?
77. was Dutch used at auctions you went to?
78. were there plays performed in Dutch?
79. did you read Dutch texts?
80. If yes, what kind of texts did you read?
   ....
81. did you write Dutch texts?
82. If yes, what kind of texts did you write?
   ....
   did you use Dutch when shopping
83. - in the stores in town?
84. - at the farmers' market?
85. did you speak Dutch to your family doctor?
86. did you speak Dutch to your mayor/the members of the board of supervisors?
87. did you speak Dutch to the animals on your farm?

Appendix: Questionnaire

88. If yes, to which?
    ....

89. did you speak Dutch to your household pets?

90. If yes, to which?
    ....

91. did you sing in Dutch?

92. If yes, what kind of songs?
    ....

93. did you use Dutch proverbs, sayings or nursery rhymes?

94. did you tell jokes in Dutch?

95. did you use more Dutch than today?
    o yes o no

96. Do you feel that you are forgetting some of our Dutch?
    o yes o no

Are there any people with whom you used to speak Dutch but speak English with now or the other way round?

97. - Dutch → English: ....

98. - English → Dutch: ....

2.3.4 Present-day language use (general)

99. What language do you usually talk in when you speak during the day?
    ....

100. With whom and how long did you speak Dutch during the last two days?
     ....

Do you ever read or write Dutch, English, Bible German and Standard German?

- read: - write:

101. - Dutch: o yes o no   105. - Dutch: o yes o no
102. - English: o   o   106. - English: o   o
103. - BG: o   o   107. - BG: o   o
104. - SG: o   o   108. - SG: o   o

What do you read in Dutch, English, Bible German, and Standard German?

	D	E	BG	SG
109. - letters				
110. - diary				
111. - notes				
112. - articles				
113. - speeches				
114. - sermons				
115. - prose				
116. - poetry				
117. - plays				
118. - other:				

....

What do you write in Dutch, English, Bible German, and Standard German?

	D	E	BG	SG
119. - letters				
120. - diary				
121. - notes				
122. - articles				
123. - speeches				

Appendix: Questionnaire

124. - sermons
125. - prose
126. - poetry
127. - plays
128. - other: ....

2.3.5 Relatives, friends, and neighbors (=N1)

A = always
B = sometimes
C = never, even though interlocutor understands PG
D = never, because interlocutor doesn't understand PG
E = doesn't apply

	A	B	C	D	E

Do you speak Dutch...

129. to a. ....?
130. to b. ....?
131. to c. ....?
132. to d. ....?
133. to your father?
134. to your mother?
135. to your brother(s) older than you?
136. to your sister(s) older than you?
137. to your brother(s) younger than you?
138. to your sister(s) younger than you?
139. to your spouse if your children are not present?
140. to your spouse if your children are present?
141. to your son(s)?
142. to your daughter(s)?
143. to your paternal grandfather?
144. to your paternal grandmother?
145. to your maternal grandfather?
146. to your maternal grandmother?
147. to your grandson(s)?
148. to your granddaughter(s)?
149. to your godfather?
150. to your godmother?
151. to your godson?
152. to your goddaughter?
153. to your uncles and aunts?
154. to your nephews and nieces?
155. to your male cousins?
156. to your female cousins?
157. to your father-in-law?
158. to your mother-in-law?
159. to other members of your family and other relatives? ....

to your neighbors
160. - who are Dutch? ....
161. - who are not Dutch? ....
162. to male neighbors?

Appendix: Questionnaire

163. to female neighbors?

    to your friends
164. - who are Dutch?
165. - who are not Dutch?
166. to male friends?
167. to female friends?

2.3.6 Work (=N2)

Do you speak Dutch...

	A	B	C	D	E

to your colleagues at work
168. - about work?
169. - about other things?

to your boss/supervisor
170. - about work?
171. - about other things?

to your subordinates/farmhands
172. - about work?
173. - about other things?

to your competitors
174. - about business?
175. - about other things?

to your clients
176. - about business?
177. - about other things?

to your customers
178. - about business?
179. - about other things?

to salespeople/dealers
180. - about business?
181. - about other things?

to your relatives working in your business/on your farm
182. - about work?
183. - about other things?

Appendix: Questionnaire

		A	B	C	D	E
184.	– about business?					
185.	– about other things?					

2.3.7 School (=N3)

		A	B	C	D	E
	Do you speak Dutch...					
186.	to your teachers in class?					
187.	to your teachers during recess?					
188.	to your male schoolmates in class?					
189.	to your female schoolmates in class?					
190.	to your male schoolmates during recess on the school playground?					
191.	to your female schoolmates during recess on the school playground?					
192.	to your male schoolmates on your way to or from school?					
193.	to your female schoolmates on your way to or from school?					
194.	to your male schoolmates about homework you don't understand?					
195.	to your female schoolmates about homework you don't understand?					
196.	to your parents about homework you don't understand?					
197.	to your male schoolmates when you play?					
198.	to your female schoolmates when you play?					

2.3.8 Religion (=N4)

		A	B	C	D	E
199.	Are certain parts of the church services in your community conducted in Dutch or Bible German?					

If yes, which parts are in |D|BG|E?|

		D	BG	E
200.	– liturgy			
201.	– hymns			
202.	– prayers			
203.	– sermon			
204.	– announcements			
205.	– other:			

Is Dutch used by the minister at the following events?

206.	– funeral			
207.	– wedding			
208.	– baptism			
209.	When you meet the minister in the street, will the conversation be in Dutch?			
210.	Shortly before or after the service, do you speak in Dutch with the other participants?			

When you make up your own prayers, do you pray for yourself

211.	– in Dutch?			
212.	– in English?			
213.	– in Bible German?			

Appendix: Questionnaire

When you use memorized prayers, do you pray for yourself

214. - in Dutch?
215. - in English?
216. - in Bible German?

Do you ever read the Bible

217. - in Dutch?
218. - in English?
219. - in Bible German?

Do you ever read church bulletins written

220. - in Dutch?
221. - in English?
222. - in Bible German?
223. - in English with a Dutch column?
224. - in English with a BG column?

2.3.9 Spare time (=N5)

225. Do you use Dutch when you talk to people while pursuing the following hobbies: ....

226. Is Dutch used at the the official activities of the PG club or PG society?

Do you use Dutch when you talk to other people at

227. - the *Versammling*?
228. - talks on Dutch language and culture?
229. - the Grundsowlodge?
230. - auctions?
231. - flea markets/craft sales?

232. - theater plays?
232. - other: ....
233. If yes, with whom? ....

Do you use Dutch when you actively participate in

234. - the *Versammling*?
235. - talks on Dutch language and culture?
236. - the Grundsowlodge?
237. - auctions?
238. - flea markets/craft sales?
239. - theater plays?
240. - other: ....
241. What official functions do you have? ....

Do you use Dutch at the home butchering speaking to

242. - the butcher?
243. - other people: ....

Do you use Dutch when you talk

244. - to the waiters/waitresses in the restaurant?
245. - the people you go out with to the restaurant?
246. If yes, who are they? ....
247. Do you use Dutch when you talk with the salespeople at country fairs or similar folk festivals?

Appendix: Questionnaire

		A	B	C	D	E
264.	Do you speak Dutch to the salespeople in the little stores in town?					
265.	Do you speak Dutch when you meet a Dutch speaking friend in such a store?					
	Do you speak Dutch to the salespeople					
266.	- at the big supermarkets?					
267.	- at the shopping malls?					
	Do you speak Dutch when you meet a Dutch speaking friend					
268.	- at the big supermarkets?					
269.	- at the shopping malls?					

2.3.11 Doctor and officials (=N7)

		A	B	C	D	E
	Do you speak Dutch to your family doctor					
270.	- at his office?					
271.	- when meeting him/her privately?					
	If you were in hospital, would you speak Dutch					
272.	- to the doctors?					
273.	- to the nurses?					
	Imagine you met the same hospital staff privately. Would you speak Dutch					
274.	- to the doctors?					
275.	- to the nurses?					
	In official business, do you speak Dutch					
276.	- to the mayor/members of the board of supervisors?					
277.	- to the other officials working at the town hall?					
	Do you use Dutch when speaking privately					

		A	B	C	D	E
248.	If yes, at which fairs or festivals?					
249.	Do you ever listen to Dutch radio programs?					
250.	Do you ever watch Dutch TV programs?					
	If yes, what kind of programs are these (news, entertainment, cultural programs, religious programs, etc.)?					
251.	- radio:					
252.	- TV:					
253.	Do you read newspapers, magazines or bulletins					
253.	- written wholly in Dutch?					
254.	- with a Dutch column?					
255.	If yes, what kind of publications are these (title, topic)?					
256.	Do you read Dutch books?					
	If yes, what kind of books are these?					
257.	- novels					
258.	- stories					
259.	- poetry					
260.	- non-fiction					
261.	- other:					

2.3.10 Shopping (=N6)

		A	B	C	D	E
262.	Do you speak Dutch to the salespeople at the farmers' market?					
263.	Do you speak Dutch when you meet another Dutch speaking customer at the farmers' market?					

Appendix: Questionnaire

278. - to the mayor/members of the board of supervisors?
279. - to the other officials working at the town hall?

2.3.12 Network beyond the borders of the Pennsylvania German speech area (=N8)

	A	B	C	D	E

Do you ever use Dutch when speaking to local people in

280. - Reading?
281. - Allentown?
282. - Lancaster?
283. - Harrisburg?
284. - Philadelphia?
285. If yes, who do you speak Dutch to and where?
   ....
286. Do you ever use Dutch with people living outside Pennsylvania?
287. If yes, who do you speak Dutch to and where?
   ....
288. Do you ever use Dutch on your travels abroad, for example in Germany?
289. If yes, who do you speak Dutch to and where?
   ....

FOR NONSECTARIANS ONLY:

290. Do/Did you ever have a chance to use Dutch while serving in the army?
291. If yes, who do/did you speak to and where?
   ....
292. When you visit Dutch-speaking relatives or friends living nearby (=inside the PG area) or when they visit you, do you use Dutch?
293. If yes, who do you speak Dutch to and where?
   ....
294. When you visit Dutch-speaking relatives or friends living outside Pennsylvania (=outside the PG area) or when they visit you, do you use Dutch?
295. If yes, who do you speak Dutch to and where?
   ....
296. Do you use Dutch inside your family when a non-PG comes to visit, or when you visit a non-PG?
297. If yes, who are those members of your family you keep speaking Dutch to?
298. Do you ever write Dutch letters to a regular penpal?
299. Do you ever write Dutch letters to relatives or friends living nearby (=inside the PG area)?
300. Do you ever write Dutch letters to relatives or friends living outside Pennsylvania (=outside the PG area)?

2.3.13 Various situations

	A	B	C	D	E

301. Do you speak Dutch to farm animals?

Appendix: Questionnaire 307

302. If yes, to which? ....

Are there specific calls you use
303. - to get cows from pastures? ....
304. - to make cows stand still during milking? ....
305. - to make horses go right? ....
306. - to make horses go left? ....
307. - to make horses stop? ....
308. - to make horses walk? ....
309. - to back horses? ....
310. - to feed chickens? ....
311. - to feed ducks? ....
312. - to feed turkeys? ....
313. - to feed pigs? ....
314. - to feed calves? ....
315. - to feed sheep? ....
316. - to feed goats? ....

317. Do you speak Dutch to your pets?
318. If yes, to which? ....

319. Imagine you stub your toe and say something, will it be in Dutch?

Do you sing in Dutch
320. - to yourself?
321. - with others (e.g. at family gatherings)?

What kind of Dutch songs do you sing?
322. - folk songs?
323. - children's songs?
324. - hymns?
325. - other: ....

326. Do you count in Dutch?
327. Do you spell words in Dutch?
328. Do you use Dutch to keep other people from knowing what you are saying?
329. If yes, who do you usually share the secret with and who do you keep from knowing it?

330. Do you use Dutch proverbs, sayings or nursery rhymes?
331. Do you tell jokes in Dutch?
332. Do you talk to yourself in Dutch?
333. If you get angry with another Dutch speaker, do you scold in Dutch?
334. Imagine you met a stranger in the street outside your house, would you address him/her in Dutch?
335. Imagine you were sitting in a bus or train with your little child and wanted to explain something to him/her. Two unknown people are sitting opposite you and hear what you are saying. Would you use Dutch?

2.3.14 Subject matter

	A	B	C	D	E

Imagine you are talking with a Dutch-speaking neighbor over the fence.
Do you discuss in Dutch
336. - family matters?
337. - local affairs?
338. - farming?
339. - the weather?

Appendix: Questionnaire

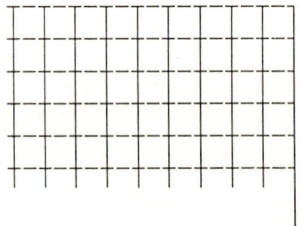

340. - religion?
341. - sports?
342. - health?
343. - fashion?
344. - cars?
345. - business?
346. - finances?
347. - national affairs?
348. - international politics?

3 Language attitude

3.2 Matched-guise test

Please rate each speaker individually on the following scales:

Speaker No. ....

1. well educated —o——o——o——o——o—— poorly educated
2. intelligent —o——o——o——o——o—— dumb
3. professional —o——o——o——o——o—— laborer
4. is in charge of things —o——o——o——o——o—— has little authority
5. has a lot of money —o——o——o——o——o—— has little money
6. honest —o——o——o——o——o—— insincere
7. dependable —o——o——o——o——o—— not dependable
8. generous —o——o——o——o——o—— stingy
9. friendly and likeable —o——o——o——o——o—— unfriendly and unlikeable

Appendix: Questionnaire 309

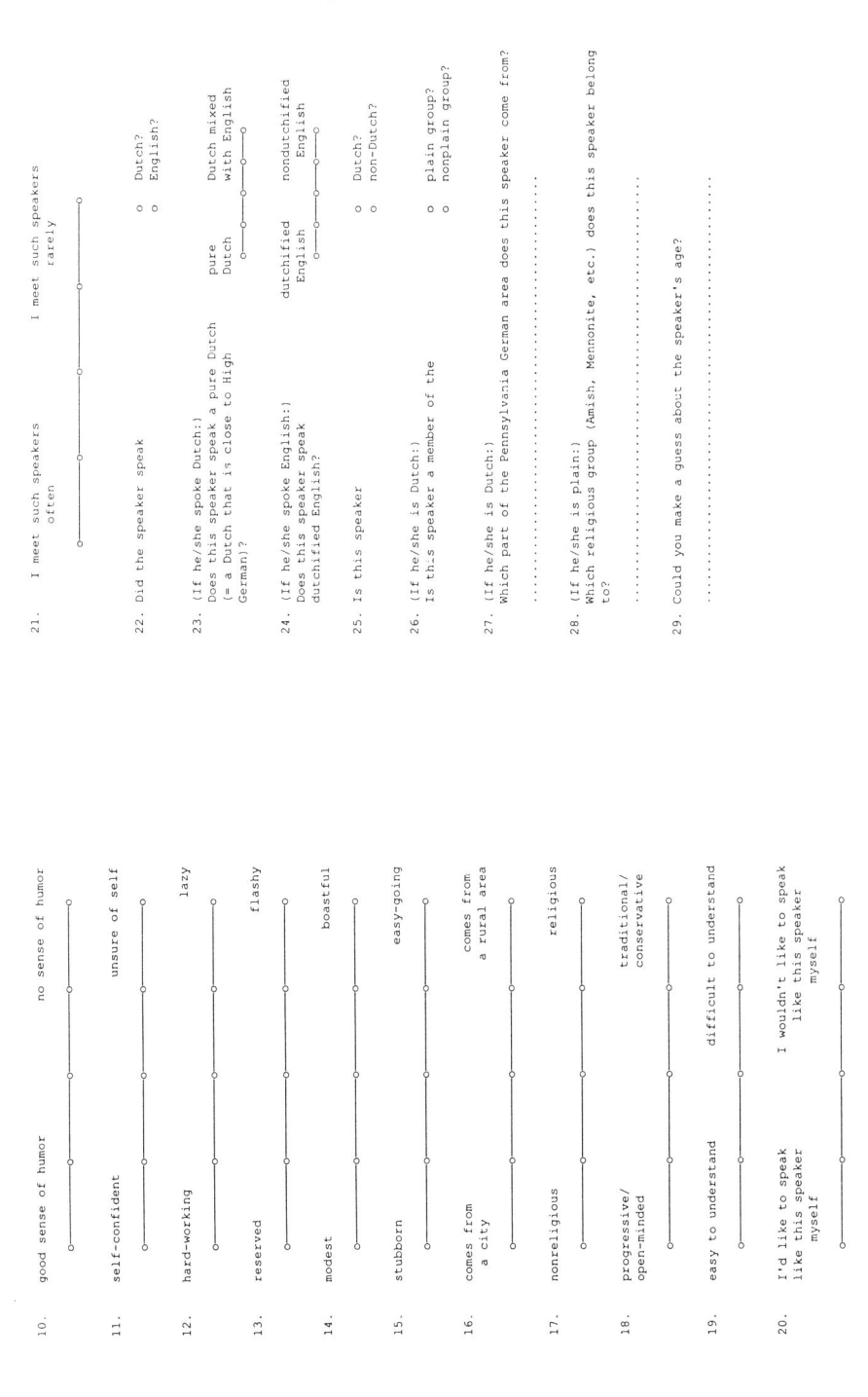

10. good sense of humor ○——○——○——○——○ no sense of humor
11. self-confident ○——○——○——○——○ unsure of self
12. hard-working ○——○——○——○——○ lazy
13. reserved ○——○——○——○——○ flashy
14. modest ○——○——○——○——○ boastful
15. stubborn ○——○——○——○——○ easy-going
16. comes from a city ○——○——○——○——○ comes from a rural area
17. nonreligious ○——○——○——○——○ religious
18. progressive/ open-minded ○——○——○——○——○ traditional/ conservative
19. easy to understand ○——○——○——○——○ difficult to understand
20. I'd like to speak like this speaker myself ○——○——○——○——○ I wouldn't like to speak like this speaker myself

21. I meet such speakers often ○——○——○——○——○ I meet such speakers rarely

22. Did the speaker speak
    ○ Dutch?
    ○ English?

23. (If he/she spoke Dutch:)
    Does this speaker speak a pure Dutch (= a Dutch that is close to High German)?
    pure Dutch ○——○——○——○——○ Dutch mixed with English

24. (If he/she spoke English:)
    Does this speaker speak dutchified English?
    dutchified English ○——○——○——○——○ nondutchified English

25. Is this speaker
    ○ Dutch?
    ○ non-Dutch?

26. (If he/she is Dutch:)
    Is this speaker a member of the
    ○ plain group?
    ○ nonplain group?

27. (If he/she is Dutch:)
    Which part of the Pennsylvania German area does this speaker come from?
    ....

28. (If he/she is plain:)
    Which religious group (Amish, Mennonite, etc.) does this speaker belong to?
    ....

29. Could you make a guess about the speaker's age?
    ....

Notes

Chapter 1. Introduction

1. For summaries of the literature, together with extensive bibliographies, *see* Kopp 1988 and Meister Ferré 1994.

2. Religio-societal insulation as displayed by the sectarian informants of the present study was identified by Kloss (1966, 206) as the most powerful factor contributing to language maintenance in the United States.

3. Short, critical accounts of the concept of the *speech community* (*Sprachgemeinschaft*) are given in Romaine 1982 and Raith 1987.

4. *See* Britto 1986. An overview of the concepts of diglossia and polyglossia is presented in Kremnitz 1987. For a summary of diglossia research and an extensive bibliography, *see* Hudson 1992. The problem of nonuniform interpretation of the term *diglossia* in Pennsylvania German studies is addressed in chapter 3, note 35.

5. For an overview of the literature on language maintenance, language shift, and language death, *see* Dressler 1988.

6. The Scotch-Irish are Scots who had settled in northeastern Ireland for a few generations before they came to America. Their language was Northern English (Baugh and Cable 1993, 381).

7. For the purpose of the present study, only the first of the three major periods of German emigration to America, namely the one from 1683 (founding of Germantown) to 1783 (end of the Revolutionary War), is relevant. The two other phases, the century from 1815 to 1914 and the time from World War I until the present day, had little or no effect on the Pennsylvania Germans.

8. For a recent introduction to *Pfälzisch*, *see* Post 1990.

9. Some scholars have attributed this to a closer affinity to the written standard of German. However, the influence of Standard German in the formation of Pennsylvania German must not be overrated.

10. Reed (1957) distinguishes three major dialect areas in the Pennsylvania German heartland, namely the Lancaster Area (including Lancaster, Lebanon, and York Counties), the Berks Area (Berks County), and the Lehigh Area (Lehigh, Bucks, and Montgomery Counties).

11. For a depiction of these migrations, *see* Redekop 1989:14.

12. Cf. the diagram in Kloss 1985, 134.

13. Here and in the following, the term *Bible High German* does not imply that the sectarians have an active command of Standard German. Rather, passages from the Luther Bible and traditional High German hymns are rendered with Pennsylvania German phonology.

14. According to Hostetler (1993, 75), the sectarians' striving for separation from the world is primarily based on two passages from the Bible: "Be not conformed to this world, but be ye transformed by the renewing of your mind that ye may prove what is

that good and acceptable and perfect will of God." (Romans 12:1) and "Be ye not unequally yoked together with unbelievers; for what fellowship hath righteousness with unrighteousness? and what communion hath light with darkness?" (II Corinthians 6:14).

15. For a detailed analysis of the Old Order Amish worship service, *see* Enninger and Raith 1982.

16. For a description of the history of Himmel's Church, *see* Carter 1936.

17. The information about the history of Klingerstown is taken from a special edition of *The Citizen Standard* of Friday, 27 April 1990.

18. The best overall study of the German-Americans in World War I is Luebke 1974. Among the more recent publications, Wiedemann-Citera's book (1993) examining the effects of World War I on the German-Americans as reflected in three New York City newspapers deserves special mentioning.

19. A key indicator was the position of the chimney. Houses following the German tradition had their chimney in the center, while in English houses fireplaces were usually located at the outside wall(s).

20. *Fraktur* was originally a German-style of black-letter text type developed in the sixteenth century, whose name alluded to the curlicues that broke up the continuous line of a word. Cf. Standard German *Frakturschrift* 'fraktur writing'.

21. Chicken catchers work at the local poultry farms and help to load chickens on trucks.

22. To create a natural situation for the use of Pennsylvania German, the fieldworker switched to his native dialect of *Pfälzisch*.

23. The French dialectologist Gilliéron (1915, 45) wryly comments on this dilemma with the words, «le questionnaire...pour être sensiblement meilleur, aurait dû être fait après l'enquête» ('The questionnaire, in order to be clearly the best, ought to be made after the survey'; quoted by Mather and Speitel 1975, 10; translated by Francis 1983, 52).

24. The wife of the b-generation couple grew up as a New Order Mennonite in Ohio. This may have influenced their decision to join the Beachy Amish community and to speak English to their children. Although rather untypical, this case shows that Pennsylvania German may well be threatened even among the sectarians in the long run.

25. Labov (1972b, 113) defines the observer's paradox as follows: "To obtain the data most important for linguistic theory, we have to observe how people speak when they are not being observed."

26. According to Dorian (1981, 98), "the most serious drawback of the questionnaire self-report, as compared to the interview self-report, is its lack of depth." Answering a questionnaire, the informants usually give very brief answers, with no supporting material. By contrast, in an interview, the fieldworker has the opportunity to expand on certain topics, thus being able to judge the validity of the answers.

27. Dorian observed her Gaelic informants during fifteen years (Dorian 1981, 97).

CHAPTER 2. THE INFLUENCE OF PENNSYLVANIA GERMAN ON THE PHONOLOGY OF ENGLISH

1. Enninger and his associates (1984, 11) describe morpho-syntactical data, as opposed to phonological data, as "notorious for their inaccessibility." Free interviews would produce relatively natural data, but constitute a rather uneconomical method with respect to comparability. However, all methods to collect comparable data in the areas of

syntax and lexicon necessarily involve translation tasks, which were rejected because of their subjectivity. The influence of the source language would be too direct to rule out atypical features.

    2. As Labov (1966, 90ff.; 1972a, 79ff.) points out, two major contextual styles have to be distinguished in verbal interaction: casual and careful speech. Casual speech is normally used among peers in private conversation, careful speech in all formal situations. Thus, in formal interviews like the ones administered in this study, careful style is most likely to be used. Casual style may at best be received at the beginning and the end of the interviews, when the tape recorder is switched off, or during interruptions such as telephone calls or visitors. Beyond careful style, Labov identifies three even more formal stages, reading style, word lists, and minimal pairs.

    3. The use of flashcards and the ultimate elicitation of word lists did not allow for a useful examination of intonation patterns, for which coherent texts are indispensable. The presence of specific intonation patterns in Pennsylvania German English was first postulated by Page (1937, 205), particularly for questions, assertions, and in spoken spellings. In several articles (1984a, 179f.; 1984b, 100; 1986a, 9f.; and 1986b, passim), Huffines shows that these intonation patterns are among the most stable Pennsylvania German English phenomena and play an important role as ethnicity markers.

    4. For the distribution, *see* chapter 2.

    5. For a detailed overview of /r/ in Pennsylvania German, *see* Louden 1987, 29–32. Louden associates the occurrence of retroflex /r/ in plain Pennsylvania German with the sectarians' practice of syllable-by-syllable hymn singing.

    6. Although in word-internal position, the affricate is in the syllable coda and could therefore be regarded as syllable-final. German *Auslautverhärtung* (unvoicing of final consonants) usually applies not only to word-final position, but also to syllable-final position.

    7. To keep the very complex topic of the phonology of voiced/voiceless stops limited and manageable in the present context, only target words with a short vowel before the final consonant were selected (possibly with the exception of *bird*). Likewise, the problem of the lengthening of the vowel before [b,d,g] as opposed to [p,t,k] has to be excluded from the present discussion. It is acknowledged that [b,d,g] are less voiced in final position than intervocalically in English. For a discussion of these issues *see* Kohler 1984, Keating 1984, and Henton, Ladefoged, and Maddieson 1992. For German, Fourakis and Iverson (1984) reject the suggestion that the neutralization of final voiced/voiceless contrast is incomplete on account of differences in vowel length.

    8. While initial and intervocalic [z] is present in the north of Germany, it is absent in all positions in most of the southern German dialects, including Pennsylvania German.

    9. In no instance was /v/ realized as bilabial [β], which only occasionally appeared in the informants' varieties of Pennsylvania German.

    10. The following sentence uttered by informant 2 and overheard by the fieldworker nicely illustrates the phenomenon that some speakers articulate and treat /θ/ as [s]. During a family dinner at the house of informants 1 and 2, the husband (informant 1) urged his wife to make sure that all the children, grandchildren, and other guests helped themselves to enough food. Informant 2 replied that "they all have mouths [mɑːsɪs] to say something." According to the "normal" rule, the plural allomorph is [ɪz] after /s/, but would be [s] after /θ/.

    11. This realization reflects an ordering relationship between rules, specifically a feeding relationship: [ð]→[θ]→[s], where final unvoicing occurs before the sibilization

of the dental fricative. If unvoicing occurred after the avoidance of the dental fricative, the result would be [ð]→[d]→[t], ergo *[smuːt].

12. The centralization of the first element in /oʊ/ is a general innovation in Pennsylvania and other areas. Labov (1994, 57) found this feature in Philadelphia in words like *bow* and *road*, but never before liquids.

13. For instance, monophthongal variants of /oʊ/ and /eɪ/ are found in the variety of St. John's, Newfoundland, which has preserved characteristics of various West Country dialects (Clarke 1991, 109). However, this is not conclusive evidence to rule out that Pennsylvania German English can produce the same phonological result through external influence.

14. Labov (1972a, 177) reports a similar feature found in the English of Yiddish-speaking immigrants in New York City. First-generation speakers do not differentiate low back rounded and unrounded vowels (e.g., in *coffee* and *cup*). The second generation reacts to this influence of the Yiddish substratum with "a hypercorrect exaggeration of the distinction," that is, a raised, tense, and over-rounded vowel.

15. The reasons Huffines (1984b, 98f.) gives are as follows: "The field records of the 'Linguistic Atlas' for this area, collected in 1939–40 by Guy Lowman, provide no indication of the monophthongization except for a few occurrences of the monophthong before /r/ as in 'our' and a lengthening of the first component of the diphthong on the part of some informants, a variant which Kurath and McDavid (1961, 17 [my addition]) call a 'slow diphthong' [aˑU] or [æU]. Pennsylvania German has the diphthong; however, Carroll Reed (1947, 272 [my addition]) states that in Pennsylvania German, 'the diphthong [au] occasionally appears as a monophthong [aː], usually with slight rounding.'"

16. Although she does not give exact numbers, Huffines (1984a, 178) implies that epenthetic [ə], which "seems to result when the articulatory position for the long vowel has been relaxed while the voicing continues," appeared more frequently in her sample. She found the feature "in the speech of Pennsylvania Germans in the middle age brackets" and suggests that "its occurrence requires that the speakers have minimal Pennsylvania German speaking ability." According to Huffines, "the feature does not occur in the speech of monolingual English speakers."

17. Weinreich (1953, 1) defines *interference phenomena* as "[t]hose instances of deviation from the norms of either language which occur in the speech of bilinguals as a result of their familiarity with more than one language, i.e. as a result of language contact." Later he adds in reference to phonic interference: "Interference arises when a bilingual identifies a phoneme of the secondary system with one in the primary system and, in reproducing it, subjects it to the phonetic rules of the primary language" (Weinreich 1953, 14). This phenomenon has also been called *negative transfer* (Appel and Muysken 1987, 84). Haugen (1956, 40) defines *interference* as "the overlapping of two languages," that is, as the stage between *switching* ("the alternate use of two languages") and *integration* ("the regular use of material from one language in another"). The issue of the inconsistent use of the term is addressed in Clyne (1975, 16). Van Coetsem (1988, 2f. and 77f.) stresses the inadequacy of Weinreichs concept of interference, as it "lacks specificity and is confusing" and "[t]he distinction between borrowing and interference is unsatisfactory" (Van Coetsem 1988, 77). At the same time, Van Coetsem (1988, 3 and passim) emphasizes the necessity to distinguish between recipient language agentivity, which results in borrowing, and source language agentivity, which results in imposition. For an application of this theory to the data of the present study, *see* chapter 5.

18. Weinreich (1953, 1) considers "two or more languages...to be IN CONTACT if they are used alternately by the same persons." This restriction to language-using individuals as "the locus of the contact" (Weinreich 1953:1) is too narrow for the present study, as the definition would not account for ethnically marked features in the speech of monolinguals. Therefore, the term *contact phenomenon* is here understood as a sociolinguistic rather than a psycholinguistic phenomenon; in some cases, the contact situation involves more than just one speaker.

19. The variant [?] is regarded as ethnically marked as it is a voiceless sound. It does not occur in the regional standard in the present context.

20. The devoicing observed here is of a higher degree than the one normally found in the regional standard for voiced plosives and fricatives in word-initial (*zipper*) or final (*because*) positions (as compared to voiced contexts, e.g., *busy*). Variants marked "°" are counted as intermediate ethnic forms as they are located somewhere between voiced and unvoiced.

21. This last figure, which is based on the score of a single informant only, should be taken with a grain of salt.

22. At any rate, the basic phonetics and phonology of an individual's speech are fairly fixed and cannot readily be assumed to change within just a few years.

23. For an overview, *see* Chambers 1992.

24. For an in-depth introduction into the use of implicational scales in English dialectology, see Pavone 1980. Dittmar and Schlobinski (1988) provide a general overview. Implicational scales were first used in the field of sociology by Guttman (1944), who surveyed U.S. combat troops during World War II. Unaware of Guttman's work, DeCamp independently developed the concept in 1958 and was the first to apply it to linguistic data (DeCamp 1971, 32).

25. According to Pavone (1980, 68f.), "one of the most important properties of a scalogram is that it is possible to deduce any subject's response pattern from a knowledge of only his total score or number of positive responses and the order of difficulty of the items....This characteristic of the scalogram model is called reproducibility and in the ideal case is 100%." Guttman (1944) considers a 90%-scalability to be satisfactory. Thus, 10% of the total number of cells can be nonpredictable responses or errors. Guttman's Index of Reproducibility (IR) is calculated according to the following formula (Pavone 1980, 69):

$$IR = 1 - \frac{\text{total number of errors}}{\text{total number of opportunities for error}}, \text{ or}$$

$$IR = 1 - \frac{\text{total number of errors}}{\text{number of items x number of subjects}}.$$

26. After the test was over and the cassette recorder was switched off, the fieldworker did actually hear informant 2 pronounce the word *vegetables* as [wetʃəte:bl̩s] ([w] for [v]). The fact that it did not appear in the actual test, although plenty of opportunities were given (two target words for forty-five informants each), suggests that this feature, along with the others that did not come up, is located at an earlier point in the process of the linguistic change and that the speech of none of the informants is conser-

vative enough to include them. It is easily conceivable that the parents and grandparents of the members of the nonsectarian a-generation quite generally had these variables in their English. According to Huffines (1984a, 176), the bilabial variant [w] of /v/ (*visit*) is one of those features that almost exclusively occur in the speech of nonsectarian native speakers of Pennsylvania German and which, as soon as this generation dies out, will pass from the spoken English of the Pennsylvania German community. This result is congruent with the findings of the present study. Elsewhere, Huffines (1984b, 98) emphasizes that "these bilabial variants, although they occur relatively infrequently for all speakers, have become a stereotypic marker of the Pennsylvania German, and it is a feature which is consciously monitored by many younger informants who seem to equate its loss from their English as 'losing their Dutch accent.'" Raith (1981) found the variables [w] for [v] (*very*), ø for [ɾ] before word-final /s/ (*teenagers*), and final [f] for [v] (*leave*) in his examination of a group of Anabaptist informants from Lancaster County, Pennsylvania.

27. According to Labov (1994, 45f.), "[t]he first and most straightforward approach to studying linguistic change in progress is to trace change in apparent time: that is, the distribution of linguistic variables across age levels." For an extensive discussion of the notions of *apparent time* and *real time*, see Labov 1994 (43–112).

28. According to Bailey (1973, 77), "[a] given change begins quite gradually; after reaching a certain point (say, twenty per cent), it picks up momentum and proceeds at a much faster rate; and finally tails off slowly before reaching completion. The result is an ʃ-curve: the statistical differences among isolects in the middle relative times of the change will be greater than the statistical differences among the early and late isolects." Bailey developed his model to describe the growth and spread of phonetic change. He observed that the introduction of a new variant is slow until it is found in about 20% of all possible words. The change then becomes very fast, before it slows down again when about 80% of all possible words have the new variant. In other words, it is easy to find speakers who have the new variant in two words, and who have it in all but two words. It is difficult, however, to find speakers who have the new variant in 50% of all possible words and the old variant in the other 50%.

29. *See* Selinker 1972 and 1992. *Interlanguage* is "the version or the variety of the target language which is part of the implicit linguistic knowledge or competence of the second-language learner" (Appel and Muysken 1987, 83).

30. This is true at least for the majority of the target words (*crown*, *houses*, *cow*, and *mouse*). *South* is the only word to present a different picture. Here, ethnically marked variants are the rule even in the non-Pennsylvania Germans' speech.

31. A similar connection will be established for the various groups of informants of the present study in chapter 3.

32. Fries and Pike (1949) claim that even monolingual speakers are able to maintain two separate phonologies. Louden (1987, 21 and 25) postulates the existence of two discrete phonemic systems (American English and Pennsylvania German) among plain Pennsylvania Germans.

33. Here and in the following, the phonetic notation is that used by the authors.

Chapter 3. The Effects of Language Competence, Acquisition and Use on Maintenance and Shift

1. A number of nonsectarian and non-Pennsylvania German informants had been to Germany. Moreover, during the introduction of all the interviews, the informants were shown German newspapers. Therefore, they knew what was meant by this descriptive term, although the informants' notion of *Standard German* is by no means a scholarly one.

2. This self-report reflects an old pattern. Pennsylvania German has basically had the function of a spoken language, and has not been used as a written code, as the lack of a standard orthography indicates. Instead of Pennsylvania German, Standard German served as the written medium before English became predominant (German newspapers until about 1900). It was not until the early twentieth century that a small corpus of Pennsylvania German literature, both in verse and prose, arose. Today, this written variety is most accessible through weekly columns in local newspapers.

3. None of the nonsectarian native speakers made this claim. A comparison between the self-report and the actual competence as found in the free interviews suggests that the members of the a-generation impose far stricter standards when rating their competence than the members of the b-, c-, and d-generations.

4. The Gaelic-dominant bilinguals are fully proficient in Gaelic. The corresponding subgroups of the nonsectarian Pennsylvania Germans examined here are the a-generation and part of the b-generation. The semispeakers speak Gaelic "with varying degrees of less than full fluency, and their grammar (and usually also their phonology) is markedly aberrant in terms of the fluent-speaker norm. Semi-speakers may be distinguished from fully fluent speakers of any age by the presence of deviations in their Gaelic which are explicitly labeled 'mistakes' by the fully fluent speakers" (Dorian 1981, 107). In the present study, some members of the nonsectarian b- and c-generations correspond to Dorian's semispeakers. Finally, "near-passive bilinguals often know a good many words or phrases, but cannot build sentences with them or alter them productively" (Dorian 1981, 107). The corresponding informants in the present study are some belonging to the nonsectarian c-generation and some members of the d-generation.

5. Mentioning similar observations made in East Sutherland, Dorian (1981, 106) points out that "it is common enough for the native speakers of a dying language to state that they value their mother tongue greatly, while doing nothing to ensure its survival—that is, while failing to pass it on to their children."

6. During the collection of data, the fieldworker had the opportunity of attending a Saturday afternoon class in Bible High German at Sunny Side Mennonite School in Millmont. It was offered to those adolescents who felt they had learned too little High German at home or at school to understand the German Bible and the hymns. The class, which was attended by five male students between the ages of twelve and twenty, was taught by two older members of the Mennonite community. The lesson consisted of reading aloud single High German words from flashcards as well as passages from the Luther Bible and a Christian text book. At the beginning and the end, hymns from the *Unpartheyisches Gesangbuch* 'independent hymnal', the Mennonite hymn book, were sung.

7. The term *language use* is preferred to *language choice*, as a large number of informants (the younger nonsectarians, all the non-Pennsylvania Germans) have no real

choice for lack of competence. For a general overview of language use and its guiding factors such as domain, role, and network, *see* Preston 1987.

8. The concept of domain was introduced by Fishman (1964, 1965/revised 1972). He uses this term for institutional contexts in which one variety is considered to be more appropriate than another. Important factors may be location, topic, or participants. Examples of domains are family, friendship, neighborhood, employment, education, religion, etc. For an overview, *see* Preston 1987.

9. As Fishman (1972, 251) notes, "each domain can be differentiated into role-relations that are specifically crucial or typical of it." Examples include such relationships as employer–employee, student–teacher, and minister–parishioner, which are characteristic of the domains workplace, education, and religion, respectively. Thus, the macroparameter domain is supplemented by a microparameter (role).

10. The most comprehensive discussion of the concept is found in the works of Lesley Milroy (first edition: 1980, second edition: 1987) and James Milroy (1992). For an overview, *see* Boissevain 1987.

11. Cf. Dorian 1981, 75: "Just how many domains exist, and what they are, must be established for any given speech community."

12. Cf., for example, Milroy (first edition: 1980, second edition: 1987) and Lippi-Green (1989) for such examinations.

13. A secondary reason is the danger of methodological involution. As Boissevain (1987, 169) emphasizes, "network analysis has borrowed heavily from mathematical graph theory. Analytical rigour easily leads to methodological refinements remote from human interaction."

14. The language of the school was Standard German until the advent of the state schools in Pennsylvania around 1840 put a damper on German language instruction. By the time of the Civil War, the shift to English was most probably completed. However, there were still families which taught their children at home how to read and write Standard German (C. Richard Beam, letter to author, 13 July 1993). As long as the public schools were mostly rural, one-room facilities, they were also attended by sectarian children. With the introduction of the school consolidation program in the late 1930s and the schools' repeal of the practice of allowing the sectarian children to repeat the eighth grade (in order to avoid having to attend high school), the sectarians established their own small, decentralized parochial schools (*see* Hostetler 1993, 257ff.).

15. The earliest German settlers in America worshipped in Standard German, using the German Bible. In the 1830s English began to replace Standard German in the nonsectarians' worship services. In some areas, however, the Lutheran Church held regular services in Standard German until World War I. During the period of transition, many congregations alternated languages in which they held services. Pennsylvania German has never been the language of the church. The present-day annual Pennsylvania German church services prevalent in the area are no more than the religious facet among the array of nostalgic and folkloristic attempts to preserve Pennsylvania German. Their presence may be taken as yet another indicator of the ongoing, rapid loss of Pennsylvania German among the nonsectarians.

16. The fieldworker established his earliest contacts with some of the informants at the annual Pennsylvania German service at Klinger's Church on 12 November 1989. The service was tape-recorded. All songs and spoken parts were in Pennsylvania German. As the regular minister was not of Pennsylvania German origin, the sermon and the prayers were delivered by an older member of the community who was a native speaker of Penn-

sylvania German. The regular minister's role in the service was restricted to a short prayer in the beginning and the blessing in the end, which he attempted to read in Pennsylvania German. The scripture and a psalm were read in Pennsylvania German by a young member of the community.

17. Apart from a number of psalms and some well-known shorter passages such as the Lord's Prayer, the gospels (Wood 1968) were the only parts of the Bible to be translated into Pennsylvania German at the time of the interviews. In 1994 a "committee for translation" consisting of Old and New Order Amish from Ohio published a Pennsylvania German–English edition of the New Testament under the title *Es Nei Teshtament: Pennsylvania Deitsh un English*.

18. Pennsylvania German card games (e.g., *Haasepeffer* < *Haasimpeffer* 'rabbit in the pepper' [cf. Lambert 1924, 78]) are played only in very few country barrooms in the area, such as Drumheller's in Rebuck.

19. In a case of participant observation on 2 December 1989, however, when the fieldworker accompanied informant 14 during a day of deer hunting in the Mahantango Valley with a group of friends, Pennsylvania German was only used among the older hunters, that is, three of fifteen, including informant 14.

20. On 20 April 1990 the fieldworker had the opportunity of attending the forty-seventh *Fersommling* at Lykens. About three hundred men were present. A full-course meal was followed by a program in Pennsylvania German including a prayer, songs, speeches, and a skit. The actress in the skit, a member of the band, and two waitresses were the only female persons admitted to the meeting. Although the language on stage was exclusively Pennsylvania German, some English was heard in the audience, especially among the younger men. It is said that in former years the participants had to pay a small amount of money if they were caught speaking English.

21. On 1 January 1990 the fieldworker took part in a home butchering by members of nonsectarian family 1 on the farm of informants 1 and 2. The butcher was informant 17, the grandson of the owners of the farm. About twenty family members were present. They helped cut the meat, fill the sausage into casings, and stir the *Pannhaas*, or scrapple, a Pennsylvania German speciality made of the broth from cooking the beef bones, buckwheat flour, and spices. For a full account of a home butchering in the Mahantango Valley, *see* Huffines and Moyer 1986. Their article includes a list of Pennsylvania German butchering terms.

22. Although the title is German, almost all the articles are written in English.

23. According to Huffines (1990b, 125), weekly Pennsylvania German columns currently appear in nine newspapers published in the Pennsylvania German area.

24. The fieldworker witnessed one such occasion during the interview with informants 1 and 2. The language used between the storekeeper and the informants was Pennsylvania German.

25. Although the two sectarian families did move from Lancaster County to Buffalo Valley in the 1960s, this migration cannot be regarded as individual geographical mobility. Many families moved together and immediately founded new religious communities.

26. Cf. the discussion of positive and negative attitudes toward Pennsylvania German in chapter 4.

27. In the case of interlocutor 20, farm animals are taken as the primary source. Only if the informant had no access to farm animals, household pets are accepted instead in order to avoid a large number of inapplicable cells.

28. Dorian (1981, 80) reports the same phenomenon for the East Sutherland speech communities in Scotland, where English was the sole language used at school: "In terms of language choice the situation was a simple one during the childhood of most surviving bilinguals: Gaelic had no place in the school domain."

29. In no case is a "wrong" symbol found in any of the three zones of "G," "B," and "E"/"e." Even if all the inapplicable cells are counted as errors, the scalability is high at 0.93. For the calculation of the scalability, cf. the discussion of figure 2.29 (chapter 2, note 24).

30. The scalability is 0.89 if "G" and "B" are set in opposition to "E" and all inapplicable cells are counted as errors.

31. In questions 303–316 (questionnaire section 2.3.13), calls for specific farm animals were collected. Some of them proved to be Pennsylvania German (e.g., *Kumm da!* 'Come here' to call cows from the pasture, *Stell dich!* 'Stand still' and *Schtop dei Gschwenzel!* 'Stop wagging your tail' to make cows stand still during milking, and *Kumm, Wutzi Wutzi!* 'Come, piggy' to feed the pigs), others were English (e.g., *Get up!* to make horses walk and *Back up!* and *Hoof back!* to back horses).

32. Dorian (1981, 82) made the same observations for Gaelic in Scotland: "In the case of a strictly local-currency language of low prestige, lacking any institutional support whatever, the home domain is clearly crucial to the continuity of the language."

33. The difficulty in gathering comparable data may be illustrated by a comparison of the answer of informant 13 with those of informants 12 and 14. All of them belong to the b-generation of nonsectarian family 2, have near-native competence in Pennsylvania German and live in roughly the same area, thus having access to the same rural stores. Nevertheless, informant 13 claims that he always speaks Pennsylvania German with the storekeepers, while informants 12 and 14 report that they cannot speak Pennsylvania German. One possible explanation is that informant 13, just like the members of the elderly and less mobile members of the a-generation (who report the exclusive use of Pennsylvania German) leads a fairly secluded life and does not go shopping that often or when he does always goes to the same stores. However, the informants might also have understood the question in different ways. The number of storekeepers who can speak Pennsylvania German has become so small that informants 12 and 14 are not even aware of them, while informant 13 based his answer on this small number.

34. How small the share of Pennsylvania German is in these latter cases may be gathered from a remark by informant 18 (c-generation). He knows one Pennsylvania German swearword, which he claims to use in situations like the one given in question 319.

35. Introduced by Ferguson in 1959, the term diglossia originally referred to two varieties of the same language (Ferguson 1959, 325). The H- and L-varieties were distinguished on the basis of nine criteria (function, prestige, literary heritage, acquisition, standardization, stability, grammar, lexicon, and phonology). Fishman (1967) reduces this catalog to function (i.e., use in certain domains and roles) and stability. Thus, diglossia is understood as bilingualism connected with compartmentalization. Following Fishman, Huffines (1980b) and Moelleken (1983) describe the linguistic situation among the sectarian Pennsylvania Germans as diglossic bilingualism. The present study follows this practice. Louden (1987) dismisses all interpretations based on Fishman and offers his own categorization: While the linguistic situation of the nonplain Pennnsylvania Germans is characterized by unstable bilingualism between Pennsylvania German and English, the sectarians show stable bilingualism between Pennsylvania German and English,

and in addition diglossia (in Ferguson's sense) between Pennsylvania German and Bible High German. Louden (1987, 27) also criticizes Enninger's (1979, 1980) claim of the sectarians being trilingual, as their competence in Bible High German is clearly passive rather than active.

36. If the thirty-one inapplicable cells are counted as errors, the scalability is 0.86. For the calculation of the scalability, cf. the discussion of figure 2.29 (chapter 2, note 24).

37. Interlocutor 13 shows that in some cases the problem of the empty cells (cf. the methodological discussion in chapter 1) is less severe than it seems. Although there are ten empty cells, the correct rank of the column can easily be determined on the basis of cultural knowledge. The fact that the language of the sectarian school is English makes hypothetical questions superfluous.

38. Similarly, during their singings on Saturday night, young sectarians like to sing English hymns, while the traditional ones used in the Sunday worship service are in German.

39. According to Kraybill (1989, 14), estimates for attrition rates in the Amish communities in Lancaster County, Pennsylvania, range between 10 and 24%.

40. This is reflected by the relatively low scalability of 0.74.

41. The direction of the shift cannot be decided on the basis of the implicational scale alone. Theoretically, the young informants may return to Pennsylvania German when they are older, in which case there would be no shift at all. However, it is possible to determine that the shift is from Pennsylvania German to English with the help of the social data. It is clear that the d-generation is completely monolingual and will never be able to develop native-like competence in Pennsylvania German. Further evidence of the direction of the shift can be gained from a comparison of the scales for childhood and present-day language use.

42. If the (retired) members of the a-generation had colleagues, some of them would probably be local age peers with competence in Pennsylvania German. Column 12 (colleagues) would then resemble interlocutor 4 (children) more than 15 (God).

43. The question whether the members of the a-generation would speak Pennsylvania German to their work colleagues if they had any depends on so many factors (colleagues' origin, workplace, age, language competence, etc.) that hypothetical questions would not have resulted in reliable data (cf. the methodological discussion in chapter 1).

44. The same tendency was found in the childhood language use of informant 12.

45. The school domain is covered in much more detail for childhood, while it is altogether inapplicable for most informants today. Likewise, the differentiation between brothers and sisters older or younger than the informants proved to be significant for childhood, but not for the adults. By contrast, the interlocutors spouse, children, and grandchildren were inapplicable for the childhood survey.

46. It is remarkable that many of the revivalist efforts tend to be led by first-in-their-family native speakers of English, beside the members of the a-generation. Quite a few b-generation informants and their age peers are actively involved with the organization of Pennsylvania German *Versammlinge*, church services, language classes, skits, radio shows, and newspaper columns. A comprehensive study of attempts to reverse language shift in speech communities all over the world can be found in Fishman 1991.

47. However, English is used in the home domain among the core-members of the family in a number of special situations and settings: when telling jokes, when relating

stories heard in English, with some handicapped children, among some siblings, as parents' secret language, when non-Pennsylvania German speakers are present, at Tupperware and Home Interior parties, and in all writing, including messages. Moreover, the quantity of English words within Pennsylvania German is considerably higher in so-called *motherese* or *Baby Pennsylvania German*, that is, the language used by adults when dealing with infants (Louden 1991, 131f.).

48. In her study of a comparable English-German contact situation, that is, a German community in central Texas, Moore (1980, 168–73) reports higher ability levels in German and more use of this language for male informants than for female ones.

49. The scalability is 0.95. For the calculation of the scalability, cf. the discussion of figure 2.29 (chapter 2, note 24).

50. The distribution of the empty cells (cf. the methodological discussion in chapter 1) over a fairly limited area between informant ranks 15 and 28 as well as on the right of the continuum of topics is an indication of the strong similarity of the columns. If the empty cells below the gradation line were interpreted as "G" or "B," the line would be almost horizontal.

51. These results are in line with Dorian's (1981, 111) findings for the Gaelic-speaking community in East Sutherland: "[D]espite the association of English with modernity and technology and the public spheres of life, no topic connected with these aspects of live forces a choice of English. If the setting and the interlocutor permit, any topic, no matter how sophisticated or remote from local life, can be discussed in Gaelic."

52. One of the first scholars to focus on these two concepts was Fishman (1964). For an overview of further research on language maintenance and shift, *see* Fasold 1984, 213–45. A recent, if somewhat different, application of the term *language maintenance* is found in Milroy 1992, 10–13.

53. Cf. Dorian 1981, 105: "The home is the last bastion of a subordinate language in competition with a dominant official language of wider currency."

54. Gal (1979, 110) reports that in the bilingual town of Oberwart in Austria parents or grandparents sometimes speak Hungarian while their children or grandchildren consistently answer in German.

55. One typical example occurred during a home butchering with nonsectarian family 1. The men, all members of the a- and b-generations, downstairs in the room where the sausage was made were speaking to each other in Pennsylvania German, deciding that they needed some wrapping paper from the women upstairs. A member of the b-generation went to the staircase and shouted up to his wife in English. His wife answered in English. This short exchange was enough to make the men in the basement switch from Pennsylvania German to English for the rest of their conversation downstairs.

56. Cf. Fasold 1984, 240. On the psycholinguistic level the so-called *decision-tree* has been used to predict an individual speaker's language choice (Rubin 1968).

57. Cf. Dorian 1981, 105: "An impending shift has in effect arrived, even though a fairly sizeable number of speakers may be left, if those speakers have failed to transmit the language to their children, so that no replacement generation is available when the parent generation dies away."

CHAPTER 4. LANGUAGE ATTITUDES: A MATCHED-GUISE TEST

1. For a preliminary report on the methodology and some of the findings, *see* Kopp 1993.

2. Parts of MacKinnon's questionnaire (1977) were used for the matched-guise test administered for the present study.

3. For a discussion of the matched-guise technique along with other methods of testing language attitudes, *see* Ryan, Giles, and Hewstone 1988.

4. As Osgood and his associates (1957, 25) point out, a sample of semantic scales represents "a semantic space, a region of some unknown dimensionality." Williams (1973, 114) describes the semantic differential scale as involving "the evaluation of a concept or stimulus by rating it on scales comprised of adjectival opposites."

5. Osgood and his associates (1957, 85) report that different numbers of alternatives given in a scale (i.e., three, five, seven, nine, or eleven steps) were variously suitable for certain groups of informants. While college students seemed to work best with seven-step scales, American Legion members preferred three alternatives; grade-school children worked best with five-grade scales. The authors note that little is known about these individual differences.

6. This cube-like framework of the data arrangement was suggested by Osgood and his associates (1957, 86) as early as 1957.

7. Factor analyses in previous matched-guise tests have led to more or less similar groupings of scales. Osgood and his associates (1957, 36ff.) isolated the three factors evaluation, potency, and activity. Shuy and Williams (1973, 88) additionally identified a complexity factor. In his study of teachers' attitudes toward their students' language varieties, Williams (1973, 116) distinguished two clusters of scales, confidence-eagerness and ethnicity-nonstandardness. The groups of scales found in the present study are almost identical with those isolated by Carranza and Ryan (1975) in their examination of attitudes held by bilingual Anglo and Mexican adolescents toward speakers of English and Spanish. In their study, four scales (educated–uneducated, intelligent–ignorant, successful–unsuccessful, and wealthy–poor) formed the so-called *status-stressing* category, while four other scales (friendly–unfriendly, good–bad, kind–cruel, and trustworthy–untrustworthy) formed the so-called *solidarity-stressing* group (Carranza and Ryan 1975, 91). Finally, Heiner (1991, 56f.) identified four factors, the first two of which are congruent with those found in the present study.

8. Because of the minimal gaps, the fact that voice 7 is at the top of the continuum, separated from the other Pennsylvania German English voices, should not be overinterpreted.

9. In a letter of 9 May 1753, Franklin wrote to Peter Collinson that "[t]hose [Germans] who come hither are generally of the most ignorant Stupid Sort of their own Nation....Few of their children in the Country learn English" (Labaree 1961, 483f.).

10. For a historical overview of the image of German immigrants to North America and detailed accounts of the terms *Palatine*, *Hessian*, and *Dutchman*, see Yoder 1980.

11. Cf. chapter 2 on Pennsylvania German English phonology. The titles of three common examples of commercial booklets promoting Pennsylvania German English reflect the stereotypes: *Ferhoodled English: A collection of quaintly amusing expressions heard among the Pennsylvania Dutch folks* (published anonymously, 1987); *How to speak dutchified English: An "inwaluble" introduction to an "enchoyable" accent of the "inklish lankwitch"* (by Gary Gates, 1987); and *A delightful bit of entertainment: Quaint idioms and expressions of the Pennsylvania Germans* (by A. Monroe Aurand, Jr., 1938).

12. Here, as earlier, a comparison of voices 1–8 with voice 9 is preferred to a comparison of voice 5 with voice 9. While the latter would offer the advantage of a genuine matched-guise, it would provide less differentiated results as to the structure of the in-

formants, particularly in those cases where the investigation relies on only one question. Here, each average would be based on a single vote, thus depending a lot more on chance and resulting in many identical difference values. Generally speaking, however, both comparisons turned out to structure the informants in the same way.

13. Cf. Huffines 1986a. The author explains that "in the Pennsylvania German community, each subgroup has devised its own strategies for maintaining Pennsylvania German and its own set of linguistic ethnic markers" (1986a, 1). Having interpreted the nonsectarians' and sectarians' language behaviors in terms of Giles's speech accommodation theory (cf. Giles, Bourhis, and Taylor 1977) and ethnic boundary model (cf. Giles 1979), Huffines comes to the conclusion that nonsectarian "native speakers of Pennsylvania German maintain Pennsylvania German within their own generation and celebrate it as a symbol of in-group solidarity....The younger, non-fluent bilinguals and monolingual speakers of English who strive toward maintenance fail in that endeavor as judged by their elders and their own report. The English of these speakers must, then, bear the symbols of community and identity. Pennsylvania Germans who natively speak English maintain ethnic boundaries by ethnicizing English" (1986a, 14).

14. Since this is a comprehensive issue concerning both chapters 2 and 4, it will be taken up again in the conclusion.

15. It should be noted, however, that of the three features found for the c-generation one ([l] for [ɫ] before a vowel unless preceded by a plosive [*lion*]) is found in all groups of informants anyway, while the other two (word-final [ɹ] for [ɾ] [*family*] and word-final [s] for [ð] [*smooth*]) are doubtful as their occurrence is rather unpredictable (*see* figure 2.31).

16. This problem was taken into account when the questionnaire was set up. One part of the question set includes characterizations which are more often associated with the nonsectarian Pennsylvania Germans, and the other part comprises adjectives which are attributed more often to the sectarians.

CHAPTER 5. SYNTHESIS AND CONCLUSION

1. For a comparison of sectarian and nonsectarian Pennsylvania German in the areas of syntax and vocabulary, *see* Huffines 1992.

2. On a closer look, the ambiguity in attitude toward Pennsylvania German ethnicity does not come as a surprise. For historical reasons, mixed feelings toward certain cultures seem to be quite common. An example could be the nonuniform image which the modern Japanese and German nations have in today's world.

3. In his influential study *Languages in contact* (1953, 74), Weinreich avoids conventional terms such as *native language, mother tongue,* and *first* and *second language,* as he deems it irrelevant in connection with interference to know which of the two systems in contact was learned first. According to Weinreich, all that matters is which language is the source and which is the recipient. Normally, the transfer of linguistic material, including interference, proceeds from the source language (sl) to the recipient language (rl). In 1988 Van Coetsem and Thomason and Kaufman, independently from each other, developed two very similar theories of language contact, both distinguishing the two basic forms of transfer mentioned above. Unlike Weinreich, however, both Van Coetsem (1988) and Thomason and Kaufman (1988, 35–64) stress the importance of a differentiation between the speakers' native (or linguistically dominant) language and their foreign (or target) language. For the differences between the two recent models, *see*

Buccini 1992, 16ff. Further discussion of the theories may be found in Guy 1990 and, along with examples of German influence on English in various parts of the United States, in Howell 1993.

4. The fact that the amount of imposition is much smaller than in the English of the nonsectarian a-generation is in line with Van Coetsem's claim that social dominance is normally more evident in (lexical) borrowing (rl-agentivity) than in (phonological) imposition (sl-agentivity).

5. The linguistic component most readily affected by convergence is syntax (Louden 1988, 31).

Bibliography

Appel, René, and Pieter Muysken. 1987. *Language contact and bilingualism*. London: Arnold.

Aurand, A. Monroe. 1938. *A delightful bit of entertainment: Quaint idioms and expressions of the Pennsylvania Germans*. Lancaster, Pa.: Aurand.

Ausbund, das ist: Etliche schöne christliche Lieder, wie sie in dem Gefängnis zu Passau in dem Schloß von den Schweizer-Brüdern und von anderen rechtgläubigen Christen hin und her gedichtet worden. 1984. First published in 1564. 13th ed. Lancaster, Pa.: Lancaster Press.

Bailey, Charles-James N. 1973. *Variation and linguistic theory*. Arlington, Va.: Center for Applied Linguistics.

Baugh, Albert C., and Thomas Cable. 1993. *A history of the English language*. 4th ed. London: Routledge.

Beam, C. Richard. 1985. *Pennsylvania German dictionary. English to Pennsylvania Dutch*. Lancaster, Pa.: Brookshire.

Boissevain, Jeremy. 1987. Social Network. In *Sociolinguistics—Soziolinguistik. An international handbook of the science of language and society—Ein internationales Handbuch zur Wissenschaft von Sprache und Gesellschaft*, vol. 1, edited by Ulrich Ammon, Norbert Dittmar, and Klaus J. Mattheier, 164–69. Berlin: de Gruyter.

Bourhis, Richard Y., and Howard Giles. 1976. The language of cooperation in Wales: A field study. *Language Sciences* 42: 13–16.

Britto, Francis. 1986. *Diglossia: A study of the theory with application to Tamil*. Washington, D.C.: Georgetown University Press.

Buccini, Anthony F. 1992. Southern Middle English *hise* and the question of pronominal transfer in language contact. In *Recent developments in Germanic linguistics*, edited by Rosina Lippi-Green, 11–32. Philadelphia: Benjamins.

Buffington, Albert F. 1937. A grammatical and linguistic study of Pennsylvania German. Ph.D. diss., Harvard University.

Buffington, Albert F., and Preston A. Barba. 1965. *A Pennsylvania German grammar*. Revised edition. Allentown, Pa.: Schlechter's.

Carranza, Michael A., and Ellen Bouchard Ryan. 1975. Evaluative reactions of bilingual Anglo and Mexican American adolescents toward speakers of English and Spanish. *Linguistics* 166: 83–104.

Carter, John H. 1936. The Himmel Church. In *The Northumberland County Historical Society: Proceedings and addresses*, vol. 8, 67–97. Sunbury, Pa.: Northumberland Historical Society.

Chambers, Jack K. 1992. Linguistic correlates of gender and sex. *English World-Wide* 13: 173–218.

Clarke, Sandra. 1991. Phonological variation and recent language change in St. John's English. In *English around the world: Sociolinguistic perspectives*, edited by Jenny L. Cheshire, 108–22. Cambridge: Cambridge University Press.

Clyne, Michael. 1975. *Forschungsbericht Sprachkontakt.* Kronberg/Taunus, Germany: Scriptor.

Committee for Translation. 1994. *Es nei Teshtament: Pennsylvania Deitsh un English.* South Holland, Ill.: The Bible League.

Crystal, David, and Derek Davy. 1969. *Investigating English style.* London: Longman.

———. 1975. *Advanced conversational English.* London: Longman.

DeCamp, David. 1971. Implicational scales and sociolinguistic linearity. *Linguistics* 73: 30–43.

Dittmar, Norbert, and Peter Schlobinski. 1988. Implikationsanalyse. In *Sociolinguistics—Soziolinguistik. An international handbook of the science of language and society—Ein internationales Handbuch zur Wissenschaft von Sprache und Gesellschaft*, vol. 2, edited by Ulrich Ammon, Norbert Dittmar, and Klaus J. Mattheier, 1014–26. Berlin: de Gruyter.

Dorian, Nancy C. 1981. *Language death. The life cycle of a Scottish Gaelic dialect.* Philadelphia: University of Pennsylvania Press.

Dressler, Wolfgang. 1988. Spracherhaltung—Sprachverfall—Sprachtod. In *Sociolinguistics—Soziolinguistik. An international handbook of the science of language and society—Ein internationales Handbuch zur Wissenschaft von Sprache und Gesellschaft*, vol. 2, edited by Ulrich Ammon, Norbert Dittmar, and Klaus J. Mattheier, 1551–63. Berlin: de Gruyter.

Enninger, Werner. 1979. Language convergence in a stable triglossia plus trilingualism situation. In *Anglistik: Beiträge zur Fachwissenschaft und Fachdidaktik. Festschrift für Eleonore Cladder*, edited by Peter Freese, Carin Freywald, Wolf Paprotté, and Willi Real, 43–63. Münster, Germany: Regensberg.

———. 1980. Syntactic convergence in a stable triglossia plus trilingualism situation in Kent County, Delaware, U.S. In *Sprachkontakt und Sprachkonflikt—Language in contact and conflict—Langues en contact et en conflit–Taalcontact en taalconflict*, edited by Peter Hans Nelde, 341–50. Wiesbaden: Steiner.

———. 1984. Funktion, Struktur und Erwerb der Varietäten Pennsylvaniadeutsch, Amisch Hochdeutsch und Amerikanisches Englisch bei den Altamischen. In *Spracherwerb—Sprachkontakt—Sprachkonflikt*, edited by Els Oksaar, 220–42. Berlin: de Gruyter.

———. 1985a. Die Altamischen (Old Order Amish) in Kent County, Delaware. In *Deutsch als Muttersprache in den Vereinigten Staaten. Teil II: Regionale und funktionale Aspekte*, edited by Heinz Kloss, 11–20. Stuttgart: Steiner.

———. 1985b. Die Altamischen (Old Order Amish): Ihr Zeichenrepertoire und Zeichengebrauch als Forschungsgegenstand. In *Deutsch als Muttersprache in den Vereinigten Staaten. Teil II: Regionale und funktionale Aspekte*, edited by Heinz Kloss, 137–52. Stuttgart: Steiner.

Enninger, Werner, and Joachim Raith. 1982. *An ethnography of communication approach to ceremonial situations: A study on communication in institutionalized social contexts: The Old Order Amish church service.* Wiesbaden, Germany: Steiner.

Enninger, Werner, and Karl-Heinz Wandt. 1982. Pennsylvania German in the context of an Old Order Amish settlement: The structural instability of a functionally stable variety. *Yearbook of German-American Studies* 17: 123–44.

Enninger, Werner, et al. 1984. The English of the Old Order Amish of Delaware: Phonological, morpho-syntactical and lexical variation of English in the language contact situation of a trilingual speech community. *English World-Wide* 5: 1–24.

Fasold, Ralph W. 1984. *The sociolinguistics of society. Introduction to sociolinguistics*, vol. 1. Oxford: Blackwell.

Ferguson, Charles A. 1959. Diglossia. *Word* 15: 325–40. Reprinted 1964 in *Language in culture and society*, edited by Dell Hymes, 429–39. New York: Harper & Row. Also 1972 in *Language and social context*, edited by Pier Paolo Giglioli, 232–51. Hammondsworth, England: Penguin.

Ferhoodled English: A collection of quaintly amusing expressions heard among the Pennsylvania Dutch folks. 1987. Gettysburg, Pa.: Conestoga Crafts.

Fishman, Joshua A. 1964. Language maintenance and shift as fields of inquiry. *Linguistics* 9: 32–70.

———. 1965. Who speaks what language to whom and when? *La Linguistique* 2: 67–88.

———. 1967. Bilingualism with and without diglossia; diglossia with and without bilingualism. *Journal of Social Issues* 23: 29–38.

———. 1972. The relationship between micro- and macro-sociolinguistics in the study of who speaks what language to whom and when. In *Sociolinguistics*, edited by J. B. Pride and Janet Holmes, 15–32. Hammondsworth, England: Penguin.

———. 1991. *Reversing language shift: Theoretical and empirical foundations of assistance to threatened languages*. Philadelphia: Multilingual Matters.

Fourakis, Marios, and Gregory K. Iverson. 1984. On the "incomplete neutralization" of German final obstruents. *Phonetica* 41: 140–49.

Francis, W. Nelson. 1983. *Dialectology: An introduction*. London: Longman.

Frey, John William. 1942. *A simple grammar of Pennsylvania Dutch*. Clinton, S.C.: J. W. Frey. Reissued with a new preface by C. Richard Beam 1981. Lancaster, Pa.: Brookshire.

———. 1945. Amish triple talk. *American Speech* 20: 85–98.

Fries, Charles C., and Kenneth L. Pike. 1949. Coexistent phonemic systems. *Language* 25: 29–50.

Gal, Susan. 1978a. Peasant men can't get wives: Language change and sex roles in a bilingual community. *Language in Society* 7: 1–16.

———. 1978b. Variation and change in patterns of speaking: Language shift in Austria. In *Linguistic variation: Models and methods*, edited by David Sankoff, 227–38. New York: Academic Press.

———. 1979. *Language shift. Social determinants of linguistic change in bilingual Austria*. New York: Academic Press.

Gates, Gary. 1987. *How to speak dutchified English: An "inwaluble" introduction to an "enchoyable" accent of the "inklish lankwitch."* Intercourse, Pa.: Good Books.

Gilbert, Russell Wieder. 1962. *A picture of the Pennsylvania Germans*. 3d ed. Gettysburg, Pa.: Pennsylvania Historical Association.

Giles, Howard. 1979. Ethnicity markers in speech. In *Social markers in speech*, edited by K. R. Scherer and Howard Giles, 251–89. Cambridge: Cambridge University Press.

Giles, Howard, and Richard Y. Bourhis. 1976. Methodological issues in dialect perception: Some social psychological perspectives. *Anthropological Linguistics* 187: 294–304.

Giles, Howard, Richard Y. Bourhis, and Donald M. Taylor. 1977. Towards a theory of language in ethnic group relations. In *Language, ethnicity and intergroup relations*, edited by Howard Giles, 307–48. London: Academic Press.

Gilliéron, Jules. 1915. *Étude de géographie linguistique: Pathologie et thérapeutique verbales*. Neuveville, Switzerland: Beerstecher.

Gumperz, John J. 1968. The speech community. *International encyclopaedia of the social sciences*, 381–86. New York: Macmillan. Reprinted 1971 in *Language in social groups: Essays by John J. Gumperz*, edited by Anwar S. Dil, 114–28. Stanford: Stanford University Press. Also 1972 in *Language and social context*, edited by Pier Paolo Giglioli, 219–31. Hammondsworth, England: Penguin.

Guttman, Louis. 1944. A basis for scaling qualitative data. *American Sociological Review* 9: 139–50.

Guy, Gregory R. 1990. The sociolinguistic types of language change. *Diachronica* 7: 47–67.

Haugen, Einar. 1956. *Bilingualism in the Americas: A bibliography and research guide*. University, Ala.: University of Alabama Press.

Heckewelder, John. 1833. *Names given by the Lenni Lenape or Delaware Indians to rivers, streams and places in the now states of New Jersey, Pennsylvania, Maryland and Virginia; and also names of chieftains and distinguished men of that nation: with their significations and some biographical sketches*. Philadelphia: American Philosophical Society. Reprinted 1940 with an introduction by Samuel H. Ziegler in *The Pennsylvania German Folklore Society*, vol. 5, 1–41. Allentown, Pa.: Pennsylvania German Folklore Society.

Heiner, Hubert. 1991. Glasgow attitudes towards language: An empirical investigation. Master's thesis. Universität Heidelberg.

Henton, Caroline, Peter Ladefoged, and Ian Maddieson. 1992. Stops in the world's languages. *Phonetica* 49: 65–101.

Horne, A. R. 1875. *Pennsylvania German manual*. Kutztown, Pa.: Horne.

Hostetler, John Andrew. 1980 (3d ed.). 1993 (4th ed.). *Amish society*. Baltimore: Johns Hopkins University Press.

Howell, Robert B. 1993. German immigration and the development of regional variants of American English: Using contact theory to discover our roots. In *The German language in America, 1683–1991*, edited by Joseph C. Salmons, 188–212. Madison, Wis.: Max Kade Institute for German-American Studies.

Hudson, Alan. 1992. Diglossia: A bibliographic review. *Language in Society* 21: 611–74.

Huffines, Marion Lois. 1980a. English in contact with Pennsylvania German. *German Quarterly* 54: 352–66.

———. 1980b. Pennsylvania German: Maintenance and shift. *International Journal for the Sociology of Language* 25: 47–57.

———. 1984a. The English of the Pennsylvania Germans: A reflection of ethnic affiliation. *German Quarterly* 57: 173–82.

———. 1984b. Language contact across generations: The English of the Pennsylvania Germans. In *Dialectology, linguistics, literature. Festschrift for Carroll E. Reed*, edited by Wolfgang W. Moelleken, 93–103. Göppingen, Germany: Kümmerle.

———. 1984c. Pennsylvania German stereotype: Particles, prepositions, and adverbs. *Yearbook of German-American Studies* 19: 23–32.

———. 1984d. Word gain and loss in the English of the Pennsylvania Germans. *Pennsylvania Folklife* 34: 30–33.

Bibliography

———. 1986a. Strategies of language maintenance and ethnic marking among the Pennsylvania Germans. *Language Sciences* 8: 1–16.

———. 1986b. Intonation in language contact: Pennsylvania German English. In *Studies on the languages and the verbal behavior of the Pennsylvania Germans I*, edited by Werner Enninger, 25–36. Stuttgart: Steiner.

———. 1989. Case usage among the Pennsylvania German sectarians and nonsectarians. In *Investigating obsolescence. Studies in language contraction and death*, edited by Nancy C. Dorian, 211–26. Cambridge: Cambridge University Press.

———. 1990a. Contact phenomena in language maintenance and shift: The Pennsylvania German infinitive construction. *American Journal of Germanic Linguistics and Literatures* 2: 95–108.

———. 1990b. Pennsylvania German in public life. *Pennsylvania Folklife* 34: 117–25.

———. 1991. Translations: A vehicle for change? Evidence from Pennsylvania German. *American Journal of Germanic Linguistics and Literatures* 3: 175–93.

———. 1992. Language change and enabling strategies of Pennsylvania Anabaptists. In *Diachronic studies on the languages of the Anabaptists*, edited by Kate Burridge and Werner Enninger, 166–81. Bochum, Germany: Brockmeyer.

Huffines, Marion Lois, and John Moyer. 1986. A family butchering in the Schwaben Creek Valley. *Historic Schaefferstown Record* 20/2: 15–43.

International Phonetic Association (IPA). 1957. *The principles of the IPA*. London: International Phonetic Association.

Keating, Patricia A. 1984. Phonetic and phonological representation of stop consonant voicing. *Language* 60: 286–319.

Kloss, Heinz. 1966. German-American language maintenance efforts. In *Language loyalty in the United States*, edited by Joshua A. Fishman, 206–52. The Hague: Mouton.

———. 1977. Über einige Terminologie-Probleme der interlingualen Soziolinguistik. *Deutsche Sprache* 3: 224–37.

———. 1985. Sprachkonservative Religionsgemeinschaften. In *Deutsch als Muttersprache in den Vereinigten Staaten. Teil II: Regionale und funktionale Aspekte*, edited by Heinz Kloss, 127–37. Stuttgart: Steiner.

Kohler, Klaus J. 1984. Phonetic explanation in phonology: The feature fortis/lenis. *Phonetica* 41: 150–74.

Kopp, Achim. 1988. Die Sprache der Pennsylvania Germans im sozialen Kontext. *Staatsexamen* thesis. Universität Heidelberg.

———. 1993. The matched-guise technique in practice: Measuring language attitudes within the Pennsylvania German speech community. In *The German language in America, 1683–1991*, edited by Joseph C. Salmons, 264–83. Madison, Wis.: Max Kade Institute for German-American Studies.

Kraybill, Donald B. 1989. *The riddle of Amish culture*. Baltimore: Johns Hopkins University Press.

Kremnitz, Georg. 1987. Diglossie/Polyglossie. In *Sociolinguistics—Soziolinguistik. An international handbook of the science of language and society—Ein internationales Handbuch zur Wissenschaft von Sprache und Gesellschaft*, vol. 1, edited by Ulrich Ammon, Norbert Dittmar, and Klaus J. Mattheier, 208–18. Berlin: de Gruyter.

Kurath, Hans. 1949. *A word geography of the eastern United States*. Ann Arbor: University of Michigan Press.

———. 1972. *Studies in area linguistics*. Bloomington: Indiana University Press.

Kurath, Hans, and Raven I. McDavid, Jr. 1961. *The pronunciation of English in the Atlantic states*. Ann Arbor: University of Michigan Press.

Labaree, Leonard W., ed. 1961. *The papers of Benjamin Franklin, vol. 4: July 1, 1750, through June 30, 1753*. New Haven: Yale University Press.

Labov, William. 1966. *The social stratification of English in New York City*. Washington, D.C.: Center for Applied Linguistics.

———. 1972a. *Sociolinguistic patterns*. Philadelphia: University of Pennsylvania Press.

———. 1972b. Some principles of linguistic methodology. *Language in Society* 1: 97–120.

———. 1994. *Principles of linguistic change, volume 1: Internal factors*. Oxford: Blackwell.

Lambert, Marcus Bachman. 1924. *Pennsylvania-German dictionary*. Lancaster, Pa.: Pennsylvania German Society. Reprinted 1977. Exton, Pa.: Schiffer.

Lambert, Wallace E. 1967. A social psychology of bilingualism. *Journal of Social Issues* 23: 91–109.

Lambert, Wallace E., R. C. Hodgson, R. C. Gardner, and S. Fillenbaum. 1960. Evaluational reactions to spoken languages. *Journal of Abnormal and Social Psychology* 60: 44–51.

Lins, J. C. 1887. *Common sense Pennsylvania German dictionary; containing nearly all the Pennsylvania German words in common use*. Kempton, Pa.: Lins.

Lippi-Green, Rosina L. 1989. Social network integration and language change in progress in a rural alpine village. *Language in Society* 18: 213–34.

Louden, Mark Laurence. 1987. Bilingualism and diglossia: The case of Pennsylvania German. *Leuvense Bijdragen* 76: 17–36.

———. 1988. Bilingualism and syntactic change in Pennsylvania German. Ph.D. diss., Cornell University.

———. 1989. Syntactic variation and change in Pennsylvania German. In *Studies of the languages and the verbal behavior of the Pennsylvania Germans II*, edited by Werner Enninger, Joachim Raith, and Karl-Heinz Wandt, 29–40. Stuttgart: Steiner.

———. 1991. The image of the Old Order Amish: General and sociolinguistic stereotypes. *National Journal of Sociology* 5: 111–42.

———. 1993. Variation in Pennsylvania German syntax: A diachronic perspective. In *Verhandlungen des Internationalen Dialektologenkongresses—Proceedings of the International Congress of Dialectologists—Communications du Congrès International de Dialectologie, Bamberg 29. 7. – 4. 8. 1990, Band 2—volume 2—volume 2: Historische Dialektologie und Sprachwandel—Historical dialectology and linguistic change—Dialectologie historique et variation linguistique: Sprachatlanten und Wörterbücher—Linguistic atlases and dictionaries—Atlas linguistiques et dictionaires*, edited by Wolfgang Viereck, 169–79. Stuttgart: Steiner.

Luebke, Frederick C. 1974. *Bonds of loyalty: German-Americans and World War I*. DeKalb: Northern Illinois University Press.

MacKinnon, Kenneth M. 1977. Language shift and education: Conservation of ethnolinguistic culture amongst schoolchildren of a Gaelic community. *Linguistics* 198: 31–55.

Mather, J. Y., and H. H. Speitel, eds. 1975. *The linguistic atlas of Scotland: Scots section*, vol. 1. London: Croom Helm.

Meister Ferré, Barbara. 1994. *Stability and change in the Pennsylvania German dialect of an Old Order Amish community in Lancaster County*. Stuttgart: Steiner.

Bibliography

Mencken, H. L. 1919. *The American language. An inquiry into the development of English in the United States.* Supplement II. New York: Knopf.

Milroy, Lesley. 1980 (1st ed.). 1987 (2d ed.). *Language and social networks.* Oxford: Blackwell.

Moelleken, Wolfgang W. 1983. Language maintenance and language shift in Pennsylvania German: A comparative investigation. *Monatshefte* 75: 172–86.

Moore, Barbara Joan Reeves. 1980. A sociolinguistic longitudinal study (1969–1979) of a Texas German community, including curricular recommendations. Ph.D. diss., University of Texas at Austin.

Osgood, Charles E., George J. Suci, and Perci H. Tannenbaum. 1957. *The measurement of meaning.* Urbana: University of Illinois Press.

Page, Eugene R. 1937. English in the Pennsylvania German area. *American Speech* 12: 203–06.

Pavone, James. 1980. Implicational scales and English dialectology. Ph.D. diss., Indiana University.

Post, Rudolf. 1990. *Pfälzisch: Einführung in eine Sprachlandschaft.* Landau/Pfalz, Germany: Pfälzische Verlagsanstalt.

Preston, Dennis R. 1987. Domain-, role- or network specific use of language. In *Sociolinguistics—Soziolinguistik. An international handbook of the science of language and society—Ein internationales Handbuch zur Wissenschaft von Sprache und Gesellschaft,* vol. 1, edited by Ulrich Ammon, Norbert Dittmar, and Klaus J. Mattheier, 690–99. Berlin: de Gruyter.

Quirk, Randolph, Sidney Greenbaum, Geoffrey Leech, and Jan Svartvik. 1985. *A comprehensive grammar of the English language.* London: Longman.

Raith, Joachim. 1981. Phonologische Interferenzen im Amerikanischen Englisch der anabaptistischen Gruppen deutscher Herkunft in Lancaster County (Pennsylvania). *Zeitschrift für Dialektologie und Linguistik* 48: 35–52.

———. 1982. *Sprachgemeinschaftstyp, Sprachkontakt, Sprachgebrauch. Eine Untersuchung des Bilinguismus der anabaptistischen Gruppen deutscher Abstammung in Lancaster County, Pennsylvania.* Wiesbaden, Germany: Steiner.

———. 1987. Sprachgemeinschaft. In *Sociolinguistics—Soziolinguistik. An international handbook of the science of language and society—Ein internationales Handbuch zur Wissenschaft von Sprache und Gesellschaft,* vol. 1, edited by Ulrich Ammon, Norbert Dittmar, and Klaus J. Mattheier, 200–08. Berlin: de Gruyter.

Rauch, E. H. 1879. *Rauch's Pennsylvania Dutch handbook—Rauch's Pennsylvania Deitsh Hond-Booch.* Mauch Chunk, Pa.: Rauch.

Redekop, Calvin Wall. 1989. *Mennonite society.* Baltimore: Johns Hopkins University Press.

Reed, Carroll E. 1947. A survey of Pennsylvania German phonology. *Modern Language Quarterly* 8: 267–89.

———. 1948. A survey of Pennsylvania German morphology. *Modern Language Quarterly* 9: 322–42.

———. 1957. Die Sprachgeographie des Pennsylvaniadeutschen. *Zeitschrift für Mundartforschung* 25: 29–39.

Reed, Carroll E., and Lester W. J. Seifert. 1954. *A linguistic atlas of Pennsylvania German.* Marburg/Lahn, Germany.

Rippley, La Vern J. 1976. *The German-Americans.* Boston: Twayne. Reprinted 1984. Lanham, Md.: University Press of America.

Romaine, Suzanne. 1982. What is a speech community? In *Sociolinguistic variation in speech communities*, edited by Suzanne Romaine, 13–24. London: Arnold.

Rubin, Joan. 1968. Bilingual usage in Paraguay. In *Readings in the sociology of language*, edited by Joshua A. Fishman, 512–30. The Hague: Mouton.

Ryan, Ellen Bouchard, Howard Giles, and Miles Hewstone. 1988. The measurement of language attitudes. In *Sociolinguistics—Soziolinguistik. An international handbook of the science of language and society—Ein internationales Handbuch zur Wissenschaft von Sprache und Gesellschaft*, vol. 2, edited by Ulrich Ammon, Norbert Dittmar, and Klaus J. Mattheier, 1068–81. Berlin: de Gruyter.

Schach, Paul. 1951. Semantic borrowing in Pennsylvania German. *American Speech* 26: 257–67.

Seel, Helga. 1988. *Lexikologische Studien zum Pennsylvaniadeutschen. Wortbildung des Pennsylvaniadeutschen. Sprachkontakterscheinungen im Wortschatz des Pennsylvaniadeutschen.* Stuttgart: Steiner.

Selinker, Larry. 1972. Interlanguage. *International Review of Applied Linguistics* 10: 209–31.

———. 1992. *Rediscovering interlanguage*. London: Longman.

Shields, Kenneth Jr. 1985. Germanisms in Pennsylvania German English: An update. *American Speech* 60: 228–37.

———. 1987. Germanisms in the English of Eastern Pennsylvania. *Journal of English Linguistics* 20: 163–80.

Shuy, Roger W., and Frederick Williams. 1973. Stereotyped attitudes of selected English dialect communities. In *Language attitudes: Current trends and prospects*, edited by Roger W. Shuy and Ralph W. Fasold, 85–96. Washington, D.C.: Georgetown University Press.

Springer, Otto. 1943. The study of the Pennsylvania German dialect. *Journal of English and Germanic Philology* 42: 1–39.

Stevens, S. K. 1976. *Pennsylvania history in outline*. 4th ed. Revised and enlarged by Donald H. Kent. Harrisburg, Pa.: Pennsylvania Historical and Museum Commission.

Stine, Eugene S. 1990. *Pennsylvania German to English dictionary*. Lehighton, Pa.: Stine.

Struble, George G. 1935. The English of the Pennsylvania Germans. *American Speech* 10: 163–72.

The local historians of Klingerstown. 1990. Klingerstown has important spot in history. *The Citizen Standard*, 27 April. Valley View, Pa.

Thomason, Sarah Grey, and Terrence Kaufman. 1988. *Language contact, creolization, and genetic linguistics*. Berkeley: University of California Press.

Tucker, Whitney R. 1934. Linguistic substrata in Pennsylvania and elsewhere. *Language* 10: 1–5.

Van Braght, Thieleman Jens. 1968. *The bloody theatre; or, martyrs mirror of the defenseless Christians*. Compiled from various authentic chronicles, memorials, and testimonies. Translated from the original Dutch edition (Dordrecht, 1660) by Joseph F. Sohm. Scottdale, Pa.: Herald.

Van Coetsem, Frans C. 1988. *Loan phonology and the two transfer types in language contact*. Dordrecht, Netherlands: Foris.

Van Ness, Silke. 1990. *Changes in an obsolescing language: Pennsylvania German in West Virginia*. Tübingen, Germany: Narr.

Veith, Werner H. 1968. Pennsylvaniadeutsch. Ein Beitrag zur Entstehung von Siedlungsmundarten. *Zeitschrift für Mundartforschung* 35: 254–83.

Weinreich, Uriel. 1953. *Languages in contact: Findings and problems.* The Hague: Mouton.

Weiser, Frederick S., and Mary Hammond Sullivan. 1980. Decorated Furniture of the Schwaben Creek Valley. In *Ebbes fer alle—ebber ebbes fer dich. Something for everyone—something for you. Essays in memoriam Albert Franklin Buffington. Publications of The Pennsylvania German Society*, vol. 14, 331–94. Breinigsville, Pa.: Pennsylvania German Society.

Wiedemann-Citera, Barbara. 1993. *Die Auswirkungen des Ersten Weltkrieges auf die Deutsch-Amerikaner im Spiegel der New Yorker Staatszeitung, der New Yorker Volkszeitung und der New York Times 1914–1926.* Frankfurt/Main: Lang.

Williams, Frederick. 1973. Some research notes on dialect attitudes and stereotypes. In *Language attitudes: Current trends and prospects*, edited by Roger W. Shuy and Ralph W. Fasold, 113–28. Washington, D.C.: Georgetown University Press.

Wilson Joseph B. 1980. The English spoken by German Americans in central Texas. In *Languages in conflict*, edited by Paul Schach, 157–73. Lincoln: University of Nebraska Press.

Wood, Ralph Charles. 1968. *The four gospels, translated into the Pennsylvania German dialect.* Allentown, Pa.: Pennsylvania German Society.

Yoder, Don. 1980. Palatine, Hessian, Dutchman: Three images of the German in America. In *Ebbes fer alle—ebber ebbes fer dich. Something for everyone—something for you. Essays in memoriam Albert Franklin Buffington. Publications of The Pennsylvania German Society*, vol. 14, 105–29. Breinigsville, Pa.: Pennsylvania German Society.

Index

accent, 21, 47, 48, 49, 50, 51, 52, 53, 54, 55, 105, 113, 212, 223, 237, 245, 272, 273, 281, 282, 283, 286, 315n. 26, 322n. 11
accommodation (linguistic), 323n. 13
adstratal, 287
advancing (phonetic), 67, 86, 91
Aesop, 220
affricate, 72, 94, 96, 120, 121, 122, 312n. 6
age, 59, 82, 90, 100, 104, 110, 112, 114, 115, 116, 117, 127, 128, 129, 130, 132, 137, 138, 139, 151, 152, 154, 155, 157, 160, 161, 162, 166, 167, 168, 169, 170, 174, 176, 179, 183, 184, 185, 186, 188, 189, 190, 191, 193, 194, 196, 197, 198, 203, 221, 223, 244, 250, 254, 258, 261, 264, 266, 275, 277, 281, 292, 297, 309, 313n. 16, 315n. 27, 316nn. 4 and 6, 320n. 43
Albany (ship), 35
Alemannic, 23
Allentown, Pennsylvania, 150, 296, 306
allomorph, 312n. 9
allophone, 82, 120
Alsace, 19, 27, 29
alveolar, 120, 121, 122
Amanite, 26
America, 18, 20, 21, 26, 34, 85, 310nn. 6 and 7, 317n. 15. *See also* North America. *See also* South America
Amish, 18, 19, 24, 26, 29–31, 39, 40, 41, 43, 45, 47, 55, 56, 58, 59, 78, 79, 82, 85, 86, 88, 89, 101, 102, 112, 114, 130, 132, 139, 143, 144, 150, 155, 164, 166, 176, 177, 178, 193, 207, 243, 244, 251, 271, 275, 309, 320n. 39; Amish Mennonite, 31; Beachy Amish, 31, 40, 41, 47, 55, 101, 176, 179, 185, 186, 190, 193, 311n. 24; Church Amish, 31; House Amish, 31; New Amish, 31; New Order Amish, 40, 47, 54, 55, 101, 130, 186, 318n. 17; Old Order Amish, 14, 29–31, 129, 131, 132, 311n. 15, 318n. 17. *See also* worship service
Amish Mennonite. *See* Amish. *See* Mennonites
Ammann, Jacob, 29
Anabaptism 19, 26, 27, 28, 31, 132, 315n. 26
apparent time, 15, 109, 315n. 27
Ausgleichsformen, 24
Auslautverhärtung, 73, 94, 312n. 6
Austria, 135, 151, 321n. 54

Baby Pennsylvania German. *See* motherese
backing (phonetic), 127
Baden, 19
Bald Eagle State Forest, 39
ban (from church), 29
bank barn, 37
barn raising, 30, 146, 153
barn-sign, 37
Beachy Amish. *See* Amish
Beam, C. Richard, 148, 317n. 14
Beissel, Konrad, 25
Berks County, Pennsylvania, 20, 32, 35, 145, 146, 310n. 10
Bern, 27
Berrisburg, Pennsylvania, 149
Berwick, Pennsylvania, 41, 56, 57, 114, 154, 178
Bethel College, 29

334

Bethlehem, Pennsylvania, 26
Bible High German, 28, 31, 39, 41, 44, 62, 134, 136, 137, 138, 139, 140, 144, 172, 173, 208, 279, 292, 294, 295, 297, 298, 299, 300, 303, 304, 309, 310n. 13, 316n. 6, 320n. 35
bilabial, 69, 120, 127, 312n. 9, 315n. 26
bilingual(ism), 13, 15, 17, 66, 97, 130, 133, 136, 145, 186, 190, 206, 207, 211, 221, 272, 277, 281, 283, 285, 286, 287, 288, 313n. 17, 316n. 4, 319nn. 28 and 35, 321n. 54, 322n. 7, 323n. 13
Birdsboro, Pennsylvania, 146
Black Bumper Mennonite. *See* Mennonites
Bloomsburg, Pennsylvania, 148
Blue Mountain, 34
borrowing, 94, 213, 214, 218, 279, 285, 286, 287, 313n. 17, 324n. 4
Boyertown, Pennsylvania, 148
Britain, 37
Brothers (ship), 34
Bucknell University, 42
Bucks County, Pennsylvania, 310n. 10
Buffalo Creek, 39
Buffalo Valley, 39, 40, 53, 54, 55, 62, 149, 318n. 25

cabinetmaking, 37
calls for farm animals, 170, 307, 319n. 31
Calvin Jean, 25
Canada, 22, 27, 29, 112, 151, 154, 211
cardinal vowel, 91
careful style, 64, 312n. 2
casual speech, 63, 64, 312n. 2
Catholic, 19, 25, 26, 38, 51, 52
centralized vowel, 66, 313n. 12
centring diphthong, 68, 69, 83
Charles II, 18
Chester County, Pennsylvania, 40, 54, 55
Chicago, 22
chi-square test, 201
Church Amish. *See* Amish
Church of England, 25
Church of the Brethren, 25
Cincinnati, 22
Civil War, 148, 317n. 14

clear /l/, 69, 106
closing diphthong, 68
cluster (in a social network), 142, 152
coal region, 32, 38, 51
code switching, 195, 196, 207, 208, 279, 280, 313n. 17, 321n. 55
Collinson, Peter, 322n. 9
Columbia County, Pennsylvania, 41, 56, 57
community (linguistic), 82, 276–77. *See also* nonsectarian Pennsylvania Germans. *See also* sectarian Pennsylvania Germans. *See also* non-Pennsylvania Germans. *See also* Amish. *See also* Mennonites. *See also* generation. *See also* speech community
Concord (ship), 18
Conestoga Valley, 22
conscientious objection, 28
Conservative Mennonite. *See* Mennonites
consonant, 66, 69, 70, 74, 80, 96, 133, 312n. 7. *See also* lenis (consonant). *See also* fortis (consonant). *See also* preconsonantal
contact phenomenon, 15, 90, 94, 97, 98, 119, 120, 122, 133, 272, 314n. 18
convergence, 16, 276, 280, 287, 288, 324n. 5
correlation matrix, 227, 230
covered bridge, 39
Crisp, Stephen, 18
Croatian, 38
Czech, 26

Daafschei, 37
Dalmatia, Pennsylvania, 149
Danville, Pennsylvania, 149
dark /l/, 69, 95, 106, 213, 216
dative case, 216
Dauphin County, Pennsylvania, 32, 126
decision-tree, 321n. 56
Delaware, 14, 22, 131
Delaware Indians, 32, 34
Delaware River, 18
density (of a social network), 142, 153, 154, 155
dental (sound), 120, 122, 313n. 11

Derr, Ludwig (Lewis), 42
devoiced/devoicing, 69, 72, 73, 74, 75, 76, 77, 80, 94, 97, 104, 122, 124, 127, 128, 131, 132, 314n. 20
diachronic, 158, 209
dictionaries, 14
Die Botschaft, 148
diglossia/diglossic, 13, 15, 17, 181, 183, 185, 186, 190, 193, 206, 209, 277, 279, 282, 283, 287, 288, 310n. 4, 319–20n. 35
diphthong, 66, 68, 69, 72, 83, 84, 86, 90, 91, 93, 95, 97, 104, 107, 108, 120, 125, 127, 133, 313n. 15
domain, 15, 17, 29, 41, 134, 140, 141, 142, 144, 149, 150, 152, 154, 155, 156, 159, 161, 162, 163, 164, 166, 169, 170, 171, 173, 178, 183, 185, 186, 187, 189, 190, 191, 192, 193, 198, 200, 202, 204, 205, 206, 208, 209, 277, 279, 280, 285, 317nn. 9 and 11, 319nn. 28, 32, and 35, 320nn. 45 and 47
Dornsife, Pennsylvania, 32
Drumheller's Store and Bar, 149, 318n. 18
duke of York, 18
dumb Dutchman stereotype, 16, 210, 234, 235, 237, 239, 244, 245, 246, 252, 253, 260, 261, 262, 272, 273, 274, 277, 278, 281, 283
Dunker, 25
Dutch, 20, 23, 27. *See also* Pennsylvania Dutch
dutchified English, 105, 106, 242, 277, 280, 281, 309, 322n. 11

East Sutherland, 136, 316n. 5, 319n. 28, 321n. 51
Eberbach, 25
Economy, Pennsylvania, 26
eigenvalue, 227, 228, 229
elicitation (of phonemes), 15, 44, 64, 131
Elizabethtown, 35
Elkhart, Indiana, 29
emigration, 19, 20, 22, 29, 310n. 7
England, 18, 20, 34, 42
Enterlein, Rev. John Michael, 34
epenthetic, 93, 95, 96, 108, 127, 128, 129, 313n. 16
Ephrata, Pennsylvania, 40
Ephrata Cloister, 25, 27
Erdman, Pennsylvania, 35, 36, 144
erstsprachige Mehrsprachigkeit, 130
es schwere Deel, 31
Essen Delaware Project Team, 14
ethnic boundary model, 323n. 13
ethnic identity, 16, 133, 208, 246, 257, 261, 262, 269, 270, 273, 274, 277, 279, 281, 282, 283, 285, 323n. 13
ethnic marking, 15, 16, 63, 66, 68, 71, 72, 73, 74, 75, 76, 77, 78, 79, 80, 82, 83, 84, 85, 86, 87, 88, 89, 90, 91, 92, 93, 94, 95, 96, 97, 98, 99, 100, 101, 102, 103, 104, 105, 106, 107, 108, 109, 110, 111, 112, 113, 114, 115, 116, 117, 118, 119, 120, 122, 123, 124, 125, 126, 128, 130, 131, 132, 133, 188, 210, 214, 231, 232, 233, 234, 235, 236, 238, 239, 240, 242, 244, 247, 249, 250, 251, 253, 254, 255, 256, 257, 259, 260, 261, 262, 265, 268, 269, 270, 271, 272, 273, 274, 275, 276, 278, 280, 283, 286, 212n. 3, 314nn. 18 and 19, 315n. 30, 323n. 13; deliberate, 269, 270, 279, 283
ethnomethodology, 16
Europe, 22, 26, 29, 37, 150, 154, 296

factor analysis, 226–31, 233, 322n. 7
factor extraction, 227, 228
factor matrix, 229, 230
Farmers' Market, 42, 43, 149, 296, 299, 305
Fasnacht, 37
Federal Penitentiary, 42
feeding (linguistic), 312n. 11
fieldwork (linguistic), 13, 33, 43, 44
Fisher Ridge, 32
flashcards, 44, 64, 291, 312n. 3, 316n. 6
Focus on the Family, 148
foot washing, 28, 29
fortis (consonant), 69, 72, 73, 74, 75, 107, 120, 127, 128, 131
Fraktur, 37, 311n. 20
Frankfurt, 18
Franklin, Benjamin, 245, 322n. 9

free speech, 63
free variant, 82, 106
free-church movement, 26
French, 20, 211, 311n. 23
fricative, 75, 76, 81, 94, 96, 120, 121, 122, 313n. 11, 314n. 20
Frisian, 26
Fuhreleit. See Mennonites

Gaelic, 136, 211, 311n. 27, 316n. 4, 319nn. 28 and 32, 321n. 51
Geist's Store, 149
gender, 59, 82, 102, 103, 104, 114, 117, 132, 151, 152, 160, 167, 168, 170, 174, 176, 184, 194, 196, 197, 203, 205, 209, 223, 244, 247, 249, 250, 251, 253, 254, 257, 258, 263, 264, 266, 275, 292, 321n. 48; language use and, 199–201
General Conference Mennonite Church. *See* Mennonites
generation: of nonsectarians (defined by acquisition patterns), 13, 36, 45–46, 158, 277–79; of sectarians, 46–47, 58; of non-Pennsylvania Germans, 47, 58; correlating with age, 116–17
German dialects, 17, 94, 136, 312n. 8
Germantown, 18, 27, 310n. 7
Germany, 18, 19, 25, 27, 37, 135, 151, 154, 172, 306, 312n. 8, 316n. 1
glottal stop, 69, 73, 74
Goshen College, 29
grammar, 14, 316n. 4, 319n. 35
Gratz, Pennsylvania, 146, 147, 149
Great Plains, 22, 36
Great Valley, 32
Greek, 51, 52
Groffdale Conference. *See* Mennonites
Grundsau, 37, 38, 295, 304

Haasepeffer (card game), 318n. 18
Harmony, Pennsylvania, 26
Harrisburg, Pennsylvania, 32, 34, 39, 150, 296, 306
Hartleton, Pennsylvania, 39, 41, 149
Hartleton County Store, 149
Hepler, Jesse, 148
Herndon, Pennsylvania, 146

Herrnhuter, 26
Hesse, 19
Hessian, 322n. 10
hex-sign. *See* barn-sign
Himmel's Church, 34–35, 62, 144, 145, 146, 311n. 16
Holland, 18, 20, 27
home butchering, 37, 61, 62, 112, 138, 147, 172, 295, 304, 318n. 21, 321n. 55
Honeybrook, Pennsylvania, 40
Hooflander Mountain, 32
Horning Mennonite. *See* Mennonites
horse-and-buggy transportation, 28, 29, 30, 39, 40, 155, 285
House Amish. *See* Amish
Hudson Valley, 20
Huffines, M. Lois, 43
Huguenot, 20
Hungarian, 321n. 54
Hus, Johannes, 26
Hutterite, 19, 26
H-variety, 165, 207, 319n. 35
hypercorrection, 313n. 14

identification, 219, 225, 233, 251, 255–60, 261, 262, 273, 274
identity. *See* ethnic identity
Illinois, 22, 150
immigration, 20, 21, 22, 23, 26, 27, 29, 34, 35, 36, 37, 38, 313n. 14, 322n. 10
implicational scaling, 44, 63, 103, 104, 105, 106, 107, 108, 110, 112, 114, 115, 121, 123, 131, 166, 168, 169, 170, 171, 183, 185, 186, 187, 188, 189, 190, 191, 192, 193, 194, 202, 205, 314nn. 24 and 25, 320n. 41
imposition, 16, 285, 286, 287, 288, 313n. 17, 324n. 4
indentured servitude, 20
Independent Bible Church, 56
Indiana, 22, 150
informants, 45–59
integration (linguistic), 313n. 17
intelligence, 211, 226, 234, 237, 238, 239, 240, 245, 251, 252–55, 257, 258, 259, 260, 261, 262, 271, 272, 281
interference, 36, 46, 64, 66, 71, 72, 78, 90,

338 Index

94, 97, 110, 113, 117, 122, 123, 130, 132, 133, 139, 213, 214, 215, 216, 217, 218, 224, 236, 241, 242, 243, 246, 249, 260, 269, 270, 271, 272, 273, 278, 279, 280, 281, 282, 293, 284, 285, 288, 313n. 17, 323n. 3
interlanguage, 122, 315n. 29
interlocutor, 15, 137, 140, 141, 157, 158, 159, 160, 161, 164, 165, 166, 167, 168, 169, 170, 171, 172, 173, 174, 175, 177, 178, 179, 180, 181, 182, 183, 184, 185, 186, 187, 188, 189, 190, 191, 192, 193, 194, 195, 196, 197, 198, 199, 200, 201, 202, 203, 205, 206, 207, 208, 209, 221, 257, 278, 301, 320n. 45, 321n. 51
intermediate phonological variants, 73, 79, 83, 84, 85, 87, 89, 97, 104, 105, 107, 108, 114, 120, 122, 123, 124, 125, 132, 314n. 20
interview, 60–61, 63, 64, 65, 71, 100, 134, 141, 169, 197, 220, 222, 245, 271, 273, 281, 311n. 26, 312n. 2, 316n. 1, 318nn. 17 and 24; free interview, 64, 134, 135, 311n. 1, 316n. 3; pilot interview, 43, 64, 211, 224, 262
intervocalic, 75, 312nn. 7 and 8
intonation, 223, 312n. 3
Iowa, 22
IPA transcription, 66
Ireland/Irish, 20, 42, 310n. 6
Iroquois Indians, 32, 34, 35
Italian, 38, 51

Japanese, 323n. 2

Kaiser criterion, 228
Kansas, 22
Karl-Ludwig (Elector of the Palatinate), 19
Kaufmann, Carl Heinrich, 34
Kent County, Delaware, 131, 132
Kentucky, 22
Kitchener, Ontario, 150
Klinger, Alexander, 35
Klinger, Johannes Philipp, 35, 36
Klinger's Church, 36, 144, 145, 317 n. 16

Klinger's Store, 149
Klingerstown (Klingerschtedtel), Pennsylvania, 32, 34, 35–36, 62, 144, 147, 149, 311n. 17
Klouser, Bill, 148
Korea, 151
Krefeld, 18, 20
Kutztown, Pennsylvania, 147

L_1-multilingualism, 130
labio-dental, 120
Lancaster, Pennsylvania, 22, 148, 150, 296, 306
Lancaster Conference. *See* Mennonites
Lancaster County, Pennsylvania, 14, 20, 24, 25, 27, 28, 32, 40, 53, 54, 55, 62, 129, 310n. 10, 315n. 26, 318n. 25, 320n. 39
language acquisition, 15, 45, 66, 111, 116, 117, 119, 122, 130, 132, 134, 137–40, 169, 170, 182, 188, 189, 191, 208, 212, 244, 260, 272, 274, 275, 277, 278, 279, 281, 284, 285, 298, 319n. 35
language attitude, 15, 16, 44, 60, 133, 137, 169, 188, 189, 207, 208, 209, 210–75, 276, 277, 278, 279, 281, 282–84, 285, 287, 308, 318n. 25, 322nn. 3 and 7, 323n. 2. *See also* school
language change, 14, 16, 18, 96–97, 108, 110, 117, 118, 119, 122, 123, 124, 133, 278, 286, 287, 314n. 26, 315nn. 27 and 28
language choice, 209, 284, 316n. 7, 319n. 28, 321nn. 51 and 56
language competence, 13, 15, 17, 23, 28, 36, 44, 45, 46, 61, 64, 66, 72, 75, 90, 97, 103, 111, 115, 116, 124, 125, 127, 133, 134–37, 138, 139, 140, 145, 151, 156, 159, 162, 169, 170, 172, 176, 177, 178, 179, 180, 181, 187, 189, 191, 192, 193, 195, 198, 206, 208, 245, 248, 260, 261, 269, 270, 274, 278, 279, 281, 282, 283, 284, 285, 288, 297, 310n. 13, 313n. 16, 315n. 29, 316n. 3, 317n. 7, 319n. 33, 320nn. 35, 41, 42, and 43. *See also* translation

Index 339

competence
language contact, 15, 16, 63, 64, 130, 133, 276, 285, 286, 287, 288, 313n. 17, 314n. 18, 321n. 48, 323n. 3. *See also* contact phenomenon
language death, 13, 15, 16, 36, 38, 138, 147, 190, 193, 206, 207, 278, 285, 287, 288, 310n. 5, 316n. 5
language loss, 22, 36, 135, 162, 190, 260, 273, 274, 279, 281, 283, 287, 288, 315n. 26, 317n. 15
language maintenance, 15, 17, 134, 140, 158, 159, 175, 179, 192, 206–08, 209, 245, 277, 287, 288, 310nn. 2 and 5, 321n. 52, 323n. 13
language shift, 15, 16, 17, 134, 140, 157, 158, 164, 182, 183, 185, 186, 187, 188, 189, 191, 192, 193, 198, 206–08, 209, 273, 281, 285, 287, 288, 310n. 5, 317n. 14, 320nn. 41 and 46, 321nn. 52 and 57
language use, 15, 16, 44, 45, 48, 61, 97, 110, 111, 113, 115, 117, 128, 130, 133, 134, 140–206, 207, 208, 209, 210, 224, 247, 253, 257, 270, 276, 277, 278, 279, 280, 282–84, 287, 288, 292, 294, 297, 314n. 18, 316–17n. 7, 319n. 33, 320n. 41, 321n. 48; in childhood and adolescence, 156–71, 298; present-day, 171–206, 300; within the family, 193–99; and gender, 199–201. *See also* school
lateral (sound), 75
laxing (phonetic), 127
Lebanon, Pennsylvania, 148
Lebanon County, Pennsylvania, 310n. 10
Leck Kill, Pennsylvania, 144, 149
Lehigh County, Pennsylvania, 20, 21, 25, 211, 212, 310n. 10
Leipzig, 34
lenis (consonant), 69, 72, 73, 74, 75, 76, 77, 80, 94, 97, 107, 120, 122, 127, 128, 131
Lenni Lenape, 32
Leola, Pennsylvania, 40
leveling (linguistic), 17, 23, 24
Lewisburg, Pennsylvania, 39, 41, 42, 43, 57, 58, 62, 114, 143, 148, 149, 154

Lewisburg Elementary School, 143
lexicon, 15, 15, 17, 23, 64, 223, 279, 280, 281, 285, 286, 312n. 1, 319n. 35, 323n. 1, 324n. 4
Line Mountain, 32, 34
Line Mountain High School, 38, 137, 138, 143
liquid (sound), 312n. 12
Little Germany, 22
loan word, 66, 94, 215, 218
Lord Baltimore, 18
lowering (phonetic), 92, 95, 96, 120
Luther, Martin, 26, 27, 28, 136, 139, 310n. 13, 316n. 6
Lutheran, 19, 25, 34, 35, 36, 38, 47, 48, 49, 50, 51, 52, 129, 130, 211, 223, 317n. 15
L-variety, 165, 179, 201, 207, 319n. 35
Lykens, Pennsylvania, 38, 62, 146, 147, 318n. 20
Lykens Valley, 34, 35, 146

Mahanoy Creek, 34
Mahantango Creek, 35
Mahantango Mountain, 32, 34, 45
Mahantango Valley, 32, 34, 35, 36, 37, 38, 39, 42, 47, 48, 49, 50, 51, 52, 53, 62, 143, 144, 149, 155, 207, 211, 212, 222, 318nn. 19 and 21
Mahantango Valley Elementary School, 143
mainstream society, 15, 101, 113, 130, 133, 207, 224, 246, 277, 279, 281, 285
majority language, 16, 206, 276, 288
Mandata, Pennsylvania, 38, 147
Mannheim, 24
marking. *See* ethnic marking
Martin's Store, 149
Maryland, 18, 22
matched-guise test, 15, 43, 44, 60, 61, 132, 210–75, 281, 308, 322nn. 2, 3, 7, and 12
Meidung, 29
Mennonites, 18, 19, 24, 26–29, 30, 31, 39, 40, 41, 43, 45, 46, 54, 55, 58, 59, 62, 73, 75, 77, 78, 79, 80, 83, 84, 85, 86, 89, 101, 102, 111, 112, 130, 139, 143,

144, 147, 149, 150, 151, 155, 163, 164, 166, 168, 173, 176, 178, 179, 186, 204, 236, 238, 243, 244, 251, 271, 275, 309, 316n. 6; Amish Mennonite, 31; Black Bumper Mennonite, 28, 150; Conservative Mennonite, 129, 130; *Fuhreleit*, 28; General Conference Mennonite Church, 27; Groffdale Conference, 28, 39; Horning Mennonite, 28; Lancaster Conference, 28; Mennonite Brethren Church, 27, 129, 130; New Mennonite, 28; New Order Mennonite, 55, 112, 211, 212, 222, 223, 241, 311n. 24; (Old) Mennonite Church, 27, 28, 129, 130; Old Order Mennonite, 28, 39, 40, 46, 53, 54, 62, 101, 130, 186; Pike Mennonite, 28; Reformed Mennonite, 28; Reidenbach Mennonite, 28; Stauffer Mennonite, 28; Team Mennonite, 28; Wenger Mennonite/Wengerite, 28; Weaverland Conference, 28; Wisler Mennonite, 28. *See also* worship service
Mennonite Church. *See* Mennonites
Mennonite Brethren Church. *See* Mennonites
Mexican, 322n. 7
Michigan, 22
Middle High German, 95
Middleburg, Pennsylvania, 62
Midwest, 22, 36, 85
Mifflinburg, Pennsylvania, 39, 40, 147
Millmont, Pennsylvania, 41, 62, 316n. 6
Milton, Pennsylvania, 39
Milwaukee, 22
minimal pair, 63, 94, 312n. 2
minority language, 15, 16, 206, 207, 209, 276, 278, 288
monolingual(ism), 13, 17, 43, 46, 47, 56, 57, 58, 64, 75, 89, 97, 98, 106, 115, 118, 119, 124, 127, 128, 131, 132, 133, 136, 138, 139, 169, 175, 176, 185, 186, 189, 193, 206, 246, 249, 253, 261, 262, 263, 267, 268, 274, 277, 278, 280, 281, 283, 284, 288, 313n. 16, 314n. 18, 315n. 32, 320n.

41, 323n. 13
monophthong, 66, 67, 68, 69, 83, 84, 85, 86, 88, 89, 90, 91, 95, 96, 97, 107, 108, 120, 121, 125, 127, 214, 215, 216, 217, 313nn. 13 and 15
Montana, 150
Montgomery County, Pennsylvania, 25, 310n. 10
Moravian, 19, 25
Moravian Brethren, 25
Mormon, 52, 145
morpheme-final, 127
morphology, 14, 17, 311n. 1
motherese, 321n. 47
Mountain View Mennonite Church, 62
multilingualism, 206
multiplexity (of a social network), 142, 153, 154, 155, 163, 164, 165, 179

Napoleonic Wars, 22, 27
nasal (sound), 82, 86
native word, 94
Netherlands, 26
network (social), 15, 16, 17, 44, 134, 140, 141, 142, 143, 144, 145, 149, 150, 151, 152, 153, 154, 155, 164, 165, 166, 169, 173, 191, 208, 276, 277, 292, 294, 297, 306, 317n. 13
neutralization (linguistic), 120, 312n. 7
New Amish. *See* Amish
New Berlin, Pennsylvania, 39
New England, 20
New Holland, Pennsylvania, 40
New Mennonite. *See* Mennonites
New Order Amish. *See* Amish
New Order Mennonite. *See* Mennonites
New Testament, 26
New World, 18, 20, 22, 23, 27
New York (state), 18, 20, 34, 150
New York City, 22, 311n. 18, 313n. 14
non-Pennsylvania Germans, 13, 41–43, 47, 58, 276–79
nonsectarian(s). *See* Pennsylvania German(s)
nonstandard English, 73, 78, 79, 86, 92, 94, 95, 102, 113, 114, 119, 133
North America, 18, 27, 29, 85, 322n. 10. *See also* America

North Carolina, 22
North Dakota, 22
North Newton, Kansas, 29
Northampton County, Pennsylvania, 20, 25
Northumberland County, Pennsylvania, 22, 32, 126

Oberwart, 321n. 54
observer's paradox, 60, 311n. 25
Odenwald, 35
off-glide, 65, 68, 84, 104, 123, 125, 292
Ohio, 22, 55, 79, 112, 118, 150, 311n. 24, 318n. 17
Oklahoma, 22
Old Mennonite Church. *See* Mennonites
Old Order Amish. *See* Amish
Old Order Mennonite. *See* Mennonites
Ontario, 22, 27, 151
Orthodox, 38
orthography, 14, 17, 220, 316n. 2
over-report, 136, 158, 169, 175, 187, 195

Paalzer, 20
pacifism, 26, 27
Palatinate, 19, 20, 21, 24, 27, 42, 60
Palatine, 20, 322n. 10
palato-alveolar, 121, 122
Pannhaas, 37, 318n. 21
participant observation, 16, 60, 61, 62, 134, 152, 158, 176, 177, 178, 195, 197, 207, 318n. 19
Pastorius, Franz David, 18
pause (in speech), 213
Peasant Wars, 26
Penn, William (father), 18
Penn, William (son), 18, 34, 35
Penns Central Railroad, 39
Penns Creek, 39
Pennsylfaanisch Deitsch, 23
Pennsylvania, 18, 19, 20, 21, 22, 24, 25, 26, 27, 29, 32, 33, 34, 62, 87, 150, 212, 245, 296, 297, 306, 317n. 14
Pennsylvaniadeutsch, 23
Pennsylvania Dutch, 23, 135, 141, 142, 143, 144, 146, 147, 149, 150, 156, 158, 159, 161, 172, 173, 175, 180, 202, 203, 211, 242, 243, 246, 272, 292, 293, 294, 295, 296, 297, 298, 299, 300, 301, 302, 303, 304, 305, 306, 307, 309, 315n. 26, 322nn. 10 and 11
Pennsylvania German(s): definition, 20, 21–24; language label, 23; number of speakers, 22–23; nonsectarian, 13, 25, 32–39, 45–46, 58, 276–79; sectarian, 13, 25–31, 39–41, 46–47, 58, 276–77. *See also* Amish. *See also* Mennonites
Pennsylvania German (newspaper) column, 148, 173, 245, 295, 296, 304, 305, 316n. 2, 318n. 23, 320n. 46
Pennsylvania German dialects, 24, 131, 243, 310n. 10
Pennsylvania German folk art, 37
Pennsylvania German Folklore Society, 37
Pennsylvania German literature, 37, 316n. 2
Pennsylvania German paradox, 15, 113, 133, 276, 279–82
Pennsylvania German Society, 37, 146, 295, 304
Pentecostal Church, 42, 56
Perth County, Ontario, 22
Pfaffen-Beerfurth, 35
Pfälzer, 20
Pfälzisch, 23, 95, 310n. 8, 311n. 22
Philadelphia, 18, 20, 22, 34, 35, 150, 296, 306, 313n. 12
phone (linguistic), 69
phone shanty, 30
phoneme, 64, 65, 69, 79, 94
phoneme system, 66, 72, 78, 97, 108, 120, 133, 315n. 32
phonetic(s), 63, 64, 65, 66–70, 78, 86, 94, 97, 98, 103, 106, 108, 116, 119, 120, 130, 188, 313n. 17, 314n. 22, 315nn. 28 and 33
phonic, 313n. 17
phonology/phonological, 14, 15, 16, 17, 23, 44, 63–133, 215, 216, 217, 236, 246, 248, 249, 269, 270, 271, 272, 273, 274, 276, 277, 278, 279, 280, 281, 282–84, 285, 286, 287, 288, 291, 310n. 13, 311n. 1, 312n. 7, 313n. 13, 314n. 22, 315n. 32, 316n. 4, 319n. 35,

322n. 11, 324n. 4
Pietist, 18
Pike Mennonite. *See* Mennonites
Pillow, Pennsylvania, 32
Pine Creek, 35
Pitman, Pennsylvania, 147, 149
plain (people), 25, 29, 30, 143, 149, 151, 152, 161, 165, 186, 242, 243, 246, 247, 280, 287, 296, 309, 312n. 5
plosive, 73, 82, 94, 104, 106, 108, 109, 114, 120, 121, 122, 125, 314n. 20, 323n. 15
polyglossia, 310n. 4
Pottstown, Pennsylvania, 57, 58
preconsonantal, 65, 71, 81, 82, 94, 106, 108, 109, 120, 122, 131
prescriptivism, 280
prevocalic, 65, 71, 81, 82, 94, 108, 109, 114, 120, 125, 323n. 15
Protestant, 25, 38, 42, 56, 57, 58
Prussia, 27

Quakers, 18, 22
qualitative, 15, 16, 61, 63, 73, 77, 84, 89, 103, 108, 120, 122, 123, 124, 125, 126, 128, 132, 133, 140, 166, 180, 181, 183, 188, 209
quantitative, 16, 61, 63, 73, 84, 89, 97, 108, 122, 123, 124, 126, 128, 133, 140, 180, 181
questionnaire, 16, 43, 44–45, 60, 61, 64, 134, 140, 141, 156, 158, 159, 168, 171, 173, 185, 199, 202, 208, 221, 224, 241, 245, 256, 273, 290–309, 311nn. 23 and 26, 319n. 31, 322n. 2, 323n. 16
quilting, 30, 37, 146

R. B. Winter Park, 39
raising (phonetic), 67, 91, 127, 313n. 14
Rappist, 26
Reading, Pennsylvania, 35, 150, 296, 306
reading text, 63, 131, 220, 312n. 2
real time, 315n. 27
Rebuck, Pennsylvania, 34, 144, 149, 318n. 18
redemptioner, 20
Reformed, 19, 25, 26, 34, 35, 36, 56, 129, 130
Reformed Mennonite. *See* Mennonites
regional standard of English, 15, 17, 42, 56, 57, 58, 65, 66, 72, 77, 82, 83, 84, 86, 87, 89, 90, 92, 94, 95, 96, 104, 110, 118, 119, 120, 123, 124, 125, 133, 210, 211, 212, 218, 221, 223, 225, 231, 232, 233, 234, 235, 236, 237, 238, 239, 240, 241, 242, 243, 244, 247, 248, 249, 250, 251, 252, 253, 254, 255, 256, 257, 258, 259, 260, 261, 262, 263, 267, 268, 269, 270, 271, 272, 273, 275, 281, 314nn. 19 and 20, 315n. 32
Reidenbach Mennonite. *See* Mennonites
Reist, Hans, 29
repertoire (linguistic), 283. *See also* language competence
reproducibility. *See* scalability
retroflex /r/, 69, 213, 215, 216, 218, 312n. 5
Revolutionary War, 20, 21, 22, 34, 310n. 7
Rhine, 18, 19, 20, 27
Rhine Frankish dialect, 23
Richfield Methodist Church, 62
rl- (recipient language) agentivity, 285, 286, 287, 313n. 17, 323n. 3, 324n. 4
role (social), 17, 140, 317nn. 7 and 9, 319n. 35
Rotterdam, 34
Rough and Ready, Pennsylvania, 144
rounding (phonetic), 67, 127, 313nn. 14 and 15
Russia, 27

ʃ-curve, 118, 119, 315n. 28
Salem Church, 144
Saxony, 25
scalability, 105, 186, 314n. 25, 319nn. 29 and 30, 320nn. 36 and 40, 321n. 49
Schaffhausen, 31
Schleitheim Confession, 27
Schnitz and Gnepp, 37
Schnitzboi, 37
Schoharie River, 34
school: of nonsectarians, 38, 317n. 14; of sectarians, 41, 207, 317n. 14; of non-

Index

Pennsylvania Germans, 43; language use at, 162, 163, 165, 171, 178, 185, 200, 299, 303, 319n. 28, 320n. 37; language attitude at, 245
Schuylkill County, Pennsylvania, 22, 32, 35, 126
Schwaben Creek Valley, 32, 34
Schwenkfelder, 19, 25
Scotch-Irish, 20, 310n. 6
Scotland/Scots/Scottish, 20, 211, 310n. 6, 319nn. 28 and 32
secondary migration, 20, 27, 34
sectarian(s). *See* Pennsylvania German(s)
self-hatred, 273
self-report, 61, 134, 135, 136, 197, 199, 311n. 26, 316n. 3, 323n. 13
Selinsgrove, Pennsylvania, 43
semantic differential scale, 211, 218, 219, 242, 322nn. 4 and 5
semispeaker, 36, 97, 136, 316n. 4
semivowel, 120
setting. *See* situation (social/linguistic)
Seventh Day Baptist, 25
sex. *See* gender
Shamokin, 32
Shamokin, Pennsylvania, 51, 148, 149
Shawnee Indians, 34
Shikallamy, 32
sibilant, 127
sibilization 312n. 11
Silesia, 25
Simons, Menno, 26
situation (social/linguistic), 140, 141, 142, 143, 156, 157, 159, 160, 162, 165, 167, 170, 171, 173, 174, 180, 181, 182, 183, 184, 185, 187, 191, 192, 202, 206, 209, 221, 280, 282, 284, 312n. 2, 319n. 34, 320n. 47, 321n. 51
sl- (source language) agentivity, 285, 286, 287, 313n. 17, 323n. 3, 324n. 4
Slovak, 38, 51, 115
Snyder County, Pennsylvania, 62, 211, 212
Snyder's Store, 149
social groups. *See* nonsectarian Pennsylvania Germans. *See* sectarian Pennsylvania Germans. *See* non-Pennsylvania Germans. *See* Amish.

See Mennonites. *See* generation
Society of Friends, 18
solidarity, 16, 233, 234, 235, 239–41, 244, 262, 263, 264, 265, 267, 268, 269, 270, 271, 273, 274, 281, 287, 322n. 7, 323n. 13
sound, 66, 69, 75, 76, 78, 79, 84, 87, 90, 91, 94, 95, 97, 119, 120, 133, 314n. 19
sound inventory. *See* phoneme system
South America, 27
Spanish, 137, 322n. 7
speech community, 16, 130, 141, 142, 143, 164, 165, 166, 195, 206, 208, 273, 279, 310n. 3, 317n. 11, 319n. 28, 320n. 46, 321n. 51
speech island, 16, 22, 276
spelling pronunciation, 83
Spracherwerbskontext, 130
Sprachgebrauchsfaktoren, 130
Sprachgemeinschaft, 130, 310n. 3
Sprachinsel, 16, 276
Spread Eagle, 35
St. John's, Newfoundland, 313n. 13
St. John's Church, 144
St. Louis, 22
St. Michael's Lutheran Church, 62, 144
Standard English. *See* regional standard of English
Standard German, 23, 46, 51, 52, 53, 90, 95, 134, 135, 136, 137, 139, 140, 145, 163, 172, 173, 243, 244, 261, 297, 298, 300, 310nn. 9 and 13, 316nn. 1 and 2, 317nn. 14 and 15
State College, Pennsylvania, 39
status, 16, 219, 225, 233, 234, 235–39, 240, 241, 244, 247, 248, 249, 250, 251, 252, 253, 254, 255, 259, 260, 261, 262, 265, 266, 267, 268, 269, 270, 271, 272, 273, 274, 281, 322n. 7
Stauffer Mennonite. *See* Mennonites
Steuben, Friedrich Wilhelm von, 20
stereotype. *See* dumb Dutchman stereotype
stop (sound), 127, 132, 312n. 7
Strasburg, Pennsylvania, 28
subject matter. *See* topic
substratal, 287, 313n. 14

Summerwascht, 37
Sunbury, Pennsylvania, 32, 148, 149
Sunday school, 28, 40, 61, 62
Sunny Side Mennonite School, 41, 62, 143, 316n. 6
superstratal, 287
Susquehanna River, 32, 39, 41, 42
Susquehanna University, 43
Swede, 21
Swiss Brethren, 26
Switzerland/Swiss, 19, 21, 22, 23, 24, 26, 27, 29, 31
syllable break, 83
syllable-final, 312n. 6
synchronic, 158, 173, 183
syntax/syntactic, 14, 17, 215, 217, 223, 280, 281, 285, 311n. 1, 312n. 1, 323n. 1, 324n. 5

target word, 65, 71, 72, 75, 76, 77, 79, 80, 81, 82, 86, 87, 88, 89, 90, 92, 93, 97, 98, 99, 100, 101, 102, 103, 105, 106, 107, 108, 109, 111, 112, 115, 120, 123, 124, 125, 131, 312n. 7, 314n. 26, 315n. 30
Team Mennonite. *See* Mennonites
tense (vowel), 313n. 14
Texas, 14, 22, 56, 321n. 48
The Citizen Standard, 148, 311n. 17
The Daily Item, 148
The Lewisburg Journal, 148
The News Item, 148
The Pathway Papers, 148
The Press Enterprise, 148
The Upper Dauphin Sentinel, 148
Thirty Years' War, 19
Tirolian, 115
tolerance (religious), 19, 27
topic, 140, 202–06, 209, 307, 317n. 8, 321n. 50
transfer (linguistic), 285, 286, 287, 313n. 17, 323n. 3
translation competence, 75, 103, 111, 112, 113, 114, 115, 117, 280
Tri Valley Junior High School, 143
triglossia, 279
trilingualism, 320n. 35
trilled /r/, 69, 215, 216, 218

Tulpehocken Path, 32, 34, 35
Tupperware party, 321n. 47

Ukrainian, 38
unaspirated (sound), 69
Union Church, 25, 35, 36
Union County, Pennsylvania, 22, 39, 42
United Church of Christ, 25, 35, 38, 48, 50, 52, 53
United Methodist Church, 42, 56, 57
United States, 13, 14, 22, 27, 29, 35, 36, 38, 42, 85, 207, 310n. 2, 324n. 3
Universitätsrechenzentrum Heidelberg, 226
Unpartheyisches Gesangbuch, 316n. 6
unrounded (sound), 313n. 14
unstressed (sound), 65, 66, 67, 127, 78, 92, 95, 292
unvoiced (sound), 69, 72, 73, 75, 76, 77, 79, 94, 96, 108, 120, 121, 122, 125, 312nn. 6, 7 and 11, 313n. 11, 314nn. 19 and 20
Upper Mahantango Township, 35
us-them concept, 206

Valley View, Pennsylvania, 148
velarization, 127
Versammling, 38, 49, 61, 62, 146, 147, 245, 260, 273, 295, 304, 318n. 20, 320n. 46
Vicksburg, Pennsylvania, 41
Virginia, 22
vocabulary. *See* lexicon
voiced (sound), 69, 72, 75, 79, 94, 120, 127, 133, 312n. 7, 313n. 16, 314n. 20
voiceless (sound). *See* unvoiced (sound)
vowel length, 66, 67, 84, 123, 125, 312n. 7, 313n. 15

Wales/Welsh, 20, 42
Washington, D.C., 57
Washington, George, 20
Waterloo County, Ontario, 22, 27
wave-model, 118
Waynetown, 35
Weaverland Conference. *See* Mennonites
Weavertown, 31
Weiser, Conrad, 32

Wenger Mennonite/Wengerite. *See* Mennonites
West Coast, 150
West Country dialect, 313n. 13
West Virginia, 14
Wisconsin, 22
Wisler Mennonite. *See* Mennonites
Womelsdorf, Pennsylvania, 32
word list, 15, 44, 60, 63, 312nn. 2 and 3
word-final, 65, 66, 69, 71, 72, 73, 76, 77, 78, 79, 80, 81, 82, 91, 92, 93, 94, 95, 96, 106, 107, 108, 109, 120, 121, 122, 125, 127, 128, 129, 131, 132, 214, 291, 312nn. 6, 7 and 11, 314n. 20, 315n. 26, 323n. 15
word-initial, 65, 72, 73, 76, 77, 78, 80, 82, 107, 108, 109, 120, 122, 129, 312n. 8, 314n. 20
word-internal, 65, 71, 76, 77, 78, 80, 106, 107, 108, 109, 120, 122, 312n. 6
World War I, 36, 207, 310n. 7, 311n. 18, 317n. 15
World War II, 28, 36, 38, 48, 151, 207, 314n. 24
worship service, 299, 303, 317n. 15; of nonsectarians, 25, 34–35, 36, 38, 204; of Amish, 31, 40, 41, 136, 144, 164, 288, 311n. 15, 320n. 38; of Mennonites, 28, 41, 62, 136, 144, 164, 288, 320n. 38; annual Pennsylvania German service of nonsectarians, 62, 144, 145, 245, 273, 317nn. 15 and 16, 320n. 46

Yiddish, 313n. 14
York County, Pennsylvania, 310n. 10

Zion Lutheran Church. *See* Klinger's Church
Zoarist, 26
Zurich, 27
Zweisprachigkeit, 130
Zwingli, Huldrych, 25, 26, 27